Gender Politics in Transitional Justic

Transitions from violent conflict and authoritarian rule are believed to be transformative moments for women, unique conjunctures in public and private, international law and domestic law, with the potential to transform the gender order of a society. Transitional justice processes, though principally concerned with providing limited accountability for human rights violations of the past, are increasingly injected with transformative social and political goals for the future. What then is the impact of transitional justice processes on the human rights of women in states emerging from political violence?

Gender Politics in Transitional Justice draws on original comparative research on women's movements in Chile, Northern Ireland and Colombia, and on legal analysis of transitional justice processes in these case studies, to confront these issues. Catherine O'Rourke argues that human rights outcomes for women of transitional justice processes are negotiated and determined in the space between international law and local gender politics.

An essential resource for students and scholars of Law, Politics and Gender Studies, this book provides critical analysis of the potentially transformative intersection between law and gender relations.

Catherine O'Rourke is based at the Transitional Justice Institute at the University of Ulster.

Transitional Justice

Series Editor: Kieran McEvoy

Queen's University Belfast

The study of justice in transition has emerged as one of the most diverse and intellectually exciting developments in the social sciences. From its origins in human rights activism and comparative political science, the field is increasingly characterised by its geographic and disciplinary breadth. This series aims to publish the most innovative scholarship from a range of disciplines working on transitional justice related topics, including law, sociology, criminology, psychology, anthropology, political science, development studies and international relations.

Titles in this series:

Transitional Justice, Judicial Accountability and the Rule of Law
Hakeem O. Yusuf (2010)

The Era of Transitional Justice: The Aftermath of the Truth and Reconciliation Commission in South Africa and Beyond
Paul Gready (2010)

The Dynamics of Transitional Justice
Lia Kent (2012)

Gender Politics in Transitional Justice
Catherine O'Rourke (2013)

Identity, Reconciliation and Transitional Justice
Nevin T. Aiken (2013)

Corporate Accountability in the Context of Transitional Justice
Sabine Michalowski (2013)

Transitional Justice Theories
Edited by Susanne Buckley Zistel, Teresa Koloma Beck, Christian Braun, Friederike Mieth (2014)

Forthcoming titles in the series:

Families of the Missing
Simon Robins

The Concept of the Civilian
Claire Garbett

Transitional Justice and the Arab Spring
Edited by Kirsten Fisher and Robert Stewart

Truth, Denial and Transition: The Contested Past in Northern Ireland
Cheryl Lawther

The Judiciary and the Politics of Transition: Saviours, Scoundrels, Scapegoats
Marny Requa

Gender Politics in Transitional Justice

Catherine O'Rourke

Routledge
Taylor & Francis Group
LONDON AND NEW YORK

First published 2013
by Routledge
2 Park Square, Milton Park, Abingdon, Oxfordshire OX14 4RN

Simultaneously published in the USA and Canada
by Routledge
711 Third Avenue, New York, NY 10017

First issued in paperback 2014

Routledge is an imprint of the Taylor & Francis Group, an informa business

British Library Cataloguing in Publication Data
A catalogue record for this book is available from the British Library

Library of Congress Cataloging-in-Publication Data
A catalog record has been requested for this book

ISBN 13: 978-0-415-82634-1 (hbk)
ISBN 13: 978-1-138-85013-2 (pbk)

Typeset in Baskerville
by RefineCatch Limited, Bungay, Suffolk

To my mum and dad, Catherine and Richard O'Rourke

Contents

Acknowledgements

This book is the product of many conversations, conferences, classes and, foremost, my doctoral research. I am indebted to the many fellow travellers I have had in conducting this research and in bringing the book to completion. The doctoral research, on which the book is based, was expertly supervised by Professor Christine Bell and Carmel Roulston. The thesis was thoughtfully examined by Professors Christine Chinkin and Fionnuala Ní Aoláin. Together, these four women have had enormous impact on my thinking and writing. The best parts of the book can be attributed to their collective input. In particular, Christine Bell has been a steady mentor and friend throughout the research. Her unfailing confidence in this ambitious project was motivating and reassuring during my own moments of doubt. Carmel Roulston gave generously of her time, her understanding of women's mobilisation in Northern Ireland and her encyclopaedic knowledge of feminist and political theory. Christine Chinkin carried out a robust probing of the thesis that provided many valuable lines of development and improvement for the book. Fionnuala Ní Aoláin's interrogation of the theoretical framework significantly strengthened the overall body of work. As I set about the long process of unpicking the case studies and organising the book thematically, these contributions of my examiners proved to be invaluable.

While the thesis research and writing was largely conducted elsewhere, the book is very much a product of its environment, both the Transitional Justice Institute (TJI) at the University of Ulster and Belfast. As a lecturer within the TJI, I have had ongoing access to an extraordinary community of gender scholars. My sincere thanks are due to Monica McWilliams, Aisling Swaine, Eilish Rooney and Fionnuala Ní Aoláin for input and feedback on the ideas and writing in the book. In particular, I wish to acknowledge Aisling and Fionnuala, my co-authors on a UN Study on Reparations for Conflict-related Sexual Violence, for enhancing my knowledge and understanding of gender and reparations. Sincere thanks also go to my friend and former TJI colleague Catherine Turner for helpful reading of the early book chapters. The book has also been very much shaped by my teaching at the TJI. I have been fortunate to be able to 'road-test' the ideas of the book to the thoughtful and talented students of the Gender and Transition postgraduate module that I deliver, and in the TJI Annual Gender Summer School. I pay tribute to my students, current and former, who provided a critical first-reading of much of the book's content. (In a period when teaching and research are so often portrayed as antagonistic in higher education, it feels important to acknowledge the ways in which they have supported each other in producing this book.) Finally, the book is a product of Belfast and the ongoing feminist efforts here to make the transition deliver on its promises of equality and human rights for women. In this regard, the book has been profoundly shaped by my involvement in recent years with Hanna's House. The thoughtful and committed colleagues who make up the Board of Hanna's House have taught me more than anyone about the challenges – and the importance – of asserting an avowedly feminist agenda in issues of transitional justice. I am indebted to Margaret Ward, Joanna McMinn, Claire Hackett, Ann Hope, Shirley Graham, Linda Kelly and Emma Rogan.

The international research was facilitated through the extraordinary kindness and hospitality of Julie Mertus at American University in Washington DC, Lidia Casas at the Universidad Diego Portales in Santiago, Chile and Isabel Cristina Jaramillo at the Universidad de los Andes in Bogotá, Colombia. I am grateful also to Cath Collins for assisting my access to human rights groups in Chile. In particular, I am grateful to the many feminist activists who met with me in Chile, Northern Ireland and Colombia to patiently explain dynamics that I struggled to understand. I have been overwhelmed by the tenacity and commitment of these women in the most difficult of circumstances. Where we disagree on our analysis, I know that it will be a friendly and constructive disagreement. The book also draws heavily on archival research. I gratefully acknowledge the Political Collection of the Linen Hall Library in Belfast, the United States Library of Congress, the human rights collection of American University and the special collections of Universidad Diego Portales and Universidad de los Andes, for access to essential primary sources.

My final thanks are to the friends and loved ones who supported me through the writing and completion of the book. They, like me, are happy to be closing this chapter. In particular, to my dearest Elizabeth, who cheerfully read and proofed the text, offered comments, finalised references, provided reassurance, as well as keeping me fed and watered through the final weeks of the book, I cannot express the depth of my gratitude. Very finally, I sincerely thank my parents for unstinting support through the many stages of study and work that led to this book. I dedicate the book to them, with much love and thanks.

Catherine O'Rourke, Belfast, January 2013

International instruments, statutes and cases

Table of Cases

United Nations Human Rights Committee

Karen Noelia LLantoy Huamán v Peru, Hum. Rts. Com., Communication No. 1153/2003 UN Doc. CCPR/C/85/D/1153/2003 (2005) 24n24, 25n33
Lyashkevich v Belarus, Hum. Rts Com., Communication No. 887/1999, UN Doc. CCPR/C/77/D/950/2000 (2003) 124n7
Validzhon Khalilov v Tajikistan, Hum. Rts Com., Communication No. 973/2001, UN Doc. CCPR/C/83/D/973/2001 (2005) 124n7

Committee on the Elimination of All Forms of Discrimination Against Women

A.T. v Hungary, Communication No. 2/2003, Views of the Committee on the Elimination of All Forms of Discrimination Against Women under Article 7, paragraph 3, of the Optional Protocol (2003) 24n25

African Commission on Human and Peoples' Rights

Amnesty International v Sudan, AfCHR, Communication No. 48/90, 50/91, 52/91, 89/93 (1999) 124n7

Inter-American Commission on Human Rights

Baby Boy v United States, Inter-Am. C.H.R., Case 2141, Report No. 23/81, OEA/Ser.L/V/II.54, DOC.9 REV.1 (1981) 176n27, 216n10
Ignacio Ellacuría et al v El Salvador, Inter-Am. C.H.R., Case 10.488, Report No. 136/99 (1999) 124n7
Raquel Martí de Mejía v Perú, Inter-Am. C.H.R., Case 10.970, Report No. 5/96 (1996) 21n10, 23n18

Inter-American Court of Human Rights

European Court of Human Rights

International Criminal Tribunals

Chile

Colombia

Northern Ireland

South Africa

UK

International instruments

National legislation

Chile

Colombia

United Kingdom

Statutes of international tribunals

International meetings

Part I

Introduction

Introduction

From the popular feminist slogan of Latin American women's movements 'Democracy in the Country and in the Home' to the contemporary feminist peace slogan of 'No to war that kills us. No to a peace that oppresses us',[1] there is evidence of an enduring feminist belief in the potential of transitions from violent conflict or repressive rule to transform the status of women and gender relations. Moreover, the adoption of United Nations Security Council Resolution 1325 on Women, Peace and Security in 2000 marked formal political and legal recognition, at the highest international institutional level, that transitions from political violence *should* be transformative for women.[2] But what role do transitional justice processes play in determining outcomes for women of transitions from political violence? Transitional justice processes, though principally concerned with providing limited accountability for human rights violations of the past, are increasingly injected with transformative social and political goals for the future. What then is the impact of transitional justice processes on the human rights of women in states emerging from political violence? To what extent does international law determine these outcomes for women of domestic transitional justice processes? Or is the role of women's movements and local gender politics determinative of how women's human rights fare in domestic processes of transitional justice?

Gender Politics in Transitional Justice sets out to answer these questions. The book is interested in the extent to which transitional justice processes redress past violations of women's human rights, secure the non-recurrence of such violations, and empower women's movements as stakeholders in post-conflict and post-authoritarian societies.

Transitional justice refers to the legal, moral, and political dilemmas of providing accountability for the mass human rights violations that occurred during periods of violent conflict and repressive rule, while assisting the transition out of political violence. Transitional justice processes typically include some combination of criminal trials, truth-seeking, reparations and institutional reform. This book

1 This is a popular peace slogan amongst Colombian feminists. See further Cockburn (2007: 46).
2 United Nations Security Council Resolution 1325 (2000), S/RES/1325 (2000).

examines feminist engagement with transitional justice processes, and their human rights outcomes for women, in the selected case studies of Chile, Northern Ireland and Colombia. The comparative study sets out to understand and explain why some transitional justice processes produce better outcomes for women than other transitional justice processes. When, why and how does international law help to deliver progressive human rights outcomes for women in domestic processes of transitional justice? What are the optimum domestic political circumstances for international law to exert such a progressive influence? What are the strategies that can be effectively pursued by feminist advocates, practitioners and women's movements to deliver progressive human rights outcomes for women in states undergoing domestic processes of transitional justice?

BACKGROUND TO THE STUDY

The study is motivated by two factors. First, the proliferation of transitional justice mechanisms and the recognition of their significance for women's status and gender relations in post-conflict and post-authoritarian contexts. Second, growing feminist unease about the gap between ostensible feminist gains in international law and the actual impact of international law on women's daily lives.

Is transitional justice transformative for women?

It is important to locate feminist approaches to transitional justice within broader feminist approaches to transitions from political violence. The adoption of United Nations Security Council Resolution 1325 on Women, Peace and Security in 2000 marked formal international political and legal recognition that both political violence and its resolution are gendered. To say that political violence and its resolution are gendered involves two linked insights: first, that the origins and maintenance of political violence are linked to gender relations in the societies in which such violence prevails; and second, that gender is a determining factor in how one experiences political violence. Neither greater policy attention, nor growing political recognition, of the gendered nature of political violence emerged from the unprompted enlightenment of the international community. Rather, women's movements, and transnational feminist advocacy to target international institutions, have been at the heart of the advancement of women in the international agenda on peace and security (see generally Reilly 2009). This focus of transnational feminist advocacy on women, peace and security has been motivated by the exigencies of political violence: the felt need to respond to widespread and egregious violations of women's rights in these contexts. But this focus is also motivated by a belief in the transformative opportunities offered for women and gender relations by transitions from political violence.

The extreme social disruption caused by political violence can allow for some loosening of gender norms and create space for women to take up atypical gender roles.[3] For example, either through the death or absence of men, contexts of political violence can offer new opportunities for community leadership by women.[4] Extremes of poverty and deprivation can motivate mass mobilisation amongst women to meet daily needs, to oppose political power-holders and to demand that greater attention be paid to the needs and rights of women.[5] Further, these mobilised groups of women may be well placed to make demands for women's rights and equality on political elites when an end to political violence is being either imposed or negotiated (Bell 2005). Moreover, substantial political and legal reforms now typically form part of transitions from political violence, often with extensive provision for the protection of human rights.[6] The advent of a panoply of new political and legal institutions in states emerging from periods of sustained political violence suggest an opportunity 'to build some of these ideas [of women's rights and women's inclusion] in with the bricks' (Mackay 2011) of post-conflict and post-authoritarian state institutions.

Feminist political science approaches to democratisation transitions were motivated particularly by the prospect of radical democratisation, and the construction of more participatory models of democracy that eschewed the exclusionary tendencies of the liberal democratic model (Jaquette 1989). Prolific feminist analysis of transitions has now turned to more sober feminist assessments. In particular, feminist analysis has questioned the transformative potential of political changes that engage exclusively with public political and legal institutions in which men predominate, to the neglect of the arrangements of the private sphere in which women experience most persistent inequality. As Georgina Waylen has cautioned: 'Institutional democratisation does not necessarily entail a democratisation of power relations in society at large, particularly between men and women' (Waylen 1994: 329).

Analysis of transitional justice has followed a similar trajectory. First, the range of important long-term and non-legal implications of transitional justice processes for societies emerging from conflict or repression has been emphasised. Transitional justice mechanisms of selective trials, truth commissions, reparations and institutional reform are now broadly linked to degrees of reconciliation (Hamber 2009), economic development (Mani 2002), security sector performance (United Nations Secretary-General 2004) and political equality (de Greiff 2007) in post-conflict and post-authoritarian societies. This realisation prompted optimistic perspectives on transitional justice, as a vehicle for the dissipating broader social conflict, and for securing the radical redistribution of political and material resources in transitional societies (Mani 2002). This optimism has, however, been dampened by more sober longer-term assessments of the political and economic dispensation of states

3 The author has written elsewhere (with Bell) about 'the perverse equality gains of war'. See Bell and O'Rourke (2007: 41).
4 For example, during the conflict in Northern Ireland. See McCoy (2000).
5 For a discussion of these dynamics in Latin America, see further Craske (1998).
6 For example, within the provisions of negotiated settlements to end conflict. See Bell (2000).

emerging from transitions (Miller 2008). There is increasing caution about a 'project of envisaging utopias recognised as elusive even in western liberal democracies, but now arrogantly attempted in the most dystopic situations where all the political precursors appear to be missing' (Bell 2009: 7). In terms of its outcomes for women, the preoccupation of transitional justice with providing accountability for public harms underpinned by political violence in transition tends to marginalise and make invisible the manifold harms experienced by women that are deemed to be private and non-political. Elsewhere (with Bell), the author identified this gendered solipsistic focus on public harms as the consequence of the perceived 'from' (male-defined political violence) and 'to' (liberal democratic frameworks) of transitional justice discourse (Bell and O'Rourke 2007: 23).

Feminism and international law

Feminist engagement with the institutions and processes of law is seldom straightforward. Feminists encounter a recurring dilemma of how to engage the law to advance a feminist agenda. Carol Smart has succinctly captured the dilemma thus: 'Law is so deaf to the core concerns of feminism that feminists should be extremely cautious of how and whether they resort to law' (Smart 1989: 2). '[W]hile some law reforms may indeed benefit some women, it is certain that all law reforms empower law' (Smart 1989: 161). The key concern of Smart, and others,[7] is the deradicalising effect that campaigns for law reform tend to have on women's movements. The very process of formulating a campaign for legal change means translating social and political problems, which require dramatic social and political responses, into legal deficiencies that require incremental technical change. In the process, initially radical feminist analysis tends to become flattened into reformist demands for more or 'better' law.

Feminist dilemmas over engagement with law are arguably more acute at the international level. The gap between law-in-the-books and law-in-action exists in peaceful democratic states; thus it would be naive to assume a correlation between the legal prohibition of a particular practice and the actual elimination of that practice at the level of individual states. It is even more naive to assume that the prohibition of particular offences or the guarantee of particular rights at the international level will achieve their stated effect as, to quote Cassese: 'the *normative* role of [international] law is more powerful and effective than its *repressive* function' (Cassese 2008: 8, emphasis in the original). The coercive capacity and compliance pull of international law is highly questionable.

The antecedents of what we now recognise as the sub-field of gender and transitional justice lie firmly within the feminist approaches to international law that emerged in the early 1990s. Feminist theoretical and practical engagement with international human rights law in that period – to both critique and reform the

7 See also MacKinnon (1983); Fineman (1992); Munro (2007).

canon – inaugurated a feminist approach to international law more generally of simultaneous engagement and critique. Feminist interventions into the terrain of international criminal law secured some prominent gains in the legal recognition and prohibition of gender-specific harms experienced by women in contexts of political violence. Over a decade has passed since the adoption of United Nations Security Council Resolution 1325 on Women, Peace and Security (2000). That period has been accompanied by further Security Council resolutions dealing with the protection of women experiencing wartime sexual violence.[8] The UN has recently reorganised its gender work to more specifically focus on issues of post-conflict justice for women. A permanent International Criminal Court, of which feminist advocates were prominent supporters, is now and up and running. Regional human rights courts have become increasingly assertive in imposing positive legal obligations on states to protect and promote the human rights of women. The application of these legal obligations to states experiencing or emerging from political violence is attracting increasing policy attention, most notably from the Committee on the Elimination of All Forms of Discrimination against Women. There is a sense in which the doctrine and institutions of international law have never been more supportive of delivering positive human rights outcomes for women from domestic processes of transitional justice. Moreover, the institutions and practice of transitional justice proliferate in contemporary responses to political violence.

However, these ostensible feminist gains in international law have more recently motivated strongly critical-reflective scholarship questioning the value of such gains to women's daily lives (see especially Otto 2009). Criticism of the gendered shortcomings of criminal trials, truth commissions, reparations programmes and institutional reform within states emerging from political violence is both trenchant and persistent (e.g. Harris-Rimmer 2010). Feminist criticism points to the frequent exclusion of women from transitional justice processes on the ground in transitional states, the elision of gendered harms and the damaging preoccupation of these processes with public harms and the 'primary' cause of political violence (Ní Aoláin 2006). This criticism suggests a chasm between feminist optimism about transitions, the promise of international law and the implementation of transitional justice on the ground in states exiting political violence.

We need to understand why this chasm exists.

OBJECTIVES OF THE BOOK

Many critical feminist scholars of international law would attribute the gap between ostensible feminist gains in international law and human rights outcomes

8 See especially United Nations Security Council Resolution 1820 (2008), S/RES/1820. See also United Nations Security Council Resolution 1888 (2009), S/RES/1889 (2009) and United Nations Security Council Resolution 1960 (2010), S/RES 1960.

for women of transitional justice to the conceptual shortcomings of international law. These conceptual shortcomings are said to privilege the use of force, the state over the individual, and the resolution of public incidences of violence over the private harms that occur daily in contexts of political violence.[9] A focus on domestic political factors might lead to the belief that immutable patriarchies hold power at the domestic level within transitional states and that transitional justice processes that emerge from elite-driven negotiated resolutions to conflict will inevitably disserve women. Alternatively, it has been suggested that negative outcomes for women of transitional justice evidence 'complementary patriarchies' operating between domestic and international actors (Ní Aoláin 2009: 1057). But none of these approaches tell us why some transitions are better for women than others, and why some transitional justice processes and mechanisms produce better outcomes in terms of women's human rights than other processes and mechanisms. Moreover, each of these approaches fails to account for women's political agency in influencing the operation and outcomes of transitional justice processes.

Consequently, we need a more subtle and nuanced understanding of when, why and how international law helps to deliver progressive human rights outcomes for women in domestic processes of transitional justice. What are the optimum domestic political circumstances for international law to exert such a progressive influence? And what are the strategies that can be effectively pursued by feminist advocates, practitioners and women's movements to deliver progressive human rights outcomes for women in states undergoing domestic processes of transitional justice?

Gender Politics in Transitional Justice sets out to answer these questions.

APPROACH AND STRUCTURE OF THE BOOK

The book draws on original comparative empirical research on women's movements in Chile, Northern Ireland and Colombia, and legal analysis of transitional justice in the case studies, to illuminate the relationship of international law to local gender politics in transitional justice. This section details the approach and structure of the book.

Comparing human rights outcomes for women

In examining the human rights outcomes for women of transitional justice processes, the book will focus on the right of women to live free from violence and women's reproductive rights. This study maintains a focus on the female body for a number of practical and conceptual reasons. To focus on the body provides a boundary to the empirical and legal phenomena under analysis. Further – and

9 For the classic statement of this critique, see Charlesworth *et al.* (1991).

at the acknowledged risk of reifying gendered shortcomings of established legal categories – substantial developments in the treatment of violence against women and women's reproductive autonomy within the international human rights canon have been made since the beginning of the 1990s. Importantly, these two issues have been selected for priority feminist concern in both local and transnational women's organising (e.g. Reilly 2009; Joachim 2007). In examining the relationship of women's mobilisation to legal change, the issues of violence and reproduction therefore suggest themselves for analysis. Principally, however, the focus on the body has been selected because it exposes the crude and arbitrary nature of a starkly gendered distinction between 'public' bodily harms cited for rebuke, retribution, redress, reparation and legal reform in transitional justice, and the 'private' bodily harms that remain invisible within the prevailing legal paradigm.

Women's movements: a term of art? Theoretical and methodological challenges

Substantial scholarly disagreement prevails in respect of how to define and identify a women's movement.[10] Disagreement persists over the size, mandate, level of autonomy and relationship to the state necessary to constitute a women's movement. In this book, the term 'women's movement' is used broadly, to refer to women's collective action, without seeking to settle the questions and differences identified in feminist scholarship. However, the term 'women's organisation' is used rather more specifically and selectively. In this volume, reference is made to women's organisations that mobilise to end violence against women and to advance women's reproductive rights. Violence against women and reproductive rights need not be the exclusive or primary concern of these organisations, but it must feature within their overall mandate. Further, reference in the book is frequently made to 'feminist' engagement with transitional justice. The women's organisations examined in the book tend to be feminist, though they are not all necessarily so. Instead, specifically feminist engagement is identified by a commitment to challenge the exploitative gender order and advance the status of women in a transitional society, and approaching transitional justice processes as an opportunity to that end. Both women's organisations and feminist organisations are distinguished from organisations and movements of which women are present or prominent (for example, mothers of the disappeared, or women in the mainstream human rights movement), but which do not principally define their mandate in terms of work to advance the status of women.

Adopting this definition does not, however, resolve definitional challenges. It can be difficult to speak coherently of often diverse and poorly co-ordinated women's organisations. The problem here is both theoretical and practical.

10 For a comprehensive overview of these debates, see Molyneux (1998).

Unified feminist positions on the questions under study are not apparent. The past three decades of feminist theory teaches us that apparently unified feminist responses to political questions should (rightly) be suspected for their hegemonic and silencing tendencies. But how is this theoretical dissonance to be translated into a coherent data collection strategy in investigating feminist engagement with transitional justice in transitional societies? The task proved both easier and harder than initially expected – easier because women's organisations often vocally disagree with one another. In each of the transitional contexts examined in the book, clear ideological cleavages existed within the women's movements that interest the book. They differed principally on their position to the state, and to the political violence in which their organising was inevitably enmeshed. They differed in their relationships to combatant women, and to human rights movements more broadly. Thus, to present unified feminist positions on the questions under study would be poor science. However, capturing diversity and disagreement within women's movements was also harder than expected for two reasons: first, protagonists of women's movements are often reluctant to articulate the reasons for disagreement, in particular to an outsider; and second, while identifying the main political cleavage within each women's movement allowed me to identify two distinct sets of 'feminist' positions, it concealed a much wider canvas of less dramatic political and theoretical differences within those movements. This limitation is acknowledged.

Comparing transitional justice?

Transitional justice is a burgeoning and proliferating field of analysis, and its exact boundaries and parameters remain highly contested. This contestation becomes particularly apparent in more recent efforts to expand the concerns of transitional justice to address socioeconomic needs in transition (Mani 2002; Miller 2008) and to include alternative 'traditional' or community-based accountability mechanisms for dealing with the past (McEvoy 2007; Lundy and McGovern 2008). To date, efforts to 'map' the field' (Bell 2009), or to document its evolution (Arthur 2009), highlight – rather than overcome – this ongoing contestation about just what is meant conceptually and substantively by the term 'transitional justice'. This confusion presents particular challenges of 'what to compare' when constructing a comparative legal and empirical study of transitional justice in three case studies. While the book does not pretend to resolve disagreements over the exact contours and components of transitional justice, the comparative study of trials, truth, reparations and institutional reform has been arrived at inductively and deductively. Deductively, the foundational work of Ruti Teitel,[11] and broader

11 Teitel organises her path-breaking study of the role of law in transitional justice around: the rule of law, criminal justice, historical justice, reparatory justice, administrative justice and constitutional justice (Teitel 2000).

gender scholarship in transitional justice,[12] posits these devices as significant for studying the outcomes for women of transitional justice. Inductively, both the cases under study, and broader gender work of practitioners in transitional justice,[13] point to the significance of trials, truth, reparations and institutional reform as sites for delivering gains to women in transitional justice. These devices are significant to outcomes of transition across the three case studies, in terms both of women's mobilisation to engage domestic transitional justice processes, and in terms of gender legal outcomes of transition.

Comparative analysis and case selection

The book explores strategies adopted by women's movements towards transitional justice, and the ultimate legal treatment of women's human rights within transitional justice, in Chile, Northern Ireland and Colombia. Comparative research proceeds from the premise that, where patterns in a given phenomenon can be discerned across different cases, 'we can learn more about any of them by comparing their dynamics than by looking at each on its own'.[14] David Nelken cautions, however, that in comparative legal research explicit attention must be 'given to clarifying what a given comparison is for and how a given aim can best be achieved' (Nelken 2005: 247). The comparative study in this book examines transitional justice devices for their implications for the legal treatment of violence against women and women's reproductive rights in the respective case studies. Strategies of local women's movements for engaging transitional justice are examined. Comparative analysis can determine whether the gender dynamics in each of the case studies is simply the product of the local political context, or whether there is a gendered pattern of compromise in the negotiation of legal change in transition that leads to common outcomes across the three case studies in terms of women's human rights.

Legal analysis of transition has been able to draw together a broader range of case studies than comparative political science analysis of transitions. The particular question of how a successor regime deals with the crimes of the past posits ground for comparative analysis across a range of democratisation and conflict-to-peace transitions. In seminal work in the area, Priscilla Hayner notes:

12 See, for example, Askin (1997) (criminal trials); Ní Aoláin and Turner (2007) (truth commissions); Rubio-Marin (2006) (reparations). Compare Nesiah (2006).

13 In 2010 the United Nations reorganised its gender work to focus more specifically on issues of post-conflict justice for women. The UN Secretary General's Action Plan for Gender Responsive Peacebuilding cites prosecutions, truth commissions, reparations programmes and rule of law reform as key areas of transitional justice activity requiring 'gender responsiveness' (United Nations Secretary-General 2010: 15).

14 This is the rationale underpinning social movements theorists McAdam, Tarrow and Tilly in their systematic analysis of the common dynamics of social mobilisation in very diverse processes of strikes, revolutions, nationalism and democratisation, through an encompassing notion of 'the politics of contention' (McAdam *et al.* 2001: 4).

> Change may come at the end of a civil war, through the downfall of a military regime, or through popular revolt against a repressive regime combined with shifting winds of international support. But in each of these very different types of political transitions, very similar questions and difficulties arise.
>
> (Hayner 2002: 5)

Whereas feminist political analysis of transition has to date eschewed this type of gender analysis across different types of transitions, analysis here suggests that gender analysis of transition could usefully adopt such a comparative approach and expand the cases under study. This book approaches transition as a process underpinned by a common set of legal devices, each with important gender implications on a range of issues such as violence against women and women's reproductive rights. Thus comparative gender analysis across democratisation and conflict-to-peace transitions is not only feasible, but also highly valuable.

The case studies represent different types of transitions. The transitions are distinguished by the underlying causes of political violence. Mass human rights violations in Chile were underpinned by ideological divisions between the secular socialist tradition of the organised left, and the conservative religious free-market commitments of the military and right (Borzutzky and Oppenheim 2006). Political violence in Northern Ireland can be attributed to ethnic divisions between the Protestant majority and the Catholic minority, linked to competing national aspirations for the territory of Northern Ireland (McGarry and O'Leary 1995). The Colombian conflict was initially attributed to ideological divisions from violent challenges to the elite-driven state posed by Marxist guerrillas. More recent conflict cycles can be characterised as largely socioeconomic in character, based on violent confrontation for the control of resources (Welna and Gallon 2007). Distinctions in the underlying causes of conflict have, in turn, led to different political and legal contexts for transitional justice in each of the jurisdictions. These are explored more fully in the respective case studies.

Significantly, the transitions under study are distinguished temporally. The Chilean transition to democracy occurred in 1990; the major peace agreement underpinning Northern Ireland's negotiated transition was signed in 1998; and contemporary transitional justice in Colombia was initiated in 2005, although it has antecedents in the process leading to the agreement of a new Constitution in 1991. This temporal range is enormously valuable to the study. Since the 1990s, accountability requirements for human rights violations have hardened substantially under international law. Further, two decades of feminist engagement with international law has led to striking developments in the legal treatment of violence against women and women's reproductive autonomy within international human rights law, international humanitarian law and international criminal law. These legal developments constitute the international legal context for the legal treatment of violence against women and the legal regulation of women's reproductive lives in domestic processes of transitional justice. Because of the temporal range in

Table 0.1 The comparative study

	Chile	*Northern Ireland*	*Colombia*
Nature of political violence	Authoritarian government	Ethnic conflict	Revolutionary/ ideological/ resources
Timing of transition	Transition to democracy 1990	Framework peace agreement 1998	Attenuated and cyclical
Main drivers of transition	Internal	Internal	Internal

the case studies, the interface of two decades of international legal developments with domestic processes of transitional justice can be traced. In particular, there is scope to examine how legal developments at the international level have impacted women's experiences of transition.

Each of the three cases involves self-reliant states and processes of transition that were largely domestically driven. International involvement in all of the cases has been relatively minor. Fletcher and Weinstein's comparative research on transitional justice emphasises the distinction between transitions in self-reliant states and internationally driven processes of transition. They identify this attribute as one of the most significant in indicating the choice and timing of transitional justice devices and determining whether or not transition is consolidated in the longer term (Fletcher *et al.* 2009). In an internationally driven process of transition, a range of international actors become significant to analysis: international institutions playing a political and technical role, and transnational women's organisations, are more significant players in the negotiation of domestic legal norms. Local political decisions are heavily influenced by global political dynamics. In effect, a much larger number of variables become pertinent for analysis. By contrast, in domestically driven processes, the interface between local women's organisations and local political and legal elites is central. Given the decision to examine transitions only in self-reliant states, the conclusion to the book makes some observations as to the applicability of the book's findings to the ever-increasing number of internationally driven transitional justice processes.

The plan of the book

The book is divided into six substantive sections. Part I, the Introduction, sets out the theoretical framework for the study. Chapter 1 draws on feminist doctrinal analysis of international law and transitional justice, together with feminist political science analysis of transitions, to elaborate an innovative analytical framework for examining the interaction of international law and local gender politics in transitional justice. Chapter 2 introduces the book's case studies. While not providing comprehensive accounts of each case study, Chapter 2 describes the harms experienced by women against the backdrop of political violence in each of the case studies. The harms are examined in terms of violence against women, infringements of women's reproductive autonomy and the manipulation of women's collective action. This discussion of harms experienced by women during periods of political violence in the case studies informs the remainder of the book. Human rights outcomes for women of transitional justice in the case studies are measured against the harms outlined in Chapter 2.

Part II of the book, Justice, examines feminist engagement with and gendered outcomes of criminal prosecutions in the case studies. Chapter 3 focuses on the strategies of women's movements to pursue criminal accountability for harms against women in the cases under study and finds a disjuncture between human rights groups and women's organisations that tend to mark civil society in periods of political violence and transition. The chapter considers the causes in international law of this disjuncture and identifies the implications of the disjuncture in terms of the failure to document human rights violations experienced by women in contexts of political violence. Chapter 4 reviews the unfolding duty under international law to prosecute serious violations of international human rights law and the evolving place of harms against women within this legal duty. The domestic implementation of this duty in each of the three case studies is examined, and the local political factors that determined diverging state responses to prosecutions are identified. The chapter finds that, despite the mooted 'new start' of transitions and the opportunity to establish new gender norms through ending impunity for harms against women, international law often works to guarantee continuities in gender norms and gender relations through transition. Nevertheless, the chapter identifies some potentially significant non-legal dividends to women of criminal accountability in transitional justice.

Part III of the book, Truth, turns to feminist engagement with, and gendered outcomes of, official truth processes in the three cases under study. Chapter 5 begins with a theoretically driven discussion of the potential gains to women and to women's movements to be derived from an inclusive and feminist-informed official truth process. The chapter then turns to empirical analysis of the truth strategies actually adopted by women's movements in the case studies, and identifies the political factors that lead to a relatively narrow and limited set of feminist political objectives being pursued in the truth campaigns of women's movements. Chapter 6 examines the treatment of harms against women in official truth processes in the three case studies, finding that ostensible feminist gains in international law tend to be mediated and diminished through local political dynamics in the implementation of domestic truth processes. The chapter further argues that many of the examples for women of official truth initiatives are promising in their deviation from international legal norms, and not in their implementation of them. Nevertheless, the chapter concludes, international law can provide a useful 'floor' to ensure a minimum of human rights gains for women, below which official processes cannot fall.

Part IV of the book addresses reparations in transitional justice. Chapter 7 argues that, while feminist theoretical literature on reparations tends to focus – optimistically – on the potential of reparations to establish women's political equality in transitional states, in practice interventions by women's movements into reparations processes in the case studies have – of necessity – been reactive and focused on resisting further damage to women's political equality in transitional justice. Chapter 8 suggests that while there is emerging consensus around a right to reparations for human rights violations in international law, transitional states adopt substantial and deliberate muddling of categories for reparations by states in order to obscure state liability for past harms, and to undercut the uniqueness of reparations as recognition and redress for past harms. The gendered consequences of these dynamics, in terms of the treatment of harms against women in domestic reparations processes under study, are explored and considered.

Part V of the book turns to institutional reform in transitional justice. Analysis of women's mobilisation in transitional states (Chapter 9) identifies women's movements at the forefront of demands for institutional reform, and these demands are often rooted in international human rights law. However, the demands tend to be framed as forward-looking, to address ongoing private harms against women unconnected to past political violence. Chapter 10 identifies institutional reform as the area of transitional justice in which obligations on states under international law are least developed and prescriptive. While states typically adopt international human rights law to frame institutional reform, this overt commitment is often undermined by informal gender constraints that manifest during the implementation phase of institutional reform.

Part VI, the Conclusion, draws on good practice identified in the case studies to sketch out a feminist law of transitional justice that addresses official processes for justice, truth, reparations and institutional reform. The book thereby includes concrete legal and policy recommendations. Nevertheless, as the book recognises, both international law and local gender politics are dynamic and evolving, and feminist strategies to secure positive human rights for women from transitional justice must negotiate these vagaries. Thus the book concludes by advocating for the feminist pursuit of gender justice in transition as the basis for more principled feminist engagement with transitional justice.

Chapter 1

Between international law and local gender politics

Women's human rights in transitional justice

INTRODUCTION

Transitions from political violence have motivated substantial feminist interest and optimism. However, feminist analysts differ greatly in whether they identify the local or the international as the key determinant of the gender outcomes of transitions. Understandably, in the context of the domestically driven transitions of the Latin American Southern Cone, and even in the more internationalised transitions of Central and Eastern Europe, feminist analysts privileged domestic political actors and local gender politics in shaping the outcomes of transition for women. The focus on the domestic was all the more justified by the absence of a robust international legal framework to guide such transitions. Contemporary conflict-to-peace transitions evidence a dramatically increased level of internationalisation. International actors and institutions are central. Such transitions operate increasingly in the shadow of international law, in which hardening international norms around accountability for past human rights violations shape domestic legal approaches to accountability. In response, contemporary feminist analysis of transitions looks consistently to the framework of international law to understand and explain the outcomes for women of transitions.

Thus, two distinct sets of feminist literatures speak to questions of transitional justice and the human rights outcomes for women of transitions from political violence. Feminist analysis of international law elucidates the potential influence of international law on domestic processes of transitional justice. In this book, this role for international law is termed 'the international frame'. This scholarship, however, relies on the often unsubstantiated assumption that international law is the key determinant of gender outcomes of domestic processes of transitional justice. Conversely, feminist political science analysis of democratisation transitions offers substantial insights concerning the local gender politics that determine human rights outcomes for women, termed here 'the local fit'. This body of scholarship says little about the role of international law or the specifics of transitional justice processes.

This chapter sets out the core thesis and theoretical framework of the book, namely that in order to understand and explain the human rights outcomes for women of transitional justice processes, the interaction between international law and local gender politics must be examined. The chapter proposes a framework for understanding the impact of international law on domestic politics and law and sets out more systematically – and modestly – the normative, legal and political ways in which 'the local fit' and 'the international frame' interact to determine the human rights outcomes for women of transitional justice.

Gender, law and transitional justice: 'the international frame'

Transitional justice is a burgeoning area of scholarship and practice. With antecedents in the post-Second World War trials at Nuremberg, transitional justice is an encompassing term that refers to the normative, legal and political concerns around how post-authoritarian and post-conflict societies provide accountability for the human rights violations of the past, while also consolidating a transition away from political violence. Political scientists exploring the nature of political transitions in southern Europe and South America dominated early scholarship in the area (e.g. O'Donnell *et al.* 1986; Huntington, 1991). Questions of transitional justice and legal accountability for past human rights violations were understood to be the outcomes of political bargains between elites, and were not therefore central to this political science analysis. Similarly, feminist political science democratisation scholarship was chiefly concerned with actors and institutions. Consequently, accountability for past human rights violations was largely understood as simply an outcome of political compromise in both mainstream and feminist political science democratisation scholarship. Decisions to prosecute and punish or to forgive and forget were all about politics, and the balance of political power between former authoritarian actors and new democratic actors such as political parties (Huntingdon 1991). As such, backward-looking decisions around accountability motivated little interest or analysis from feminist political scientists studying democratisation, who were more centrally concerned with forward-looking policy issues of domestic violence and abortion and levels of women's political participation in new democratic institutions. Against this ambitious feminist agenda for transformation, questions of accountability for human rights violations of prior non-democratic actors appeared peripheral and of relevance to only a very small constituency of direct victims and their immediate family members.

Contemporary transitional justice scholarship is more clearly identified with the normative work of human rights lawyers of the early 1990s, who argued that international human rights standards were applicable to and should be enforced during political transitions in order to hold perpetrators of serious violations to account (e.g. Roht-Arriaza 1990; Orentlicher 1991). With the emergence of normative legal work in the study of transitions, which articulated a duty on post-authoritarian states to prosecute perpetrators of the prior regime under international human rights law (e.g. Roht-Arriaza 1990; Orentlicher 1991), the precise scope of the legal obligation – for what offences, in what circumstances – motivated very substantial doctrinal analysis.[1] However, the advent of attention from international human rights lawyers in questions of accountability in democratisation transitions did not at this early stage motivate feminist analysis, as human rights in transitional justice was found to be doggedly male-centric, exclusively concerned with the male political actor. Within this emerging conversation concerning legal obligations to prosecute past wrongdoers for a defined and narrow set of offences, feminist legal scholars were largely silent.

But the early 1990s was also a seminal period in feminist scholarly and political interventions into international human rights law, to demand the protection and promotion of a new set of women's human rights,[2] most notably in terms of violence against women (e.g. MacKinnon 1993; Thomas and Beasley 1993). Women's reproductive rights were also prominent (Plata 1994; Heise 1995: 238). Specific demands from feminist international lawyers for past-focused accountability for offences by a prior non-democratic regime did not, however, emerge. In common with feminist political science analysis of transitions, past-focused accountability demands motivated relatively few scholarly interventions or analyses from feminist international lawyers. In both feminist legal and political analysis of transitions, feminist priorities were forward-looking to the political, legal and social ordering of the new state, with little interest in backward-looking questions of accountability for civil and political rights violations of an (overwhelmingly) male group.

Rather, it was the shattering revelations of widespread sexual violence against female civilian populations in the Balkans conflict that motivated concerted feminist scholarship and advocacy seeking the prosecution of certain offences committed against women in contexts of political violence. Groundbreaking work of the mid-1990s by international legal scholars such as Rhonda Copelon (1994), Christine Chinkin (1994), Kelly Askin (1997), Judith Gardam (1997) and others identified the potential to prosecute rape and sexual violence against women within the contemporary body of international criminal law and international humanitarian law, and also proposed substantial legal reform to better capture such violence under international law. Although principally linked to backward-looking concerns of securing accountability for past incidences of conflict-related sexual violence against women, this belated feminist engagement with questions of transitional justice was also motivated by a growing appreciation of the contemporary and forward-looking significance of improved accountability for these gendered harms against women. Three broad rationales can be discerned for the attribution of contemporary significance by feminists to securing accountability for past conflict-related sexual harms against women. First, securing accountability for conflict-related sexual violence was linked to initiatives to end impunity

1 For a contemporary statement of the relevant law, see Mallinder (2008).

2 Paradigmatically, see Bunch (1990). See generally Cook (1994).

for violence against women more broadly.[3] In a related vein, efforts to activate criminal accountability under international law for violence against women offered an important site for advancing broader normative developments in international law concerning women's rights (Reilly 2009: 93–115). And finally, there was a belief that progressive developments in the criminalisation and prosecution of sexual violence under international law could potentially lead to positive norm transfer from the international to the domestic realm in the legal treatment of gendered harms against women (Green *et al.* 1994; Ní Aoláin 1997).

Legal analysis of gender and transition thus emerged as distinct from the transition scholarship of feminist political science.[4] The feminist legal scholarship does, to some limited extent, continue the analysis of women's mobilisation that is prominent in feminist political science (e.g. Bedont and Hall Martinez 1999). However, feminist legal scholarship of transition has radically expanded the institutional focus of analysis by bringing in a range of legal and quasi-legal mechanisms and institutions. The most prominent of such mechanisms are justice initiatives involving selective prosecutions and wider amnesties,[5] truth recovery and truth-telling processes (e.g. Ross 2003; Ní Aoláin and Turner 2007), reparations (Rubio-Marin 2006b) and the reform of institutions most directly complicit in the human rights violations of the past. Specifically legal analysis of gender and transition has brought transitional justice processes under the investigation of feminist scholars considering the transformative potential of transitions for women. One of the key questions motivating such analysis has consistently been the definition of harms against women under international law.

The evolution of harms in international law and transitional justice

The term 'harms' refers to women's lived experiences of political violence, and is to be distinguished from legal categories of criminal offences or human rights violations. Feminist legal scholars have pointed to the critical role that law plays in shaping the social understanding of harm (West 1991; Conaghan 1996). As this section documents, while harms experienced by women in contexts of political violence remain relatively consistent during the period under analysis, legal capture[6] of those harms, as violations of international human rights law and

3 As noted by Christine Chinkin (1994: 341), 'recent steps within the international community to ensure that women's rights are recognised as human rights and to enhance the accountability of governments for violence against women are as much an integral part of the overall counter-attack on the war against women as are the more publicised and dramatic responses to events in the former Yugoslavia'.

4 For an introductory account of this scholarship, see Bell and O'Rourke (2007).

5 This literature is too extensive to cite in full, but see generally Askin (1997).

6 For a discussion of legal capture of gendered harms, see Ní Aoláin (2000a).

offence under international criminal law and international humanitarian law, has evolved substantially over time.

Public/private

In gender analysis of international law, the identification of a public/private divide in harms falling within the purview of international law, and those falling outside legal classifications, has been key (Charlesworth and Chinkin 2000). Classical liberalism draws a sharp distinction between the public world of government and commerce, and the private world of family and home. The former is deemed political and consequently requiring state regulation. The latter, by contrast, concerns apolitical matters governed by free individual choice (Mill 1859). The private is the realm in which individuals are entitled to assert their autonomy from state interference. Feminist analysis has revealed the gendered nature of this divide – that women spend most of their lives in the private realm – and how, in turn, this division of public and private makes invisible a range of harms experienced by women within the private realm.[7] Continuing impunity around violence within the home (Amnesty International 2001b), and the relatively unrestricted availability of pornography (MacKinnon 1993), are identified as the practical discriminatory outworking of the public/private divide.

Feminist analysis has traced the consequences of the public/private divide in the gendered deficiencies of the human rights framework (Bunch 1990) and the normative structure of international law (Charlesworth *et al.* 1991; Charlesworth and Chinkin 2000). The prioritisation of civil and political rights in the human rights canon reflects and perpetuates the prioritisation of the public over the private: civil and political rights govern the relationship of an individual's 'public' life and their relationship with government. While women are also beneficiaries of this guarantee, the public is not the realm in which women most need this guarantee of protection. The traditional canon of human rights was the subject of heavy feminist critique for its focus on violations of civil and political rights of political activists by state agents (a catalogue of human rights violations that Charlesworth (1993: 8) has damningly characterised as 'what men fear most will happen to them').

The implications of this focus on the male political actor, and the harms he incurred in contexts of political violence, was to cast women's experience of harm in such contexts as vicarious, through the familial relationship to the male political actor. In early transitional justice women's experiences of harm could be characterised as *secondary victimhood*: women have most often been visible as 'indirect' victims of harms in contexts of violent conflict and political repression. The harms that are most prominent in a focus on women's secondary victimhood is the absence and loss of a close family member, the disruption to family life and

7 The seminal text in this area is Pateman (1988).

harmony caused by such loss, and the hardships encountered by those women in their campaigns for justice for the loss of a family member.

'Adding women'

Although the autonomous political actor is classically understood as male (Elshtain 1981), there is extensive evidence of women as political actors in the public sphere. In turn, women political actors have been subjected to similar forms of torture and extrajudicial killings as their male counterparts, and this has activated the same human rights concerns as in respect of male victims.[8] (Indeed, when Amnesty International was first approached to work on the human rights of women in 1981, the organisation responded by saying that it could only work on the issue of 'women as political prisoners'.[9]) Over time, international human rights law has been forced to acknowledge certain instances in which *women experience the same physical harms as men in contexts of political violence.* In this way, women are recognised as enduring the same physical harms as men while performing roles traditionally held by men within traditionally male domains.

Feminist-informed revelations around *the different physical harms women experience in similar circumstances as men in contexts of political violence* has marked an important expansion in the harms to women that are visible to international law and to transitional justice. Although performing similar roles in similar circumstances as men, women political activists can also suffer different gender-specific forms of harm. Most notable in this category of harms is rape and other forms of sexual victimisation that women experience in conflict and detention. This recognition of sexual violence perpetrated by state actors as torture was achieved in the 1990s through landmark jurisprudence of the regional human rights bodies.[10] Recognition of the different physical harms women experience during political violence has longer antecedence in international criminal law and international humanitarian law. The post-Second World War trials at Nuremberg were silent on the sexual violence experienced by female civilians, despite significant evidence of rape by both Allied and Nazi forces during the war (Brownmiller 1993). However, in the International Military Tribunal for the Far East (IMTFE), offences of rape were included within war crimes charges, though the IMTFE Charter did not enumerate rape as a prosecutable violation.[11] It was the shattering revelations of widespread sexual violence against female civilian populations in the Balkans conflict that motivated concerted feminist scholarship and advocacy seeking the prosecution of rape and sexual violence against women committed in

8 See, for example, Amnesty International (1985) on the detention of women prisoners.

9 Account from Reilly (2009: 69).

10 *Raquel Martí de Mejía v Perú*, Inter-Am. C.H.R., Case 10.970, Report No. 5/96 (1996); *Aydin v Turkey*, ECHR, Application Number 57/1996/676/866 (1997).

11 See further Askin (1997).

the course of armed conflict.[12] Central to the changes secured in international law was the recognition of women's experiences of sexual violence in armed conflict as amongst the most serious crimes of war by including rape within the definitions of a 'grave breach' of the Geneva Conventions,[13] of crimes against humanity[14] and of genocide.[15] The Rome Statute of the International Criminal Court (ICC) codified these developments and went beyond them by explicitly recognising rape, sexual slavery, enforced prostitution, pregnancy and sterilisation, and other forms of sexual violence as crimes against humanity and as war crimes.[16] More recently, the Special Court for Sierra Leone, established jointly by the Sierra Leonean government and the United Nations to prosecute serious violations of domestic criminal and international humanitarian law, held forced marriage to be an element satisfying the requirements of crimes against humanity.[17]

Gendered contradictions

Recognition of the gender-specific forms of public harm endured by women in contexts of political violence, in particular their sexual victimisation, has been important in revealing gendered contradictions in the concerns of transitional justice. There have been substantial gains in international human rights law in recent years in terms of requiring states to prohibit, prevent and punish violence perpetrated by private actors. A proliferation of soft law instruments and consensus documents emerging from international human rights conferences has asserted that women's rights are human rights. Doctrinal developments have been most pronounced in respect of the rights of women to live free from violence, and to a lesser extent the rights of women to reproductive autonomy. Treaty-monitoring bodies and the jurisprudence of regional human rights bodies have articulated obligations on states to prohibit, prevent and punish violence against women and to guarantee the rights of women to exercise reproductive choice without coercion or discrimination. Developments around the horizontal application of human rights standards, in particular in respect of state obligations to prevent, prohibit

12 For an overview of feminist mobilisation in this area and account of the development of the relevant international legal norms, see Bedont and Hall Martinez (1999).

13 *Prosecutor v Tadic*, No. IT-94-1-T (7 May 1997).

14 Statute of the International Criminal Tribunal for the Former Yugoslavia, UNSC Res 827 annex, Article 5(g) (25 May 1993), 32 ILM 1203 (1993); Statute of the International Criminal Tribunal for Rwanda, UNSC Res 955 (8 November 1994), 33 ILM 1398 (1994); Rome Statute of the International Criminal Court [hereinafter Rome Statute], 17 July 1998, 2187 UNTS 3, Article 8; Statute of the Special Court for Sierra Leone, annex to Agreement on the Establishment of the Special Court for Sierra Leone, 16 January 2002, UN-Sierra Leone.

15 *Prosecutor v Jean-Paul Akayesu*, ICTR-96-4-T Delivered on 2 September 1998. The Court's reasoning in holding rape as constitutive of genocide has not been pursued in further jurisprudence by either the ICTR or ICTY, and remains highly controversial in feminist circles (Engle 2005).

16 Rome Statute, Articles 7 and 8.

17 *Vasiljevic*, IT-98-32-A, Appeals Chamber, 25 February 2004, para 165.

and punish domestic and sexual violence, have worked impressively to propel the global problem of violence against women to the mainstream of the human rights canon. Sustained feminist political mobilisation and engagement with human rights instruments secured recognition in the human rights canon of how women can suffer different gender-specific harms in the same contexts as men, in particular in respect of sexual violence and rape of women detainees.[18] The regional human rights courts have grown increasingly assertive in their articulation of state obligations to prohibit, prevent and punish violence perpetrated against women by private actors. In *MC v Bulgaria*, the European Court of Human Rights held that the state's failure to investigate an alleged rape case was in violation of the positive obligations under the prohibition of torture, inhuman and degrading treatment, and, significantly, that this 'obligation cannot be considered limited to cases of ill-treatment by state officials'.[19] Further, in *Opuz v Turkey* the European Court went on to find the state's failure to prevent and protect the applicant from the violence of her spouse not just a violation of the positive obligations under the prohibition of inhuman and degrading treatment, but by attributing the state's failure to the general attitudes of the local authorities, such as the manner in which women were treated at police stations when they reported domestic violence, and judicial passivity in providing effective protection to victims, the Court held that the state's behaviour constituted discrimination against women.[20] More recently, in the *Campo Algodonero* decision concerning three in a series of unsolved and poorly investigated rapes, disappearances and killings of young women in Ciudad Juarez on the Mexico–United States border, the Inter-American Court of Human Rights affirmed the state's extensive positive obligation to prevent and investigate violence against women by private actors.[21] The Court examined the human rights issues in the context of mass violence against women and structural discrimination, and held that the violence was gender-based and the state's inadequate response constituted discrimination.[22] In these landmark decisions the human rights canon demonstrated the manifold public obligations that pertain to ostensibly private harms of domestic and sexual violence perpetrated by private actors. Moreover, in the jurisprudence emerging from the individual complaints mechanism of the Optional Protocol to the Convention on the Elimination of All Forms of Discrimination against Women (CEDAW), the CEDAW Committee has focused

18 First in the groundbreaking decision of the Inter-American Commission on Human Rights in *Raquel Martí de Mejía v Perú*, Inter-Am. C.H.R., Case 10.970, Report No. 5/96 (1996), and subsequently in the application of the *Mejía* jurisprudence by the European Court of Human Rights in *Aydin v Turkey*, ECHR, Application Number 57/1996/676/866 (1997) and more recently by the Inter-American Court in *Miguel Castro-Castro Prison v Peru* (Merits, Reparations and Costs), IACtHR, Series C 160 (2006).

19 *MC v Bulgaria*, ECHR, Application No. 39272/98 (2003), para 151.

20 *Opuz v Turkey*, ECHR, Application No. 33401/02 (2009), paras 192–198.

21 *Caso González y otras ('Campo Algodonero') v México*, IACtHR, Series C No. 205 (2009), pp 67 (prevent) and 75 (investigate).

22 *Caso González y otras ('Campo Algodonero') v México*, IACtHR, Series C No. 205 (2009), p 100.

on the articulation of the state's due diligence obligations in respect of domestic violence (Sokhi-Bulley 2006). This jurisprudence displays an increasing, and increasingly sophisticated, understanding of how the private sphere poses particular risks to women, and the resulting responsibilities of states to ensure that public institutions respond to the particular circumstances of violence in the private sphere. Furthermore, human rights developments in the arena of reproductive rights have established the responsibility of states to guarantee the physical integrity of women carrying pregnancies that pose a risk to their life or health,[23] including the risk to their mental health.[24] Jurisprudence has been prominent in respect of states' obligations to provide information to women in respect of their reproductive rights,[25] and not to restrict access to information concerning abortion services abroad.[26] In *Tysiac v Poland* the European Court articulated the state's obligations to ensure effective access to legal abortion by establishing appeals and review mechanisms for medical decisions about abortion, to regulate the practice of conscientious objection and to institute other procedural safeguards, as constitutive of the state's positive obligations to ensure the right to private and family life.[27] Again, this human rights jurisprudence marks the articulation of public (state) obligations in respect of intimately private matters of pregnancy and reproduction. Moreover, the state is not permitted to blithely justify the restrictive regulation of women's private reproductive conduct out of deference to perceived 'public morals'.[28] Thus, the state's advancement of political ideologies that rest on the politicisation of women's private reproductive roles is also highly antithetical to human rights law and principles.

The development of the doctrine of horizontal application of human rights has been dramatic in its amelioration of a public/private divide in human rights, especially in respect of women's reproductive rights and the right of women to live free from violence. The canon is no longer exclusively concerned with violations perpetrated by state agents against male political actors. Rather, there has been a dramatic escalation of state responsibility for harms perpetrated against women by private actors. The perpetration of these harms indicate failings in state institutions of policing,[29] criminal justice,[30] prisons,[31] institutions for the guarantee of

23 *Tysiac v Poland*, ECHR, Application no. 5410/03 (2007).
24 *Karen Noelia LLantoy Huamán v Peru*, UNHRC Communication No. 1153/2003 (2005).
25 *A.T. v Hungary*, Communication No. 2/2003, Views of the Committee on the Elimination of Discrimination Against Women under Article 7, paragraph 3, of the Optional Protocol (2003).
26 *Open Door and Dublin Well Woman v Ireland*, ECHR, Application No. 64/1991/316/387–388 (1992).
27 *Tysiac v Poland*, ECHR, Application No. 5410/03 (2007).
28 See especially *Open Door and Dublin Well Woman v Ireland*, ECHR, Application No. 64/1991/316/387–388 (1992) para 68: 'The Court cannot agree that the State's discretion in the field of the protection of morals is unfettered and unreviewable.'
29 See, for example, *Caso González y otras ('Campo Algodonero') v México*, IACtHR, Series C No. 205 (2009).
30 *Caso González y otras ('Campo Algodonero') v México*, IACtHR, Series C No. 205 (2009).
31 *Aydin v Turkey*, ECHR, Application Number 57/1996/676/866 (1997).

equality and human rights,[32] hospitals[33] and schools (e.g. Committee on the Elimination of All Forms of Discrimination Against Women, 2005). While it would be misleading to set out an unduly rosy picture of international human rights law and its treatment of women, it must be acknowledged that substantial and important inroads have been made into the public/private distinction that traditionally defined the canon.

However, as this book reveals, the scale and severity of human rights violations in contexts of political violence leads to the prioritisation of 'most serious' harms in transitional justice. This category of harms concerns a much smaller set of human rights violations, generally those deemed 'most serious' under international human rights law, recognised offences under international criminal law and war crimes under international humanitarian law (Mallinder 2008). Thus, international law in transitional justice rests on, and reinforces, a very particular set of gendered binaries. In particular, transitional justice rests on a traditional and highly gendered understanding of 'public' 'political' violence. Transition is defined as the movement away from political violence perpetrated by state actors and/or non-state armed groups. Within this typology, so-called 'private' violence within homes and communities can continue unseen and unaddressed by the dramatic changes to legal norms and institutions undertaken in transition. Rape in detention or in the context of armed conflict falls within the concerns of transitional justice. Sexual violence perpetrated by an enemy combatant falls within the remit, but rape perpetrated within the violent and militarised context of political violence by a non-combatant falls outside the remit of transitional justice. Forced pregnancy and forced sterilisation as part of a 'widespread or systematic attack on a civilian population' fall within the concerns of transitional justice,[34] but widespread infringements of women's reproductive autonomy that characterise contexts of political violence do not fall within the scope of transitional justice. These contradictions reveal the practical legal outcomes of a gendered public/private division that structures transitional justice. In political and legal decision-making to narrow the range of harms to be recognised and addressed by transitional justice, feminist gains in human rights are lost, and multiple gender-specific harms experienced by women are returned to the private sphere.

Does international law matter for local gender justice?

Implicit in feminist study and critique of international law in transitional justice is the assumption that international law is the most important determinant of

32 *Opuz v Turkey*, ECHR, Application No. 33401/02 (2009).

33 *Karen Noelia LLantoy Huamán v Peru*, UNHRC Communication No. 1153/2003 (2005).

34 To constitute a 'crime against humanity', rape must be part of a 'widespread or systematic attack on a civilian population'. Rome Statute, Article 7(1).

women's experiences of domestic processes of transitional justice. In practice, the actual impact of international law on the human rights outcomes for women of transitional justice is opaque and little understood. While there is some single case analysis of the impact of international law on domestic human rights outcomes for women of transitional justice (see especially Buckley-Zistel and Stanley 2011), and comparative work on the impact of international law on the human rights outcomes for women of particular transitional justice mechanisms (e.g. Rubio-Marin 2006b; Ní Aoláin and Turner 2007), a framework for understanding the impact of international law on human rights outcomes for women in domestic processes of transitional justice that has analytical power across a range of transitional contexts has not yet been developed. The introduction to the book noted the weak enforcement mechanisms attached to international law and the widespread belief that its normative significance is greater than its repressive function. How then are we to understand and identify the impact of international law on human rights outcomes for women in domestic processes of transitional justice?

This book has developed the following framework for understanding the distinct, though related, ways in which international law can matter to human rights outcomes for women of domestic processes of transitional justice, namely normatively, doctrinally and politically.

Normatively

Within transitional justice scholarship, the observation is frequently made that, in societies emerging from mass violations of human rights, domestic law is generally deemed corrupt, biased, deficient or ineffective.[35] International law is identified as significant in filling this legal vacuum in transitional societies. To quote Teitel:

> Positive international law norms are defined in conventions, treaties, and customs. Moreover, in its circumspection of the most heinous abuses, international law offers a source of normative transcendence.
>
> (Teitel 2000: 21)

Feminists, too, have been much exercised about the normative significance of international law. In their path-breaking feminist entry into international law in 1991, Charlesworth, Chinkin and Wright observed the masculinist normative structure of international law, that 'rests on and reproduces' the public/private divide of the domestic legal order, and privileges the state over individuals (Charlesworth *et al* 1991: 625–6). More recent feminist elaborations of this early critique have focused on the theory and method of international law, the

35 Paradigmatically Teitel (2000). See also Campbell and Ní Aoláin (2005); Dugard (2005).

relationship of international law to national and international security, and larger questions of local and global justice.[36]

More optimistically, however, most feminist engagement with international law also maintains a belief in the positive potential for women of international law's normative significance. International law norms change and evolve. New norms emerge. To the extent that positive international law norms are defined in conventions and treaties, these legal instruments show progressive development in the protection of women's rights[37] and socioeconomic rights more broadly,[38] and require increasing levels of individual criminal accountability for harms against women.[39] In each of these respects, international law stands to have a potentially positive normative impact on the shape of transitional justice in domestic states. The criminalisation under international law of individual acts of gender-based violence can set an important marker for the post-conflict and post-authoritarian society of the moral repugnance of these offences. It can shine a light on the structural gender inequalities that enable such offences. Within the legal understanding of the harm under international law lies the potential to progressively reshape social understanding of the harm in the domestic transitional context.

Doctrinally

In transitions from authoritarianism and conflict, substantial – even dramatic – changes to legal regimes of the transitioning state create a rupture or lacuna in the regulatory framework. Old laws, constitutions and legal institutions are dispensed with; new laws, constitutions and legal institutions are introduced and must attempt to build legitimacy. In this period of substantial flux in the legal order, international law offers a consistent and continuous frame for the domestic legal order (Teitel 2000: 20). In providing this continuity, international law preserves the rule of law in the transitional state. However, it also enables transformation, in facilitating accountability for past harms (for example, former East German border guards tried in the 1990s for killing fugitives as they attempted to escape to West Germany were explicitly prosecuted under international law (Geiger 1998)) and in providing a legal framework for reforms to law and legal institutions. For example, new constitutions often incorporate international human rights treaties into the domestic legal order.[40]

36 This scholarship is too extensive to cite comprehensively. For a snapshot of contemporary feminist scholarship in international law, see Kouvo and Pearson (2011).

37 See, for example, the adoption of the Optional Protocol to Convention on the Elimination of All Forms of Discrimination Against Women, 6 October 1999, 2131 UNTS 83.

38 See, for example, the adoption of the Optional Protocol to the International Covenant on Economic, Social and Cultural Rights, 10 December 2008, GA Res. 832, UN GAOR, 63rd Session, UN Doc A/RES/63/117 (2008).

39 See, in particular, the Rome Statute.

40 For a discussion of the incorporation of international human rights treaties into domestic constitutions as part of negotiated settlements, see generally Bell (2000).

Moreover, in transitional justice local decisions around accountability are made with reference to international law. A legal obligation upon transitioning states to prosecute those who bear greatest responsibility for – at a minimum – genocide, crimes against humanity and war crimes, means that domestic compromises around accountability in transitional states operate in the shadow of international law (Mallinder 2007). Recognising this central role of international law in transitions, feminist legal analysis has been principally concerned with the evolving definition of harms against women under international law (e.g. Copelon 1994), and securing legal recognition of rape as a war crime (e.g. Meron 1993), crimes against humanity (Chinkin 1994) and a constitutive act of genocide (e.g. MacKinnon 1994).

International law can guide domestic legislation on related matters of transition and transitional accountability. For example, the famous Pinochet arrest in London and subsequent legal proceedings through the UK courts hinged on section 134 of a domestic statute, the Criminal Justice Act 1988, which incorporated the Convention Against Torture into UK law, and thereby created a new crime under UK law: the crime of torture.[41] Further, there are manifold incidents in which domestic courts deliver positive accountability outcomes through the application of international human rights treaty law to domestic cases. Such examples pertain across domestic litigation initiatives to deliver criminal accountability for past crimes[42] and to vindicate the positive duty on states to prevent discrimination against women in the response of criminal justice institutions to sexual violence.[43]

Politically

The potential political impact of international law on domestic processes of transitional justice is twofold: first, international law can be valuable in affirming women's political equality by, for example, supporting the presence of women in transitional justice processes, and second, international law can play an important role in the strategies adopted by women's movements in their engagement with domestic processes of transitional justice. In terms of the impact of international law on the strategies of women's movements more generally, the findings of Beth Simmons' definitive empirical research on the domestic impact of international human rights treaties are highly relevant (Simmons 2009). The study demonstrates that domestic impact does not turn on interstate relations or peer enforcement by states of the human rights regime. Rather, it was concluded that it is in

41 *Regina v Bow Street Metropolitan Stipendiary Magistrate, ex parte Pinochet Ugarte*, [1999] 2 WLR 827 (HL).

42 See, for example, Collins (2006: 732) for discussion of the application of international treaty law to domestic prosecution and civil actions for past crimes in Chile and El Salvador.

43 *Carmichele v Minister of Safety & Security & Another* 2001 (10) BCLR 995 (CC) (S. Afr.) para 62, applying the CEDAW.

the empowerment of domestic actors to mobilise successfully to secure domestic implementation that international treaties hold their significance (Simmons 2009). The Simmons study points in particular to the effectiveness of this strategy with respect to the Convention Against Torture and the Convention on the Elimination of all Forms of Discrimination Against Women, two treaties with the greatest potential significance for the human rights outcomes for women of transitional justice. The 'consistently important role [international human rights treaty law and related mobilisation] has played in polities in which institutions are changing, evolving, and in flux' is noted (Simmons 2009: 360). Moreover, the Simmons study concludes, the supportive international legal framework can promote and reinforce the legitimacy of the domestic demands of women's movements (Simmons 2009: 357).

In the specific case of repressive or authoritarian states, transnational co-ordination between local civil society and with civil society in other states to push international institutions to press for improved human rights performance of recalcitrant governments has been found to be critical to the effectiveness of domestic civil society mobilisation (Keck and Sikkink 1998). Transnational co-ordination by women's movements to enhance the rights of women to live free from violence has been identified as a particularly salient and effective case (Keck and Sikkink 1998: 165–98). The existence of a supportive international legal framework was critical in facilitating this transnational co-ordination and in providing a common language and tools for such co-ordination across women's movements in diverse nations and cultures (Keck and Sikkink 1998: 165–98). Whether or not local women's movements could look to neighbouring women's movements and a transnational feminist network to support their claims was, in part at least, dependent on a supportive international framework to facilitate such co-ordination. The parallel NGO forum at the 1995 UN Fourth World Conference on Women is regarded as paradigmatic of the mutually constitutive relationship of the framework of international law and women's transnational mobilisation (Friedman 2003; Reilly 2009).

Further, this transnational co-ordination is critical in fostering peer enforcement by states of international human rights obligations. In the early 1990s, for example, human rights networks co-operated to pressurise the USA and European states to impose human rights reforms on non-compliant states of Central America by de-funding the repressive military governments of El Salvador and Guatemala (Burgerman 1998).

In a related vein, developments in the international legal framework can also facilitate new alliances across movements. Paradigmatic here is the belated and hard-won adoption of violence against women as a human rights issue within the mainstream human rights NGO community. Women's organisations co-ordinated to press the institutions of, in particular, the United Nations to work on women's rights within their human rights agencies (Joachim 2007: 122–30). Amnesty International and Human Rights Watch began, in turn, to document and report on human rights violations experienced by women. These developments at the international and transnational level have, in certain instances, facilitated domestic co-ordination between human rights organisations and women's movements in the advancement of women's rights.

'The international frame'

While the impact of international law on the human rights outcomes for women of domestic processes of transitional justice may be opaque and little understood, it is clear that several valuable related lines of inquiry have been pursued within broader feminist scholarship in international law and human rights. International law is identified as particularly significant in defining categories of harm in domestic processes of transitional justice and, correspondingly, in determining legal requirements of accountability within those processes. The significance of international law in setting the normative framework for domestic processes of transitional justice has been identified. Moreover, the starting point for feminist interventions into transitional justice has critiqued the flawed 'from' and 'to' of transition, in which ending the public harms of the 'primary' conflict has been prioritised (see especially Bell and O'Rourke 2007). Politically, international law is identified as potentially significant in affirming women's political equality and shaping the interventions of women's movements into domestic processes of transitional justice. International law can form the basis of co-operative working relationships between women's movements transnationally and between women's movements and other social movements, most notably human rights movements. Conversely, international law can foster competition between such movements as they vie for the normative and material resources of international law. In this book, the term 'the international frame' refers to the potential threefold normative, doctrinal and political role of international law in determining the human rights outcomes for women of domestic processes of transitional justice.

WOMEN, POLITICS AND TRANSITION: 'THE LOCAL FIT'

Feminist analysis in international law identifies several important grounds for both concern and optimism in the operation of international law within domestic processes of transitional justice. However, what we lack to date is an understanding of when, how and under what domestic circumstances international law acts progressively to advance the human rights of women in transitional justice normatively, legally and politically. Succinctly stated, we do not know enough about the local gender politics that influence the human rights outcomes for women of transitional justice. What are the key factors? Who are the key actors? What are the key issues in which international law can play a progressive role?

In unpicking local gender politics, and its role in shaping the domestic implementation of international law in transitional justice, substantial insights are already on offer from feminist political science studies of transitions. Feminist political science analysis of transitions offers an invaluable analytical framework for considering the most pertinent domestic factors in determining gender outcomes of transitions. As this chapter outlines, the domestic factors identified to be most pertinent are the location of women's movements within the local political opportunity structure, the relationship of women's movements to civil society allies and the resonance of women's movements' demands with the dominant narrative of transition.

Feminist scholarly analysis of transition emerged in response to the democratisation transitions of the Latin American Southern Cone and Eastern and Southern Europe. This scholarship, a subfield of political science and comparative politics, emerged as a challenge to the mainstream political science democratisation literature, disputing the focus on democratic elections and related procedures within mainstream literature.[44] Inspired by the scale of broad-based women's mobilisation, and the 'opening' in the political system created by transitions, this initial feminist analysis – preceding or coinciding with the 'transitional moment' – was optimistic in tone (see especially Jaquette 1989). Analysts were duly excited by the prospects of a new and more participatory model of politics that might emerge. The prominence of women's organisations in movements for democracy suggested that new state institutions might be more accommodating to their presence and receptive to their demands.

More sober feminist assessments of transition were, however, soon to follow. Feminist scholarship in the early 1990s, based on empirical analysis of transitions, demonstrated that 'institutional democratisation does not necessarily entail a democratisation of power relations in society at large, particularly between men and women' (Waylen 1994: 329).[45] The particular focus of this literature was the under-representation of women in new democratic institutions (Jaquette 1994), and the tendency for transitions to be accompanied by the large-scale retreat of women from the public sphere of protest and politics to the retrenched (though reorganised) private sphere of domesticity and capitalist development (e.g. Fitzsimmons 2000).

Subsequently, less sanguine feminist transition scholarship turned to the impact of transition on particular policy issues, such as domestic violence or abortion, examining whether transition had resulted in an improved state response to policy areas of particular concern to women (e.g. Htun 2003). This policy focus generated interest in the bespoke institutions established by newly democratic governments to advance the substantive and symbolic representation of women in politics, known generically as national women's machineries (NWMs).[46] The

44 For an excellent review of the relationship of gender and transition literature to mainstream political science, see Waylen (2007: 1–48).

45 Sonia Alvarez's 1990 study of gender and transition in Brazil was the path-breaking study in this area.

46 See generally Rai (2003). For a discussion of transition politics and NWMs, see Waylen (1996). The Chilean case has been particularly prominent in this literature.

relationship of NWMs to established women's organisations, and the effectiveness of NWMs in advancing contentious policy initiatives, has been of particular interest in this scholarship (Waylen 1996; Rai 2003). This renewed attention to policy issues has also prompted close attention to the impact of a re-established public sphere (free elections, democratic institutions) on the ostensibly private concerns of body, home and family (see especially Htun 2003). In particular, the increased regulation of women's sexuality and reproductive capacities that tends to be imposed by newly democratised political systems (Fuszara 1991; Htun 2003; Blofield 2006) has demonstrated the potentially non-linear and illiberal trajectory of transition for women.

Geographically, feminist transition scholarship remained largely confined to democratisation transitions of Latin America, and to a lesser extent Eastern Europe. A particular analytical frame and common set of research questions is therefore apparent in analysis. The recurrent motif was attention to women's mobilisation, and in terms of state institutions analysis was largely restricted to national parliaments and NWMs. The South African transition, however, generated some important new departures in feminist political science analysis of transition. First, the turn to South Africa signalled a new geographical focus within transition scholarship. Moreover, the South African transition involved a conflict-to-peace axis, in addition to the democratisation focus of earlier transition scholarship.[47] Perhaps most significantly, the centrality of legal change – in particular the new constitution and the assertive and progressive constitutional court – to the transition first posited constitutional change in transition as significant for feminist analysis (e.g. Albertyn 1994; Murphy 2003). Notably, this turn in scholarship has facilitated comparative feminist analysis of constitutional change across a range of transitional and non-transitional contexts, such as Canada, the European Union, Iraq and Afghanistan (Dobrowolsky 2000; Dobrowolsky and Hart 2003). To date, this scholarship has tended to confine analysis to women's mobilisation to impact constitutional design and the substance of women's rights given constitutional recognition, and has even prompted a revisiting of earlier transitions with this revised research focus (e.g. Waylen 2006). Hence, the South African transition has marked an expansion of focus of feminist transition literature to attend also to legal reform in transition.

As the period of time and number of cases for analysis expands, feminist transition literature has retrospectively attempted to draw global 'lessons' or 'conclusions' about the gendered legacy of transition.[48] 'What do we know?' (Waylen 2003: 157). By focusing on the interplay of actors and institutions (women's movements, political parties and the extent of the 'rupture' in transition between repressive regimes and their democratic successors), this literature attempts to discern

47 For this discussion of 'axes' of transitions, see Campbell and Ní Aoláin (2005).

48 In particular, the work of Georgina Waylen has been central to this area: see Waylen (2003), (2004), (2007).

the circumstances for 'optimum gender outcomes' in transition (see especially Waylen 2003). Optimum gender outcomes are assessed with reference to the substantive and symbolic representation of women in politics, and particular policy outcomes around domestic violence, reproductive health, marriage and divorce laws, and family and property rights (Waylen 2003: 170).

This evaluative turn in feminist transition scholarship prompted greater reflection on the factors that determined the success (or otherwise) of feminist engagement with the transitional state. In a thoughtful application of social movements theory, feminist scholars of transitions gave more specific consideration to the relative power of actors within the formal political system (in particular, 'gatekeeper' political parties) and outside the political system (such as the church, the former non-democratic regime leaders and male-dominated left-wing social movements) that influenced the outcomes of transition for women (Molyneux 1985, 1998). Further, the relative openness of the new state's institutional arena (which Waylen has categorised as electoral, constitutional and bureaucratic) was also identified as important in the *political opportunity structure* (Waylen 2007: 203). These studies suggested that, while activists targeted the institutions most open to them, access to only one institutional arena made success unlikely (Waylen 2007: 203). In addition, studies of the dynamics of women's organising revealed the significance of the relationship of women's organisations to other social and political organisations in determining their success. Observing this relationship was an effective shorthand for determining a women's movement's *resource mobilisation* in the transitional context. Autonomous women's organisations appeared less successful than those who were able to mobilise additional resources through alliances with, in particular, political parties.[49] Further, the success of women's movements' strategies seemed to turn on whether the *framing* of such strategies resonated with the dominant political narrative of the transition. Waylen offers the South African experience of women's movements framing feminist demands as demands for human rights as an example of effective feminist framing that fitted within the political narrative that the transition would mark the beginning of widespread respect for human rights.[50] Finally, feminist scholarship of transitions revealed the importance of adopting a disaggregated approach to distinct gender policy areas. In her review of legal reform on abortion, divorce and family law in transitions in Argentina, Chile and Brazil, Mala Htun shows how each of these issues were embedded in different logics behind the state's role in regulating private lives and thus could not be collapsed into a single area of 'gender policy reform' analysis (Htun 2003). In practical terms, feminist scholars of transitions have documented how proposals for policy reforms in distinct gender issues mobilised different

49 For a discussion of the strategies of either 'double militancy' or autonomy adopted by such movements, see Schild (1997).

50 The 'findings' from the gender and transition scholarship are summarised in the tour de force opening chapter of Waylen (2007: 1–48).

Table 1.1 Understanding local gender politics in transitions: 'the local fit'

Political opportunity structure	Relative power of actors within the political system (political parties, bureaucrats), and actors outside the political system (church, left-wing social movements) Openness of electoral, constitutional and bureaucratic arena
Resource mobilisation	Relationship of women's organisations to potential allies in political parties, human rights groups, popular sector organisations, left-wing social movements
Framing	Resonance of demands of women's organisations with dominant political narrative of transition
Disaggregating gender policy issues	Different gender policy issues mobilising different oppositional groups, with varying levels of political power

oppositional constituencies, with different degrees of political power, and gave rise to different policy outcomes (Alvarez 1990; Blofield 2006).

Feminist political science analysis of transitions therefore offers an invaluable analytical framework for considering the most pertinent domestic factors in determining gender outcomes of transitions. These factors are termed in this book 'the local fit'. It refers to the location of women's movements within the local political opportunity structure, the relationship of women's movements to civil society allies (resource mobilisation), and the resonance of women's movements' demands with the dominant narrative of transition (framing). Moreover, it is wise to be alert to the different prospects for feminist success on different gender policy issues.

NEGOTIATING 'THE INTERNATIONAL FRAME' AND 'THE LOCAL FIT': A NEW FRAMEWORK FOR ANALYSIS

Given the discussion so far, it should be clear by now that this book rejects either the local or the international as chiefly determinative of the outcomes for women of transitional justice. Rather, feminist political and legal insights into transitions together indicate a dynamic and interactive relationship of international law and local gender politics in determining the human rights outcomes for women of domestic processes of transitional justice. To illustrate: the relative power of local political parties and social movements may determine the location of women's movements within the political opportunity structure of the transitional state, but international law can empower women's movements by reinforcing the legitimacy of their demands in transitional justice processes. The openness of the electoral, constitutional and administrative arena to non-elites may determine the likely success of women's movement demands on the state, but international law can impact the domestic legislative and constitutional framework and foster more sympathetic responses from domestic institutions of transitional justice.

Similarly, the relationship of women's movements to potential allies in human rights movements and women's movements in different jurisdictions may depend on their effectiveness in domestic resource mobilisation, but international law also underpins the normative and doctrinal framework for collaborative political work between these different social movements as they engage transitional justice processes. Moreover, where international law recognises women's rights and affirms women's political equality, this can support the raising of feminist consciousness within local women's movements. In terms of framing, the resonance of women's movement demands in transitional justice processes with the dominant political narrative of transition may be an important indicator of the success of those

Table 1.2 Bridging 'the Local Fit' and 'the International Frame': determining human rights outcomes for women in transitional justice

Political opportunity structure	Supportive international law can • empower women's movements in their engagement with transitional justice processes by reinforcing the legitimacy of their demands; and • impact the domestic legislative and constitutional framework of transitional justice processes and foster more sympathetic response from state institutions to women's movements' claims
Resource mobilisation	International law can underpin co-operative working relationships with women's movements and • other social movements (especially human rights organisations) engaging transitional justice processes and • with women's movements in other jurisdictions and operating internationally Raising feminist consciousness
Framing	International law can influence the dominant political narrative of transition to make it more accommodating to demands of women's movements
Disaggregating gender policy issues	International law, is potentially more progressive and prescriptive in respect of certain gender issues than other law in transitional justice processes

demands. However, international law also plays an important normative role in influencing the dominant narrative (the 'from' and 'to') of transition and the extent to which structural gender inequalities are identified and redressed. Finally, different gender policy issues may progress with different levels of success in domestic transitional justice processes, but international law is also more progressive and prescriptive on certain human rights of women than others.

QUESTIONS MOTIVATING THE BOOK

This book is fundamentally concerned with understanding why some transitional justice processes deliver more progressive human rights outcomes for women than other such processes, and the relative role of international law and local gender politics in determining those outcomes. This book aims to contribute to theoretical debate in feminist political science by introducing a framework for systematically considering the impact of international law on domestic gender politics in transitions. Further, the book contributes to feminist scholarship in international law through detailed grounded case study analysis of the domestic impact of international law on violence against women and reproductive rights in transitional states and illuminating the most important local political factors that determine this impact. In exploring why some transitional justice processes produce better human rights outcomes for women than other such processes, this book addresses a critical set of questions rarely considered by analysts of either gender outcomes of transitions or critical feminist scholarship of international law, namely: in transitional justice processes, under what domestic political conditions does international law reinforce the legitimacy of women's movements' demands and positively influence the legal framework in which women's movements make their demands? Under what domestic circumstances does international law affirm women's political equality, underpin co-operative working arrangements between women's movements and other social movements (in particular human rights organisations), and raise feminist consciousness of local women's movements? Does international law influence the dominant political narrative of transition to make it more accommodating to demands of women's movements engaging transitional justice processes? In the implementation of international law in domestic processes of transitional justice, on what gender issues is international law more prescriptive and progressive?

Chapter 2

Justice for what?

Recognising a web of gender-based harms against women in transitional justice

INTRODUCTION

So far, this book has used the term 'human rights outcomes for women' in the context of transitional justice rather uncritically. Chapter 1 signposted the evolution of human rights and international law in the recognition of women's experiences of political violence, from women as secondary victims to women as primary victims of the same – and different – physical harms as men. The definition of women's human rights in transitional justice is, therefore, a moving target. Moreover, efforts to expand the definition of women's human rights have been critical terrain in feminist engagement with transitional justice.[1] Feminist engagement with human rights and transitional justice has always worked on two fronts, seeking both the protection of the human rights framework for violations against women, while also seeking to challenge and redefine the narrow understandings of violations that fall within the human rights frame.

In this same spirit of simultaneous engagement and critique, this chapter sets out the understanding of women's human rights that underpins the remainder of the book. The chapter seeks to work creatively within the strictures of the human rights canon, to reveal a web of public *and* private harms against women in contexts of political violence.

'Starting from women's lives'[2]: public and private harms as different, though complexly related

The approach advocated here is a nuanced understanding of how gender hierarchies interact with other political cleavages and dynamics to determine women's experiences of harm in contexts of political violence. In the account of women's experiences of public and private harms that follows, this chapter sets out the manner in which public harms of violent conflict and political repression

1 See further Ní Aoláin and O'Rourke (2010).
2 Bunch (1990: 496).

exacerbate and alter the nominally 'private' harms of violence against women in the home, on the body, the repressive regulation of women's reproductive lives, and the manipulation of women's collective organising. In capturing this account of different though complexly related public and private harms, a web of harms against women is proposed. The image of the web is apt: the web describes the connections between different types of harms against women, identifying the relationship of public to private harms. However, the collapse of those harms into a single indistinguishable set is eschewed.

Four aspects of how the context of political violence exacerbates women's private experiences of harm are emphasised and documented in the case studies:

1. First, political violence has a negative impact on the state's capacity to prohibit, prevent and punish private harms against women.
2. Second, political violence gives rise to the militarisation of everyday life, which erodes any notion of a private sphere for women free from the state's negative infringement of her bodily integrity. This manifests in sexualised harms to women political activists.
3. Third, heightened gender ideologies in periods of political violence lead to the acute public regulation of women's private reproductive lives.
4. Fourth, women often enter the public sphere during periods of political violence on the basis of the private maternal role and the need to provide for one's family and community. However, recognition of the subversive potential of women's collective action results in the public political manipulation of women's organising.

While this account of harms in the case studies is necessarily brief, the discussion identifies and articulates the relationship between private and public harms against women in contexts of political violence on which analysis in the remainder of the book relies.

Private violence against women and the state's deficient public response

In each of the cases under study, the context of political violence exacerbated the private incidences of domestic violence against women. In particular, the state's prioritisation of political violence over and above private violence meant that victims of domestic violence could not rely on the state's protective role against their victimisers. Through state inaction, this violence was invisible and implicitly condoned. The manifold deficiencies of public institutions exacerbated private incidences of violence. As this section will detail, whereas deficiencies in the police response were particularly evident in Northern Ireland, in Chile the complicity of the judiciary in perpetuating domestic violence was particularly significant. Moreover, in particular in Colombia, the militarisation of society created a climate of impunity for violence generally, that had a specifically gendered impact on the manifestation of domestic violence in the country.

Chile

In Chile, the socialist presidency of Salvador Allende was deposed by military coup in 1973 (Borzutzky and Oppenheim 2006). Political opposition was brutally suppressed under the military regime. Following the coup, approximately 6,000 individuals were arrested in a mass round-up by the new regime in Santiago. In this period repressive methods were unpredictable: courts-martial, summary executions, trial or indefinite detention (Frühling 1983). On 17 June 1974 the Bureau of National Intelligence (DINA) was created and empowered to arrest and detain people in secret locations. This marked the centralisation of the state's repressive apparatus. Within six months of the coup, the military had arrested 80,000 persons, and 160,000 suffered politically motivated job dismissals. An estimated 200,000 persons, including political refugees and their families, went into exile. The regime expelled 30,000 students, and replaced thousands of university professors with military personnel (Baldez 2002: 125). In the regime's first 18 months, one in every ten Chilean families was affected by arrest, detention or exile, and thousands of Chileans were executed (Americas Watch 1983a: 3). Detentions, disappearances and deaths continued at a high level until 1977.

In Chile, the impact of military rule on domestic violence was most pronounced in the response of the judiciary. The military junta formally respected the independence of the judiciary.[3] In practice, however, the courts were almost idle in respect of supervision of the legality of the regime's activities. Indeed, of over 5,400 habeas corpus petitions filed with the Chilean courts between 1973 and 1983, all but 10 were rejected, as the courts willingly accepted the official explanation that detained individuals had gone missing only after they had been released by the military or police (Hilbink 2007: 1). Judicial complicity in the perpetration of violence was not confined to habeas corpus petitions. Feminist organisations such as *La Morada* and DOMOS were active on the issue of domestic violence during the dictatorship. The first legal survey on domestic violence in Chile, carried out between October 1987 and December 1988, demonstrated the extent of judicial complicity in the impunity surrounding domestic violence in the country (Gonzales 1989). The study analysed the files of court cases from three regions for the crimes of injury, parricide and homicide of a wife or companion filed in 1986, and reviewed the rulings of the Court of Appeals and the Supreme Court from 1980 to 1986 for these same crimes. The study found that in the cases of the lower courts examined, no case resulted in a punishment set for the assailant. Analysis of judicial reasoning in the Court of Appeals and Supreme Court found that domestic violence tended to be justified or excused, rather than punished. Clear patterns

3 Decree Law No. 1, Diario Oficial, 11 September 1973.

were evident in the judicial response to domestic violence and more widespread failure of the Chilean judiciary to protect the human rights of individuals during this period.[4]

Northern Ireland

In Northern Ireland, the political conflict has lengthy historical roots, but hinges on the competing national aspirations of the minority Irish (largely Catholic) nationalist community, who seek a united Ireland, and the majority British (largely Protestant) unionist community, who seek to remain part of the United Kingdom. In parallel with the emergence of peaceful civil rights agitation in the 1960s (Northern Ireland Civil Rights Association 1978), the prospect of physical force resistance to the state gathered momentum. The response both directly by the state and by pro-state mobs was hostile, often violent. As civil unrest and violence spiralled, the British government authorised the mobilisation of units from the garrison force of the British Army in August 1969. In 1970 the recently remobilised paramilitary organisation, the Irish Republican Army, split into the Official IRA and the Provisional IRA (IRA or 'the Provisionals'), the latter of which was to pursue Irish independence through a campaign of violence. In response to continued unrest, the Northern Ireland executive introduced internment without trial on 9 August 1971 under the Civil Authorities (Special Powers) Act 1922 with British government approval. Within the first six months of its operation, sweeps by the police and army led to the arrest of almost two-and-a-half thousand individuals, all but a handful from the Catholic/Nationalist community (Foster 1988). It was the shooting dead of 13 unarmed civilians by the British Army at a banned anti-internment march in the city of Derry in 1972 that finally prompted the proroguement of the Northern Irish parliament. Northern Ireland was to be governed through direct rule by the British government in London.

Over the course of the conflict, political violence in Northern Ireland was to pose the most grave of challenges to a liberal democracy: 'how can a country cope with organised lawlessness pursued for ostensibly political purposes?' (Ewing and Gearty 1990: 211). A policy of 'criminalisation' was to be used toward proponents of political violence. A slew of anti-terrorist legislation followed. Although internment would continue until 1976, as many cases as possible were to be processed through the courts as criminal charges. The British government's longer-term legislative response to the political violence in Northern Ireland was to set in train the steady erosion of due process requirements within the criminal justice system, most notoriously through the suspension of jury trials for paramilitary offences,[5]

4 The Chilean Truth and Reconciliation Commission found that 'During the period in question the judicial branch did not respond vigorously enough to human rights violations' (Chilean National Commission on Truth and Reconciliation 1993: Chapter 4A).

5 See further Jackson and Doran (1995).

but also through making confessions given involuntarily more easily admissible in criminal trials, allowing convictions based solely on the testimony of informers,[6] allowing inferences from the accused's silence,[7] and the extensive empowerment of the police and army.

In Northern Ireland, the impact of the conflict on individual experiences of domestic violence was most pronounced in relation to the policing of domestic violence. The greater number of legally and illegally held guns in Northern Ireland meant that guns were more commonly used in physical attacks on women than in either Britain or the Republic of Ireland (McWilliams and McKiernan 1993). The policy of 'criminalisation' pursued by the state in response to political violence, and the continued operation of the criminal justice system adjusted by emergency legislation, meant that the police operated at the frontline of the state's response to conflict violence in the jurisdiction.[8] The police were considered a 'legitimate target' of Republican violence. This highly militarised police role (the Royal Ulster Constabulary was the only routinely armed police force in the UK; the police were accompanied by the military on patrol; and police vehicles were heavily armed) (Walker, 2000: 175) gave rise to broad alienation of the police from the community. This alienation was experienced most acutely by the Catholic community. The overwhelmingly Protestant composition of the police force (Independent Commission on Policing for Northern Ireland 1999: 2), compounded by recurrent allegations of security force collusion in Loyalist violence,[9] led to perceptions – and compelling evidence – of one community (Protestant) policing the other major ethnic group (Catholic). The position of the police force at the frontline of the conflict led, unsurprisingly, to a 'suspicion of outsiders',[10] a suspicion that limited opportunities for constructive collaborative relationships with women's organisations such as Women's Aid that addressed domestic violence in the jurisdiction.

The absence of confidence in the police meant that domestic violence reporting remained very low throughout the period of the conflict.[11] The security concerns of the police around entering Catholic communities exacerbated the situation. For example, when a report of domestic violence was made, it was common practice to wait an hour and phone the number from which the call was made, in order to ensure that the phone call was not intended to lure police officers to

6 See further Greer (1995).

7 Criminal Evidence (Northern Ireland) Order 1988.

8 The dynamics are comprehensively described in Ní Aoláin (2000b: 26–71).

9 Aspects of these allegations concerning the deaths of Patrick Finucane, Robert Hamill, Rosemary Nelson and Billy Wright are documented in Cory (2004).

10 Eileen Calder, Director of Belfast Rape Crisis Centre, Belfast, personal communication, 29 June 2007.

11 Avila Kilmurray recounts that during the 1970s, there was simply no reporting to the police. Further, in Women's Aid's dealings with the Housing Association, there was no expectation from them that any reporting was taking place. Kilmurray, personal communication, 2 July 2007.

harm. There are recorded incidents of police responding to domestic violence reports in rural Republican areas with the support of snipers and army helicopters (McWilliams and McKiernan 1993). In the context where even to call the police resulted in great stigma, these sort of police responses further eroded women's confidence in reporting incidences of violence. The question 'don't you know there's a war going on?' was often posed in similar terms to women reporting domestic violence (Montgomery and Bell 1985: 53; McWilliams and McKiernan 1993). It captured the prioritisation by the police of the security situation over women's experiences of intimate violence.

Colombia

Colombia has endured the longest-running armed conflict in the Western Hemisphere. Successive waves of confrontation among guerrilla groups (most notably, the Fuerzas Armadas Revolucionarias de Colombia (Revolutionary Armed Forces of Colombia), or FARC, but also the urban-based M-19[12] and the Cuban-inspired Ejército de Liberación Nacional (ELN)), the armed forces (which have traditionally maintained a high degree of autonomy from government, allowing them to block attempts by the government to reach a negotiated settlement with the guerrilla groups, while being heavily complicit in the violence and criminality of paramilitary groups)[13] and paramilitary groups that emerged in the 1960s as part of a counter-insurgency tactic of the state to stem the spread of the perceived communist threat, have caused enormous loss of life and forced displacement and weakened the rule of law. The conflict has been marked by patterns of victimisation, drug trafficking and political crime. The new Colombian Constitution of 1991 was a landmark attempt to bring all political factions within the country into a reformed and reconstituted political infrastructure. The peace agreement character of the new Constitution was evident in its drafting, in the broad participation in its negotiation, and most literally in the 'right to peace' enshrined in the resulting constitutional text.[14] The Colombian Constitutional Court was called upon to facilitate Colombia's movement away from violence and injustice. However, the political pact that underpinned the 1991 Constitution, and initially held the political and military elites to principles of non-violence, quickly disintegrated. Increasing violence by paramilitary actors occurred in parallel with the diminution of state capacity in the country. By the end of the 1990s Colombia teetered on the verge of failed statehood. The collapse of a peace process with the FARC guerrillas coincided with heavy US investment in the

12 The group's full title was Movimiento 19 de Abril (19 April Movement). It took this title from the date of the presidential elections of 1970, in which the populist candidate Gustavo Rojas Pinillo was denied an electoral victory in an outcome that the group regarded as fraudulent.

13 For an early account of this relationship, see Amnesty International (1988a).

14 Constitution of Colombia, 1991, Article 22.

Colombian military, and renewed state determination to achieve a military defeat of the guerrilla forces. While levels of violence have waxed and waned, and its chief protagonists have varied, political violence has been a constant in Colombia since the 1940s (Welna and Gallon 2007).

The widespread impunity that surrounds violence perpetrated by the state and armed groups has contributed to a broader climate of impunity for all types of violent acts. The state's almost exclusive concern with political violence and narcotrafficking permitted the increase of other forms of violence. Research in 1987 found that the percentage of murders in Colombia resulting from subversion did not exceed 7.51 per cent in the years under analysis, and therefore over 90 per cent of violent killings were not considered to be of a political nature (Comisión de Estudios sobre la Violencia 1987: 18). Feminist and civil society organisations have long resisted the state's prioritisation of guerrilla-perpetrated violence. In the 1980s Latin American women's organisations began to raise the issue of domestic violence. The Colombian Casa de la Mujer in Bogotá, established in 1982, was one of the very first such organisations.[15] CAMI Mujeres was established in Cali in the same year, with the three political priorities of increasing women's political participation, advancing women's reproductive rights and ending violence against women.[16] Further, one of the first studies on the prevalence of domestic violence in Latin America was conducted in Bogotá in 1985.[17] These women's organisations have consistently sought to articulate the connections between the economic, social and political context of conflict violence, and levels of violence in the private ambit:

> [I]ntrafamily violence has not been the focus of attention for profound investigation in the way that political violence has, nor has it been sufficiently criminalized, which has permitted its reproduction under a climate of impunity and, why not say it, tacit social acceptance.
>
> (Casa de la Mujer 1988: 12)[18]

15 Larrain Heiremans (1994) (listing Casa de la Mujer in Colombia and La Morada in Chile as the first two Latin American women's organisations to advocate on domestic violence). Examples of Casa de la Mujer publications addressing domestic violence in this period include: Casa de la Mujer, *La Violencia: lo Impensable la Impensado* (Bogotá, Colombia: 1990), Casa de la Mujer, *Nuevos Espacios y Otros Retos: Propuesta a Las Mujeres* (Bogotá, Colombia: 1986), Casa de la Mujer, *Violencia en la Intimidad* (Bogotá, Colombia: 1988).

16 See http://www.camimujeres.org/ (last accessed 1 March 2013).

17 The study was conducted by A. Berenguer on the basis of 233 interviews with women who had personal injuries attended to by the Instituto de Medicina Legal Bogotá in 1982. He recorded the civil status, age and socio-economic level of the women. The study also uncovered child abuse. Domestic violence was associated with alcoholism, irritability and accusations of infidelity against the woman. A. Berenguer, *Violencia Conyugal*, edn Colectivo Cuéntame tu Vida, No. 9, Cali, Colombia 1986, cited in Larrain Heiremans (1994).

18 Comments of the advisor to the President for the Plan Nacional de Rehabilitacion (the Plan proposed by the reformer President Barco in 1988 for social investment in conflict zones).

The consequences for Colombian women of this impunity and disregard was heightened vulnerability to staggering levels of violence, including domestic violence, illustrated by the address of the Colombian delegation to the 1987 Feminist *Encuentro* (meeting) in Taxco, Mexico, which opened with the words:

> We, Colombian women, have brought in our suitcases, in our backpacks, in our bodies, pieces, fragments from the moment our country is living . . . We couldn't nor wanted to leave behind, at the border, the trace of violence in Colombia.
>
> (Quoted in Morgan 1992: 367)

Privatised violence against women by public actors

In the discussion of human rights law in Chapter 1, it was observed that the classic political actor was understood to be male. This has had grave consequences for the construction of human rights protections around the needs of the male political actor. The assumption of political activity as male has meant that, in addition to being punished for political subversion, female political dissidents have been targeted for gender-specific forms of violence to punish their deviance from received gender norms (Corcoran 2006). Moreover, the sex-based nature of the harms has allowed perpetrators to portray this harm as 'private' and a manifestation of individual personal motivation ('lust'), and to resist its inherently political character as violence perpetrated by state actors against female political dissidents. These same gender dynamics can be traced in Chile and Northern Ireland, in terms of the deliberate targeting of female political dissidents for sexualised brutality, and in Colombia in the brutal regulation of the reproductive lives of female combatants through compulsory contraception and forced abortions. While these sexualised harms against combatant women and women in detention fit most neatly within the range of gender-specific harms against women currently recognised in transitional justice, the political character of these harms was in fact contested and resisted in each of the case studies.

Chile

In Chile, the repression by the military dictatorship was experienced directly and violently by women, most notably by women in detention. Female dissidents were systematically targeted for sexual violence and torture (Bunster 1985, 1991). Their departure from the traditional maternal role provoked a brutal and highly sexualised response from the state (Acuña Moenne 2005). The work of Ximena Bunster was particularly important in bringing this violence to light in the 1980s, exposing the torture of women that was consciously and systematically directed at her female sexual identity and female anatomy (Bunster 1985: 307; 1991). Physical and psychological sexual violence was inflicted on women by the military, either for direct involvement in dissident activities, or for her relationship to a politically active male. Further, 'family torture' was perpetrated by the military regime, whereby state agents tortured children in front of their mothers in order to coerce information from these women about the subversive activities of their husbands (Bunster 1985). The regime's brutal practice of torture thereby reinforced the regime's gendered ideology of maternity and family: deviance from the maternal role was violently suppressed, and the valorised protected family bond was used against individual dissident women who were forced to witness the torture of a family member.

Ideologies and ideals of womanhood were not exclusive to the military regime. They were replicated in the attitudes of the women's fellow political prisoners, as is graphically illustrated by the account of former political prisoner Hernán Valdés of the sexual relations between female detainees and soldiers he witnessed while in detention:

> We couldn't figure the women's behaviour out. Were they participating [by consorting with the soldiers] out of fear, sheer despair, cynicism or pleasure? . . . We [the men] were all outraged. Someone recalled how in the National Stadium the women prisoners had preferred to be shot rather than let the soldiers lay a finger on them. We couldn't explain this kind of collusion.
>
> (Hernán Valdés, quoted in Baldez 2001: 29)

The modes of survival adopted by these women were condemned for their deviation from the pure and self-sacrificing feminine 'ideal'. Further, the women's behaviour was presumed to emanate from their private personal preference, and not the public political circumstances of their detention.

Northern Ireland

In Northern Ireland, against a backdrop of emergency powers and high levels of imprisonment, prisons have always been key sites of the political conflict.[19] In 1976 the British government withdrew political status from prisoners arrested for paramilitary activity in Northern Ireland, prompting prison protests as Republican prisoners refused to wear the newly assigned prison uniform (they instead wore only blankets, in a protest that became known as the blanket protest). The blanket protest escalated into a 'no wash' protest, then the 'no slop-out' protest, and finally the 'dirty protest', which involved prisoners spreading excrement along the walls of their prison cells. Republican prisoners in Armagh women's prison joined the protest for political status first by refusing to work, and later in the adoption of a 'no wash' protest in 1980. While these prison events were landmarks in the escalation of the conflict in Northern Ireland, it was the strip-searching of women

19 For the authoritative account of the relationship of prisons to the political conflict, see McEvoy (2001).

prisoners that has been the lightning-rod issue of the political detention of women in Northern Ireland.

In 1982 the normal procedural practice of strip-searching a prisoner on reception at Armagh women's prison was extended on a random and frequent basis to prisons in Northern Ireland. Strip-searching was carried out with much greater frequency on female inmates in Northern Ireland than in prisons in England and Wales (National Council for Civil Liberties 1986). According to the women subjected to the practice, the searches were being used to discipline and punish female prisoners.[20] Amnesty International routinely condemned the practice of strip-searching female prisoners in Northern Ireland, voicing concerns that the practice was being carried out 'with the deliberate intention of degrading and humiliating the women' (Amnesty International 1986: 4; 1991b: 22). The women prisoners themselves publicly condemned the practice:

> What we are saying is that, in Armagh, intensive strip searching is currently being used in a way that constitutes sexual harassment, specifically to break the spirit of women who are regarded by the authorities as a political threat to the British state.
>
> (Letter from Armagh women prisoners, cited in Hackett 1995: 111)

The prevalent conservative ideologies of womanhood dominated the campaign against strip-searching at Armagh (Father Dennis Faul 1983). One campaign pamphlet states:

> This new procedure has been a traumatic experience for young Catholic girls and older women, all of whom were reared and educated in Catholics houses and schools where the strictest standards of modesty were impressed upon them as a matter of conscience . . . they were taught to be pure and chaste like the Blessed Virgin and St Brigid and St Maria Goretti.
>
> (Father Dennis Faul 1983)

This language reified cultural values deeply antithetical to women's autonomy and stands in stark contrast to the language with which women experiencing strip-searching condemned the practice. This characterisation of the treatment as antithetical to the passive and chaste images of Catholic femininity evacuated the women and their treatment of its clearly political character.

Colombia

In Colombia, the First Report on the Human Rights Situation in Colombia conducted by the Inter-American Commission on Human Rights in 1981

20 *The Irish Times* (1980) as quoted in Loughran (1988: 64).

catalogued civil and political rights violations in the country during the previous four years. The report was particularly concerned with the executive's capacity to declare states of emergency,[21] extra-judicial killings,[22] habeas corpus,[23] ordinary and military justice[24] and military operations in rural zones.[25] 'Other rights' included freedom of religion and conscience, freedom of thought and expression, the right to assemble, freedom of association and political rights.[26] With strong resonance to Chile and Northern Ireland, specific mention of women's human rights was confined to female prisoners. Allegations of the abuse and torture in detention of a small number of female members of M-19 and FARC were investigated. The Commission noted the 'vile insults' that were made against 'the honour and dignity' of these women, while naked and enduring 'every type of abuse'.[27]

Much later reports noted similar sexualised victimisation of female combatants. In her 2001 Report, the UN Special Rapporteur on Violence Against Women noted the sexualised violence experienced by women within armed groups, in particular in terms of sexually transmitted infections, forced contraception and abortions.[28] The public political activity of these female combatants was giving rise to the brutal regulation of their private reproduction, as women's reproductive roles were deemed incompatible with their public combatant roles.

In terms of the gendered binary of public and private harms in transitional justice, these sexualised harms against combatant women and women in detention fit most neatly within the range of gender-specific harms against women currently recognised in transitional justice. Nevertheless, as the foregoing account illustrated, the political character of these harms was in fact contested and resisted in each of the case studies.

The public regulation of women's private reproductive lives

The control of women's reproductive functions by men and/or the state has long been critiqued by feminists as the cornerstone of women's oppression (see especially Petchesky 1986). The denial of women's reproductive autonomy can result in compulsory maternity for women, confining them to the private domestic sphere and restricting their access to the public sphere, as the gendered construction of the public sphere excludes women with caring roles. This analysis neatly

21 Inter-American Commission on Human Rights, 1981: Chapter 1, Political and Normative System.
22 Ibid, Chapter 2, Right to Life.
23 Ibid, Chapter 3, Right to Personal Liberty.
24 Ibid, Chapter 5, Right to Due Process.
25 Ibid, Chapter 7, Military Operations in Rural Zones.
26 Ibid, Chapter 6, Other Rights, A.
27 Ibid, Chapter 4, Right to Security and Personal Integrity, D.6.
28 United Nations Special Rapporteur on Violence Against Women: Radhika Coomaraswamy, 2001: para 56. See also Human Rights Watch (2003: 56–8).

reveals the highly public nature and consequences of the ostensible private matter of reproduction and mothering. Further, the heightened gender ideologies that tend to prevail in contexts of political violence mean that public political ideologies often involve the politicisation of a private maternal role (Yuval-Davis 1997). These observations on the centrality of reproduction to the political status of women bear particular resonance in times of heightened political change or threat. As 'the bearers of the collective' (Yuval-Davis 1997: 26), when the collective is threatened through insurgency or other forms of widespread political violence, regulation of women's fertility and reproduction can become central to maintenance of the collective. These dynamics manifested in distinct though related ways across each of the three case studies.

Chile

In developed and developing nations, the regulation of women's reproductive functions has been effective shorthand for revealing the ideology of the governing regime. This was nowhere more obvious than in the institution of a cult of maternity, and the practice of compulsory maternity, by the military junta in Chile. The militarisation of everyday life in Chile under the military junta led directly to further restrictions on women's reproductive freedom. Official state pro-natalism was motivated and justified by appeals to 'national security'. The size of families was a priority concern of the military regime, as evidenced in a 1979 Office of Planning (ODEPLAN) publication that stated:

> It should be kept in mind that every threat to the integrity of the family seriously affects the quality and quantity of the population, arthrologically reducing the number of inhabitants and their integral formation. It has been proven that the birth rate decreases substantially with the disintegration of the family and increases with family stability. An affectionate, stable family life is the best environment for the development of children.
>
> (Parson 2005: 83)

In 1980 the military's Director of Health, General Eduardo Diaz, expressly linked the regime's concern with family size to the doctrine of national security: 'We need conscription, but who is going to put on a uniform if we only have men of 60 or boys of 15?' (*Revista Hoy*, 23 July 1980, quoted in Acuña Moenne 2005: 156).

Against this backdrop, advancements made under the Allende government in public health family planning programmes, and reducing the number of backstreet abortions, were immediately and dramatically reversed with the installation of the military regime.[29] Therapeutic abortion was finally criminalised by the

29 For discussion see Casas (2004).

military regime in 1989; however, accounts of the evolving approach to abortion within the Chilean health system note that the 1989 legal development marked the logical conclusion of the medical practice ushered in by the military usurping power in 1973 (Red Chilena contra la Violencia Doméstica y Sexual 2008). It did not constitute a dramatic change in medical practice from the previous 17 years. Rather, the coup had been the critical moment in the change of behaviour of medical practitioners towards abortion. The considerably more sympathetic approach of medical practitioners that prevailed under the Allende administration, respectful of women's wishes and their socio-economic circumstances, ended with the installation of the military regime.[30] The coup marked the onset of the punitive public regulation of women's private reproductive lives.

Northern Ireland

Spiralling political violence in Northern Ireland in 1972 prompted the British government to prorogue the Northern Irish parliament, and to institute direct rule of the jurisdiction from ministers in central government in London. The circumstances of inter-communal political violence resulted in a high degree of deference by central government to what were perceived to be shared local sensibilities on social issues in the jurisdiction. Cross-religious consensus against women's reproductive autonomy, in particular in terms of access to abortion, has been consistently used by the state to shore up otherwise fragile political consensus in the jurisdiction. Central government demonstrated a reluctance to legislate progressively on issues in Northern Ireland contrary to the preferences expressed by the main religious communities. This was most clearly demonstrated in respect of liberalising legislation on abortion.

This unwillingness to institute progressive legal change has had particular gendered consequences for women, as, in respect of abortion, this issue was not even cited for possible legislative action by the British government. Liberalising legislation was introduced in England and Wales in 1967, and this was not extended to Northern Ireland by the local parliament. According to the administrative headquarters for the exercise of executive power in the jurisdiction, the Northern Ireland Office (NIO):

> Since the introduction of direct rule in 1972 the view has been taken not to introduce a measure to change the abortion laws in Northern Ireland unless it is likely to command broad support among the people of the Province. Such support does not exist at present.
>
> (Letter of Northern Ireland Office Minister Nicholas Scott to Ken Weetch MP, 21 March 1985, cited in Furedi 1995: 97)

30 Gloria Maria Vargas, Santiago, September 2008 at launch of Red Chilena contra la Violencia Doméstica y Sexual (2008).

The NIO relied on a motion passed the previous year by the Northern Irish Assembly and affirmed by 14 of the 26 local district councils stating their opposition to the extension of the Abortion Act 1967 to Northern Ireland. Thus, in deference to these overwhelmingly male-dominated political fora, restrictive legal regulation of women's reproductive lives continued in the jurisdiction, to devastating effect on women living there. Between 1967 and 1994, it is estimated that 40,000 women travelled from Northern Ireland to England and Wales to obtain an abortion, with the added financial, health and emotional burden entailed by that travel (Rossiter 2001: 6). In the context of inter-communal political violence, central government preferred to defer to perceived shared local sensibilities on private matters, irrespective of the impact on women.

Colombia

In Colombia, also, the struggle for public order and the state's survival during violent conflict has operated to limit the reproductive autonomy of individual women. During the 1990s violence spiralled and Colombia verged on failed statehood. Against this backdrop, the Constitutional Court's interpretation of the right to peace as a collective right served to permit the state to reassert its authority and to monopolise violence within the national territory. In consistent jurisprudence during the 1990s, the Court interpreted the right to peace as collective rather than individual, and consequently imposed a duty on all citizens to accept, for example, the violent consequences of having a police station in close proximity to their homes.[31]

The Court's determination to support the state in establishing public order in this period extended into the reproductive lives of individual women. In 1994 the Court first considered the constitutionality of the blanket prohibition of abortion in the country.[32] The Court was asked to consider whether a blanket ban on abortion was in violation of the state's duty to protect the right of citizens to freedom of conscience and religion, given that there was a diversity of beliefs in the country on when life begins. In affirming the constitutionality of the blanket ban, the Court noted that rights to freedom of conscience and religion can be constitutionally limited on the grounds that they pose a threat to public order. Further, the Court noted, 'public morality forms part of the concept of public order.'[33] Thus,

31 This rationale was clear in two cases decided by the Court in 1993, in which *tutela* applications by citizens seeking the removal of recently installed police stations, because they were targets for guerrilla violence, were rejected by the Constitutional Court. Corte Constitucional de Colombia, *Sentencia No. T-139/93*, magistrado ponente Jorge Arango Mejía, Corte Constitucional de Colombia, *Sentencia No. T-255/93*, magistrado ponente Fabio Morón Diaz.

32 Corte Constitucional de Colombia, *Sentencia No. C-133/94*, magistrado ponente Martha Sachica de Moncaleano.

33 Corte Constitucional de Colombia, *Sentencia No. C-133/94*, magistrado ponente Martha Sachica de Moncaleano, 10.

the individual's right to freedom of conscience and religion was subject to restriction where it clashed with perceived societal consensus on particular issues of 'public morality'. Giving express legal protection to the position of anti-choice opinion in the country was deemed constitutive of maintaining public order. In effect, the state worked to maintain its authority by submitting individual reproductive autonomy of women to the collective public morality.

Women's public political organising on the basis of private reproductive roles

There is a theoretical and practical tendency to counterpose women and private domesticity with the major political concerns of international politics.[34] However, the patterns in which women in repressive or conflicted times enter the public realm through the politicisation of their private interests have attracted substantial feminist analysis.[35] The maternal identity ('militant motherhood') (Alvarez 1990: 57) and the need to provide for one's family and community ('consumption-based mobilisation') (Craske 2003: 65) were the leitmotifs of this mobilisation. Feminist scholars are divided as to the potential of this sort of privately motivated mobilisation to secure a feminist reorganisation of political life, concerned that it reifies understandings of women's caring roles as natural and inevitable.[36] Whatever one's position on the question of feminine versus feminist political mobilisation by women, there is a much clearer distinction between women's self-organisation in the pursuit of collectively agreed goals and the manipulation of women's collective action to pursue externally decided goals by state or non-state armed actors (Molyneux 1985). In each of the cases under analysis, political elites were alert to the significance and subversive potential of women's political organising, and consequently sought to manipulate its political character. Women entered the public sphere often on the basis of their private maternal roles, but were met by public attempts to diminish the political character and to reassert the private character of women's collective action.

Chile

The circumstances surrounding the military coup in Chile fostered the heavy politicisation of women's maternal role from the outset of the regime. Women were perceived to have been key instigators in the military's usurpation of power.[37]

34 For discussion and critique of the distinction between 'big-P' and 'little-P' politics, see Cockburn (1998: 3).
35 See, for example, the paradigmatic work of Molyneux (1985, 1998).
36 For an overview of this debate, see Molyneux (1998).
37 See the discussion of the March of the Empty Pots in Baldez (2002: 76–97).

The Allende government's dramatic programme of wealth redistribution prompted unrest in commercial and agricultural spheres, leading to massive shortages of food and other consumer goods. The food shortages, and the perceived attack on the Catholic Church, mobilised a large female constituency in opposition to the Allende government, culminating in a massive protest of women from the upper, middle and popular sector on 1 December 1971. They marched to the Presidential Palace, banging their empty pots and pans. In this heavily gendered symbolism, the Allende administration was being condemned for forcing women – through its failure to guarantee adequate provision of food – to neglect their familial duties and to enter the public world of protest and politics. In 1972 the leaders of the march formed 'Feminine Power' (El Poder Feminino) to co-ordinate women's groups in opposition to Allende. This mobilisation sealed popular perceptions of the coup as motivated by the demands of women on the Chilean military. Indeed, in the early aftermath of the coup, junta leader General Pinochet specifically invoked the mobilisation of women in order to legitimate the military's actions:

> They knew even then, the Chilean women, that the country was in danger and that, with the inefficiency of political action thus demonstrated, only in the Forces of Arms and of Order existed the salvation of Chile. Now that the path of our history has been rectified by the military *movimiento* of the 11th of September, it would not be right to forget the agreement we made with the women of our country. Their voice was for us the voice of the country, that called upon us to save it.
>
> (Augusto Pinochet, *El Mercurcio*, 24 April 1974, quoted in Baldez 2002: 118)

Within the context of highly restricted political expression, General Pinochet sought to marshal women's political activity, in their private maternal role, behind the military regime. Just as the military had drawn on heavily gendered ideology of the Chilean mother to justify overthrowing the democratically elected government, protection and valorisation of the Chilean family was to prove a potent ideological force in maintaining the dictatorship. The dictatorship actively sought to recruit Chilean women to this ideology of family. Thus, the theme of abnegation[38] and sacrifice by women (principally mothers) was to prove popular and enduring. The extensive network of Mothers' Centres (Centros de Madres, CEMAs), established in the 1950s by church and charity groups to train women in crafts, and thereby to allow them to earn an extra family income, proved ready recruiting ground for the military regime. By 1973 30,000 such centres existed through the country. Immediately after the coup, in October 1973, Pinochet created the National Secretariat of Women (Secretaría Nacional de la Mujer,

38 To refuse, relinquish or deny oneself certain rights.

SNM). Also during October 1973, he reorganised the Mothers' Centres. Pinochet's wife, Lucia Hiriart de Pinochet, became the director of both organisations. These efforts were designed to build on support provided by 'Feminine Power', and to marshal the support of Chilean women behind the military regime:

> The Chilean woman has understood how to achieve her duties, reestablishing in the soul of the people her role as a mother, the feeling of nationality, and faith in the destiny of our Fatherland.
>
> (Lucia Hiriart de Pinochet, at the inauguration of the International Year of Women, 4 April 1975, quoted in Parson 2005: 82)

The private maternal role of women was manipulated to further the public political objectives of the military regime.

Northern Ireland

Since the re-escalation of conflict in the 1960s, women's organising has been a mainstay of the jurisdiction (Roulston 1997: 65). However, the emergence and evolution of women's civil society organisations in Northern Ireland has not been immune to the political divisions that structured violent conflict in the jurisdiction (Roulston 1997: 56). Rather, women's civil society organising in Northern Ireland has been very largely determined by these prevailing political divisions. As Rick Wilford has observed: '[E]fforts to forge [a united] women's movement in Northern Ireland ha[ve] foundered over the mutually reinforcing cleavages of nationality and religion' (Wilford 1996: 41). The detention conditions of women in Armagh prison prompted intense pressure on the Northern Ireland Women's Rights Movement (NIWRM), as the Republican women engaged in 'dirty protests' in order to receive official recognition of their imprisonment as political. Nell McCafferty captured the dilemma confronting feminists with graphic detail as she wrote in the *Irish Times* that year: 'the smell of menstrual blood on the walls of Armagh prison smells to high heaven. Shall we turn our noses up?' (McCafferty 1980). Nevertheless, the NIWRM refused to take a position on political status, as it was 'not a feminist aim' (Loughran 1988: 59). There were concerns that supporting the women's protest would be perceived as supporting the IRA's armed campaign. The inadequacy of feminism as a unifying political agenda was painfully apparent, as 'Armagh became a metaphor for everything that has kept Irish women divided from each other' (Ward, 1991: 156). The fraught political backdrop of ethnic divisions, inter-communal violence, and routine presence of highly militarised security forces, meant that women's mobilisation in Northern Ireland during the conflict came to be defined by the practical co-operation of women on issues of material survival for the family and community (Rooney 1995: 45). Hence, rather than a 'women's movement' per se, Northern Ireland has been home to a 'women's sector' since the 1970s. This 'women's sector' consists of a large network of organisations of, and for, women, defined not by their avowed feminist commitments, but by their common concern for material survival issues of women and families.

In Northern Ireland, the proroguement of the local parliament and the institution of direct rule from London over the jurisdiction in 1972 resulted in an absence of obvious sites and targets of political participation. Consequently, alternative sites of political participation had to be forged in order to influence state decision-making. Civil society organisations flourished during the period of direct rule. Tenant associations, trade unions, civil rights movements, Left politics and community development emerged initially in a spirit of self-help. Over time, these organisations gained capacity and the 'professional' bodies responsible for decision-making in health and social services, employment and training, education, the environment and agriculture sought broader input in their decision-making. Consequently, in the interests of 'getting the business of government done', several civil society organisations came to have significant policy influence in Northern Ireland.[39] Further, this development of a vibrant civil society was not without gender implications. Women proliferated in these organisations, as volunteers, staff members and service-users (Meehan 2003). The response of state institutions was to selectively include and validate certain forms of women's organising, while attempting to exclude and delegitimate other forms, principally in order to depoliticise women's organising. The state wielded its influence in this regard through government funding and regulating access to public decision-making.

In 1985 the British government introduced the *Hurd Principles* for determining the eligibility of community organisations for state funding, in which organisations deemed to be directly or indirectly advancing the aims of paramilitary groups were precluded. In the implementation of these principles, various community organisations, largely from the Catholic community, were either denied funding or had their funding withdrawn. The specifically gendered impact of this political vetting became apparent in 1990 when Belfast City Council refused to continue to grant aid to the Falls Women's Centre in Republican West Belfast. This prompted the coming together of the Downtown Women's Centre and the Shankill Women's Centre in Loyalist West Belfast in solidarity with the Falls Women's Centre to protest at the City Council's decision, and ultimately the decision was reversed.[40]

The general trend in non-governmental organisations, as they have increased in size and influence, was to move from advocacy work to service-provision.[41] With this institutionalisation of their role as service-providers, they have increasingly become government 'partners' in state provision of social services, with attendant influence in state decision-making (Morison and Livingstone 1995). However, the privileging of women's activism in social service provision over

39 See further Hadfield (1989: Chapter 5).

40 See further Cockburn (1998: 76).

41 Avila Kilmurray, Director of the Community Foundation for Northern Ireland and Founder Member of Northern Ireland Women's Coalition, personal communication, 2 July 2007.

more overtly political activity works to reinforce notions of women's caring role as both natural and inevitable.

Colombia

The threat to women's political organising in Colombia has been of a more overtly violent nature. Writing in 2001, the UN Special Rapporteur on Violence Against Women noted the heavy toll that the conflict violence was taking on women's organisations, as the groups were losing their organisational processes and also losing their autonomy to armed actors (UN Special Rapporteur on Violence Against Women 2001: 23). This concern over the impact of the conflict on the autonomy of women's organisations has been reiterated in feminist analysis of the reinsertion element of the current demobilisation process of paramilitaries taking place under the auspices of the 2005 Justice and Peace Law. A Report examining the reintegration process of paramilitaries in Tierralta concluded that the process was imposing further limitations on the rights of free associations and expression of women as a consequence of the hegemony of paramilitarism in the zone (Corporación Humanas 2007).

There is overwhelming evidence of the more direct targeting of women civil society leaders for violence and threats of violence. This violence is generalised across women's movements making demands through the justice and peace process. It reached a head in 2007 with the four high-profile assassinations of women leaders within a period of two months.[42] In response to these assassinations, women's peace organisation Iniciativa de la Mujeres por la Paz (IMP) brought a *tutela* application for the protection of 13 named women, drawn from IMP leaders and high-profile victims being supported by IMP. The application ultimately reached the Constitutional Court. The Court held that the existing programme for protection of victims and witnesses[43] was inadequate to protect the applicants' constitutional rights to life and security, and that the Minister for Justice and National Office of the Prosecutor were under a legal obligation to establish a programme of protection within six months that specifically addressed the added vulnerability of women victims seeking to avail themselves of the justice and peace process.[44]

These examples demonstrate not just the direct targeting of women political activists by paramilitaries, but the failure of state institutions to effectively protect and defend the rights of those women to politically organise.

42 Yolanda Izquierdo Berrio, Carmen Cecilia Santana Romaña, Osiris Jacqueline Amaya Beltrán, Judith Vergara Correa.

43 Established further to Presidential Decree 3570 of 2007.

44 This account is taken from Iniciativa de Mujeres Colombianas por la Paz (2009).

Table 2.1 The Web of Harms: the relationship of public to private harms against women in contexts of political violence

	Chile	*Northern Ireland*	*Colombia*
Private violence and deficient state response to that violence	Deferential judiciary, failing to protect rights and security of individuals	Police neglecting domestic violence, prioritising political violence	State's prioritisation of conflict violence, general climate of impunity for violence against women
Privatised violence against women by public actors	Sexualised torture of female political dissidents	Strip-searching of women political prisoners	Brutal regulation of the reproductive functions of combatant women
The public regulation of women's private reproductive lives	Linking 'national security' and state pro-natalism	Conservative political consensus on women used to balance otherwise violently opposed parties	Privileging 'public morality' over women's individual autonomy
Women's political organising on the basis of a private role	Manipulating mothers' centres	Privileging women's apolitical organising	Direct targeting of women civil society leaders for violence and threats of violence

THE WEB OF HARMS: NORM, DOCTRINE, POLITICS

This final section of the chapter elaborates the normative, doctrinal and political merits of placing the notion of a web of gender-based harms against women at the centre of feminist engagement with transitional justice.

The web of harms: a normative construct

Chapter 1 outlined the grounds for sustained feminist critique of the public/private divide, namely the tendency for this divide to neatly separate the harms in women's lives from the concerns (and obligations) of the state, and to consign women to an apolitical space. Notwithstanding this critique, feminists have seldom completely rejected the public/private distinction. Instead, feminist focus has attached to the mutability of the public/private divide (Landes 1998), and how individuals and groups with resources have great discretion in determining where the divide is drawn.[45] Those without resources, however, must endure the most exploitative probing of the 'private', in particular to access the public resources of the state (Fineman 1995). The control of women's reproductive functions reflects this exploitative drawing of the public/private divide. For example, the requirement that, in order to access abortion services restricted to cases of rape and incest or fatal foetal abnormality, individual women must endure investigation of the most intimate areas of their lives. Consequently, rather than a rejection of the public/private divide altogether, many feminists have called for the distinction to be drawn in a way that is less exploitative of women (see especially Lacey and Frazer 1993).

The value of a private sphere, respected by the state, resonates all the more in cases of transition. Often the prior regime was characterised by the perpetration of violence in the 'private' sphere, for example through house searches of civilians or strip-searching prisoners. In this context, establishing a private sphere, free of interference from a state of still dubious legitimacy, is an understandable priority. Further, for women's movements seeking to make gains through the transitional state, the overall project of rehabilitating the public sphere is helpful. The state can thereby become a legitimate site of feminist activity and feminist gains.

The public/private divide is a potent theoretical tool in gender analysis of political violence and transitions out of such violence. To surrender such a tool can only weaken gender analysis of transitions. Rather, the web of harms retains the public/private divide, and focuses on revealing the relationship of the public to the private and the ways in which this relationship changes during transition.

The web of harms: a doctrinal framework

The doctrinal motivation for the web of harms against women, which is also – admittedly – a pragmatic motivation, is rooted in the understanding of harm within established legal categories in transitional justice. As noted, transitional justice is typically concerned with widespread human rights violations of a 'most serious' nature. Even mechanisms ostensibly more flexible than courts, such as truth commissions, borrow from established legal categories in their definition of harm (Ní Aoláin and Turner 2007). Similarly, administrative reparations programmes in transitional justice respond to a 'traditional catalogue of civil and political rights violations' (de Greiff 2006: 7). Thus the common legal devices of transitional justice turn upon the very designation of public civil and political rights violations, as explicitly distinct from private harms that occur in contexts of political violence. Against this backdrop, the strategic wisdom of articulating the commonality in women's experiences of harms before, during and after political

45 See especially Nancy Fraser's (1998) enlightening analysis of the Anita Hill–Clarence Thomas hearings, in which Thomas could successfully assert the 'private' nature of his behaviour, while Hill's behaviour was exposed to repeated and intense scrutiny.

violence is questionable. As Margaret Urban Walker observes: 'In a perspective that looks to violence with an eye to *reparations* for victims, the individual victim's experience of catastrophic *discontinuity* needs to hold central place' (Urban Walker 2009: 29, emphasis in original).

Efforts to establish a continuum of state responsibility for public and private harms against women have secured remarkable gains in recent years, in terms both of state obligations to prohibit, prevent and punish violence perpetrated against women by private actors, and in the responsibility of states to guarantee the physical integrity of women carrying pregnancies. States are now bound by overlapping positive obligations in respect of private harms against women. While, formally, political violence does not exempt states from their due diligence obligations, in practice the political exigencies that pertain in contexts of political violence result in the loosening of legal obligations on those states in respect of their positive obligations. As experience tells us, in the context of transitional justice instituted in the aftermath of widespread political violence, these legal devices rely on a traditional, smaller and less exacting catalogue of negative obligations on states to refrain from the direct perpetration of harms against its citizens.

By articulating the qualitative impact of political violence on private harms against women, as undertaken in this book, it may be possible to articulate a different, though related, set of obligations on the transitioning state in respect of violence against women and women's reproductive rights. The web of harms provides a framework for nuanced engagement with legal categories in transitional justice that emphasises the importance of ensuring accountability for past public harms against women, but by also revealing the impact of past political violence on women's private experiences of harm, demonstrates the need for transitional justice to provide some form of redress also to those exacerbated private harms.

The web of harms: a political tool

The final, and most significant, reason for adopting a web of harms thesis concerns the political context for feminist engagement with transitional states. Advancing the notion of state responsibility for private harms against women is a difficult political agenda. The length of time required to secure today's modest gains is a vivid illustration of the challenges involved in making private harm a public responsibility. Nevertheless, securing state accountability for the public harms of the past is also a thorny political agenda in transitional states. Demands to 'look to the future' and to 'move on' and 'close the book' on harms of the past are potent in contexts in which the past is deemed difficult, divisive and potentially destabilising to a transition (Fletcher *et al* 2009). It is important, therefore, for feminists to avoid an undifferentiated approach to seeking accountability for past 'public' harms and ongoing 'private' harms. This sort of undifferentiated approach would be insufficiently sensitive to the deeply *political* context in which demands for state accountability are made in transitional contexts. States, eager to break from the past, may view any question of state liability in past harms as antithetical to the transitional project and damaging to the recuperation of state legitimacy. Conversely, demands to address ongoing private harms, such as domestic violence, may offer the new state an opportunity to demonstrate its commitment to human rights and non-violence without costly reminders of the state's relationship to past harms. Women's movements would be well advised against being naive about the extent to which feminist demands can legitimate powerful political narratives of states in transition. To draw on Elizabeth Spelman's groundbreaking feminist analysis of overlapping systems of disadvantage:

> Ironically, the categories and methods we may find most natural and straightforward to use as we explore the connections [between harms may] confuse those connections rather than clarify them.
>
> (Spelman 1990: 115)

The web of harms, by contrast, encourages political sensitivity to the differential position of the state to past and future harms, and to public and private harms, and for feminists to strategise accordingly, in order to ensure the recognition and redress of the widest possible range of harms against women, both public and private.

CONCLUSION

Defining harms in transitional justice has been one of the key sites of feminist intervention and contestation in this field. This chapter has sought to draw empirical analysis of women's experiences of violence, infringements of reproductive autonomy and political manipulation, together with feminist theoretical elaboration of those harms, in order to speak to dominant categories of harms in transitional justice. Findings and analysis in this chapter underpin the remainder of the book, as it examines human rights outcomes for women in terms of this web of harms against women. Normatively, do transitional justice processes recognise the exacerbating impact of public on private harms against women? Doctrinally, do transitional justice processes provide accountability for this web of harms? Politically, do transitional justice processes affirm women's agency as they mobilise around a web of harms against women?

Part II

Justice

Chapter 3

Defining 'justice'

Patterns in human rights advocacy

INTRODUCTION: THE INTERNATIONAL FRAME: NORM, DOCTRINE AND POLITICS

In transitional justice it is by now axiomatic that understandings of justice are heavily shaped by understandings of prior injustice (Teitel 2000: 6). This chapter posits human rights advocacy, in particular documented accounts of harm in human rights reports, as central to understanding past harms in transitional justice. Chapters 1 and 2 revealed the normative and doctrinal blind spots of the international human rights canon and its concern with the male political actor. This chapter focuses, in turn, on international law as a site and outcome of social movement politics.

The chapter tells a story of an international human rights movement preoccupied with male political actors and male experiences of harm, and the imprint of this solipsism on documented accounts of harm in the cases under study. The chapter further charts the emergence of a transnational women's movement beginning to challenge this bias and to assert women's rights as human rights, in order to shape the documented account of harms requiring justice in the cases under study. The chapter thereby maps a dialectic of local human rights advocacy, international law and transnational feminist politics.

HUMAN RIGHTS DOCUMENTATION AND TRANSNATIONAL ADVOCACY NETWORKS

The critical importance of NGOs to the emergence and development of the international human rights system is widely documented and accepted.[1] When international human rights law is viewed also as a product of an international human rights movement, the feminist critique of human rights law moves from more abstract notions of sovereignty, national interest and separate spheres, to

1 See further Keck and Sikkink (1998: 121–64).

more concrete issues of human rights mobilisation and documentation. Concerted empirical examination has been given to how civil society actors make human rights norms matter on the ground within states (e.g. Brysk 1993; Collins 2010). A key motivating question was to understand why states departed from traditional motivations of self-interest in order to comply with externally determined human rights standards (Burgerman 1998). Transnational advocacy networks (TANs) activity is central to creating a consensus amongst states against behaviour that violates individual human rights.[2] In this telling, transnational advocacy actors co-operated, for example, to pressurise the USA and European states to impose human rights reforms on non-compliant states of Central America in the early 1990s (Burgerman 1998). The identification of a new civil society phenomenon, namely TANs, is essential to this understanding. TANs describe the operation of domestic NGOs in documenting human rights abuses at the local level, the communication of these findings to international human rights NGOs and the mobilisation of international NGOs to publicise these violations.[3] In a process known as the 'boomerang pattern', local human rights advocates collaborate with international actors in order to bring external pressure upon non-compliant states (Keck and Sikkink 1998: 12). 'Information politics' constitutes the modus operandi of transnational advocacy networks (Keck and Sikkink 1998: 18). The successful operation of TANs hinges on both *local documentation* of human rights violations and *international verification* of reported violations, as the input and output of information politics.

The reliance on local NGOs for the documentation of human rights abuses, and on international actors to communicate this information to an international audience, locates information and its transmission as the central organising feature of TANs. Local NGOs are alternative sources of information that challenge the dominant state narrative of the situation on the ground. In this regard, domestic advocates have leverage and influence through their local knowledge and expertise and access to information – their capacity to provide detailed and specific accounts of the human rights situation. In their documentation work, local NGOs typically rely on a combination of technical/statistical information about the scale of violations with testimonial information to humanise victims (Keck and Sikkink 1998: 19–21). International actors, by contrast, cannot provide this level of local information and expertise. They can, however, add legitimacy to the reports of local actors (who may be discredited as rebels or insurgents or militants) through verification and transmission of the reports of local actors. Moreover, international actors can access neighbouring states, intergovernmental institutions and the wider public to secure change in the behaviour of the violating state.

2 For a discussion of these dynamics in relation to violence against women, see Joachim (2007).
3 The paradigmatic work on TANs is Keck and Sikkink (1998).

Central to the practice of 'information politics' is human rights reporting. As Stan Cohen elaborates:

> A major part of human rights work is the production of written reports. The report is usually seen as a means to an end. Information is collected, checked, standardized, and disseminated as part of a wider strategy to prevent violations and implement universal standards. Reporting also may become an end in itself: The belief that even without results there is an absolute duty to convey the truth, to bear witness.
>
> (Cohen 1996: 517)

Further, there is considerable evidence of human rights documentation directly informing transitional justice processes. For example, as discussed further in Chapter 6, the Chilean Truth and Reconciliation Commission relied on the records of the two main domestic human rights organisations, the Vicaría de la Solidaridad and Corporation for the Promotion and Defense of People's Rights (Corporación de Promoción y Defensa de los Derechos del Pueblo, CODEPU), when documenting the human rights violations that occurred under the military dictatorship. Even where the work of human rights organisations does not so directly inform transitional justice mechanisms, civil society initiatives can be important in setting agendas around accountability in transitional states. The Northern Ireland example is instructive, in that the civil society initiative 'Healing Through Remembering' gained considerable influence in official policy circles and came to be substantially emulated by subsequent official efforts to deal with the past. In Brazil, civil society documentation of past abuses was so central that it in fact came to supplant any official truth-seeking initiative.[4]

The conceptualisation and identification of TANs marks an important advance in understanding how civil society narratives influence not just international norm generation, but also the domestic enforcement of those international norms. It also helps us to understand the significance of the human rights documentation work of civil society to outcomes of official transitional justice processes.

TANs and contesting meaning

Insights from Keck and Sikkink and others revealing the operation of TANs provide a useful and important basis for empirical investigation of the extent to which such TANs featured harms against women within their information networks and politics. Moreover, the transnational space is not just a site for the physical exchange of information; it is also an important site for the negotiation of meaning. Robert Cover's paradigmatic work reveals how interpretative communities create

4 See further Backer (2003).

law and give it meaning (Cover 1983). In terms of international law, norm-generation occurs in a space in which meanings are heavily contested (e.g. Charlesworth 1998), and in which social movements constitute 'interpretative communities' that that add shape and definition to international law. Movement actors are involved in production and maintenance of meaning, as they frame how TAN members and observers understand a particular issue or problem, such as the targeting of civil society for state violence or the strip-searching of women prisoners.

TANs must, therefore, also be understood as political spaces in which differently situated actors negotiate – formally or informally – the social, cultural and political meanings of their joint enterprise. In this respect, TANs constitute 'communicative structures' (Keck and Sikkink 1998: 2). Celebratory work on TANs (Keck and Sikkink 1998; Mertus 2000) appears to assume (implicitly at least) that the meanings that emerge from such transnational mobilisation are progressive. (Such implicit assumptions are evident in the identification of TANs as constructed around 'principled-issues', consisting of actors motivated by a self-less commitment to social struggles of the disenfranchised and the need to circumvent the recalcitrance or opposition of the violating state.) Analysis in this chapter suggests that this assumption may not be entirely correct. While human rights TANs co-ordinate around largely progressive agendas of individual rights and state accountability, this chapter reveals space within these larger narratives for regressive sub-themes seeking, most notably, the regressive regulation of women's sexuality.

Plan of the chapter

This chapter advances three key claims: first, that the international frame offered by international human rights law in the 1970s, 1980s and early 1990s was critically flawed and failed to provide either normative or doctrinal recognition of harms against women in contexts of political violence. Second, the chapter adopts the TANs thesis of Keck and Sikkink as a theoretical framework for the empirical investigation of the place of harms against women within the information politics operated in the human rights TAN under study. The chapter argues that these shortcomings of the international frame resulted in heavily male-dominated accounts of harm to emerge in the political documentation work of human rights NGOs in the case studies. Moreover, the shortcomings of the international frame were overlaid with regressive gender norms in domestic gender politics. The final claim is that women's autonomous organising resulted in a more comprehensive documentation of harm in the cases under study and that women's organisations began to organise transnationally in order to target international human rights law as a site of potential feminist gains.

THE LOCAL FIT: DOMESTIC HUMAN RIGHTS ADVOCACY AND DOMINANT GENDER NORMS

Documenting harms and regressive gender norms

Chile

In Chile, local human rights-based activism was characterised by some important gender dynamics that worked to mitigate against the documentation of harms against women. The dictatorship's valorisation of family and maternity was oddly reflected in the parallel maternalist bent in much domestic Chilean human rights advocacy. The centrality of the Roman Catholic Church to Chilean human rights advocacy reinforced these more conservative gender dynamics. As this section reveals, this context of maternalist and Church-dominated human rights advocacy was contributory to some of the most egregious gendered oversights of this advocacy, most notably the failure to document sexual violence perpetrated by the military dictatorship against female political dissidents.

The Catholic Church was an important protagonist and guardian of human rights activism in Chile. Traditional forms of Church aid to the poor were increased after the coup and the Church leadership began to speak out explicitly against the repressive policies of the state (Frühling 1983). This relief role expanded into overt challenges to the state's use of terror with the establishment of Vicaría de la Solidaridad in 1976, which was housed within the former residence of the archbishop alongside the Santiago cathedral (Frühling 1983: 510–12). Over the course of the dictatorship, the organisation became more professional, routinely bringing writs of *amparo* (habeas corpus) and documenting and reporting human rights violations (Frühling 1983: 513). Writs of habeas corpus, and seeking legal redress for the military regime's use of torture, were filed starting from the first months of military rule and this continued throughout the period of the regime in police stations and detention locations. Because of the ongoing legal work of the Vicaría, the Chilean dictatorship is described as unique: the number of human rights violations that were committed can be counted by reference to judicial proceedings (Garretón 2005). The human rights work of the Vicaría was supplemented over the years by the emergence of the Christian Churches Foundation for Social Assistance (Fundación de Ayuda Social de las Iglesias Cristianas, FASIC) in 1975, the Chilean Human Rights Commission, which was established in 1978 to draw attention to the regime's use of torture, and the CODEPU, which emerged in 1980. The protective role of the Catholic Church was essential to the continued operation of such human rights advocacy.

Moreover, human rights-based opposition to the dictatorship evidenced a strong maternalist bent. In demands for justice of human rights advocates, Chilean women have an abiding iconic status. Small groups of Chilean mothers – carrying photos of their (overwhelmingly) male family members 'disappeared' by the military regime and demanding to know 'Where are they?' ('*¿Dónde están?*') – endure as the abiding public image of justice demands on the dictatorship. Moreover, the gender of these human rights advocates was not incidental to their activism; rather it was fundamental to the activism and its effectiveness. In terms of domestic Chilean rights-based advocacy under the dictatorship, the military regime felt the perverse and contradictory effects of the reactionary ideology it espoused. The justification for the military coup was the perceived attacks of the Allende administration on the key institutions of Chilean national life, namely the family and the Church (Schirmer 1988). Thus, the military's repression of political opposition was always tempered by the recognition that state-sponsored attacks on the family or the Church threatened to undo the very ideological basis of the regime (Schirmer 1988). As Schirmer observes on the strong maternalist bent to the Agrupación de Familiares de Detenidos-Desaparacidos (AFDD):

> [T]he experience of these groups reveal the ironic circumstances created by the repressive state. On the one hand, the state valorises motherhood and the family, on the other hand, it simultaneously undertakes systematic repression through the use of forced disappearance. As a result, the repressive state has found itself confronting new forms of resistance based precisely on motherhood and the family. Using the language of sacrifice and the traditional values associated with motherhood as both political protection and political tools, these women have been willing to take public action during the worst years of repression in Argentina, Guatemala and Chile.
>
> (Schirmer 1988: 42)

The imprint of this maternal profile of activists can be seen on the harms and victims that secured documentation, and those that did not. In one of only two publications by mainstream human rights organisations to specifically document the victimisation of women by the military regime, in 1990 CODEPU published *Todas Íbamos a Ser Reinas* (And We Were All Going To Be Queens), which documented the nine known instances of pregnant women who were detained and then disappeared by the military regime.[5] The particular political orientation of the AFDD meant that, while this mobilisation clearly occupied a feminine space, there was no overt connection with feminism. In addition, the targeting of men by the regime – largely due to the perceived 'apolitical' nature of women's collective activity[6] – meant limited attention was paid during this period to the particular ways in which the regime targeted female political actors. The mothers' groups pursued accountability for violations against their *male* relatives.[7] As noted Chilean feminist and human rights advocate Lorena Fries recounts:

5 This figure was later revised upward to ten women: see CODEPU (2002).

6 For discussion, see Chuchryk (1989, 1994).

7 AFDD reports only dealing with disappeared men, except for a single report in 1986 that dealt with disappeared women.

> The movement for human rights for the violations of the dictatorship was lax about women. Women fought for their gendered experience, concerning their relatives – men. Therefore there was no gendered perspective on this. That was one part of it. The men who worked on the violence, the human rights violations of the past, did not know and were not sensitised to the theme of gender. Consequently, they didn't incorporate [gender-specific human rights violations] either.
>
> (Lorena Fries, Corporación Humanas, Santiago, personal communication, 27 October 2008)

This gap is most pronounced in respect of the failure to document sexual violence perpetrated by the dictatorship against female political dissidents. The work of Chilean feminist Ximena Bunster to document the various forms of sexual violence perpetrated against women political dissidents in Chile has already been noted. However, despite the (justly) celebrated documentation work of Vicaría and other local human rights groups during the Chilean dictatorship, no such incidences of sexual violence formed the basis of legal action at the time (Garretón 2005).

> It did not appear in the registers of the *Vicaría*. It didn't appear in the CODEPU. It didn't appear in any of the organizations acting in defence or support of the victims. What's more, there existed the myth that there had not been any sexual violence.
>
> (Lorena Fries, Corporación Humanas, Santiago, personal communication, 27 October 2008)

Reflecting more recently on the reasons for this failure to document sexual violence in human rights reporting in Chile, former lawyer for the Vicaría, Roberto Garretón, attributes this absence to a combination of personal factors (the 'modesty' of the individual women victims) and structural factors (legal action with the potential for practical effect was prioritised: whereas the detained and disappeared might possibly be released or returned, there was little prospect of effecting change through legal action for victims of execution or torture, including rape) (Garretón 2005).[8] Gender is not considered, however, to be a structural factor, in terms of the regressive gender norms that otherwise informed the advocacy, or as underpinning a flawed international framework.

8 See also Roberto Garretón, El Capitulo Chilena del Ombudsman (formerly Vicaría de la Solidaridad), Santiago, personal communication, 30 October 2008.

Northern Ireland

In Northern Ireland, also, some distinct gender dynamics can be discerned from local human rights advocacy that militated against the documentation of harms against women during the conflict. First, and predictably given the flawed international frame, human rights advocacy was principally concerned with male political actors. Second, to the extent that women feature as rights-holders within local rights advocacy, the advocacy betrays a disproportionate concern with the 'purity' of the women in question. Finally, while piercing the private veil of the home was a persistent feature in human rights violations during the Northern Irish conflict, it was considered to be particularly egregious in the case of the privacy of women.

Human rights activism in Northern Ireland has always been a fraught activity. The state-based nature of human rights obligations meant that it was the state's activities that were subjected to scrutiny by rights-based advocacy and international law in Northern Ireland. In a conflict defined by opposing positions on the legitimacy of the state, it was very difficult to posit the exclusive legal scrutiny of the state's conduct of the conflict as a politically neutral activity (Bell and Keenan 2004). Further, the determination of the British government to characterise the conflict as an internal criminal problem insulated paramilitary forces, most notably the IRA, from international legal scrutiny under international humanitarian law. (Throughout the Troubles, the consistent assertion of the government was that neither the 'war of national liberation' regime of Protocol I of the Geneva Conventions, nor the 'civil war' regime of Protocol II, nor the 'internal armed conflict' standards of Common Article 3 of the Geneva Conventions were applicable to the conflict.[9]) Thus perceptions prevailed in the jurisdiction of international law and human rights as a political and legal discourse 'owned' by the minority Catholic–nationalist community. This perception militated against broad-based civil society advocacy to document human rights violations. Instead, legal representatives of Republicans made increased use of judicial review on prison administration matters, with frequent recourse to the European Court of Human Rights (McEvoy 2000). The state's powers of arrest[10] and detention,[11] and unlawful killings by security forces,[12] were the primary concern of this litigation at the European Court.

9 Protocol Additional to the Geneva Conventions of 12 August 1949, and relating to the Protection of Victims of International Armed Conflicts (Protocol I), 8 June 1977, 1125 UNTS 3; Protocol Additional to the Geneva Conventions of 12 August 1949, and relating to the Protection of Victims of Non-International Armed Conflicts (Protocol II), 8 June 1977, 1125 UNTS 609. For analysis, see Bell (2000: 59); Ní Aoláin (2000b).

10 *Murray v UK* [1996] ECHR 3, (1996) 22 EHRR 29, 22 EHRR 29 (1994).

11 *Brogan v UK*, ECHR, Application No. 11209/84 11 EHRR 117 1988 (1988).

12 *McCann v UK*, ECHR, Application no. 18984/91 (1995).

Human rights advocacy more broadly in the jurisdiction focused on the erosion of due process requirements in the criminal justice system detailed above, the official ban on broadcasting statements made by political organisations and the use of plastic bullets by security forces. The Belfast-based Committee on the Administration of Justice, established in 1981, was one of the few indigenous human rights organisations to operate in the jurisdiction during the period of the Troubles.[13]

Predictably, this local human rights advocacy and documentation work involved the experience of male victims. Nevertheless, women were active within the IRA and their mistreatment in detention began to alert the attention of human rights advocates in 1982 with the introduction of routine strip-searches to Northern Irish prisons. Controversy surrounded the frequency of the searches and the way in which they were being carried out.[14] Women inmates claimed that a high degree of force was used on non-complying prisoners, that prisoners were frequently subjected to derogatory sexual remarks during the searches, and that searches were also conducted on babies and children visiting or resident with mothers in the prison (Father Dennis Faul 1983; London Armagh Group 1984; Irish National Caucus 1993). Local human rights group CAJ (Committee on the Administration of Justice) condemned the practice in a 1983 leaflet on prison reform (CAJ 1983).

However, in terms of opposition to strip-searching female prisoners, appeals to international legal standards were overlaid with arguments around Northern Ireland's cultural specificity. Chiefly, it was argued that given the dominance of two highly conservative religious faiths in the jurisdiction, this type of human rights violation was particularly damaging to women in Northern Ireland. To illustrate, the campaign against strip-searching at Armagh was initiated by two Catholic priests (Father Dennis Faul 1983). In a campaign pamphlet produced by Father Dennis Faul, it states:

> This new procedure has been a traumatic experience for young Catholic girls and older women, all of whom were reared and educated in Catholics houses and schools where the strictest standards of modesty were impressed upon them as a matter of conscience . . . they were taught to be pure and chaste like the Blessed Virgin and St Brigid and St María Goretti.
>
> (Father Dennis Faul 1983)

This language stood in stark contrast to the language with which women experiencing strip-searching condemned the practice:

13 Dermot P. J. Walsh, Application for Finance for the Committee on the Administration of Justice, 14 October 1981, quoted in Whelan (1992: 157).

14 It was established that strip-searching was being carried out with much greater frequency on female inmates in Northern Ireland than in prisons in England in Wales. See National Council for Civil Liberties (1986).

> What we are saying is that, in Armagh, intensive strip searching is currently being used in a way that constitutes sexual harassment, specifically to break the spirit of women who are regarded by the authorities as a political threat to the British state.
>
> (Letter from Armagh women prisoners, quoted in Hackett 1995: 111)

Further, it is a minor point, but nevertheless interesting, that in all the years of Republican legal challenges brought to the European Court of Human Rights, only one of these cases featured a challenge under Article 8 ('private and family life')[15] to the practice of house searches by security forces. This case, *Margaret Murray v UK*, was also one of the rare cases brought by Republicans that featured a woman as the first applicant.[16] This piercing of the private sphere appeared to be particularly egregious in the case of women.

Colombia

In contrast to Chile and Northern Ireland, Colombian feminists arguably encountered a more sympathetic civil society environment to their claims that violence in the family and private sphere was linked to the broader political violence engulfing the country. The multi-actor, multi-causal nature of violence in Colombia has received popular (and occasional official) recognition.[17] To illustrate, the definitive domestic 'diagnosis' of the violence in Colombia continues to be the 1987 report commissioned by the then Colombian government to enquire into the nature of violence in the country, and to make recommendations towards its resolution: *Colombia: Violencia y Democracia, Informe presentado al Ministerio de Gobierno* (Comisión de Estudios sobre la Violencia 1987).[18] From its outset, the Commission sought to reconsider the nature of violence in Colombia, and determined that the violence's socio-economic, sociocultural and territorial aspects would be considered (Comisión de Estudios sobre la Violencia 1987: 11). The Commission's central thesis was that while recent governments had concentrated their attention on the political violence and narcotrafficking:

15 European Convention for the Protection of Human Rights and Fundamental Freedoms 1950 213 UNTS 221.

16 *Murray v UK*, [1996] ECHR 3, (1996) 22 EHRR 29, 22 EHRR 29 (1994). The challenge under Article 8 was rejected by the Court.

17 The philosophical approach of the Colombian state to the armed conflict has varied with each change of president over the past several decades. For discussion, see Gallon (2007).

18 The commissioning of such a report by the Colombian government had only one precedent: a report commissioned in 1958 by the military junta into how to address the then still ongoing La Violencia. This report was responsible for proposing the National Front.

> [T]hey had observed with indifference the alarming increase of other types of violence which altogether was generating a much greater percentage of victims and affecting the daily lives of Colombians.
>
> (Comisión de Estudios sobre la Violencia 1987: 11)

Examining the forms of violence, the actors and modalities, the report discusses violence in the form of: organised crime; guerrilla violence (Comisión de Estudios sobre la Violencia 1987: 19); state violence; random acts of violence between individuals; and co-ordinated acts of violence between individuals (against those perceived to be 'social deviants' such as homosexuals, prostitutes, ex-convicts, drug dealers, with this violence often executed by death squads) (Comisión de Estudios sobre la Violencia 1987: 20). Of particular interest here was the final category of analysis: violence between individuals in their private lives (Comisión de Estudios sobre la Violencia 1987: 21). In discussion and recommendations, this section was examined under the heading of 'Intrafamily Violence' (Comisión de Estudios sobre la Violencia 1987: 150). Furthermore, the Commission solicited the Casa de la Mujer to contribute this section of the report.

The reasons for the different experience in Colombia, in terms of the uniquely integrated understanding of harms within local advocacy, are multiple, but some factors are worthy of particular mention. The first is the question of the scale of violence: unlike in Chile and Northern Ireland, where it was conceivable to disaggregate 'political' from 'private' violence, the extraordinary homicide levels in Colombia defied any such disaggregation.[19] Similarly, the use of violence to achieve social control of villages and communities, by both guerrilla and paramilitary groups (Comisión de Estudios sobre la Violencia 1987: 20), meant that social and political violence were completely imbricated. Third, in stark contrast to Chile and Northern Ireland, the Colombian case evidences some early coalescence between feminist and human rights groups, largely due to the prominence of the conflict in Colombian feminist advocacy. Consequently, Colombian human rights advocacy did not evidence the same regressive gender norms identified in Chile and Colombia.

Women's rights and human rights: a tale of two movements

A sharp divide prevailed between the human rights and women's movements across at least two of the three case studies during the period under study. The international human rights frame offered little in terms of a common agenda to these two movements. As this section has demonstrated, the prioritisation of civil and political rights within the international human rights canon, combined with regressive gender norms in human rights advocacy, operated to the effective

19 As illustrated by the approach adopted in Comisión de Estudios sobre la Violencia (1987).

exclusion of women's experiences of harm. The overwhelming priority given to ending political violence in the three case studies worked to reinforce the perceived 'private' character of harm routinely experienced by women.

THE INTERNATIONAL FRAME: INTERNATIONAL HUMAN RIGHTS ADVOCACY AND DOMINANT GENDER NORMS

This section focuses on the gender dynamics of this advocacy, namely the default male political actor that structures this advocacy, the consistent undermining of the political character of women's organising, and the emphasis on female purity throughout advocacy for the rights of female political detainees.

While scholars of human rights activism disagree on the relative significance of international and domestic human rights developments to human rights accountability in transitional states, they each note the significance of the Chilean experience of human rights advocacy to constituting an international human rights civil society, and to establishing its modus operandi.[20] For example, the International Commission of Jurists (ICJ) was the first international NGO to report on Chile and was present on the ground in the country in the immediate aftermath of the coup. That reporting focused on arrest and detention of trade unionists and members of left-wing political parties (International Commission of Jurists 1974, 1976). Similarly, Americas Watch maintained consistent scrutiny on restrictions to political organising in Chile (Americas Watch 1983a, 1988). The ICJ, Americas Watch and Amnesty International regularly published reports documenting the human rights abuses of the military dictatorship. Throughout this reporting, the default 'male political actor' is striking, most notably in the occasional 'women's actions' circulated by Amnesty International and Human Rights Watch (e.g. Amnesty International 1991c, 1992b). It is trite, but nevertheless illuminating, to note that no such 'men's actions' were ever circulated.

The priorities evidenced in human rights reporting by international NGOs in Chile are repeated across the case studies. A review of international human rights documentation and advocacy work on the three case studies reveals five themes to this advocacy, organised along a traditional catalogue of civil and political rights protections, namely: access to justice,[21] the state's use of force (National Council for

20 Collins (2010) emphasises the significance of the local, while Sikkink (1993) emphasises the transnational diffusion of norms.

21 The National Council for Civil Liberties prioritised its work in Northern Ireland on campaigning against specific measures around access to justice, such as non-jury courts and the use of paid informants to obtain convictions. For overview, see National Council for Civil Liberties (1986). See also Helsinki Watch (1991), which included a focus on access to justice. Lawyers Committee for Human Rights prioritised issues around access to justice (Lawyers Committee for Human Rights 1993, 1996).

Civil Liberties 1986),[22] states of legal exception (National Council for Civil Liberties 1986),[23] restrictions on political organising (including human rights defending) and the treatment of prisoners (see National Council for Civil Liberties 1986).

The issue of restrictions on political organising and the targeting of human rights activists for state violence motivated extensive reporting and advocacy by international human rights NGOs. In 1987 Americas Watch dedicated an entire report to the work of the Vicaría, noting that 'Chile's human rights abuses are the most widely known in Latin America because of the human rights organisations, especially the Vicaria' (Americas Watch 1987: 1). The report documented threats against Vicaría staff and affirmed: 'Such pressure is a reminder, if one were needed, that even so prestigious a human rights institution is continually at risk and deserves the concerted support of the international human rights community' (Americas Watch 1987: 7). The work of no women's organisation in Chile was venerated in the same terms as that of the Vicaría.

Similarly in Northern Ireland, Helsinki Watch (now Human Rights Watch) published a report in 1991, *Human Rights in Northern Ireland*, revealing the limitations imposed on political organising by emergency legislation that restricted freedom of movement and freedom of expression (Helsinki Watch 1991). Lawyers Committee for Human Rights prioritised the intimidation of defence lawyers as the targeting of human rights defenders (Lawyers Committee for Human Rights 1993, 1996). The specific impact of this difficult context on women's political organising was not documented (despite the considerable manipulation of women's organising documented in Chapter 2).

In Colombia, human rights reporting by international NGOs turned very directly in the 1980s to the organisation of civil society in the country and the impact of the conflict on such organisation, most notably in terms of violence against trade unionists (Amnesty International 1988a) and ongoing disappearances of members of human rights groups (Americas Watch 1989; Amnesty International 1991a). Work by Amnesty International documenting *Human Rights Defenders under Attack* focused on the Committee for Solidarity with Political Prisoners (Comité de Solidaridad con los Presos Políticos), the Regional Committee

22 The work of Amnesty International on Northern Ireland followed a similar pattern, focusing in turn on a series of reports on killings by security forces, later expanding into 'political killings'. See Amnesty International (1988b, 1994a). Helsinki Watch (1991) focused on the use of lethal force by security forces (and paramilitary groups). In Colombia, reporting during the 1980s highlighted the large sections of the country in which the armed forces were the only form of government, and that such governance was brutal and characterised by torture, and the role of paramilitary death squads in supporting the rule of the armed forces. See Americas Watch (1982, 1983b, 1986); Amnesty International (1994b).

23 Helsinki Watch (1991) focused on detention conditions, the use of lethal force by security forces (and paramilitary groups) and the limitations imposed by emergency legislation on freedom of movement and freedom of expression. Lawyers Committee for Human Rights (1993, 1996) also prioritised issues around emergency laws.

for the Defence of Human Rights (Comité Regional para la Defensa de los Derechos Humanos), the Coordinating Team for the Defence of Human Rights (Equipo Coordinadora para la Defensa de los Derechos Humanos) and the Regional Indigenous Council of Cauca (Consejo Regional Indígena del Cauca) (Amnesty International 1992a). None of the organisations included in this review of 'human rights defenders' could be characterised as women's organisations or were active on issues of gender-specific concern to women.

Normatively, this inattention by international human rights NGOs to the invaluable organising by women in the case studies, and the extraordinarily difficult circumstances in which these women organised, worked to undermine and undervalue the political nature of the work being done by women's organisations.

Uniquely, it was the treatment of prisoners that motivated the only documentation of women's gender-specific experiences of human rights violations in the international advocacy under study. In Chile, international human rights NGOs reinforced the blind spots of domestic advocacy, in that the documentation of torture made no reference to sexual violence against female detainees.[24] In addition to the reinforcement of gendered gaps and silences from the international legal framework that underpinned human rights advocacy in the case studies, there is also evidence of the regressive gender norms structuring the information politics that underpinned this advocacy. The omission of sexual violence from the information networks that monitored and reported human rights violations in the case studies was not a benign oversight. The torture of a female dissident in detention is a classic example of a civil and political rights violation. She is being tortured by a state agent within a prison as punishment for political opposition to the repressive state. Hence this form of violence and injustice was visible to the human rights legal framework, as evidenced by its mention in the Inter-American Commission on Human Rights (1974) Report on Chile. Mistreatment of prison detainees fits within the category of 'what men most fear will happen to them' (Charlesworth 1993: 8). The specifics of sexual violence against women confronted the tendency for human rights observers, advocates and lawyers to regard the harm as 'private'. Although conducted by a state agent against a prisoner, acts of sexual violence were deemed to be motivated by 'private' pursuit of sexual relations, and thus not in the public capacity of that state agent. The harm lay outside the realm of human rights. The inherently political character of such violence, as strategic in the state's targeting of women to punish such women for their deviance from gender norms and to emasculate their male counterparts, is made invisible within the 'privatised' understanding of the harm.

Evidence of conservative gender norms underpinning human rights information networks is perhaps even more stark in the documentation of strip-searching as a

24 The reporting of Amnesty International in Chile came later than either International Commission of Jurists or Americas Watch, was less frequent and focused in particular on the regime's use of torture. See Amnesty International (1983).

human rights violation in Northern Ireland.[25] In 1986 the London-based National Council of Civil Liberties (NCCL) conducted an inquiry into the strip-searching of women remand prisoners at Armagh women's prison. The inquiry concluded that the practice of strip-searching was not meeting its stated objective of improving prison security, was being carried out almost entirely on Catholic women and was subject to abuse by prison guards, and consequently should be reduced to pre-1982 levels (National Council for Civil Liberties 1986).[26] Similarly, Amnesty International routinely condemned the practice of strip-searching female prisoners in Northern Ireland, voicing concerns that the practice was being carried out 'with the deliberate intention of degrading and humiliating the women' (Amnesty International 1986: 4; 1991b: 22). However, in terms of opposition to strip-searching female prisoners, appeals to international legal standards were overlaid with arguments around Northern Ireland's cultural specificity. Chiefly, it was argued that given the dominance of two highly conservative religious faiths in the jurisdiction, this type of human rights violation was particularly harmful to women in Northern Ireland. Even the NCCL, in its report on the practice of strip-searching, observed that given the 'moral strictness which pervades the homes and schools of Protestants and Catholics alike . . . strip searching may be experienced as especially traumatic' (National Council for Civil Liberties 1986: 29). With this language, the NCCL was reifying cultural values deeply antithetical to women's autonomy, without contextualising the 'moral strictness' as a broader harm to the women affected.

THE WEB OF HARMS AND HUMAN RIGHTS ADVOCACY

The description of the web of harms in Chapter 2, which documented the manifold ways in which public political violence in the case studies impacted women's ostensibly private experiences of harms, relied heavily on documentation efforts of women's organisations during periods of political violence. The determination to reveal continuities and connections, in defiance of an Archimedean viewpoint that disaggregates the public and private, has been a foundational tenet of feminist thinking (e.g. Olsen 1985). The evidence reviewed in this section shows that it has also been central to feminist activism.

25 The work of Amnesty International on Northern Ireland followed a similar pattern, focusing on, amongst other themes, the treatment of people in detention. In the early to mid 1990s US-based international NGOs also began to make contributions to human rights monitoring in Northern Ireland. For example, Helsinki Watch (1991) focused on detention conditions. See Amnesty International (1991a).

26 By contrast, the body established by the UK government, the Standing Advisory Commission on Human Rights (SACHR), reported in the same year and found that the practice was within the terms of the UK's human rights obligations, and could not be discontinued due to security requirements. See Standing Advisory Commission on Human Rights (1986).

This section documents efforts by women's movements on the ground in the cases under study to reveal a more comprehensive range of harms and, in particular, to reveal the ostensibly 'private' impact of public harms related to the political violence, in terms of domestic violence. Further identified is the resistance of the mainstream human rights community to recognise and mobilise around the prima facie human rights violations that resulted from the denial of reproductive autonomy to women in the case studies. Finally, the section documents how, rather than retreating from the sphere of international human rights law, increasing feminist co-ordination at the transnational level fuelled feminist energy to challenge the masculinist definition of harms within that body of law, as women's movements formed their own TAN to agitate for the recognition of women's rights as human rights.

'Democracy in the Country and in the Home' was the slogan adopted by the Chilean women's movement, as it agitated for an end to the repressive military regime and sought to install feminist demands within the broader democratisation agenda. This powerful invocation of change to both the public and private hinged on important educational and theoretical work undertaken by the Chilean women's movement during the 1980s. In particular, the intellectual work of the prominent Chilean feminist Julieta Kirkwood fostered a deeper understanding within the women's movement of authoritarianism within the public and the private, and feminism as a negation of authoritarianism within both spheres (Kirkwood 1983). This connection of public and private was evident within the 'Feminist Manifesto: Feminist Demands for Democracy',[27] which was principally concerned with inequality within the family.

The explicit linkage between public and private violence was also made by local feminist movements in Colombia. As the discussion of *Violencia y Democracia* illustrated, feminists in Colombia operated with an acute understanding of the manifold ways in which political violence pervaded everyday life within the ostensibly private sphere.

While the women's movement in Northern Ireland was also confronted by the persistent bleeding of public violence into the private lives of individual women, there were fewer overt attempts to link the broader context of political violence to, for example, domestic violence. These Northern Irish dynamics could, in part, be attributed to the difficult space occupied by feminists opposing violence against women in Northern Ireland. State action and state resources were essential to practical service provision in the area of violence against women; however, the legitimacy of the Northern Irish state was at the heart of political violence, and acceptance of state resources by women's organisations could be regarded as a collusive activity.[28] Equally, opposition to violence against women perpetrated by

27 Reproduced in Gaviola *et al* (1994).

28 Consider, for example, the case of Derry Women's Aid, which endured threats from Republicans for allowing the responsible government minister to attend the launch of the domestic violence shelter in 1977. Avila Kilmurray, personal communication, 2 July 2007.

paramilitary groups exposed women activists to further threats of paramilitary violence.[29] Similarly, the state's consistent prioritisation of resources and attention to political violence over the daily quotidian harms of domestic violence revealed the difficult context in which women activists operated. (The question 'don't you know there's a war going on?' was often posed in similar terms to women reporting domestic violence to police in Northern Ireland.[30]) These factors worked together to discourage local women activists from making overt linkages between public and private violence against women. These factors also reveal the subtle though manifold ways in which the 'private' violence against women in this context was never really private.

The inattention of the local and international human rights movement to the various ways in which women's private experiences of violence intersected with the prevailing political violence is already apparent, and is perhaps unsurprising given the critical questions of extra-judicial killings, non-jury trials and the state's use of force that motivated human rights advocacy in this period. However, the criminalisation of abortion that prevailed in each of the case studies during the period under study constituted prima facie violations of manifold civil and political rights, and might therefore have more readily mobilised local and international human rights advocacy. For example, in Chile the legal prohibition of abortion resulted in the imprisonment of women, most of whom did not have access to defence council, and also a widespread practice of withholding medical treatment for botched abortions until details of who performed the abortion were disclosed.[31] In Northern Ireland, even the state's human rights monitoring body, the Standing Advisory Committee on Human Rights, identified the lack of clarity on the legal grounds for abortion in Northern Ireland as a violation of the legal certainty requirements of the freedom on expression guaranteed in the European Convention on Human Rights (Standing Advisory Commission on Human Rights 1993). In neither case did evidence of these civil and political rights violations mobilise any domestic or international human rights advocacy.

The chapter began by noting the doctrinal and normative limitations of international human rights law during the period under study, in terms of its exclusive focus on the rights of the male political actor. This brief review of the web of harms within human rights advocacy has documented the practical gendered consequences of international human rights law's focus on the male political actor,

29 Derry Women's Aid confronted Republicans once again, as they took the decision to condemn so-called 'punishment beatings' of women, and their protest was met with scorn, including from a female Republican members of Women's Aid. They took this stance in response to a particularly brutal incident in which a female member of the Irish Republican and Socialist Party was shot through the calves and buttocks for having used her gun in 'private enterprise' (a single parent, she had used the gun in a robbery for herself). Avila Kilmurray, personal communication, 2 July 2007.

30 Avila Kilmurray, personal communication, 2 July 2007. See also Montgomery and Bell (1985).

31 See generally Center for Reproductive Law and Policy and Open Forum on Reproductive Health and Rights (1998).

both in terms of the *inability* of the human rights movements in the cases under study to understand private violence as a concern of their work, and their *unwillingness* to advocate on the clear human rights violations that resulted from the prohibition of abortion. Nevertheless, this dramatic disconnect between the concerns of international human rights law and the lives of women did not lead the women's movements in the case studies, and transnationally, to retreat from the international sphere and the potential doctrinal, normative and political dividends of international human rights law. Rather, a transnational women's movement emerged during this period to forge a unified response to harms against women that transcended borders. The emergence and dynamics of this movement is already well documented in studies of TANs (Joachim 2007) and in feminist analysis of human rights (Reilly 2009), and fuller elaboration is beyond the scope of this book. Instead, this final section briefly reviews the roles of the local women's movements under study within these transnational developments.

Feminist *Encuentros* (meetings), consisting of grassroots and professional feminist activists from throughout Latin America and the Caribbean, have taken place biannually in Latin America since 1981. Although attended by feminists from 15 different countries of Latin America and the Caribbean, the first feminist *Encuentro* in 1981 was principally organised by Colombian feminists, for whom violence was an unavoidable political priority (Sternbach *et al* 1992). Chilean feminists were also prominent at this first *Encuentro*, largely due to widespread awareness at the meeting of their advocacy 'in the face of one of the continent's most nefarious military dictatorships' (Sternbach *et al* 1992: 432). (Indeed, to keep faith with Chilean feminists, at the Bogotá *Encuentro*, it was agreed that the feminist *Encuentro* would be held in Chile as soon as democracy was restored in the country.) Feminists present at the *Encuentro* were thus acutely aware of the manifold forms of state violence being perpetrated against women across the Latin American region. The Bogotá *Encuentro* proved highly significant in the emergence of violence against women – in its 'public' and 'private' forms – onto the international feminist agenda. The *Encuentro* provided a forum for the airing of experiences of violence common to women from a very diverse range of countries and backgrounds. The global nature of violence within the family was thereby revealed. Whether from a context of civil wars, military regimes or abject poverty, stories of personal experiences of violence emerged from the women participating in the meeting. Demonstrating the new prioritisation of violence against women as a feminist priority, it was the 1981 Bogotá *Encuentro* that first declared November 25 to be International Day to End Violence against Women.[32]

The emergence of the *Encuentros* was a Latin American manifestation of a broader global dynamic, namely the increasing transnational co-ordination of women's movements and feminist organisations. A key player in the early stages of this co-ordination was ISIS International, which formed in 1974 in Rome to

32 This account is taken from Sternbach *et al* (1992: 432).

assist in communication and knowledge transfer between women's organisations operating in different countries. Recognising the centrality of Latin American women's movements to the gathering pace of transnational feminist organising, in 1984 ISIS established an office in Santiago, Chile, to co-ordinate Latin American and Caribbean work.[33]

The leadership shown in transnational feminist organising, in beginning to articulate the relationship of so-called public and private incidences of violence against women, and in identifying violence against women as a global issue, entered the international United Nations women's agenda with the UN World Conference for Women in Nairobi in 1985.[34] Although Nairobi marked the third such conference (the first was held in Mexico in 1975 and the second in Copenhagen in 1980), Nairobi was the first to address violence against women.

As evidence of both the exchange (or dialogue) of expertise from the transnational feminist movement to international organisations, and the exchange of local and global feminist expertise, the 1988 UNIFEM report on violence against women in Latin America merits mention. In 1988 UNIFEM commissioned ISIS to prepare a report on violence against women in Latin America. It was this state-of-the-art report that identified the prevalence of violence against women and the absence of an appropriate legal framework in which to address the issue. Being led by the Santiago-based ISIS office, these global dynamics had an important influence on the domestic agenda of Chilean feminists. Chilean feminist and former ISIS worker Isabel Duque recounts:

> It was a milestone. [The Report] brought the issue of violence here to Chile and started here in Chile a very strong movement . . . The 25th of November, and the women's groups that were emerging under the dictatorship, started to bring in violence against women in 1986/'87. Every 25th of November . . . women's groups were out asking for policies and – more than asking for policies – it was taking the issue out of the house . . . It was domestic violence at that time. After, they started with sexual violence and women's rights.
>
> (Isabel Duque, personal communication, 15 October 2008)

By the end of the 1980s, due to a coalescence of global and local dynamics, a feminist TAN active in particular on the issue of violence against women was firmly evident and targeting the institutions of international law. And the successes of this TAN were quickly evident: in 1992 the Committee on the Elimination of Discrimination Against Women adopted its landmark General Recommendation 19 in which violence against women was identified as both a cause and

33 See http://www.isiswomen.org/index.php?option=com_content&view=article&id=30&Itemid=82 (last accessed 3 April 2013).

34 Report of The World Conference to Review and Appraise the Achievements of the United Nations Decade for Women: Equality, Development and Peace, Nairobi, 15–26 July 1985, passim.

consequence of women's historical position of inequality and consequently a violation of rights guaranteed under the CEDAW.[35] In June 1993 the United Nations World Conference on Human Rights in Vienna produced a consensus document that stressed the importance of working to end public and private forms of violence against women, and that 'violations of human rights of women in situations of armed conflict are violations of the humanitarian principles of international human rights and humanitarian law'.[36] At the end of that same year the UN General Assembly adopted the Declaration on the Elimination of Violence Against Women, which stated in its Preamble that violence against women constituted a human rights violation.[37] And in 1994 the UN Commission on Human Rights appointed its first ever Rapporteur tasked with a gender-specific mandate, namely the Special Rapporteur on Violence Against Women, its Causes and Consequences.[38]

CONCLUSION

This chapter has revealed the interaction of the local fit and international frame to ensure the omission of women's experiences from documented accounts of harms. Moreover, the chapter has demonstrated the regressive gender norms that underpinned and overlaid this advocacy at both the domestic and international levels. Nevertheless, women's organisations continued to mobilise across the three case studies, to reveal and redress the harms experienced by women. This domestic mobilisation by women was to spark a transnational movement to take on the processes and institutions of international law, with enormous significance for the legal treatment of harms against women within transitional justice.

35 UN Doc. A/47/38, 30 January 1992.

36 World Conference on Human Rights, Vienna Declaration and Programme of Action, 25 June 1993.

37 GA Res. 48/104, 20 December 1993, UN Doc. A/CONF. 157/23. II, para 58.

38 Commission on Human Rights, Res. 1994/45, UN Doc. ESCOR, 1994. Supp. no. 4, 140, 11 March 1994. See further Charlesworth and Chinkin (2000: 71–7).

Chapter 4

Criminal accountability and harms against women

INTRODUCTION: THE INTERNATIONAL FRAME: NORM, DOCTRINE, POLITICS

International law in the post-Second World War period was notorious for its inattention to harms experienced by women. Sexual violence, although falling within culpable behaviour under the Geneva Conventions, was not prosecuted by either the Nuremberg or Tokyo tribunals. Chapter 3 documented early progressive developments in the recognition of violence against women as a violation of international human rights law. The relationship between developments in the criminalisation of sexual violence in the International Criminal Tribunal for the Former Yugoslavia (ICTY), and the broader women's human rights campaign of enhancing state accountability for violence against women, is widely acknowledged. As Christine Chinkin observed in 1994 when writing on rape and sexual abuse in international law:

> [R]ecent steps within the international community to ensure that women's rights are recognized as human rights and to enhance the accountability of governments for violence against women are as much an integral part of the overall counter-attack on the war against women as are the more publicized and dramatic responses to events in the former Yugoslavia.
>
> (Chinkin 1994: 341)

Doctrinal developments in international law, in particular growing recognition of violence against women as a human rights violation, formed the critical backdrop to gradually enhancing criminal accountability for harms against women in contexts of violent conflict and political repression. International criminal law was an emerging area of positive law in this period; however, its precise scope and contours were indeterminate and therefore subject to influence from particular interest groups. Co-ordination between feminist scholars and advocates around a common mission of securing the criminalisation of the most grievous harms experienced by women influenced the development of international criminal law.[1]

The early 1990s marked the consolidation of a defined body of international criminal law, articulated in the statutes and jurisprudence of the ad hoc criminal tribunals for the former Yugoslavia (ICTY)[2] and Rwanda,[3] achieving codification in the Rome Statute of the International Criminal Court.[4] The United Nations Security Council (UNSC) Resolution establishing the ICTY specifically mentioned systematic rape.[5] Feminist activists and lawyers were significant in influencing this area of law, attempting to secure legal recognition and prohibition of gender-specific harms experienced by women in situations of violent conflict. There was particular energy surrounding the need to secure prohibition of rape within international criminal law, and recognition of rape as a grave breach of the Geneva Conventions, and as constitutive of crimes against humanity and genocide (see Chinkin 1994; Copelon 1994; Green *et al* 19904; Gardam 1997).

Format of the chapter

This chapter documents the ways in which the activation of criminal liability in international law operated on the ground in the case studies. Most notably, the chapter finds that criminal accountability for harms against women does not occur in a vacuum: broader accountability for harms of political violence is a prerequisite. In a process of *piggy-backing*, local women's movements have harnessed domestic political dynamics for accountability to specific accountability demands for harms against women. Second, the chapter finds that, through a strategy of *grounding*, greater domestic criminal accountability for harms against women can be positively attributed to doctrinal changes in international law. However, these progressive developments in international law are not sufficient to alter the more troubling gender norms evident within human rights advocacy patterns. Rather, international law tends to reaffirm these more problematic gender norms through transition. Finally, the chapter finds that retributive justice for harms against women can, nevertheless, deliver important political gains to local women's movements on the ground in transitional states.

1 For overview, see Halley (2008).

2 Statute of the International Criminal Tribunal for the Former Yugoslavia, S.C. Res. 827, U.N. Doc. S/RES/827 (25 May 1993).

3 Statute of the International Criminal Tribunal for Rwanda, S.C. Res. 955, U.N. Doc. S/RES/955 (8 November 1994).

4 Rome Statute of the International Criminal Court, 17 July 1998, 2187 UNTS 3 [hereinafter Rome Statute].

5 UN Security Council, Resolution 827, (1993), 25 May 1993, S/RES/827 (1993): 1.

THE LOCAL FIT: CRIMINAL ACCOUNTABILITY AND GENDER JUSTICE

Chile: piggy-backing gender justice

The Chilean case is a remarkable story of late justice for past human rights violations. In terms of the political opportunity structure, the difficult context of the transition, in which the military regime was narrowly voted out of formal power but retained substantial political and institutional influence, was inauspicious for securing broad criminal accountability.[6] Instead, acutely mindful of divided public opinion on the legitimacy of the military dictatorship and the military's still tentative return to the barracks, the new democratic president, Patricio Aylwin, formulated the distinctive Chilean approach to justice in the aftermath of the dictatorship: 'the whole truth and justice to the extent possible' (Chilean National Commission on Truth and Reconciliation 1993: 15). The truth section elaborates in much greater detail the varying fortunes of the Chilean women's movement as it came to target truth recovery and the evolving place of harms against women within the official truth narratives to emerge from the Chilean process. As is common with transitional justice processes, individual mechanisms do not operate discreetly. Developments in the official truth processes were to have important doctrinal and political significance for the prosecution of harms against women. This chapter will attempt to focus, however, on the detail of the prosecutions.

The 1978 self-amnesty law cast a long shadow on attempts to secure criminal accountability in Chile.[7] Consistently interpreted in a maximalist way by a largely unreformed judiciary, the amnesty acted to prevent even the investigation of past crimes (Roht-Arriaza 2005: 42). Experts differ on the relative significance of domestic rights litigation or international human rights advocacy to the renewal of human rights prosecutions in Chile. Country specialists emphasise ongoing domestic human rights advocacy (Collins, 2010), domestic judicial reforms (Hilbink 2007) or changes in domestic judicial attitudes (Huneeus 2010). Those more interested in identifying cross-jurisdictional patterns in prosecutions emphasise the so-called 'Pinochet effect' and the significant expansion of the legal norm of universal jurisdiction in the latter days of the 1990s and the early part of the 2000s (see especially Roht-Arriaza 2005). Those who privilege international developments differ on the relative significance of the international legal norm or transnational political mobilisation. Nevertheless, all commentators agree on the significance of the unexpected arrest of General Pinochet in London in 1998 to at least catalyse justice campaigns in Chile.

6 For a comprehensive account of earlier and more recent processes of accountability for past harms in Chile, see Collins (2010).

7 Decree Law No. 2191, Diario Oficial, 18 April 1978.

Throughout the attempted extradition, the Chilean government consistently called for Pinochet's return to Chile so that he would be tried in his own country (Roht-Arriaza 2005). Having made this commitment, the government was expected to deliver. Further, the high level of international scrutiny also prompted some introspection from the Chilean public. The pact of silence was showing signs of wear and tenacious local human rights advocates were poised to exploit these changed circumstances. Still hindered by the military regime's sweeping self-amnesty law of 1978, the judicial 'old guard' of the Supreme Court had continued throughout most of the 1990s to reject the so-called 'Aylwin doctrine' that offences potentially covered by the amnesty law must first be investigated in order to determine whether the amnesty law was applicable. Up until 1996 the Supreme Court was firm in its majority opinion that, as the amnesty law existed, no offence had been committed and thus there was no basis for an investigation (Roht-Arriaza 2005: 72). From 1998, however, international scrutiny, changing domestic attitudes, but also – critically – domestic judicial reforms, began to disrupt this majority opinion of the Chilean Supreme Court (Roht-Arriaza 2005: 72–5). By 1998 a judicial consensus was emerging in the upper courts in favour of the Aylwin doctrine – by the end of 1998 more than half of the Supreme Court was made up of post-Pinochet appointees – and cases formerly commandeered by recalcitrant military courts were being transferred to civilian jurisdiction, due also to this new pro-accountability judicial consensus.

But the application of the Aylwin doctrine was only sufficient to permit investigation of the offences. It did not provide grounds for proceeding with a prosecution. Two further developments were required to catalyse domestic prosecutions: first, in terms of prosecutions for forced disappearances, two 1998 decisions of the Supreme Court allowed the reopening of the cases on grounds that disappearance is a 'continuing crime', so neither the amnesty law nor the statute of limitations could apply until the body was found.[8] Second, in terms of securing prosecutions for non-lethal offences, in particular torture, the domestic application of international law was to prove critical.

This radically changed domestic context was the catalyst for specifically feminist interventions into processes of criminal accountability. Relying on already-defined terms of engagement and – more practically – available documentation, the submission of the feminist NGO Instituto de la Mujer in 1998, together with numerous other women's organisations and parliamentarians, presented to Judge

8 The characterisation of forced disappearances as a continuing crime was first signalled in the litigation surrounding the attempted extradition of Pinochet from Britain to Spain. It hinged on a legal fiction that, as the fate of those disappeared was unknown, the disappeared individual could potentially still have been kidnapped. It was on these grounds that campaigning Judge Juan Guzmán Tapia was able to pursue his investigation into charges against Pinochet, specifically concerning executions and forced disappearances occurring as part of the infamous 'Caravan of Death'.

Guzmán in the form of a *Téngase Presente*,[9] expressed their concern about the fate of the women who were detained and disappeared while pregnant. 'This was one of the few initiatives – if not the only one – designed to report and bring attention to the grave human rights violations experienced by women in this period' (Fundación Instituto de la Mujer 2003: 21). Although not primary instigators of legal action for criminal accountability, women's organisations were poised to insert specific justice demands for women who disappeared while pregnant. The framing adopted by the women's organisations in this intervention resonated with the broader civil society push for criminal accountability and the new court receptiveness to such demands.

Nevertheless, the centrality of the continuing crime rationale to the pursuit and delivery of criminal accountability for past crimes in Chile also signalled the continuing (more subtle) obscuring of past harms against women. This continuing crime rationale was sufficient to permit investigations of offences of forced disappearances. As noted, however, female victims of such offences were few, seldom documented, and to the extent that women were recognised as victims of forced disappearance, their experiences had garnered attention only as women who were pregnant when they disappeared (CODEPU 2002). In reality, this concerned a tiny and very particular group of women. There is a clear relationship here to past patterns of human rights advocacy, in which the gaps, blind spots and limited appearance of harms against women translates into limited accountability around only a very particular set of harms against women.

Unlike the offence of forced disappearance, which was characterised as a continuing crime under the Chilean penal code, the Chilean courts could only decline to apply the amnesty law to cases of torture with reference to the supremacy of international law and the incompatibility of allowing amnesty for torture with the Chilean state's international human rights obligations.[10] In 1998, in the landmark *Poblete Cordova* decision, the Chilean Supreme Court for the first time approved reopening a case based on the superiority of international law over the amnesty law.[11] This opened the doors to prosecutions for torture, including (potentially) the sexualised torture of women political dissidents. Nevertheless, as observers of the march to late justice in Chile repeatedly observe: 'Deaths and

9 Secretaria Criminal. Escrito *Téngase Presente*, presentado en Causa Fuero Rol N°2182–98 ante Juez de Fuero Juan Guzmán Tapia, 1998.

10 The case had already been closed by the military courts; however, the Supreme Court recognised the supremacy of international treaties under Article 5 of the Chilean Constitution. The Court held the applicable treaties to include the 1949 Geneva Conventions, which required (under Article 3) humane treatment of those who were unarmed and the imposition of penal sanctions against those who commit grave breaches of the Conventions.

11 *Caso Poblete Cordoba*, Rol. No. 469–98, Corte Suprema, 9 September 1998. There is a technical problem with this argument. The grave breaches provisions of the Geneva Conventions, and the obligation to prosecute offenders, are placed in the sections on international armed conflict, not civil wars. No decision of the Chilean courts has focused on the distinction.

disappearances have been prioritized' (Collins *et al* 2011: 24). Data from December 2011 reveals that only two dozen cases concerning torture survivors have been entered in the courts, 'which means that over 38 thousand survivors of political imprisonment and torture have not received recognition' in terms of criminal accountability (Collins *et al* 2011: 24).

Even within the cases concerning torture, only a tiny number have concerned women victims. Importantly, in terms of resource mobilisation, these cases have been brought not by the traditional human rights community but by Chilean women's organisations. The Chilean case is therefore familiar, in that complaints of sexual violence have been late to emerge and have seldom formed the basis of initial *querellas* (complaints). Instead, evidence of sexual violence has been uncovered in the course of fuller investigation (Maturana 2011). Most notably, the legally focused feminist NGO, Corporación Humanas, has now brought a series of *querellas* concerning sexualised acts of torture perpetrated against female victims during the dictatorship. In December 2010 the first *querella* was presented in Chile for sexual violence as a form of torture committed during the dictatorship. Patricia Herrera, lawyer for Corporación Humanas, considers that these actions will help to make visible the systematic nature of the practice. In January and February 2011 four further *querellas* for sexual violence were added (Collins *et al* 2011: 31).[12] This unfolding Chilean story of late justice for female victims of sexual violence reveals the imbrication of broad criminal accountability with gender-specific accountability for women's experiences of political violence. Nevertheless, the legacy of old established patterns and gaps of human rights advocacy is evident in the need for a feminist NGO to take forward gender justice demands within the Chilean process of criminal accountability.

Northern Ireland: hyper-legalisation of gender justice

The endurance of legal oversight (no matter how impotent) over political violence in Chile is regarded as one of the distinguishing features of efforts to deliver criminal accountability in that jurisdiction. In Northern Ireland, similarly, judicial processes of accountability persisted – though somewhat tweaked by emergency legislation – throughout the period of the political violence. Criminal prosecutions of Republican (and to a lesser extent, Loyalist) paramilitaries proceeded in large numbers throughout the conflict (Shirlow and McEvoy 2008: 2). In that sense, the Northern Ireland case can also be regarded as peculiarly judicialised. Courts continued to function throughout the Troubles, and amnesties have been rare and select (Mallinder 2008: 31).[13]

12 These women are Catalina Palma, Carmen Gloria Díaz, Elizabeth Rubio and Gimena Zavala.

13 In the Belfast Agreement, early prisoner release was agreed, but amnesty was not. Agreement Reached in the Multi-Party Negotiations, Ir–UK, 10 April 1998 available at http://cain.ulst.ac.uk/events/peace/docs/agreement.htm (last accessed 27 February 2013). See generally McEvoy (1999).

Whereas criminal accountability has been heavily one-sided in targeting IRA paramilitaries (and to a lesser extent Loyalist paramilitaries), formal findings of human rights violations have concerned state actors (police, army, criminal justice). This has led to curious unevenness in criminal accountability for past offences in Northern Ireland. To quote Fionnuala Ní Aoláin regarding findings against the state of the European Court of Human Rights concerning the use of lethal force in Northern Ireland:

> [T]hese cases represent an enormous accountability gap for the State. The story about these cases is a missing narrative about the role of the State during the conflict itself.
>
> (Ní Aoláin 2002: 588)

The very particular context of Northern Ireland, within the model liberal democracy of the United Kingdom and the exacting regulatory rights framework of the European Convention and the Council of Europe, has meant that the UK has had to confront questions to the human rights compliance of its response to political violence regularly and systematically to an extent that is unique. In this regard, it is important to note that the UK government is bound by a detailed set of legal obligations concerning the effective investigation of killings carried out by state agents. These obligations arise from decisions of the European Court of Human Rights on procedural obligations of the European Convention's Article 2 guarantee of the right to life.[14] While these four cases concerned male victims of lethal force, the precursor to this jurisprudence was the controversial 1994 decision of the European Court of Human Rights concerning the use of lethal force against three members of the IRA in 1988.[15] Among these three IRA members was Mairéad Farrell. Farrell was both a combatant in the conflict and also ultimately a victim of the conflict. Her death and its circumstances activated a substantial set of interlocking legal obligations that has made her visible within the process of criminal accountability. The protagonists of Northern Ireland's proud tradition of women's community activism, or the women who more prosaically managed daily community survival during the conflict, could make no such claim on criminal accountability processes.

Efforts to deliver criminal accountability for past harms in Northern Ireland therefore evidence a pattern of *hyper-legalisation*, which has been exclusionary to women's organisations and damaging more broadly to efforts for accountability for harms against women. Chapter 3 showed how the centrality of legal processes

14 See *Jordan v United Kingdom*, ECHR, Application No. 24746/94 (2001); *Kelly and Others v UK, ECHR, Application No. 30054/96 (2001); McKerr v UK*, ECHR, Application No. 28883/95 (2001); *Shanaghan v UK*, ECHR, Application No. 37715/97 (2001).

15 *McCann v UK, ECHR, Application No. 18984/91 (1995)* is the acknowledged precursor to the *Jordan* case. See Bell and Keenan (2005: 72).

to the conflict in Northern Ireland was inauspicious to the involvement of women's organisations in human rights advocacy and documentation work. Its implications were longer term, in that in no real sense were women's organisations considered 'players' in devising official responses to documented harms.

Institutional initiatives to pursue prosecutions for historical cases have principally taken place through the Historical Enquiries Team (HET) established within the Police Service of Northern Ireland in 2005,[16] and the Police Ombudsman Office empowered to investigate past misconduct of the police and recommend appropriate criminal or disciplinary action against police.[17] The mandate of the HET is confined to cases resulting in death, and the Police Ombudsman's mandate is restricted to 'grave or exceptional' cases. The narrow scope of their respective mandates does not bode well for comprehensive understanding of the harm and violence of the conflict emerging from these legal processes. The evidential burdens to prosecution are substantial (in particular, the time passed and unreliability of evidence mean that it is widely acknowledged that the HET will be performing well if even a handful of prosecutions result from its enquiries, not to mention convictions). As such, the HET is bound by rigorous standards of the European Convention and procedural obligations of the Article 2 right to life. Moreover, the HET's mandate is to review over 3,500 conflict-related deaths. Given the overwhelmingly male profile of these deaths (in common with Chile), accountability for deaths has been prioritised over accountability for harms experienced by the living injured, for example.

This narrow scope would be less problematic from a gender perspective if other institutional avenues existed for the comprehensive articulation of harm. However, the HET and Police Ombudsman Office constitute one of a small number of official avenues for investigation and articulation of past harm.[18] Moreover, in contrast to Chile, this obscuring of harms against women is compounded by the fact that sexual violence was not a systemic feature of the conflict in Northern Ireland. Whereas in Chile the issue of sexual violence against female political dissidents has provided an entry-point for feminist intervention into the process for criminal accountability, no such entry-point exists in Northern Ireland. The focus on women's experiences of sexual violence within international legal developments in criminal accountability and transitional justice is often critiqued by feminists for essentialising women as passive victims in contexts of political violence, and of exacerbating regressive understandings of women's 'purity' (e.g. Ní Aoláin 2000a;

16 See further Lundy (2009).

17 See further www.policeombudsman.org/ (last accessed 5 March 2013).

18 Indeed, the Office of the Police Ombudsman for Northern Ireland (2008: 8) itself noted that:

> Absent any other societal resolution to issues surrounding the Past, I will need more resources to continue doing what I am required by law to do. Victims do need resolution. While I do not believe that the Police Ombudsman can effectively provide resolution for the majority of people victimised by 'the Troubles', at present the Office is one of the few means available.

Nesiah 2006; Otto 2009). The Northern Irish case suggests, however, that in addition to these concerns, a narrow focus on sexual violence as the exclusive female experience of political violence will politically marginalise women's organisations from criminal accountability processes in contexts that do not evidence widespread patterns of sexual violence.

The Northern Irish process for criminal accountability evidences patterns of *hyper-legalisation* that are exclusionary to both women's experiences of conflict and to women's organisations. The legacy of human rights advocacy patterns documented in the previous chapter is evident, as harms against women that were not the subject of human rights advocacy and litigation are similarly excluded from a criminal accountability process in which the European Court of Human Rights is a key protagonist. Equally, the absence of any history of collaboration between women's and human rights organisations mean that there is limited potential to find common ground in the current process of criminal accountability.

Colombia: grounding gender justice and persistent gendered contradictions

Colombia has the unfortunate distinction of being the site of the longest running civil war in the Western hemisphere (International Center for Transitional Justice 2009). The country has been in an almost permanent state of civil strife since the 1940s. Side-by-side with this violence, Colombia boasts the longest running electoral democracy in Latin America. Democratic elections have been interrupted only once since independence, for a brief period of military rule in the mid 1950s. This is the paradox of Colombia's conflict: protracted and widespread violence within a constitutional democracy. There have been ongoing attempts to resolve this conflict through legal innovation:[19] from the repressive measures imposed through states of emergency through the 1980s (Americas Watch 1992); to the bold attempt of the 1991 Constituent Assembly and Constitution to transform the democratic order and restore the rule of law; to repeated compromises on accountability to secure the demobilisation of violent actors.

The most recent amended form of criminal accountability has been pursued through the framework of the so-called Justice and Peace Law of 2005, which has involved the disarmament, demobilisation and reintegration of AUC (Autodefensas Unidas de Colombia) rank-and-file, facilitated through economic and legal benefits to the demobilised within large designated demobilisation zones.[20] The contemporary process of transitional justice has operated, importantly however,

19 This reliance on legal innovation to achieve social transformation is captured by the quote from General Santander inscribed above the entrance to Colombia's Palace of Justice: 'Colombians: Arms have given you independence, laws will give you freedom'.

20 Ley 782 of 2002, Decree 128 of 2003, Decree 3360 of 2003 (which together have regulated the demobilisation of up to 35,000 paramilitaries).

under the shadow of international law.[21] Though largely supportive of the demobilisation initiative, the need to establish a comprehensive legal framework to ensure that demobilisation was consistent with international law, most notably in terms of guaranteeing criminal accountability for war crimes, crimes against humanity and genocide, has shaped the Colombian approach to criminal accountability.[22] Further, the International Criminal Court expressed early interest in the Colombian process.[23]

Efforts to mediate the state's push for amnesty and demobilisation with international legal demands for criminal accountability for the most serious crimes resulted in the Justice and Peace Law to regulate the prosecution of leaders of paramilitary groups.[24] The law established a *sui generis* judicial process for the realisation of paramilitary testimonies of their criminal activities (*'versiones libres'* or literally 'free versions'), and the conditions for participation of victims and their representatives in these testimonies. In turn, 'alternative penalties' to the deprivation of liberty for between five and eight years would be imposed on those demobilised, provided that the individual admitted responsibility for each of his/her criminal acts. The law has a residual application, to those who did not accede to benefits under the earlier Presidential Decrees, due to the nature of the crimes committed. Hence, the Justice and Peace Law provided for a measure of investigation, adjudication and sanction of those responsible for crimes against humanity, such as massacres, extrajudicial killings, forced disappearances, rape and sexual abuse, as well as forced displacement of civilian populations. The law has motivated extensive international scrutiny.[25]

21 The Organization of American States, the Inter-American Commission on Human Rights and the International Criminal Court have all exercised some degree of scrutiny over the Justice and Peace Process.

22 Permanent Council of the Organization of American States, Resolution CP/RES. 859 (1397/04) 'Support to the Peace Process in Colombia'. See also Inter-American Commission on Human Rights (2004); United Nations High Commissioner for Human Rights (2005).

23 Visits from the ICC Chief Prosecutor demonstrated the Court's concern with widespread amnesties in the country and reiterated its complementary jurisdiction over genocide and crimes against humanity in Colombia. When ratifying the Rome Statute in 2002, Colombia availed itself of the possibility of postponing the Court's jurisdiction over war crimes for a further seven years.

24 An amended criminal justice process, pursued through bespoke Justice and Peace Tribunals, allowed for the demobilisation of the leadership of the paramilitary 'blocks'. Finally, on 25 July 2005, the Justice and Peace Law (Ley de Justicia y Paz) was approved by Congress.

25 See especially *Case of the 'Mapiripán Massacre' v Colombia*, 2005, Inter-American Court of Human Rights (ser. C) No. 134 (15 September 2005): para 241 (the investigation does not fulfil the standards of access to justice and the right to judicial protection set forth in the American Convention). For discussion of this decision, see further Laplante and Theidon (2007). The Inter-American Commission immediately criticised the law for, in particular, inadequate measures to guarantee the clarification of individual crimes and inadequate resources to implement the law, particularly the establishment of a dedicated unit within the prosecutor's office consisting of only 20 prosecutors, and the short time limits to allow for investigation of alleged crimes. The Inter-American

Feminist criticism of the law has developed in two distinct though related veins, reflecting the divisions within the Colombian women's movement (see especially Wills 2007). Ideological divisions on the appropriate feminist approach to the state crystallised in the 1970s and early 1980s. The traditional anti-state posture of Colombian feminism was challenged by those who viewed the state as complex and disjointed, and potentially offering space for feminist gains. In terms of women's mobilisation to end violence and injustice, diverging philosophical approaches to the state have given rise to diverging mobilisation tactics. The justice and peace process has prompted the re-emergence of old divisions within the Colombian feminist movement, explains feminist historian María Emma Wills:

> Nowadays the division would be called by another name, but there is a division between those who campaign and work with the state and have a vision of the state as complex with fissures and ruptures. Because of these ruptures they regard the state as something to be worked with and within. There is another camp that works from a conception of civil society, from the *popular*, from the horizontal. [This camp has] nothing to do with hierarchies; nothing to do with the state. These old divisions were reproduced once again when confronted by the Justice and Peace Law. There are genealogies to these disputes. It's not that each one is a critical moment, creating new divisions and alliances. These are alliances of much longer term . . . So, the last rupture obviously had to do with the Justice and Peace Law.
>
> (Maria Emma Wills Obregón, Bogotá, personal communication, 3 December 2008)

Court held that the Justice and Peace Law did not provide sufficient incentive for exhaustive confessions and that the state must remove all actual and juridical obstacles to an exhaustive judicial examination of the violations. A decision of the Colombian Constitutional Court modified aspects of the law. Most notably the Court introduced a requirement that the *version libre* must be true and complete. If a crime is omitted from the testimony and subsequently revealed, the demobilised combatant would lose all benefits under the Justice and Peace Law. See Corte Constitucional de Colombia, *Sentencia No. C-370/06* (2006). The Inter-American Commission endorsed the Constitutional Court's judgment and continues to advise on measures to improve implementation of the law (Inter-American Commission on Human Rights 2005, 2006). See, for example, Inter-American Commission on Human Rights (2007). See also the website of the OAS Mission to the Support the Peace Process, http://www.oas.org/documents/OEA-Colombia/ConvenioOEA-ColombiaE.asp (last accessed 5 March 2013). The ICC Prosecutor, Moreno Ocampo, began to examine the investigations and proceedings for crimes against humanity in Colombia in 2005. This examination has been ongoing, including official visits by the ICC Prosecutor to the country in 2007 and 2008. After years of examination, no formal investigation has been opened ('ICC Prosecutor visits Colombia', 21 August 2008, available at: http://www.reliefweb.int/rw/rwb.nsf/db900SID/AMMF-7HQHAL?OpenDocument, last accessed 5 March 2013).

First, women's civil society organisations criticised the operation of the law for the almost complete absence of disclosures surrounding sexual violence in the *versiones libres* (Mesa de Trabajo Mujer y Conflicto Armado 2008: 57). In this response to this identified shortcoming of state-led prosecutions, Colombian women's organisations have specifically drawn on international law to push for prosecutions for conflict-related sexual violence (Corporación Humanas 2009: 14). The Colombian office of Corporación Humanas considers that greater knowledge of the Rome Statute and the arguments, forms of testimony and procedural guarantees that have been developed through the international courts in relation to criminal gangs who carried out sexual violence, can 'open up possibilities for new arguments and tougher investigations' (Corporación Humanas 2009: 12). Moreover, feminist organisations have had an input in the training of prosecutors in the prosecution of sexual violence, drawing on the Rome Statute in order to educate them about the potential to pursue criminal prosecution of cases of sexual violence as constitutive of torture, crimes of war and crimes against humanity (Corporación Humanas 2009: 14). The Colombian case is a compelling example of dedicated feminist effort to *ground* gender justice by ensuring that international legal developments in the criminalisation of sexual violence are brought to bear on the domestic process of criminal accountability.

It is necessary to acknowledge how isolated these sorts of feminist prosecution initiatives are in Colombia and that this level of feminist technical engagement is not necessarily broad-based. Rather it has emerged from specific organisations, most notably from Corporación Humanas. The important difference, however, between this feminist legal activism in Colombia and the Chilean feminist prosecution strategy is that in Colombia it is supported by mainstream human rights groups, in particular the Colombian Commission of Jurists.[26] Again, in terms of resource mobilisation, the legacy of human rights advocacy patterns is evident in contemporary feminist interventions into criminal accountability processes.

The second vein of feminist criticism of the justice and peace process has emerged from more radical feminist elements and has focused on the security costs to women of the demobilisation strategy that has accompanied the criminal accountability process.[27] Stated feminist concerns are that the disarmament, demobilisation and reintegration (DDR) of armed actors, which involves a largely

26 See, for example, the Colombian Commission of Jurists' membership of Mesa de Trabajo Grupo Mujer y Conflicto.

27 The disarmament, demobilisation and reintegration (DDR) strategy was a central element of President Uribe's policy of 'Democratic Defense and Security Policy', which was launched by him in June 2003. The main thrust of the policy has been to adjust and improve the military's position by increasing the capacity of armed forces to hold territory and by creating incentives for the armed groups to demobilise. Another important aspect of the democratic security initiative has been the incorporation of civilians en masse into the war effort through initiatives such as a 'network of informants' to inform state forces of illegal activities in return for monetary compensation (Presidencia de la República Ministerio de Defensa Nacional República de Colombia 2003).

male group of former combatants being reintegrated into largely female civilian communities, has resulted in the trading of public violence (against military and civilian populations in general) for private violence (largely against women and girls within homes and communities) (Mesa de Trabajo Grupo Mujer y Conflicto Armado 2005; Ní Aoláin and O'Rourke 2010: 115–43). Without ignoring the presence of women in combatant forces or the prominence of men in civilian populations, there is nevertheless an often unspoken gender piece to DDR: namely, that the process involves the reintegration of a largely male (former) combatant group into a disproportionately female civilian population. By and large, DDR processes are directed at societies in which there have been significant non-state sources of violence. The gender differential between returning and receiving communities means that, although DDR is officially concerned with ensuring the conditions that enable former combatants to cease violence and return to their communities of origin, DDR can also ignite a series of new challenges for women's security within the community.[28]

Feminist organisations noted alarming increases in levels of domestic violence, as relationships were forged or reignited between former combatants and members of the civilian population (Corporación Humanas and UNIFEM 2005: 73). In this catalogue of harms, the material consequences of the public/private distinction in transitional justice are directly confronted. Teenage pregnancy, poor sexual health and domestic violence fall within the sphere of private harms. Perceived as unrelated to the public violence of paramilitary groups, the proliferation of such harms against women does not inform political calculations of costs and benefits in the negotiation of demobilisation. The broader problem is 'the evident disconnect between the planning of DDR programs – as well as the benchmarking of their success – and the lived experience of women in the receiving communities' (Ní Aoláin and O'Rourke 2010: 134).

CONCLUSION: REALISING GENDER JUSTICE THROUGH CRIMINAL ACCOUNTABILITY, REALISING A WEB OF HARMS

Criminal accountability is the most formally legalised aspect of transitional justice examined in this book. Arguably, it is the high level of legalisation that narrows

28 In order to illustrate some of the 'new' gender dynamics of violence that can accompany processes of DDR, it is instructive to draw on empirical research conducted by Colombian women's organisations examining the impact of DDR on the lives of women living in the rehabilitation and consolidation zones. Based on analysis of the short- and long-term impacts, such research has regarded the process of reintegration under the terms of the Justice and Peace Law as a threat to the security of women. Early on in the DDR process, women's organisations monitoring the reintegration process in Tierralta, Córdoba identified an increase in levels of prostitution, sexually transmitted diseases and teenage pregnancy (Corporación Humanas and UNIFEM 2005: 67).

the understanding of harm and limits the potential of criminal accountability in transitional justice to deliver transformative outcomes for women. In Northern Ireland, for example, it is the hyper-legalisation of the process of criminal accountability that has proven highly exclusionary to women's organisations. Nevertheless, the substantial mobilisation of women motivated by justice demands across both transnational feminist advocacy and the Chilean and Colombian case studies makes it clear that women's movements are unlikely to abandon criminal accountability as a site of feminist engagement in transitional justice. Indeed, in broader literature on law and social movements, the distinction between legal victory and victory 'on the streets' is carefully noted (McCann 2006). It is acknowledged that legal processes can deliver both legal and non-legal dividends. Moreover, non-legal dividends of legal processes are attributed typically not to the strict legal outcome of any legal process. Rather, non-legal dividends are typically attributed to the social mobilisation required in initiating, pursuing and following up any legal process. More specifically, in feminist engagement with law and criminal justice processes, Liz Schneider has identified the important 'dialectic' that occurs between the feminist movement and any legal campaign. She observes that women's movements:

> assert rights not simply to advance legal argument or to win a case, but to express the politics, vision, and demands of a social movement, and to assist in the political self-definition of that movement. We understood that winning rights will not be meaningful without political organizing to ensure enforcement of and education concerning those rights.
>
> (Schneider 1986: 605)

Similarly, this section concludes, the pursuit of criminal accountability and retributive justice should also be considered for its non-legal dividends. This chapter points to important – though non-legal – gains delivered by the pursuit of criminal accountability in the cases under study, that provide opportunities for the realisation of a web of harms in transitional justice, and the relative role of international law and domestic gender politics in delivering these gains.

Most notably in Chile and Colombia, processes for criminal accountability in transitional justice have motivated substantial feminist engagement. Demands for the prosecution of sexual violence have framed extensive feminist intervention into ongoing processes for criminal accountability. The effectiveness of criminal accountability as a mobilising frame for women's movements and feminist demands, across both the international and domestic political sphere, means that retributive justice cannot be underestimated as an area of feminist engagement in transitional justice.

In terms of the relative significance of the local fit and international frame in retributive justice outcomes for women, international norms must always work their influence through the filter of domestic structures and domestic norms, which can produce important variations in compliance and interpretation of these norms. Typically, this involves a process by which domestic 'norm entrepreneurs' who advocate a minority position use international norms to strengthen their position in domestic debates (Sikkink and Finnemore 1998: 896). The importance of norm entrepreneurs to this feminist work in retributive justice is illustrated by the centrality of the same feminist NGO in both Chile and Colombia, namely Corporación Humanas, to the pursuit of prosecutions for sexual violence against women in criminal accountability processes. This chapter has revealed that, even in inauspicious domestic political contexts, feminist-informed developments in international law have provided an important mobilising frame for local feminist advocates seeking either to piggy-back or ground gender justice within broader domestic criminal accountability initiatives for harms against women.

Moreover, the feminist pursuit of retributive justice in the case studies delivered some important and progressive changes to the official institutions at which they targeted their advocacy. For example, in Colombia feminist pursuit of prosecutions for conflict-related sexual violence has reportedly enhanced capacity within the formal criminal justice for sexual violence prosecutions unrelated to the conflict.[29] The issue of criminal accountability may provide an entry point into the institutions of criminal justice, with longer-term positive implications for the state response to a web of harms against women. Thus, while the international frame may have emphasised prosecutions for politically motivated sexual violence, the local fit may mean that the relationships engendered between women's movements and security sector institutions lead to enhanced state performance across a range of harms against women.

Finally, in terms of criminal accountability in transitional justice and advancing recognition of a web of gender-based harms against women, a growing body of literature indicates that legal frameworks have a significant impact on how individuals understand their interests and even their identities. Sally Engle Merry's work has emphasised, in particular, the importance of a supportive international human rights framework to local understandings of women as rights-holders and of violence against women as both a rights violation and as criminally culpable (see Merry 2003). The doctrinal developments in international law noted in the beginning of the chapter therefore provide a potent educational tool locally in the moral repugnance of violence against women and of the state's duty, as a matter of international legal obligation, to prohibit, prevent and punish such violence (Merry 2003: 343).

29 Cecilia Barraza, Corporación Humanas, Bogota, personal communication, 9 December 2008.

Part III

Truth

Chapter 5

Feminist truth strategies

Looking backward, moving forward

INTRODUCTION

The difficulties of securing criminal justice in transition has given rise to the practice of truth-seeking for crimes of the past. Official efforts to establish who were the wrongdoers, what were the wrongs, who were the victims and survivors, is often posited as a supplement to limited criminal accountability.[1] The practice of official truth-seeking largely emerged from the political expediency of pacted transitions in the Latin American Southern Cone (Hayner 2002). Despite these dubious origins, however, the principle of truth-telling in transition is now broadly regarded as an important and appropriate element of contemporary transitional justice (see especially Hayner 2002). Legally, the proliferation of truth-telling mechanisms in transitional societies is grounded in the state's duty to investigate human rights violations of the previous regime,[2] and hardening international legal standards that require investigation as constitutive of reparations[3] and measures to combat impunity.[4]

This chapter advances three key claims: first, that despite reasons for lofty feminist ambitions in much truth scholarship, feminist truth strategies are generally forged within an inhospitable political opportunity structure. Second, feminist truth strategies defy any assumptions around unified women's agendas in official truth processes and consequently are undertaken with very limited available resources for mobilisation. Finally, for all of these reasons, feminist truth strategies in practice tend to focus on a narrow and modest set of objectives.

Why truth matters, to women, and to women's movements

Feminist optimism about truth processes is grounded in the perceived informality, or at least the lesser formality, of truth processes compared to criminal processes.

1 The principal overview of these initiatives is Hayner (2002).
2 A duty initially and forcefully articulated in *Velasquez Rodriguez Case*, Judgment of 29 July 1988, IACtHR, Series C No. 4 (1988), para 174.
3 See Van Boven (1993) regarding Article 3 (the scope of the obligation including investigation).
4 See Orentlicher (2005) regarding Principle 2 (the inalienable right to truth).

Legal categories of harm can be either expanded or abandoned as truth processes do not lead to convictions. Similarly, a broader range of evidence can be relied on and standards of proof and requirements of due process do not constrain truth processes (Orford 2006). More policy-oriented interventions into gender and truth-seeking emphasise that:

> Truth Commissions . . . can provide an extraordinary window of opportunity to highlight neglected abuses, research the enabling conditions of gendered violations, provide a forum for victims and survivors, recommend reparations that redress injustices, and leave a long-term legacy that is responsive to women's history and quest for reform.
>
> (International Center for Transitional Justice 2006: 2)

Although there may be disagreement about the stakes involved, there is at least agreement that truth matters for women. Feminist ambitions in truth processes, that these processes recognise and express rebuke for harms experienced by women, that they reveal the structural gender inequalities that make women vulnerable to particular types of harms and affirm women's agency, establish truth as an important site of feminist engagement in transitional justice (Ross 2003; International Center for Transitional Justice 2006; Ní Aoláin and Turner 2007). Mark Osiel notes that the cultivation of collective memory has both a retributive component that looks to the past and a deterrence function that is directed to the future.[5] In a backward-looking sense, truth processes provide a forum for the cathartic (re)telling of past experiences of harm. More broadly, they provide an opportunity for the societal expression of moral condemnation of past wrongs (Hayner 2002: 25). Moreover, the potential for broad acknowledgement and recognition of the individual's experience of harm is said to offer healing effects (Hayner 2002: 28). In its backward-looking functions, truth in transition is emphasised for its normative and expressive effects (Hayner 2002: 28). Truth in transition is said to be linked to the deterrence of future human rights violations (Hayner 2002: 154), to promoting democracy and social healing (Campbell and Turner 2008: 375) and to educating towards a human rights culture (Campbell and Turner 2008: 375). By providing a vehicle for a shared societal narrative of the wrongs of the past, and thereby establishing the foundations for a shared non-violent future, truth-seeking is linked to notions of reconciliation and social healing.[6] In its forward-looking function, by contrast, Osiel's observations suggest a highly instrumentalist rationale to the cultivation of collective memory in transitional states. Collective memory shapes a consensus about what harms of the

5 'As an aim for criminal law, the cultivation of collective memory resembles deterrence in that it is directed toward the future, where enhanced solidarity is sought. But like retribution, it looks to the past, to provide the narrative content of what is to be shared in memory' (Osiel 1997: 12).

6 For a critical review of these arguments, see Campbell and Turner (2008).

past are to be targeted for rebuke, and an agreed prioritisation for the future about the harms to be deterred. This forward-looking function of truth can underpin, for example, institutional reforms intended to guarantee the non-recurrence of past wrongs (Hayner 2002: 154). Less prosaically, in its forward-looking guise, truth crafted in official truth processes seek to underpin new societal consensus for moving forward in the context of a deeply divided past. (It is not uncommon for truth commissions to be charged with the task of reconciliation in their very titles.) As the case studies in the book illustrate, truths moulded from official processes are intended to assist, and not interrupt, efforts to move away from political violence.

The instrumentalist understanding of truth processes, as dedicated to the creation and reinforcement of narratives to unify divided groups and, in particular, to move forward a political process of transition, has motivated some trenchant critique. Wilson observes that:

> The symbolic impact of these commissions lies in how they codify the history of a period . . . Popular memories of an authoritarian past are multiple, fluid, indeterminate and fragmentary, so truth commissions play a vital role in fixing memory and institutionalizing a view of the past conflict.
>
> (Wilson 2001: 16)

Most developed in respect of the South African case, observers such as Richard Wilson have emphasised the function of truth and truth commissions in 'nation-building and a hegemonic project of state formation' (Wilson 2001: xvi). Wilson posits the writing of a 'new official memory' as central to state-building efforts in the context of a state that contains many elements of the past (Wilson 2001: xvi). Arising from the Australian process of truth recovery for the forcible removal of Aborigine children from their families, Anne Orford builds on the idea of truth as serving broader political functions of legitimating the state, understanding truth commissions as a symbolic act to illustrate both the state's break with the past and the state's capacity for self-correction. In common with Wilson, she considers the roles of these 'commissioned truths' in producing a sense 'of a unified past and a shared future' (Orford 2006: 881).

However, there is no reason to suggest that consolidating an account of the past that serves forward-looking objectives is unique to official truth initiatives. In an instructive application of Foucault's 'regimes of truth' (Foucault 1980: 131), Rolston and Scraton identify hegemonic official discourses of truth and counter-hegemonic discourses that emerge from community-based truth initiatives (Rolston and Scraton 2005). The latter are deemed to 'challenge rather than sustain regimes of truth' (Rolston and Scraton 2005: 560). To identify civil society truth initiatives as 'counter-hegemonic' should not, however, diminish their potential significance. In particular in contexts where an overarching official truth account of the past has yet to be crafted, civil society accounts of the past carry enormous potential influence and can also be motivated by instrumentalist forward-looking objectives that inform official truth processes. 'Truth' has functionality well beyond the official sphere, as alternative political groupings consolidate past truth accounts that advance their contemporary political objectives.

Constructing such a shared truth narrative amongst women is not easy. There are several reasons for the relatively limited engagement by women's movements with the truth campaigns in the cases under study. First is the legacy of the exclusionary patterns of human rights advocacy identified in Chapter Three. The narrow definition of harms that underpinned human rights advocacy meant that truth processes offered little obvious potential to advance feminist objectives, in particular in the context of acute material need that accompanies the aftermath of conflict or repression. These largely external factors are complemented by factors internal to women's organising. Truth is a complex and fraught area of women's activism. Even regarding the ostensibly non-contentious question of women's participation in truth processes, it is difficult to de-link the procedural claim for women's participation from substantive claims about what past must be examined and what truths must be told.[7] In one reading, truth processes have implications for the entire post-conflict or post-authoritarian society. According to this rationale, women constitute half of society and the exclusion of women from that decision-making is manifestly unjust (Phillips 1995: 81). However, dealing with the past is not necessarily understood as the concern of all members of society. Many would argue that victims, however defined, should have stronger moral claims for inclusion in this process (Mani 2002). Others would argue that the 'buy-in' of formerly warring parties is needed to ensure an effective and inclusive process for dealing with the past. Many feminists would argue that to acknowledge only formerly violent actors as stakeholders in dealing with the past structurally excludes women, given their statistically lower presence amongst armed actors (Bell and O'Rourke 2007: 25). Moreover, feminists argue that women were victims of the conflict, but recognising their victimhood requires a broader understanding of harms than currently underpins most official processes to deal with the past (Ní Aoláin 2000a). The question of who recovers the truth, and women's inclusion amongst those ranks, links inevitably to what truth should be dealt with. It is difficult to assert the ostensibly non-contentious claims for women's participation in truth processes without entering into the fraught political terrain of just what constitutes 'the truth'. This is terrain around which there may be little unity amongst women, women's movements or feminists.

Because of the difficulty of forging unified feminist positions into the past, and the limited identifiable gains to women's movements resulting from truth processes, women's movements can be reluctant to engage with truth processes. To the extent that they do engage, instrumentalist and forward-looking positions carry great appeal.

7 These dynamics are examined in greater detail in O'Rourke (2012).

CHILE: LOOKING BACKWARD, CLOSING THE BOOK

Political opportunity structure: the 'politics of agreement' and the long shadow of the past

When the newly elected centre-left coalition Concertación de los Partidos por la Democracia agreed its government programme in 1989, the issue of human rights was addressed in the opening paragraph. The human rights violations of the dictatorship were characterised as having consequences not only for direct victims but for all Chileans and consequently for the political future of the country. When President Aylwin took office in 1990, he listed the new democratic government's human rights goals as threefold: first, to provide an official truth of the past human rights violations; second, to provide reparations to victims; and third, to guarantee legal, social and political conditions that would prevent the recurrence of human rights violations (Lira 2006a: 5).

As to the first objective, 'an official truth', the Chilean case is paradigmatically designated a 'pacted' transition, in that the departure from power of the military dictatorship was negotiated between political elites and happened within the institutional and legal framework of the dictatorship's own design, namely the 1980 Constitution (e.g. Waylen 1994). The 1978 amnesty law was consistently interpreted in a maximalist way by an unreformed judiciary up until the late 1990s (Amnesty International 2001b). The 1980 Constitution provided that the new democratic parliament would be dominated by appointed senators sympathetic to the military including a lifetime seat for Pinochet, complemented by right-wing senators elected through a deliberately distorted electoral mechanism (Valenzuela 1992).[8] Concerns about the willingness of the armed forces to relinquish governmental power prohibited robust confrontation with the political leadership of the armed forces on questions of either accountability for past human rights violations or dismantling of the 'authoritarian democracy' constructed by the military regime in the 1980 Constitution (Americas Watch 1991: 2). Moreover, although the 1988 plebiscite marked a clear victory for pro-democracy forces, 46 per cent of voters favoured maintenance of the military regime.

The country was deeply polarised. Indeed, Chile in 1991 was characterised as a 'nation of enemies' (Constable and Valenzuela 1991). The democratic government's commitment to an 'official truth' had to be undertaken with a broader objective of advancing national reconciliation (Americas Watch 1991). As a result, the new democratic government's commitment to reveal and recognise the most serious violations of the dictatorship was avowedly undertaken with a view to stimulating a wider process of national reconciliation. 'Truth' and 'reconciliation' were the dual objectives of the 1991 Commission. They were offered in lieu of a robust approach to justice:

8 For analysis of the impact of the distorted electoral system on legislative developments in Chile, see Londregan (2000).

> Laden with Catholic associations, the concept [of reconciliation] as promoted by the government, and particularly by President Aylwin, implies forgiveness for past abuses by the victims and repentance by the victimizers in the interests of national coexistence.
>
> (Americas Watch 1991: 5)

This inauspicious context meant that demands for accountability were reconciled with the continuing power of the military through a formula of 'the whole truth and justice to the extent possible'.[9]

Resource mobilisation

A tale of two movements

The posture of the Chilean women's movement towards truth campaigns and processes was heavily determined by historical patterns of human rights advocacy, in which neither the direct victimhood experiences of women, nor collaboration with the women's movement, was prioritised by human rights groups. Preoccupied with installing a feminist agenda in the new democratic government, truth was, in turn, not a feature of women's movement campaigns. Indeed, there is evidence of overt antagonism between the agendas of women's rights and past-focused human rights in the 1990s. In 1996 Chilean feminists expressed concern about the need to 'recuperate' human rights as applying to all individuals, and not just to those disappeared by the military regime (Red Chilena Contra la Violencia Domestica y Sexual 1996: 12). As late as 1999 Chilean women's organisations expressed concern at the refusal of certain elements of Chilean society to acknowledge domestic violence as a human rights violation (e.g. DOMOS and Corporación de Desarrollo de la Mujer 1999). The tenacity of this gap between the women's movement and human rights organisations in Chile was further illustrated in a 2002 study by the Ford Foundation of the human rights movement in Chile. The study concluded that, legally and in popular perception, human rights in Chile remained confined to violations perpetrated by the dictatorship and as a result the membership and agenda of the Chilean human rights movement was very restricted (Saba 2002). In the study, Roberto Garretón (former lawyer for the Vicaría de la Solidaridad) asserted that, in Chile, human rights are synonymous with victims of the dictatorship and that 'it's not possible to overcome this barrier'.[10] He specifically used the example of gender-based violence to reveal the limitations of the prevailing human rights agenda in Chile. He observed that, in

9 President Aylwin formulated this approach to dealing with the past in Chile upon taking office. See Americas Watch (1991).

10 Quoted in Saba (2002: 5).

Chile, to describe the violence of a husband against his wife as a human rights violation would be 'stretching too much the concept of human rights'.[11]

This tension between human rights organisations and the women's movement in Chile had profound consequences for the Chilean feminist approach to truth. Limited resources were available for feminist truth campaigns in terms of civil society allies. Instead, the women's movement was more concertedly focused on forward-looking concerns of the democratisation period, most notably domestic violence. Meanwhile, the human rights groups of the past faced increasing marginalisation for troubling the democratisation agenda (Wilde 1999). A change in human rights dynamics in civil society organising would be the prerequisite to change in the feminist posture towards truth. The arrest of General Pinochet in 1998 set in motion the events that would provide the necessary catalyst for changes to the domestic civil society context.

'Recently, the truth has begun to live again in Chile': the tentative emergence of a feminist truth account

'Recently, the truth has begun to live again in Chile' was an observation made in the preface to the 2002 reissue of *Todas Íbamos a Ser Reinas* (And We Were All Going To Be Queens), the documented account of the nine known instances of pregnant women who were detained and then disappeared by the military regime (CODEPU 2002). A general resurgence of interest in the Chilean past was prompted by attempts to try General Pinochet in Chile. Given the context of renewed attention to violence of the past, it was felt that a reissue of the publication was timely. Motivated by a local incident in which a female ex-prisoner publicly accused a serving armed member of the police of sexual abuse during the dictatorship and was accused of lying (Human Rights Watch 2004), in 2002 women in Chile first set about trying to create an account of the sexual violence experienced by women under the dictatorship. Former female political prisoners made a statement confirming that they too had been victims of sexual violence while detained.[12] Further, a small colloquium was organised in Santiago in September of that year to examine the issue.[13]

Since 1997 Chilean women's organisations have held popular tribunals to investigate violations of women's human rights in Chile (Fundación Instituto de la Mujer 1997, 1999, 2001). Demonstrating the impact of the international on local feminist organising, these popular tribunals were modelled on the feminist 'tribunals' on violations of women's human rights undertaken by transnational feminist advocates

11 Quoted in Saba (2002: 5).

12 'Declaración Pública de Mujeres Detenidas durante la Dictadura con Motivo de la Denuncia de Violencia Sexual Ejercida por un alto Funcionario de Investigaciones', reproduced as an annex to Fundación Instituto de la Mujer *et al.* (2005).

13 'Las mujeres víctimas de violencia sexual como tortura durante la represión en Chile (1973–1990) – un secreto a voces' (2003).

at the UN World Conferences in Vienna and Beijing (Bunch and Reilly 1994) and operated without input from Chilean human rights groups. In 2003, for the first time, one of these tribunals investigated violations of women's human rights under the dictatorship, namely sexual violence perpetrated against female political prisoners under the military regime. Noting the extended passage of time that had been necessary before such violence could finally be exposed, the Tribunal noted:

> Thirty years have passed . . . thirty years is much time – it's a generation. Only today can we speak of human rights violations of women – only today can we affirm that there was a specific form of torture for women, only today can we denounce the rape and sexual abuse that was a general phenomenon in all locations of detention, in the house searches, in the military barracks.
>
> (Fundación Instituto de la Mujer 2003: 18)

Further, the Tribunal challenged the gender gaps of previous institutional and civil society work on truth and justice in Chile:

> Did the women who were victims of this violence reveal these acts? If they did, how were they registered by the organizations who took on this work in the past and present?
>
> (Fundación Instituto de la Mujer 2003: 22)

An initiative entitled 'Memories of Occupation' further illustrated renewed feminist attention to uncovering the truth of the past. Influenced by the changed context locally, and the increasing prominence of rape and sexual violence as tools of war at the international level, women's groups began to consider the situation of women who opposed the government during the dictatorship (Fundación Instituto de la Mujer *et al.* 2005: 10).

As well as establishing a truth account of the torture of women that had taken place, the initiative also prompted an important reconsideration of the human rights work that had taken place during the period of the repression. In his contribution to 'Memories of Occupation', one of the main lawyers of the Vicaría de la Solidaridad, Roberto Garretón, conceded that, although his organisation had always been proud of their role in documenting every detention, disappearance and incidence of torture that took place under Pinochet, he now realised a terrible falsity in that assertion: sexual violence was not registered and even less often formed the basis of judicial action (Garretón 2005). The Vicaría's records provided only an 'incomplete picture' because they provided no record of the sexual violence experienced by women (Garretón 2005: 52).

Framing: an international frame

Feminist civil society in Chile was influenced by the changed context locally, in terms of the increasing prominence of official efforts to deal with the past (e.g.

Lagos 2003). But it was not only local dynamics that led to the increasing prioritisation of truth campaigns within the Chilean women's movement. Rather, the increasing prominence of rape and sexual violence as tools of war at the international level was explicitly cited by Chilean women as motivating women's groups to consider the situation of women who opposed the military dictatorship in Chile: 'We wanted to know if these women, militants as well as sisters, daughters, and wives of militants, suffered – as is typical in every conflict – sexual violence as torture' (Fundación Instituto de la Mujer *et al.* 2005: 10). Developments at the international level prompted local Chilean feminist recognition of the potential significance of truth to ensure acknowledgement and recognition of past harms experienced by women under the dictatorship.

Revealing the extent of sexual violence perpetrated by the military regime against women did, in the Chilean instance, open the door – arguably for the first time – for bridging the local narrative of human rights and truth, which focused on male experiences of violations, with developments at the international level in recognising women's gender-specific experiences of political violence. It also suggested the tentative emergence of forward-looking feminist objectives in truth, as a basis to advocate for progressive change in the future. A Shadow Report to the Chilean State Report to the Monitoring Committee of the Convention against Torture (CAT) in 2004, co-ordinated by an alliance of Chilean feminist organisations, illustrated these new dynamics (Fundación Instituto de la Mujer *et al.* 2004). The Shadow Report marked the *first*, either in scholarly or policy literature, sustained gender analysis of institutional efforts to deal with the past in Chile. It was also the first Shadow Report submitted to the CAT Monitoring Committee from Chile dealing with gender-specific instances of torture, prompting the first set of Concluding Observations from the CAT Monitoring Committee to Chile dealing with gender-specific concerns about torture in the jurisdiction (United Nations Committee against Torture 2004). In addition, a 2008 report of the Chilean Network against Domestic and Sexual Violence explored the relationship between sexual violence and abortion in Chile. The Report examined under-reporting of sexual violence in present-day Chile in the context of the legacy of the Pinochet era in which notions of dishonour and community shame were strongly attached to violations of women's sexual purity (Red Chilena contra la Violencia Doméstica y Sexual 2008: 64). In this regard, feminist organisations sought to exploit the backward-looking functions of truth, in its expressive and normative effects, to condemn the fetishisation of female sexual purity under the dictatorship. Moreover, the women's organisations in question then advocated for a more liberal approach to women's sexuality, specifically the decriminalisation of abortion, in drawing on the forward-looking function of truth to guarantee the non-recurrence of past harms.

These nascent efforts did not, however, demonstrate the penetration of such ideas within the broader Chilean women's movement. Indeed, in launching the popular women's human rights tribunal to investigate sexual violence against political dissidents under the military regime, the initiative was explicitly distinguished from the focus of earlier popular women's human rights tribunals. Whereas the earlier tribunals focused on cases that were representative of human rights violations experienced by women in Chile, the cases concerning sexual violence by past political dissidents were deemed to 'not have the transcendent quality of the other Tribunals of the Rights of Chilean Women' (Red Chilena contra la Violencia Doméstica y Sexual 2008: 11). As Lorena Fries, former director of Corporación Humanas, observes:

> I believe that [feminist engagement with truth recovery] is very important – important because it has also to do with what is made visible in the past . . . It touches another theme, which is to what extent are women political subjects. If you don't recognize women as political subjects in the past, historically, they will not be recognized in the present.
>
> (Lorena Fries, Corporación Humanas, Santiago, personal communication, 27 October 2008)

Rather than understanding the sexual violence of the past as linked to a broader pattern of violations of women's human rights, it is submitted, this past-focused advocacy was an act of acknowledgement for women victims of the past and an attempt to close the chapter. To the extent that it was understood to have contemporary relevance, this mobilisation was understood as an act of solidarity with women in situations of conflict and political repression internationally.[14] The Chilean women's movement looked backward in order to close the book.

NORTHERN IRELAND: LOOKING FORWARD, OVERLOOKING THE PAST

The Northern Irish case evidences a persistently difficult political opportunity structure, in which little or no political consensus surrounds the issue of dealing with the past, and there is little recognition of gender as a determinative factor of one's experience of past harms. Resource mobilisation is also limited, in that a gendered pattern of labour continues to divide the (largely male) protagonists of campaigns for accountability and the service provision work of (largely female) victims groups. Against this inauspicious backdrop, compounded by the impossibility of forging a unified feminist agenda in an area so fraught as dealing with the past, a largely instrumentalist approach to the past has been adopted by women's organisations in Northern Ireland. Truth accounts that emphasise women's contribution to family and community survival during the conflict underpin claims for continued political recognition and resourcing of women's organisations.

14 For further evidence of this dynamic, see Corporación Humanas (2008b).

Political opportunity structure: invisible inequalities

While the Chilean context was inauspicious for truth-seeking, there was at least a formal commitment to an official truth process. In Northern Ireland, by contrast, the Belfast Agreement was characterised by forward-looking emphasis on institutional reforms and the establishment of new or reformed institutions, without any provision for backward-looking accountability mechanisms. Indeed, this avoidance of the past is explicit in the agreement, in which it is stated:

> The tragedies of the past have left a deep and profoundly regrettable legacy of suffering. We must never forget those who have died or been injured, and their families. But we can best honour them through a fresh start, in which we firmly dedicate ourselves to the achievement of reconciliation, tolerance, and mutual trust, and to the protection and vindication of the human rights of all.
>
> (Belfast Agreement: Declaration of Support, 1998: para 2)

The forward-looking focus of the Agreement arose primarily out of pragmatic political considerations: attempts to agree a cross-party approach to truth recovery would likely have brought the entire negotiations to grief. However, the consequence of this forward-looking approach is that an important political and ideological battle remains unresolved in transitional Northern Ireland. In the absence of an agreed mechanism for truth recovery, a 'piecemeal' and 'ad hoc' approach has instead been adopted (Bell 2003). Truth recovery continues through a series of 'surrogate' processes and institutions, such as public inquiries into conflict-related deaths and police enquiries into historical deaths.

The political opportunity structure for truth recovery in Northern Ireland is further complicated by the exigencies of the political divide that continue to structure politics in the jurisdiction. The underlying conditions of political violence are typically related to inter-ethnic tensions, oppositional ideological commitments or the grossly unequal distribution of economic resources. Persistent (or structural) gender inequalities do not fit neatly within this frame. Societies do not divide along gender lines in the same way that they divide along, for example, linguistic or religious axes. Women do not constitute a group in the sense that the group's existence constitutes a threat to national unity. To state it plainly: 'no one really expects women to secede' (Phillips 1995: 15). Concerns about the need to both understand resistance and ensure the participation of, for example, Unionists and Loyalists in truth recovery in Northern Ireland (e.g. Rolston 2006; Lawther 2013) have not been replicated in terms of women's participation.

The tendency to focus on singular axes (or structures) of inequality or difference in contexts of political violence obscures the manifold ways in which race, class and ideology intersect with gender to determine both one's experience of harm during political violence, and also – importantly – the circumstances under which people seek to protect themselves from harm in that context. For example, the

South African case has been subjected to extensive feminist critique for its failure to acknowledge the extent to which gender, as well as race, structured political violence and inequality under apartheid.[15] In Northern Ireland, these dynamics interact to cast truth as a political issue with limited potential to either acknowledge the past experiences of women or as a basis to advocate for progressive feminist change.

Resource mobilisation: a gendered division of labour

In Northern Ireland, in the aftermath of the Belfast Agreement, more general civil society initiatives to deal with truth-telling and the past began to emerge. Most significant in this regard was *The Report of the Healing Through Remembering Project* (Healing Through Remembering 2002), an impressive proposal of possible options for truth recovery, commemoration and advancing reconciliation in Northern Ireland. Those responsible for the Report consulted widely and involved a large number of civil society organisations. However, of all of the groups and organisations either targeted or submitting consultations, the only dedicated women's organisation consulted was the women's political party, the Women's Coalition. The *Healing through Remembering* initiative drew heavily on international expertise; however, international gender expertise was not specifically sought or included. The Report did little to ensure that the learning curve undertaken internationally in enhancing the treatment of women and gender issues in truth-seeking processes would be adopted in local truth-seeking initiatives.

The lack of engagement of or with women's organisations in *Healing Through Remembering* signalled a more fundamental divide between the concerns of those dealing with the past and the concerns of feminists and organised women's groups in post-conflict Northern Ireland, who were dealing variously with the socio-economic legacy of the conflict, forward-looking human rights concerns of women and resisting women's exclusion from the new political institutions established by the peace agreement. In the context of a 'piecemeal' and 'ad hoc' approach to truth recovery in Northern Ireland, resource mobilisation for a feminist truth strategy has proven difficult. The Northern Ireland victims sector has a distinctively female composition. A review of the victims sector found that the victims organisations were largely made up of women. Further, clients of services offered by these organisations were predominantly women (Potter 2004). Women were found to be in decision-making positions in these organisations. Indeed, the Review concluded:

> A predominance of women in the victims sector suggests that victims' issues are to a certain extent gender issues. Negating the needs of victims primarily affects women.
>
> (Potter 2004: 70)

15 See especially Meintjes (2009). See also Fullard (2004).

Further, it was the Northern Ireland Women's Coalition that was responsible for ensuring that the Belfast Agreement did specifically mention the needs of victims in its provisions (McWilliams and Kilmurray 1997).

Conversely, however, Northern Ireland's women's sector has not traditionally been prominent within civil society organising for truth, justice and reparations for the harms of the conflict. The past agenda does not tend to feature prominently in the demands of the women's sector.[16] Moreover, in terms of women's involvement in the victims sector, it has been found that there is:

> a gender division . . . in the role of groups, those being 'self-help' groups in nature largely being led by women (examples being given were WAVE, SAVER/NAVER, Cross, Lifeline and Shankill Stress) and those having a more political role being male-led.
>
> (Potter 2004: 49)

In short, it was found: 'the more political it gets, the more masculine it gets' (Potter 2004: 49).

There is evidence, therefore, of a gendered division of labour in dealing with the past in Northern Ireland. Through their involvement in the women's and victims sector, women deal with the (private) material consequences of the conflict (such as trauma, poverty, lack of education and training) deemed to be 'apolitical'; men deal with the 'political' consequences of the conflict (truth, prosecutions, public enquiries, police investigations). This gendered division of labour reinforces perceptions that truth constitutes a site of very limited potential feminist gains.

Framing: women transcending structural inequalities

Against a backdrop of official resistance to truth recovery, and the preoccupation of women's organisations with the material consequences of the conflict, it took almost a decade from the signing of the Agreement for avowed truth-seeking initiatives to emerge from women's organisations in Northern Ireland.[17] The framing adopted by women's organisations in their truth campaigns evidences a reluctance to engage with the political cleavages that underpinned the conflict.

16 Take for example the 'Women's Manifesto' agreed by a range of women's organisations in the two most recent elections of the Northern Ireland Assembly. Dealing with the past did not feature in any way in either manifesto. Both manifestos can be accessed at http://www.ictuni.org/ (last accessed 6 March 2013).

17 See especially Women's Support Network (2009); Women's Resource and Development Agency and Women's Centres Regional Partnership (2008); Coiste na n-Iarchimí and Relatives for Justice (2010: 3). See generally http://www.wrda.net/Women-[amp]-Dealing-with-the-Past.aspx (last accessed 6 March 2013).

They emphasise instead common or shared experiences of women as carers for family members and as stalwarts of the community during the conflict.[18] 'It is arguable that women have suffered disproportionately as a result of the conflict. Many were left without partners and were required to maintain families in very difficult circumstances' (Women's Support Network 2009: 3.19). The absence of men, through exile, imprisonment or death, was a prominent narrative in this account of the past.[19] The consequent added burden on female heads of household, in terms of managing families and family poverty, was highlighted (Women's Support Network 2009: 3.19). The impact was elaborated in terms of the increased family responsibilities on girls,[20] the shortages of basics of food and energy borne disproportionately by female family members,[21] the emotional, time and resource burden of visiting imprisoned male relatives[22] and crippling concerns for family safety carried by female heads of household.[23] Of these 'common' or 'shared' experiences, motherhood was most prominent:

> While the specific focus of women's worries and fears as mothers occasionally differed slightly, overall, the sentiments expressed by rural and urban and Protestant and Catholic women as mothers across the past four decades shared many similarities.[24]

While differences between women are noted ('rural and urban and Protestant and Catholic'), it is without the attribution of any political significance to these differences. Conversely, women who perpetrated violence were absent from view. 'Arrests and imprisonment' were something that happened to 'family members', and not to women themselves.[25]

Importantly, in terms of the forward-looking purpose of truth, these shared experiences of women ground claims to be heard:

18 These dynamics are discussed in greater detail in O'Rourke (2012).

19 See Women's Support Network (2009: 3.19); Women's Resource and Development Agency and Women's Centres Regional Partnership (2008: 12).

20 See Women's Resource and Development Agency and Women's Centres Regional Partnership (2008: 13–14).

21 See Women's Resource and Development Agency and Women's Centres Regional Partnership (2008: 4).

22 See Women's Resource and Development Agency and Women's Centres Regional Partnership (2008: 22).

23 See Women's Resource and Development Agency and Women's Centres Regional Partnership (2008: 14–15); Women's Support Network (2009: 3.28).

24 See Women's Resource and Development Agency and Women's Centres Regional Partnership (2008: 18).

25 See Women's Resource and Development Agency and Women's Centres Regional Partnership (2008: 12); Women's Support Network (2009: 3.19); Coiste na n-Iarchimí and Relatives for Justice (2010: App.1, 1–3).

> Community-based women's centres, groups and projects work tirelessly to meet the needs of women in disadvantaged areas, who have suffered greatly from the conflict, and continue to suffer its legacy today. We would therefore emphasize again that their voices are heard and heeded.
>
> (Women's Support Network 2009: 4.5)

They are also linked to the 'priority issues' that are articulated (namely mental and general health service provision,[26] safer streets and communities, public transport, community policing and tackling anti-social behaviour, improved education funding and access to education, community regeneration and job creation[27]).

This emphasis on shared experience in the interventions of women's organisations into truth recovery in Northern Ireland did not emerge in a political vacuum. Rather, it reflects the terms of engagement that had been developed within women's organising over the long period of the conflict. As discussed in Chapter 2, in order to achieve practical agreement and shared action on a limited set of policy issues, an unspoken consensus of 'Don't mention the war' had come to define women's organising in Northern Ireland (Rooney 2006: 362). These terms of engagement continue to operate in the context of a fragile peace (Rooney 2006: 356). They underpin a forward-looking and instrumentalist approach to truth by women's organisations in the jurisdiction.

COLOMBIA: LOOKING BACKWARD, MOVING FORWARD

In the context of a particularly pernicious and long-running conflict, Colombian feminists have managed to articulate the most comprehensive and challenging engagement with official truth processes. This can be largely attributed to the contested legitimacy of this official truth process.

Political opportunity structure: transitional justice without transition

Truth recovery under the Justice and Peace Law has occurred within the context of a highly contested transitional justice process. The process has been variously labelled 'transitional justice without transition', 'transitional justice without transformation', or 'the use and abuse of transitional justice' (Uprimny *et al.* 2006; Uprimny and Saffon 2008). The process has been greeted by suspicion and distrust

26 See Coiste na n-Iarchimí and Relatives for Justice (2010: 2); Women's Resource and Development Agency and Women's Centres Regional Partnership (2008: 58).

27 See Women's Resource and Development Agency and Women's Centres Regional Partnership (2008: 66–8).

from feminists, human rights advocates and peace and victims groups. In reality, international actors have been crucial to catalysing a domestic process of truth recovery.

In terms of the truth emerging from the judicial process, the principal obstacle identified to truth is the ongoing nature of conflict violence, compounded by the inadequate protection of women victims and witnesses (Grupo de Trabajo Mujer y Género 2008: 43). Manifold material obstacles exist to articulating women's gender-specific victimhood, including problems with the training of investigators and prosecutors leading to the prioritisation of perceived 'most serious' crimes such as assassinations and forced disappearances within judicial processes, at the expense of crimes perceived as less serious, such as forced displacement and sexual violence. This shortcoming, in turn, discourages the reporting of 'less serious' crimes (Grupo de Trabajo Mujer y Género 2008: 48). Practical barriers to the participation of women in the *versiones libres*, such as the cost of travelling to sites where they are recounted, are also endemic (Grupo de Trabajo Mujer y Género 2008: 55). Ultimately, the combined effects of these conceptual and practical limitations of the justice and peace process is that the substance of women's gender-specific experiences of the conflict has been occluded in the truth account emerging from the judicial process (Grupo de Trabajo Mujer y Género 2008: 55). A difficult context and process thus provides the backdrop to multi-level and diverse feminist truth campaigns in Colombia.

Framing: an international frame

Feminist approaches to truth in Colombia, and the prioritisation given to the area by women's organisations, is intrinsically linked to the prioritisation of the armed conflict in Colombian feminist organising. Human rights developments at the international level had an important impact on domestic feminist organising in Colombia in the latter part of the 1990s. It was during this period that the armed conflict and displacement became more prominent in the mobilisation of Colombian women. The link to an international feminist agenda, in particular the series of United Nations world conferences, brought about increasing internationalisation of the Colombian women's movement, which opened up both the movement and its agenda (Wills 2007: 229). The Fourth World Conference on Women in Beijing in 1995, with its three priority issues of equality, development and peace, was very significant in bringing together the themes of feminism and peace. Locally, concerns were being expressed in particular about the situation of women in the badly conflict-affected city of Uraba Antioqueño on the Caribbean coast (Wills 2007: 231). There is also evidence of women's organisations increasingly co-ordinating around the urgency to end the war.[28] Significantly, on International

28 See Wills (2007: 236); Olga Lucía Ramírez, Vamos Mujer, Medellín, personal communication, 23 July 2009.

Day to End Violence against Women (25 November) in 1996 several women's organisations gathered in the region of Antioquia to demand an end to the war and the inclusion of women in the peace negotiations that were taking place at the time. Thus, a feminist event that had traditionally focused on violence within the family adopted conflict violence as its central concern.

The international agenda around women's human rights has provided an important framework for feminist truth campaigns. In Colombia in September 2000, the group Women and Armed Conflict (Mujer y Conflicto Armado) was formed,[29] consisting of a wide range of women's rights, peace and – importantly – mainstream human rights organisations, initially in order to seek a visit from the United Nations Special Rapporteur on Violence Against Women. The group reports frequently and comprehensively on the gender-specific experiences of violence of women and girls (Mujer y Conflicto Armado 2001a, 2001b, 2004, 2005, 2008).

These practical technical interventions of women's groups, to seek the most comprehensive account possible of women's gender-specific victimhood, are supplemented by the more radical approach of organisations such as La Ruta Pacifica and Vamos Mujer, who have focused on revealing structural gender inequalities that enable violence in Colombia, with avowedly forward-looking motivations. The organisation of women against the war, and the abuses perpetrated by armed actors, produced some interesting innovations in women's mobilisation in this period. First, it politicised the maternal bond, as women sought the end to conflict violence for the protection of their loved ones: the slogan adopted by La Ruta Pacifica stated that 'women don't have sons and daughters for the war' (Las mujeres no parimos hijos e hijas para la guerra).[30] The politicisation of motherhood was also significant in revealing the toll that the war was taking on the bodies of women. This gave rise to the second notable trend in feminist organising in truth: increasing attention to the particular forms of violence experienced by women as a result of the conflict. Principally, prominence began to be given to sexual violence perpetrated against female civilians by armed male actors. Elements of the movement began to link sexual violence in the armed conflict to endemic forms of gender-based violence: '[We don't want] the war, neither in our

29 The group consists of Asociación Juana de Arco, Asociación Nacional de Mujeres Campesinas e Indígenas de Colombia (ANMUCIC), Programa Mujer y Familia de la Asociación Nacional de Usuarios Campesinos – Unidad y Reconstrucción (ANUC-UR), Corporación Casa de la Mujer, Colectivo de Mujeres Excombatientes, Colectivo María María, Comisión Colombiana de Juristas, Corporación de Apoyo a Comunidades Populares (CODACOP), Fundación Educación y Desarrollo (FEDES), Humanizar, Instituto de Derechos Humanos 'Guillermo Cano' de la Escuela Superior de Administración Pública (ESAP), Ruta Pacífica de las Mujeres, Liga Internacional de Mujeres por la Paz y la Libertad (LIMPAL), Liga de Mujeres Desplazadas de Bolívar, Organización Femenina Popular (OFP), and Red Nacional de Mujeres Bogotá. The Group also receives support from the Gender Study Program of the Universidad Nacional de Colombia.

30 See further http://www.rutapacifica.org.co/home.html (last accessed 6 March 2013).

country nor in our homes.'[31] For example, La Ruta Pacifica has asserted the right of women to:

> [T]he truth that knows and understands the facts that consistently make us victims; the truth that recognizes the crimes committed against us in war and in peace, in public and in private spaces.
>
> (La Ruta Pacifica *et al.* 2009)

The truth campaign co-ordinated by Vamos Mujer in Medellín is exemplary of the creative and innovative approach to truth adopted by the radical feminist pacifist element of the Colombian women's movement. Entitled 'Scrutinize the Skin' ('Deletrear la Piel') (Corporación Vamos Mujer 2006), the truth campaign centres on the physical toll of violence in Colombia on the bodies of women, designating the bodies of women as 'the location of memory'. By contrast, the state's preoccupation with asserting its presence in every part of the Colombian national territory, and the use of forced displacement by guerrillas and paramilitaries as a deliberate tactic of war, posits land and territory as the location of memory in Colombia. The focus on the flesh of women offers a feminist counter-account of the conflict, moving away from a geographical or territorial understanding of the conflict, highlighting the consistent toll of the conflict on the bodies of women:

> Truth in the voice and testimony of women victims, survivors, women who have overcome multiple forms of violence lived on the body.
>
> (Corporación Vamos Mujer, 'Deletrear la Piel' Tribunal Announcement, 2006)

This focus on the body as 'the location of memory' grounds a truth campaign that articulates and contests women's experiences of sexual violence in the conflict,[32] domestic violence in the home[33] and restrictions on women's sexual and reproductive rights.[34] It is thus a comprehensive account of women's gender-specific victimhood, but is also clearly tied to forward-looking objectives of ending those harms in the future. The campaign has taken the form of a 'Symbolic Truth Tribunal for Women',[35] a festival for sexual and reproductive rights[36] and the public signing of a pact for sexual equality with men.[37] This radical feminist

31 Declaration of the Organizacion de Mujeres de Pavarando, Organizacion de Mujeres Campesinas del Bajo Atrato, Uraba, Colombia, 23 December 1997, quoted in Wills (2007: 235).

32 See Corporación Vamos Mujer, 'Deletrear la Piel' Campaign Launch, 2006.

33 See Corporación Vamos Mujer, 'Deletrear la Piel' Campaign Launch, 2006.

34 See Corporación Vamos Mujer, 'Deletrear la Piel' Press Release, 2007.

35 See Corporación Vamos Mujer, 'Deletrear la Piel' Tribunal Announcement, 2006.

36 See Corporación Vamos Mujer, 'Deletrear la Piel' Press Release, 2007.

37 See Corporación Vamos Mujer, 'Deletrear la Piel' Press Release, 2007.

pacifist approach to truth has been undertaken with the avowed objective of interrupting and opposing the official truth-telling process established under the Justice and Peace Law:

> Women, the ignored victims of public and private wars that continue in our country, have names, faces, stories, and rights. However, today, just as yesterday, there is an attempt to spread oblivion and erase memory. The truth is being manipulated . . . Today more than ever, we must read out the skin!
>
> (Corporación Vamos Mujer, 'Deletrear la Piel' Boletin Lanzamiento, 2007)

The Colombian example is not only unique because of the subversive approach to truth being adopted by women's organisations, but also because of the prominence given to truth and truth processes by the women's movement.

Resource mobilisation: feminist disagreement

Divisions apparent in Colombian feminist engagement with the justice component of the contemporary process are replicated in the diverging responses of these organisations to the truth and historical memory component of the justice and peace process. Substantial feminist co-ordination has also been evident in more technical interventions into the truth process initiated by the Justice and Peace Law (Grupo de Trabajo Mujer y Género 2008). Meanwhile, the radical feminist approach to truth is impressive in its consideration of a diverse range of gender-specific harms to women, its identification of structural gender inequalities and its avowed forward-looking focus.

Nevertheless, the Colombian approach conceives of women's political subjectivity exclusively as civilian victims in the conflict. Despite the substantial presence of women in armed groups in Colombia, in particular in the guerrilla groups demobilised in the early 1990s, the claims of these women to history and truth have never been integrated into mainstream feminist truth campaigns (Luz Maria Londoño and Nieto 2009). An increasing degree of co-ordination among ex-combatant women, and attention from academics, has led to the recent emergence of demands from former female combatants 'for the right to have a past' (Luz María Londoño and Nieto 2007: 67). The stigma, rejection and guilt encountered by these women for transgressing established behavioural patterns for women is contrasted with the prestige accruing to male combatants (Luz María Londoño and Nieto 2007: 67). This stigma acts as a further barrier to recounting their truth of the conflict and the past. However, the issue of female combatants and female perpetrators of violence presents enormous challenges to feminist activism and feminist theory alike and in Colombia can find no place in a feminist pacifist truth campaign founded on solidarity with civilian victims of the conflict.

CONCLUSION

Despite the breadth of potential backward- and forward-looking feminist gains from truth, on diverse grounds, identified in theory, this chapter documented the much narrower set of political objectives that women's movements tend to pursue in their engagement with official truth-telling. Truth was typically not a political priority for women's movements. This conclusion reflects on the reasons for such diverse feminist strategies adopted to truth in the three different case studies.

Framing: the toxicity of the past

In Chapter 1 'framing' was explained to refer to the extent to which women's movement strategies resonated with the dominant political narrative of the transition. Each of the three case studies is at a different point in its engagement with the past and as the case studies reveal, the dominant political narrative of transition evolves as states move further along the transition axis. Women's movement strategies will likely evolve in turn. Chile, for example, has completed two decades of democratic government since the end of the military dictatorship. In the interim, General Pinochet was found to have engaged in massive financial fraud, was arrested in London and faced subsequent trial (though not conviction) in domestic Chilean courts, but then died. The Chilean context over time arrived at a more mature engagement with its troubled past (Wilde 1999: 474). As the justice section illustrated, against this backdrop the priority of the Chilean women's movement immediately post-transition was to focus on forward-looking rights issues of women, and the advancement of women within the new Chilean democratic regime. The gradual amelioration of the divisiveness of the past created a more accommodating context for more recent feminist engagement with the past in Chile. This is reflected in feminist truth campaigns in Chile, in terms of their more recent engagement with the past, but also in terms of understanding that engagement as an issue of little relevance to *contemporary* feminist concerns.

In Northern Ireland, by contrast, the past continues to determine the political landscape of the present. Political violence is sporadic, though it continues. The ethnic divisions that underlie the violent conflict persist, though in more peaceful form. Political affiliations in the jurisdiction are still principally determined by one's ethnic group. Memories of the toxic divisions that split the nascent Northern Ireland women's movement over the political status of female prisoners may be increasingly distant. Nevertheless, the terms of engagement that the experience determined, in the form of a tacit agreement not to mention the war, largely persist in women's political organising. Instead, for the moment, the past is fraught terrain and engagement with the past is on narrow terms, and with largely instrumentalist goals to access resources and influence in the future. These contemporary dynamics do not, importantly, foreclose the opportunity for more meaningful feminist engagement with the past as the transition continues to unfold.

In Colombia – a transition without transition, a peace process with neither peace nor process – feminist engagement with truth is not a campaign related to the past; it is a campaign very much of the present. In the context of an ongoing war, feminist truth campaigns incorporate a range of feminist issues and also seek to articulate a way out of conflict.

Political opportunity structure: the depth of the transition

Clearly related to the passage of time since the transition in determining feminist truth strategies, the depth of the transition is also a significant factor. Of the three case studies, the Chilean transition marked the clearest rupture with the past. There is, in the Chilean case, a more clearly defined 'past' that is distinct from the contemporary political context. This has facilitated unified feminist engagement with that past without the need to confront feminist divisions on contemporary political issues.

In Northern Ireland, by contrast, the transition has been much more incremental. While 1998 witnessed a comprehensive peace agreement, it has been followed by a halting process of implementation and renegotiation, and ongoing acts of political violence. As a result, it is more difficult to speak of the 'past' in Northern Ireland with any clear sense of feminist or societal agreement as to what and when that 'past' refers. The past bleeds into the present and ongoing political divisions around which there is little feminist unity. Forging a unified agenda in truth amongst feminist and women's organisations is thus deeply challenging.

In Colombia, as noted, conflict violence does not belong only to the past. Inevitably, contemporary feminist issues – and divisions – are incorporated into feminist truth campaigns. This has led to a productive and creative tension between technical and transformative feminist engagement with truth.

Resource mobilisation: the relationship of the women's movement to the mainstream human rights movement

The final local determining factor in feminist truth strategies concerns the relationship of the women's movement to the human rights movement in the transitional state. The analysis of human rights advocacy presented in Chapter 3 described the disconnection between human rights groups and women's organisations that tend to mark civil society during periods of violent conflict or political repression. Consequently, in Chile, when the past agenda was perceived as being owned by the human rights community, with that community's overwhelming concern with male victims of the regime, the Chilean women's movement instead sought to 'recover' the human rights agenda from the past. Over time, however, international human rights law came to provide a legal vocabulary and a mobilising platform for feminist engagement with the past in Chile. In Colombia, similarly, the institutions and doctrine of international human rights law have fostered co-operation between the human rights community and women's organisations in, for example, the Women and Armed Conflict group.

In Northern Ireland, by contrast, perceptions of the human rights agenda as being 'owned' by the nationalist community have been reinforced by the overwhelming prioritisation by the local human rights community of civil and political rights violations of largely male actors, all to the general exclusion of women's rights and women's organisations. Local women's organisations mobilise on human rights concerns of women, such as the development of a Bill of Rights in the jurisdiction,[38] though with little reference to past-focused accountability issues.

38 See, for example, Bill of Rights Women's Working Group (2008).

Chapter 6

Global standards, local truths

Harms against women in truth processes

INTRODUCTION

Human rights outcomes for women of truth processes are not determined only by domestic political factors. Rather, international law plays an important role in defining the harms investigated and acknowledged by truth processes, and the extent to which such processes recognise structural gender inequalities and affirm women's political agency. This chapter examines the international frame for gender outcomes in truth processes and advances three arguments. First, that although truth processes are styled as more flexible than prosecutions, with greater transformative feminist potential as a result, truth processes in fact rely heavily on established categories of harms in international law. Second, that this reliance on international law limits the recognition of gender harms, women's agency and structural gender inequalities by official truth processes in transitional justice and in this regard should not function as a ceiling to truth processes. Nevertheless, the chapter concludes that international law provides an important floor below which domestic truth processes cannot fall, in particular in their recognition of gender harms in difficult domestic political contexts of truth recovery.

THE INTERNATIONAL FRAME: INTERNATIONAL LAW, THE RIGHT TO TRUTH AND HARMS AGAINST WOMEN

While there is no explicit statement of the right to truth in a human rights treaty, the right to know the truth has been read from several overlapping international legal instruments. For example, the Universal Declaration of Human Rights recognises a 'right to seek, receive and impart information'.[1] Additional Protocol 1 to the Geneva Conventions also recognises the right of families to know the fate

1 Universal Declaration of Human Rights, 10 December 1948, GA res. 217A (III), UN Doc. A/810 at 71, Article 19.

of their relatives.[2] Moreover, the Convention Against Torture requires states to conduct a preliminary inquiry into the facts, make prompt report of the findings and conduct a prompt and impartial investigation where there are reasonable grounds to suspect torture.[3] The Inter-American system has proven particularly important to the development of the right to truth, first in its early affirmation of the state's duty to investigate the disappeared and disclose information to relatives,[4] and subsequently in having interpreted the right to know the truth as a direct remedy in itself.[5] The belief that the verification of facts and disclosure of the truth constitutes a partial remedy for human rights violations is also endorsed by the United Nations Commission on Human Rights.[6]

In terms of the right to truth and harms against women, three particular aspects require elaboration in this section. First is the material scope of the right: what harms activate state obligations under the right to truth and to what extent do harms against women fall within this scope. Second is the treatment of collective or societal harms: to what extent does the right to truth recognise and acknowledge collective harms against women and the structural gender inequalities that led to these harms. The final aspect requiring elaboration concerns the means for delivering truth, namely the tools or mechanisms available to states to discharge the right to truth and the extent to which they affirm women's political agency.

The right to truth is activated by gross human rights violations and serious violations of human rights law. International human rights bodies have recognised the right to truth in cases of gross violations of human rights, in particular enforced disappearances, extrajudicial executions and torture, and serious violations of international humanitarian law. This is supported by the jurisprudence of international and regional human rights bodies and courts.[7] Chapter 3 detailed

2 Protocol Additional to the Geneva Conventions of 12 August 1949, and relating to the Protection of Victims of International Armed Conflicts, 8 June 8 1977, 1125 UNTS 3, Articles 32 and 33.

3 Convention Against Torture and Other Cruel, Inhuman or Degrading Treatment or Punishment, 10 December 1984, 1465 UNTS 85, Article 6.

4 *Velasquez Rodriguez Case*, Judgment of 29 July 1988, IACtHR, Series C No. 4 (1988).

5 *Case of Castillo-Páez v Peru* (Reparations and Costs), Judgment of 27 November 1998, IACtHR, Series C No. 43 (1998), paras 103–107.

6 United Nations Basic Principles and Guidelines on the Right to a Remedy and Reparation for Victims of Gross Violations of International Human Rights Law and Serious Violations of International Humanitarian Law, GA Res. 60/147 U.N. Doc. A/RES/60/147 (21 March 2006), Principle 22 (b).

7 Resolution II of the XXIV International Conference of the Red Cross and Red Crescent, Manila, 1981; *Lyashkevich v Belarus*, Communication No 887/1999, UN Doc. CCPR/C/77/D/950/2000, paras 9.2. and 11; *Validzhon Khalilov v Tajikistan*, Communication No. 973/2001, UN Doc. CCPR/C/83/D/973/2001; *Tas v Turkey*, ECHR, Application No. 24396/94 (2000); *Cyprus v Turkey*, ECHR, Application No. 25781/94 (2001), para 136; *Amnesty International v Sudan*, Communications No. 48/90, 50/91, 52/91, 89/93 (1999), para 54; UN Human Rights Committee (1996), para 25 (African Commission on Human and Peoples' Rights, Principles and Guidelines on the Right to a Fair Trial and Legal Assistance in Africa, Doc/Os(XXX)247 (2001)). See, for example, *Ignacio Ellacuría et al v El Salvador*, Inter-Am. C.H.R, Case 10.488, Report No. 136/99 (1999), para 221; *Tibi v Ecuador* (Preliminary Objections, Merits, Reparations and Costs), IACtHR, Series C No. 114 (2004).

the relevant doctrinal changes, most notably the recognition of rape as torture, a war crime and as a grave breach of the Geneva Conventions. While this renders a relatively narrow scope of the right to truth, the rights-holder is very often the relative of the direct victim. In this regard, the right to truth affirms secondary victims as rights-holders.

In addition to this individual dimension, the right to truth has a collective dimension. Included in the Updated Principles to Combat Impunity is affirmation that:

> Every people has the inalienable right to know the truth about past events concerning the perpetration of heinous crimes and about *the circumstances and reasons that led*, through massive or systematic violations, to the perpetration of those crimes.
>
> (Orentlicher 2005: Principle 2, emphasis added)

It is in this collective or societal aspect that the right to truth may offer some potential to uncover the structural gender inequalities that made women vulnerable to particular forms of human rights violations.

Normatively, feminist critique of the international frame attributes the privileging of 'public' political harm, and singular axes of conflict and identity in transitional justice, to the gendered and individualised hierarchies of harm in international law. However, the contributions of Wilson (2001), Orford (2006) and others (Rolston and Scraton 2005; Lawther 2013) caution us to be attentive to the inherently local political factors and objectives that drive truth recovery in any transition. Ultimately, almost all critical contributors to the discussion of truth and its value in transitional societies attribute overwhelming power to the state to determine the hegemonic truth discourse (see especially Rolston and Scraton 2005). They point to the state's need to establish a break with past state wrongdoing and a unifying and stabilising truth narrative as the transitional society moves forward. These contributions put into stark relief the tension between the backward-looking and forward-looking functions of truth. If values expressed concerning past wrongs must be subservient to the grand reconciliatory narrative constructed in the forward-looking function of truth processes, what of values that underlie broad societal consensus but are antithetical to women's equality? As Ní Aoláin notes: 'gender hierarchies are typically a very effective stabilising force in a transitional society, but they are also deeply harmful' (Ní Aoláin 2008). This chapter will show how the local and international are often in tension with one another.

Finally, in order to put the case studies in context, it should be noted that truth commissions (TCs) are recognised as one of the main 'tools' for the state to ensure the right to truth, in particular in the case of 'societies that have experienced heinous crimes perpetrated on a massive or systematic basis' (Orentlicher 2005: Principle 5). Also important here in this emphasis on TCs is the potential for an open and exploratory approach to the past, to investigate the social or societal causes of harm, and not only the forensic details of perpetrator, victim and violation. The merits of the truth commission are also in its process-based approach to truth. Individuals can recount their stories, and receive acknowledgement and affirmation. Similarly, groups can be drawn on for evidence and information. Group harms can be affirmed. Indeed, the Sierra Leone Truth and Reconciliation Commission maintained:

> It is with [the right to truth] that truth and reconciliation commissions excel. Indeed, they can generally respond to the needs of truth-seeking better than the alternatives, such as criminal prosecutions.
>
> (Sierra Leone Truth and Reconciliation Commission, 2004: Vol. 1, 44–5, para 77)

While truth commissions remain the most high profile mechanisms for delivering the right to truth, the case study analysis reveals that other mechanisms are also available, and are typically closely linked to justice and reparations mechanisms in transitional justice. Further, criminal processes can also be charged with delivering a measure of truth, as in the Colombian case. Public inquiries remain an alternative approach to truth recovery and have been prominent in the Northern Ireland case. Although they are typically more formalised and legalised than truth commissions, they nevertheless share the forward-looking priorities of reforming for the future. Moreover, while the right to truth under international law establishes some minimum requirements upon states in the delivery of truth, states have substantial discretion to surpass these requirements and provide a more holistic measure of truth to a broader range of harms.

CHILE: INTERNATIONAL LAW AS A FLOOR . . .

The Chilean case is instructive because its truth process involved two separate phases. Despite the noted limitations of the Chilean transition from military rule, the first democratic government to succeed the military dictatorship delivered on its election commitment to establish a National Commission on Truth and Reconciliation (TRC), established by Presidential Decree.[8] While it was envisaged that the work of the TRC would inform official efforts to secure criminal prosecutions of those responsible for deaths and disappearances,[9] an unreformed judiciary consistently adopted a maximalist interpretation of the military regime's self-amnesty law.[10] Instead, after the TRC, transitional justice in Chile preceded

8 Supreme Decree No. 355, Diario Oficial, 25 April 1990.

9 Supreme Decree No. 355, Diario Oficial, 25 April 1990, Article 2 (providing for files to go to the prosecuting authority).

10 Decree Law No. 2191, Diario Oficial, 18 April 1978.

through a comprehensive programme of reparations to the families of those who lost their lives under the military regime.[11] Throughout the 1990s there was a general receding of demands for justice for the harms of the past, deemed to be too divisive and disruptive to the transition, from Chilean public life (Wilde 1999). It was not until the arrest of General Pinochet in London in 1998 that renewed demands for justice from victims and the relatives of victims gained international – and subsequently, domestic – prominence, and criminal prosecutions of individual perpetrators continue to the present day in Chile.[12] The TRC's exclusive focus on those who lost their lives meant that survivors of torture and political imprisonment had been completely overlooked in official transitional justice initiatives. In 2003, on the thirtieth anniversary of the coup, a commission was established to investigate the practice of torture and political detention under the military regime.[13]

As this section reveals, developments in international legal doctrine underpinned dramatic changes (and improvement) in the recognition of harms against women, in particular in terms of sexual violence, in truth processes in Chile. Despite this progress, however, developments in international doctrine were insufficient to reveal a broader range of harms to women. Most notably, reproductive harms experienced by women under the dictatorship remained invisible within the official truth account, as the local gender values that structured the truth process cut against progressive doctrinal developments in international law. Moreover, advancements in the recognition of women as political agents in the past also remained circumscribed, and the recognition of structural gender inequalities non-existent. Nevertheless, this section concludes, developments in international legal doctrine provided an essential floor to domestic truth processes in Chile, in ensuring at least some formal recognition of primary harms against women.

Doctrinal: defining harms

The Chilean National Truth and Reconciliation Commission

The Presidential Decree establishing the Chilean National Truth and Reconciliation Commission (TRC) provided for the TRC to 'clarify in a comprehensive manner the truth about the most serious human rights violations'.[14]

11 See further Lira (2006b).

12 The Human Rights Observatory (Observatorio Derechos Humanos) at the Universidad Diego Portales monitors these cases. See http://www.icso.cl/observatorio-derechos-humanos/ (last accessed 7 March 2013).

13 Supreme Decree No. 1040, Diario Oficial, 11 November 2003.

14 Supreme Decree No. 355, Diario Oficial, 25 April 1990, Article 1.

Adopting the framework of international human rights, 'serious violations' were defined as 'persons who disappeared after arrest, who were executed, or who were tortured to death'.[15] Consistent with patterns in human rights advocacy under the dictatorship, the TRC Report casts women exclusively as secondary victims.

For example, the Report examined 'The Impact of the Most Serious Human Rights Violations on Families and Social Relations' (Chilean TRC 1993: 997–1021) in which the devastating impact of the regime on family members and familial relationships was formally acknowledged. These secondary harms (such as loss and grief, prolonged uncertainty, damage to personal integrity, disturbances in mental and physical health (Chilean TRC 1993 997–1021), disruption caused to family life (Chilean TRC 1993: 1073–4), 'social and economic hardship' (Chilean TRC 1993: 1012)) are documented and acknowledged in the Report. The decision to restrict the mandate to abuses considered 'most serious' limited the recognised primary victims to those who lost their lives under the dictatorship. Ní Aoláin and Turner note that:

> The effect of these definitional limitations was to leave out a range of harms, which not coincidently overlapped with those rights violations most often experienced by women.
>
> (Ní Aoláin and Turner 2007: 251)

Similarly, reflecting the narrowly masculinist terms within which torture was understood under the prevailing regime of international human rights law, the Commission's discussion of torture cast women in the role of secondary victims. Although not formally within the Commission's mandate unless resulting in death, the general practice and circumstances of torture were examined (Chilean TRC 1993: 158). While the Report went on to list examples of such methods (for example, violent and continual beating, denial of food and water) as definitive findings of the Commission, uniquely 'sexual degradation and rape' were recorded as 'accusations' (Chilean TRC 1993: 158). The Report noted that 'Torture for women prisoners was sexual, and took many and bizarre forms' (Chilean TRC 1993: 160); however, in its further discussion this gender-specific form of torture was not elaborated on and no specific recommendations were made to address it. The section listed the torture of individuals in front of family members (Chilean TRC 1993: 158). As noted by Ximena Bunster, forcing female family members to witness the torture of a male relative was a common tactic of the military regime for extracting information about dissident activities from women

15 Supreme Decree No. 355, Diario Oficial, 25 April 1990, Article 1. The statute asserted the 'moral responsibility' of the state to address these activities conducted by state agents. The Commission was also to examine the activities of the armed left ('kidnappings and attempts on the life of persons committed by private citizens for political purposes').

(Bunster 1985, 1991).[16] However, this activity was not identified as a primary harm to the family member witnessing the mistreatment of their loved one. (Recognition of harm to relatives as a primary harm then had no basis in international law and would take some time to emerge.[17]) Consequently, in the discussion of torture the Report again cast women as secondary victims.

Indeed, of the 2,279 confirmed victims recognised by the TRC Report, only 126 (or 5.5 per cent) were women. Thus, while the restrictive mandate of the TRC was borne of both difficult domestic circumstances in terms of the highly negotiated character of the Chilean transition, and the gendered shortcomings of the prevailing international human rights regime, the political compromise to focus only on loss of life was not a gender-neutral phenomenon. It worked to call women into view only as secondary victims within the official truth account.

The Chilean National Commission on Political Imprisonment and Torture

Importantly, however, the story of truth recovery in Chile does not end with the Chilean TRC. The Comisión Nacional sobre Prisión Política y Tortura (the National Commission on Political Imprisonment and Torture), established by Supreme Decree of President Ricardo Lagos in 2003 to identify the victims of imprisonment and torture for political reasons under the dictatorship, would finally prove to be the site of official acknowledgement of women's gender-specific experiences of political repression.[18] Signalling the dramatic change in the recognition of harms against women, in launching the Report of the Commission, President Lagos drew particular attention to the Commission's findings on the extent of sexual violence against women:

> How can this horror be explained? What could provoke human conduct such as what appears here? . . . How can it be explained that, of the 3,400 women who gave testimony, almost all indicated having been subjected to sexual violence?
>
> (Comisión Nacional sobre Prisión Política y Tortura 2005: Prologue)

The 12 years that passed between the first and second phases of official truth recovery in Chile witnessed dramatic changes in activation of criminal

16 This tactic of the regime is noted in gender-neutral terms by the Chilean National Commission on Truth and Reconciliation (1993: 1057–120).

17 In this regard, see for example decisions of the Inter-American Court of Human Rights, which recognise the families of the disappeared as victims solely by virtue of their status as next of kin: *Villagran Morales et al v Guatemala* (the 'Street Children' case), IACtHR, Series C No. 63 (1999); *Bámaca Velásquez v Guatemala*, IACtHR, Series C No. 70 (2000).

18 Supreme Decree No. 1040, Diario Oficial, 11 November 2003.

accountability and state obligations for violence against women under international law. Hardening international legal requirements concerning truth, justice and reparations for human rights violations meant that the mandate of the Commission was firmly grounded in international law. The Torture Commission located its mandate to investigate sexual violence within the broader legal tapestry of rape as an act of aggression in war (Comisión Nacional sobre Prisión Política y Tortura 2005), and the Report even detailed the shortcomings of the Geneva Conventions and Protocols in respect of sexual violence against women, noting concern at the limited reach of the provisions on women, addressing women almost exclusively as mothers (Comisión Nacional sobre Prisión Política y Tortura 2005). The Rome Statute's recognition of rape as potentially constitutive of a war crime or crime against humanity was also noted (Comisión Nacional sobre Prisión Política y Tortura 2005). Thus, contemporary international legal treatment of rape was applied to the historical acts under investigation.

The Torture Commission did not specifically inquire into sexual violations experienced by female prisoners (Comisión Nacional sobre Prisión Política y Tortura 2005: 252), in that the questionnaire to be completed by all those testifying to the Commission did not specifically mention sexual violence (an oversight later criticised by feminist groups) (Fundación Instituto de la Mujer *et al.* 2004). Rather, the testimony 'emerged spontaneously from those giving statements' (Comisión Nacional sobre Prisión Política y Tortura 2005: 252). Nevertheless, in Chapter 5 of the Commission Report, which details methods of torture uncovered by the Commission, a separate section was dedicated to sexual violence against women. The section began:

> It seems necessary to highlight separately the situation of sexual violence experienced by women detainees, taking into consideration the characteristics of the violence, as well as its moral and cultural significance in Chilean society.
>
> (Comisión Nacional sobre Prisión Política y Tortura 2005: 251)

At the end of the process, 28,459 persons were recognised as victims by the Commission (Comisión Nacional sobre Prisión Política y Tortura 2005). Of the total number of victims, 3,621 victims were women (12.72 per cent) (Comisión Nacional sobre Prisión Política y Tortura 2005). Of the women listed, almost all of them reported being victims of sexual violence. This dramatic expansion of the recognised victim group, and the movement from casting women as secondary victims to uncovering women's primary victimhood, can be attributed quite directly to the doctrinal changes in international law.

Normative: revealing or reinforcing structural gender inequalities?

Analysis of the treatment of reproductive harm in both the early TRC and the subsequent Torture Commission reveals much about the gender values that structured the pursuit of 'reconciliation' in Chile. The introduction posited the concern that the reconciliatory and unifying values in the forward-looking function of truth might be antithetical to women's equality. The Chilean case evidences some grounds for this concern, as the expansion in the recognition of female primary victimhood and harms against women under the Torture Commission did not extend to the recognition of reproductive harms experienced by women under the dictatorship, despite related progressive developments in international law.

Finally emerging in 1998, a study by the New York-based Center for Reproductive Law and Policy provided an authoritative account of the manifold ways in which the activities of the Chilean military regime towards abortion constituted violations of even the most narrowly defined civil and political rights.[19] The study examined the experience of women prosecuted for abortion in Chile in 1983–84.[20] The study demonstrated how the restrictive legal context for abortion violated the rights of women to liberty and security, as well as, in many cases, their right to life. In addition, fundamental human rights were shown to have been violated by the methods by which women were reported to the police and the criminal process they underwent. Abortion providers and their 'accomplices' were subjected to violations of rights such as the right to due process, the right to privacy and the right of a criminal defendant to be afforded an attorney.[21]

However, this form of civil and political rights violation was invisible to the TRC. The circumstances of poverty, and the lack of publicly funded family planning under the military regime, did not feature in the Commission's account of the 'Political Context' (Chilean TRC 1993: 63–90) of rights violations in that period. Violations of women's rights to life, liberty and security, and due process for those accused of abortion-related offences, did not feature within the overview of human rights violations provided by the Report (Chilean TRC 1993: 152–595). (Withholding medical care to those seeking emergency medical assistance after botched abortions, until they disclose the identity of those who assisted them in procuring the abortion, was subsequently recognised by the CAT Committee as a violation of the Convention Against Torture (UN Committee against Torture 2004). This was routine practice under the dictatorship (Red Chilena contra la Violencia Doméstica y Sexual 2008).)

In the much later Torture Commission, because of the staggering levels of sexual violence revealed, a section of the Report dealt with pregnancies resulting from these sexual attacks. However, the issue of forced pregnancy, whilst raised in

19 See Center for Reproductive Law and Policy and Open Forum on Reproductive Health and Rights (1998).

20 See Center for Reproductive Law and Policy and Open Forum on Reproductive Health and Rights (1998).

21 See Center for Reproductive Law and Policy and Open Forum on Reproductive Health and Rights (1998: 8).

some surrounding civil society interventions into the Commission (Copelon 2003) and by now a recognised offence under international criminal law,[22] was simply absent from the Report. In a description of its legal framework, the Report stated that the Commission looked for violations of personal liberty and right to integrity and security of person committed for political motives, and looked to international law for definition of these concepts, as well as juridical backing in domestic law (Comisión Nacional sobre Prisión Política y Tortura 2005: 23). Formulation of the crime of 'forced pregnancy' has been particularly contentious within international criminal law.[23] The 1998 Rome Statute of the International Criminal Court was the first international treaty to expressly criminalise and define the offence as:

> [T]he unlawful confinement of a woman forcibly made pregnant, with the intent of affecting the ethnic composition of any population or carrying out other grave violations of international law.
>
> (Rome Statute of the International Criminal Court, 17 July 1998, 2187 UNTS 3, Article 7(2)(f))

The text of the Rome Statute provision was very carefully negotiated in order to preclude any possibility of the offence of 'forced pregnancy' being used to challenge restrictive abortion laws of states.[24] A sentence was added to the definition of the offence explicitly to that effect: 'This definition shall not in any way be interpreted as affecting national laws relating to pregnancy.'[25] The sentence shields domestic abortion laws from ICC scrutiny. Nevertheless, while the Torture Commission discussed the sexual torture identified by the Commission in the context of surrounding international human rights developments, and the account is otherwise comprehensive, no investigation or mention was made of forced pregnancy.

Meanwhile, the Commission showed substantial creativity in finding the children of women who were tortured while pregnant also to be included within the Commission's mandate, due to the torture they were deemed to have experienced in the womb. There is a striking contrast here. The Commission failed to interpret its mandate to include an offence established in international criminal law (namely, forced pregnancy), while reading into its mandate a form of victimhood without any clear international legal precedent (vicarious torture of a foetus through the torture of a pregnant woman).

Grounded in international legal developments, the Torture Commission was able to reveal women's gender-specific experiences of physical harm that took

22 Rome Statute of the International Criminal Court, 17 July 1998, 2187 UNTS 3, Articles 7(2) and 8.

23 For discussion, see Boon (2001: 655).

24 See further Boon (2001: 659).

25 Rome Statute of the International Criminal Court, 17 July 1998, 2187 UNTS 3, Article 7(2)(f).

place in the same locations as where men experienced political violence (namely in detention). Unlike the much earlier TRC, the Torture Commission identified gender as a determining factor in one's experience of harm under the dictatorship. However, from this premise, the Torture Commission did not go on to explore the restrictive regulation of women's reproductive lives, despite the manifold human rights violations involved. In addition, there is evidence of selective invocation of international legal categories even in the recognition of public harms against women, as the issue of forced pregnancy was treated as a harm to the child ultimately born and not to the woman who was forced to continue with the pregnancy in a situation of detention.

On the whole, therefore, the Chilean case evidences the vulnerability of doctrinal developments around reproductive rights at the international level to more regressive gender politics at the local level.

Political: affirming women as agents?

The Chilean National Truth and Reconciliation Commission

The narrowly gendered terms of the Chilean TRC, in which women were cast only as secondary victims, also meant that the resistance of women to the dictatorship was largely invisible to the Commission. For example, in investigating 'relevant prior circumstances' of the military dictatorship, the Chilean TRC again relied on available documentation and the opinion of experts in the area (Chilean TRC 1993: 39–40). Thus established accounts of harms, and the traditional circle of actors, were reprivileged in this process. No effort was made to introduce silenced narratives or alternative accounts of the harms of the past. Little space was provided for investigating and highlighting the abuses neglected by these established sources.[26] An important opportunity to recognise and validate this organising by women was lost, and the potential to advance women's citizenship within the new democratic government was not explored. In deciding which cases to consider, the Commission drew on the lists of victims of the major human rights NGOs (CODEPU, FASIC, the Vicaría and victims' groups such as the AFDD) (Chilean TRC 1993: 29–37). Women's organisations were not consulted and the list of victims would replicate the gendered silences of the mainstream human rights advocacy during the dictatorship. Further, this was to have important implications for the account of torture that featured in the Report. In addition, the failure to acknowledge women's groups as either operating in the defence of human rights, or as organised 'victims' of the regime, led to substantial gendered lacunae in the official 'truth' that emerged from the Report. The opportunity to

26 The ICTJ Handbook posits TRCs as a mechanism for 'highlighting neglected abuses' (International Center for Transitional Justice, 2006: 2).

recognise and validate women's political activism, and to expand the basis of citizenship in the new democratic administration, was missed.

The Chilean National Commission on Political Imprisonment and Torture

That the Torture Commission was critically important in finally giving this recognition to women as political actors in the past is beyond dispute. Nevertheless, the initiative has not been received uncritically by Chilean feminists and women victims. Lorena Fries contrasts the broad diffusion of the Report of the TRC with the limited reach of the Torture Report. While the TRC Report was published in full as an insert to a Chilean national daily paper, the Report of the Torture Commission was only made available on the internet. 'It's had a reduced impact. It has not yet become part of the historical legacy.'[27]

Substantial doctrinal developments in the criminalisation of sexual violence under international law were documented in Chapter 4. These developments have contributed, however, to further grounds for feminist unease with the ostensible gains of international law. Principally, these concerns focus on the essentialisation of women as passive victims of sexual violence. The passage of time since the adoption of the Rome Statute has created space for greater reflection and evaluation of perceived feminist 'gains' in international criminal law (e.g. International Criminal Law Review 2010: 11(3)). With the emergence of a more reflective and evaluative feminist approach to international criminal law, there is marked disillusionment at the continuing low number of prosecutions of sexual violence and the persistence of age-old evidential obstacles to accounting for women's experiences of sexual violence. There is a suspicion that perceived feminist 'victories', secured over the course of a decade, have in fact shown much in form, but little in substance.[28]

The Chilean example makes a compelling counter-case in the consideration of truth processes. The dramatic shift from women's political subjectivity in the TRC, as secondary victimhood based exclusively on women's maternal role, to the Torture Commission and its recognition of women's direct sexualised victimhood, reveals the impact of international law in affirming different forms of women's political subjectivity. This section reveals that the focus on sexual victimisation did at least begin to displace the overwhelmingly dominant narrative of political motherhood that existed prior to the Torture Commission's revelations. It points to the important role that international law has played as a floor to the Chilean truth process, guaranteeing at a minimum the recognition and acknowledgement of sexual violence experienced by women victims of torture and political imprisonment. As evidenced by the treatment of reproductive harms

27 Lorena Fries, Corporación Humanas, Santiago, personal communication, 27 October 2008.
28 For a particularly trenchant critique, see de Londras (2009).

in both the TRC and the subsequent Torture Commission, more ambitious objectives around the holistic recognition of the rights that were impacted, and the multidimensional understanding of the harms suffered, proved elusive.

COLOMBIA: . . . BUT NOT AS A CEILING

In Colombia, a process of both micro and macro truth recovery is being pursued. Whereas the search for micro-truths, grounded in categories of harm in international law, has proven narrow and exclusionary to women and women's gender-specific accounts of harm, the macro process has evidenced impressive innovation and originality in departing from established categories of harm (in international law) and linking conflict harms to broader issues of structural gender inequality. This section details, therefore, the importance of international law functioning as a floor, but not a ceiling, to official truth processes.

The international frame: defining and decontextualising harms, obscuring structural inequalities and negating women's agency in a judicial process of micro-truth recovery

One of the most trenchant and sustained feminist critiques of dominant approaches to transitional justice is the focus on individual harms (Ross 2003). This focus is said to dislocate harms from the context in which they occur and obscure the structural gender inequalities that make women particularly vulnerable to certain types of harm. Findings in Colombia evidence how the reliance on (international) legal categories of harm within truth processes underpin and perpetuate such decontextualisation. The Justice and Peace Process was also designed to include a truth-telling component, by means of the *versiones libres* of the participating paramilitaries. These individual accounts of perpetrators would thereby give rise to micro-truths about the Colombian conflict. The judicial process established by the Justice and Peace Law was intended to satisfy victims' rights to truth. Nevertheless, manifold problems have been identified in the quality of truth emerging from the process. Practical obstacles such as the insufficient number of prosecutors and lack of resources mean that the paramilitaries, and not the state nor the victims, are directing the *versiones libres*.[29] Civil society observation of the *versiones libres* has attested to the very small number of offences being admitted to, the frequent response to questioning with simple 'yes' or 'no', and the prosecutors' lack of time and resources to redress this very limited truth emerging from the process (International Federation for Human Rights 2007). These practical obstacles have

29 For a detailed account of the operation of the Justice and Peace Law, and its non-compliance with international human rights standards, see International Federation for Human Rights (2007).

functioned effectively to silence women victims and have done little to affirm their agency.

In terms of recognising collective harms and revealing structural inequalities, critics complain that the process is providing a forum for paramilitaries to justify and defend their activities either as defending the community against guerrillas, or as the 'social cleansing' of prostitutes, rapists and drug dealers (International Federation for Human Rights 2007: 60). Women's organisations have noted that sexual violence is not appearing at all in the *versiones libres*, and to the small extent that it does feature, the practice is presented as rare and isolated rather than widespread and systematic (International Federation for Human Rights 2007: 62; La Ruta Pacifica *et al.* 2009). One of the most significant criticisms from Colombian women's organisations of the *versiones libres* is that the focus on isolated offences by individual perpetrators is contributing nothing to the clarification of the relationship between the paramilitaries and state forces, economic interests or political parties (International Federation for Human Rights, 2007: 63). The 'truth' of paramilitary activities emerging from this process thus appears to be isolated acts of criminality, justified by 'social cleansing' objectives of the perpetrators, and without any gender-specific impact on women. Consequently, the systematic and widespread practice of sexual violence is being minimised and made invisible by the process (International Federation for Human Rights 2007: 44). Similarly, gendered practices involved in the control of territories by armed actors – such as invading people's homes and imposing guidelines for behaviour on the women who live there, and demanding domestic labour such as cooking and cleaning by women – are perceived as 'a consequence of the *normal* dynamics of conflict' and do not feature in the truth narrative emerging from the judicial process (International Federation for Human Rights 2007: 44).

The local fit: historical memory and recontextualising harms

Interestingly, it is the process of macro-truth recovery, removed from categories of harm in international law, that has led to the recontextualisation of conflict harms within Colombia. Micro-truths from the *versiones libres* have also been supplemented in the contemporary process with attempts to reach a macro-truth of the conflict through the work of the Group on Historical Memory (Grupo de Memoría Historica, GMH) established by the Corporación Nacional de Reparación y Reconciliación (CNRR).[30] This independent group of academics was constituted to produce the report on the causes of the emergence and development of illegal armed groups in Colombia. The group's membership and autonomy means that the working group is unique in terms of its legitimacy

30 The CNRR was acting on its mandate for historical memory, as set out in the Ley 975 de 2005, Article 52.2.

among a wide number of civil society organisations, including the human rights community and the victims sector (Diaz 2007). While the mandate given to the group by the CNRR was quite specifically to investigate the origins and emergence of paramilitary groups since 1964, the group has chosen to interpret its mandate widely, announcing that:

> [T]he GMH seeks to construct a comprehensive memory . . . a memory that integrates the voices not only of all of the armed actors, but also of all of the victims, as the foundation of understanding and transformation of the conflict.
> (Comisión Nacional de Reparación y Reconciliación y Grupo de Memoría Historica, 2007: 1.2)

The GMH case also evidences the autonomy that such groups can carve, free from the controlling state, once established. In terms of women, one of the Group members is María Emma Wills Obregón, a leading feminist activist and scholar and one of the principal scribes of the Colombian women's movement (Wills 2007). Further, the Group's progressive and integrated approach to gender has been amply demonstrated in its work to date. The GMH's Plan of Research explicitly acknowledges 'the political character of memory', 'a site of contestation in which the view of the past that prevails . . . is constructed from asymmetrical power relations'.[31] Thus, 'not all memories accede in conditions of equality to the public sphere'.[32] Early on, the Group committed to an agenda of work to facilitate the recovery of historical memory from women and minority groups.[33] The Group also committed to deepening the quality of democracy in the country by pursuing historical memory through an inclusive process of dialogue.[34] Here we see commitment to open and contextual values of openness and equality, rather than strict reliance on international legal categories, to guide the operation of the Group.

The Group on Historical Memory has proceeded through examination and reporting on a series of emblematic cases. The first such case concerned the experiences of the town of Trujillo in the Valle region in the north of the country, which endured several massacres over two decades at the hands of state, paramilitary and guerrilla forces.[35] The GMH Report clearly worked from a premise that gender is determinative of one's experience of harm and from a commitment to reveal structural gender inequalities. Moreover, from this premise, the Report moved quickly from its focus on the public harms of the massacres to expand that to deal also with ostensibly private harms experienced by women. In fact, the

31 See Comisión Nacional de Reparación y Reconciliación y Grupo de Memoría Historica (2008b: 1.2).
32 Ibid.
33 Ibid., 1.2b.
34 Ibid., 1.2.
35 See Comisión Nacional de Reparación y Reconciliación y Grupo de Memoría Historica (2008a).

Report adopts a gender perspective to challenge the very terms of its own investigation: thus the 'before' and 'after' of the massacres were acknowledged to be misleading terms, when one considers the gender-based violence that pervades normal life in Trujillo. The section brought out gender-specific experiences of violence and discrimination within families in the area, concluding that:

> [M]any of the accounts that emerged about 'before the massacre' and ordinary life demonstrate how the lives of women proceeded within practices of violent masculine domination . . . For them, the 'before' does not appear to have been an idyll of peace and respect for their rights in the domestic ambit.
> (Comisión Nacional de Reparación y Reconciliación y Grupo de Memoría Historica, 2008: 220)

It articulated the relationship of public to private harms, and violent consequences for women of that relationship within the private sphere.

In terms of affirming women's agency, the section on the memories of women concluded with a consideration of the impact of violence on women's citizenship in Trujillo and how the reparations process might be used as an opportunity to restore women in that community to a position of equal citizenship.[36] The Report acknowledged that in organising to resist the violence, and in surviving the economic hardship of the violence, women's participation in the public sphere increased as a consequence of the violence in Trujillo.[37] However, the Report noted that the discourse of human rights of women, and the recognition of women's sexual and reproductive rights, had not entered the agenda of the victim demands. The slogan of 'democracy in the house and in the plaza',[38] which has inspired the struggle of women in other contexts for their full citizenship, had not resonated in Trujillo.

The understanding of structural gender inequalities in the Report was highly sophisticated. The Report concluded that, in spite of the way the violence destabilised some of the gender strictures of the society, this did not result in the overcoming of 'dominant violent masculinity'.[39] Moreover, this understanding of structural gender inequalities underpinned the Report's forward-looking aspect, in considering the processes of reparation as an opportunity, not to return these women to their victimhood in places of exclusion and violent subordination, but to provide a route to their full citizenship in public spaces as well as private.[40] The relationship between recognising a broad range of harms, revealing structural gender inequalities and affirming women's agency in truth processes is clearly

36 Ibid., 227–9.
37 Ibid., 228.
38 Ibid., 228.
39 Ibid., 228.
40 Ibid., 228.

evident in the Colombian official process of historical memory: the Report recognises that, for these transformative objectives around women's equal citizenship to be achieved, there must first be a recognition that men and women experience conflict differently, and that this difference is a consequence of the discrimination that women experience in social, political and cultural spheres prior to conflict.[41] This enlightened gender work has continued and is evident in the methodology developed by the group (Grupo de Memoría Histórica 2009: 50–124) and each of the group's reports (e.g. Grupo de Memoría Histórica 2010: 291–392), and is further developed within the group's reports that are dedicated to questions of gender and memory (Grupo de Memoría Histórica 2010).

International law as a floor, but not a ceiling

In Colombia, there is a striking contrast between the range of harms being revealed by the GMH, with its more flexible mandate, and the justice and peace process, which, although deferring to international legal categories, is not providing a forum for official acknowledgement of even women's sexual victimisation, much less structural gender inequalities and women's agency. In Colombia, the most clearly judicialised process, expressly drawing on international legal categories, provides no venue for interrogation of structural inequalities. (Indeed, many critics would argue that its focus on individual perpetrators is deliberately designed to prevent such an interrogation of structural inequalities (e.g. Uprimny and Saffon 2008).) By contrast, the more flexible and contextual approach of the GMH has offered impressive scope for the interrogation of structural gender inequalities. It is in the section addressing the memories of women that the Report makes explicit consideration of the impact of the massacres not just on individual victims and their families, but on the social fabric of the Trujillo community, in particular through the intergenerational transfer of grief, and the economic toll of the violence.[42] This section also highlights the role of the violence in determining relations between men and women, and negative constructions of masculinity and femininity in the community: the privileging of violent masculinity, the exclusion of women from decision-making roles in the community and 'the profound devaluation of the feminine' in the violent context of Trujillo.[43]

The Colombian case can be identified as exemplary in recognising gender as a determinative factor in one's experience of harm, revealing structural gender inequalities and in affirming women's political subjectivity. However, it is in its deviation from international law, and not in its domestic implementation of it, that the Colombian case has achieved its unique success. The unique status of the GMH, as a group that has carved substantial autonomy from the state-led justice

41 Ibid., 228–9.
42 Ibid., 227.
43 Ibid., 229–30.

and peace process, has allowed the group to craft a counter-hegemonic truth discourse that simultaneously challenges the state's truth narrative and reinforces women as agents within truth processes.

NORTHERN IRELAND: INTERNATIONAL LAW AS STRAITJACKET?

The discussion in Chapter 5 of women's organisations in Northern Ireland characterised their approach as instrumentalist, in choosing not to engage with the political divisions that underpin the conflict and in articulating a vision of the past that strategically advanced their contemporary agenda. This reluctance to take on deeply divisive political initiatives in engaging with official truth processes must be understood in the context of an absence of official truth initiatives and the close imbrication of official truth initiatives with formal justice processes.

Truth recovery processes in the aftermath of wide-scale human rights violations confront substantial obstacles of ownership and legitimacy. These obstacles are closely tied to an issue flagged in Chapter 5, namely the depth of the transition. Where states can convincingly establish that the wrongdoers of the past no longer hold sway in contemporary political structures, there is potential for a state-sponsored truth process to garner both broad ownership and legitimacy from the community and from victims. Northern Ireland's constitutional status, as a devolved jurisdiction within the United Kingdom, presents a unique twist to questions of political transition and state continuity in the cases under study. In Northern Ireland, the continuity of the British state frames the substantial reform that has taken place within Northern Ireland political structures. These dynamics of state continuity are a dominant factor in truth recovery efforts in Northern Ireland. As Bell has documented, the official approach to dealing with the past in Northern Ireland has been largely defined by a range of 'ad hoc' and 'piecemeal' initiatives (Bell 2003: 1098), rather than a bespoke mechanism to deliver truth, justice and reparations. In the absence of a bespoke truth mechanism, a tapestry of formal legal processes (prosecutions, inquests, public inquiries, police investigations) emerged to provide a truth narrative in Northern Ireland. All of these initiatives have taken place within existing state structures. While both the prosecution service and the police service in Northern Ireland have undergone substantial reform, without broader accountability for the human rights violations in which these institutions were complicit in the past, a dark shadow hangs over their capacity to deliver any measure of truth in the current context.[44] Moreover, public inquiries are an established mechanism within British public law that coincided

44 On the police and resistance to change, see O'Rawe (2003). On the problems of the past-related inquiries conducted by the police and their limitations, see Lundy (2009). On the persistent problems within the Public Prosecution Service, see Committee on the Administration of Justice (2012).

with the establishment of the Northern Irish state,[45] and to the extent that this model has been revised in recent years, it has been to substantially limit – and not expand – its independence from government.[46] Truth recovery in Northern Ireland must engage, therefore, with the complexities of states telling their own truths about the past. As foreshadowed earlier, and as sensitively recognised by the Colombian GMH, 'not all memories accede in conditions of equality to the public sphere'.[47] Rather truth recovery in Northern Ireland takes place 'in the full glare of the British state' (Rolston and Scraton 2005).

Doctrinal: defining harms

Interestingly, against this backdrop, recourse to international law has proven to be a critical backstop to state efforts to limit and control truth recovery in Northern Ireland. Because of broad victim distrust of state institutions investigating their own complicity in the state's use of lethal force, a series of cases brought from Northern Ireland to the European Court of Human Rights established exacting procedural requirements upon the state in its discharge of obligations under Article 2 of the European Convention on Human Rights.[48] Many victims and civil society organisations cling to international law, most notably Article 2 of the European Convention, as the only meaningful guarantee of accountability in the face of a recalcitrant state.

Because of the different patterns of harms in the Northern Ireland conflict, in particular the absence of distinct patterns of sexual violence, feminist-informed developments in international law have offered relatively little doctrinal and normative traction for feminists on the domestic truth process. Moreover, although the Women, Peace and Security agenda inaugurated by UNSC Resolution 1325 has proven popular as a shared mobilising platform amongst women in Northern Ireland,[49] the British government's refusal to acknowledge the existence of a

45 Tribunals of Inquiry (Evidence) Act 1921.

46 Inquiries Act 2005. The main problems with the model established under this Act concern the introduction of substantial ministerial control over inquiry processes, public access to proceedings and information released to victims and the public. See further Requa (2007).

47 See Comisión Nacional de Reparación y Reconciliación y Grupo de Memoría Historica (2008b: 1.2).

48 Investigations into suspicious killings must be independent, prompt, subject to sufficient public scrutiny and capable of leading to a determination of whether the force used was or was not justified in the circumstances and to the identification and punishment of those responsible. The state must initiate an investigation on its own accord – instead of relying on family members to seek an investigation – and involve the next-of-kin to the extent necessary to safeguard their legitimate interest. *Jordan v United Kingdom*, 2001-III ECHR; *Kelly v United Kingdom*, 2001-III ECHR; *McKerr v United Kingdom*, 2001-III ECHR; *Shanaghan v United Kingdom*, 2001-III ECHR. See further Ní Aoláin (2002); Bell (2003); Bell and Keenan (2004); Requa (2007).

49 See, for example, the popular tribunal on 1325 organised by Northern Ireland's Women's European Platform (2004).

conflict in Northern Ireland means that the resolution has not garnered domestic legal or policy traction in dealing with the past (Hegarty 2011). This reality is evidenced most strikingly in the absence of any reference to Northern Ireland in the UK's National Action Plan for the implementation of UNSC Resolution 1325 (United Kingdom Government National Action Plan 2012).

This gendered shortcoming in truth in Northern Ireland does not, however, mean that international law has failed to influence official truth processes in Northern Ireland. On the contrary, in fact, truth-seeking in Northern Ireland has remained heavily determined by international law, but not by feminist-informed doctrinal developments. Procedural requirements of the right to life under the European Convention on Human Rights constitute the dark shadow that hangs over all official truth initiatives in Northern Ireland (Bell and Keenan 2005). While alternative non-legal processes are proposed, their parameters and priorities remain determined by legal categories. Article 2 requirements on the state have inaugurated and reinforced a truth process in Northern Ireland that focuses, almost exclusively, on the loss of life. In particular, a number of Troubles-related inquiries are currently operating within Northern Ireland under the UK public inquiries model. Most prominent amongst these has been the Saville Inquiry into the shooting dead of 13 unarmed civilians by the British army in 1972, an incident widely known as 'Bloody Sunday' (Lord Saville 2010). These inquiries pose a rich seam of investigation. One such public inquiry concerns the death of a woman, namely the Inquiry into the Killing of Rosemary Nelson.[50]

As in Colombia, the shortcomings of the narrowly legal approach adopted to truth recovery in Northern Ireland, which has been heavily critiqued for its exclusionary effects,[51] prompted efforts to pursue a macro-truth. The highly legalised process of truth recovery was to change in 2007, when the British government finally announced its intention to begin to address the most obvious 'missing piece' of the infrastructure of Northern Ireland's transition from conflict – a bespoke mechanism to consult across the community and to provide recommendations towards truth, justice and reconciliation for human rights violations that occurred during the conflict (Northern Ireland Office 2007). To this end, the Consultative Group on the Past was appointed by the Northern Ireland Secretary of State.

While the Consultative Group on the Past was established with the avowed intention of providing an alternative to legal processes, as this section reveals, it has in fact operated with priorities and categories of harm determined by law. Finalisation of the report was delayed and it was finally published on 23 January 2009. The flagship recommendation of the Consultative Group on the Past was to

50 See 'Chairman's Initial Statement', available at http://www.rosemarynelsoninquiry.org/current-key-documents/4/ (last accessed 27 February 2013).

51 See, for example, Consultative Group on the Past (2009: 124–33). This chapter of the Report deals with 'Legal Processes: the Arguments for Change'.

establish a single body (the 'Legacy Commission') to combine the heretofore distinct processes of reconciliation, justice and information recovery (Consultative Group on the Past 2009: 6). The overarching objective of the Commission would be to promote peace and stability. The Commission's mandate would be fourfold: to help society towards a shared future; review and investigate historical cases; conduct a process of information recovery; and examine linked or thematic cases emerging from the conflict (Consultative Group on the Past 2009: 27).[52] The Report proposed that the mandate of the Legacy Commission run for five years, and at that point the Commission proposes that 'a line might be drawn . . . so that Northern Ireland might best move to a shared future' (Consultative Group on the Past 2009: 9).

The Report of the Consultative Group on the Past, though comprehensive and impressive in many ways, once again repeated the patterns of earlier related initiatives in denying women any stake in the past. Focusing on deaths in the conflict, and the state's concomitant obligations to investigate those deaths (Bell and Keenan 2005), the Report made no specific mention of women, even in the context of secondary victimhood. Practical exclusions of the Report were evident in recommendations such as the proposed five-year operation of the Legacy Commission. There is substantial evidence that women take longer than men to come forward to report experiences of violence, in particular in cases involving sexual violence (Herman 2001). Thus the recommended short duration of the Legacy Commission would have a disproportionate impact on women.

More significantly, there is evidence of a deeper conceptual exclusion within the Report that conceives of dealing with the past as if gender were not a determining factor of one's experience of that past. The Report betrays a narrowness of concerns, a narrow understanding of the harms of the past, which serves to exclude women. The Group recommended that the Legacy Commission should focus on historical cases resulting in death (Consultative Group on the Past 2009: 27). Local experience and international best practice (International Center for Transitional Justice 2006) cautions that an exclusive focus on deaths establishes and reinforces a narrative of the conflict that posits men as the only victims of the conflict. Further, the Report's overwhelming focus on deaths resulting from the conflict works to obscure a broader range of harms,

52 Hence, there would be four strands of activity within the Commission. First, the Commission would identify areas of activity to address society issues arising from the conflict, for example tackling sectarianism and working towards reconciliation. Second, the Commission would undertake review and investigation of historical cases that resulted in death, to establish whether a realistic chance of prosecution existed. Third, the Commission would pursue a process of information recovery, after completion of the review and investigation stage, to provide families of victims with individual historical cases. Fourth, the Commission would undertake thematic investigations into issues such as collusion, which would not involve hearings or adversarial procedures.

most pronounced in the Report's failure to deal with socio-economic harms of the conflict.[53]

Political: affirming women's agency

The Report of the Consultative Group provided an important opportunity to acknowledge the women's sector as stakeholders in the debate on the past. Instead, the involvement of women's organisations was not actively sought during the consultation process, and despite having received the interim and final reports of the *Women and the Troubles* project,[54] the documents were not even acknowledged in the Report as having been consulted by the Commission.

The potential for official efforts to deal with the past to advance women's equal citizenship appears very limited, in particular when viewed in tandem with the conduct of the one public inquiry that was established to inquire into the murder of a woman. The Catholic lawyer Rosemary Nelson was murdered in 1999, in circumstances that suggested either deliberate act or negligent omission by the security forces (Rosemary Nelson Inquiry 2011). Nelson was a controversial figure. She provided legal representation to prominent individuals accused of IRA involvement. She also represented the residents of the nationalist Garvaghy Road in the parading dispute involving the Loyalist Orange Order, and the family of Robert Hamill, a young Catholic man openly kicked to death in circumstances that suggested failure by nearby police to intervene.[55] Most notably, she was lawyer for Colin Duffy. Duffy was convicted for the murder of a British soldier in 1993, though the Court of Appeal overturned the conviction in 1996 due to unreliability of a key prosecution witness.

The Inquiry reported in May 2011 (Rosemary Nelson Inquiry 2011). During its investigation, it was marked by familiar gender dynamics, as questions of the victim's sexual morality were placed centre stage. The argument was advanced in the Inquiry that it was due to a romantic affair between Nelson and Colin Duffy that Nelson was murdered by Loyalists.[56] In the Inquiry established

53 To the extent that socio-economic issues are acknowledged in the Report, the account is oddly masculine. The impact of bombs on businesses, of deterring tourists and boycotts of businesses by one community are documented (Consultative Group on the Past 2009: 28). However, there is no acknowledgement of the poverty exacerbated by the conflict, the difficulties experienced by families and communities in meeting basic needs. The account of the Report bears no relationship to the accounts of 'poverty and hardship' articulated by women in popular truth initiatives emerging from the women's movement (Women's Resource and Development Agency and Women's Centres Regional Partnership 2008: 18).

54 Margaret Ward, Women's Resource and Development Agency, Belfast, personal communication, May 2009.

55 A preliminary state-appointed inquiry into Robert Hamill's death recommended a full public inquiry (Cory 2004).

56 See, for example, Document No. RNI 806–182, available at www.rosemarynelsoninquiry.org/ (last accessed 7 March 2013).

to investigate the possible complicity of state forces in Nelson's murder, the examination of the victim's 'moral integrity'[57] consumed much of its time. There is an obvious resonance between the dynamics of the Nelson Inquiry and the strong tendency of criminal prosecutions for rape to put the victim's sexuality on trial (Lees 1997). In dedicating such attention and resources to the affair, the handling of the Nelson Inquiry demonstrated the high cost to individual women who engage with the political divisions that structure the conflict, and who feature in the truth process in that capacity. The conduct of the Inquiry is a telling backdrop to the emphasis on the 'shared' experiences of women adopted by women's civil society organisations. It signals the high cost to individual women of overt political engagement with dealing with the past and questions of state liability for past harms.

The ultimate Report was highly critical of the state. In its 'Overall Conclusions', the Inquiry found that: Nelson had been abused and assaulted by police; there were serious failures of the police force, with little or no analysis of threats or abuse by officers; and there were leaks in intelligence that must have increased the risk to her life (Rosemary Nelson Inquiry 2011: 465). The Inquiry found that the police publicly abused her on the Garvaghy Road, which had the effect of legitimising her as a target. Police also made threatening remarks about her to her clients (Rosemary Nelson Inquiry 2011: 466). Revealing the depth of institutional failures, neither the Special Branch nor the Chief Constable had accepted any complaints against the police unless it was proven to the standard of beyond a reasonable doubt by the police complaints procedure, which was not practical (Rosemary Nelson Inquiry 2011: 465). And in relation to the Northern Ireland Office, the administrative headquarters for the exercise of executive power in the jurisdiction during the Troubles, the Inquiry found 'deference' to the police force (Rosemary Nelson Inquiry 2011: 286). It found 'irritation' with the international and national NGOs who made representations on her behalf (Rosemary Nelson Inquiry 2011: 311). State institutions showed no appreciation of the risks to which she was exposed and no proactivity in relation to her safety. The Inquiry concluded that the state failed to take reasonable and proportionate steps to protect and guard her (Rosemary Nelson Inquiry 2011: 466).

The Report of the Rosemary Nelson Inquiry set out the state's manifold failures to protect women, not just from private intimate violence as detailed in Chapter 2, but also from public political violence that structured the conflict. While in its conduct the Inquiry did little to affirm women's agency, in its outcomes it makes a powerful case for enhanced state activity to affirm women's political equality in the future.

57 For discussion and critique of these dynamics, see Committee on the Administration of Justice (2009).

Normative: revealing structural gender inequalities

The Report of the Consultative Group on the Past avowedly set out to provide a forum for investigating the broader context and consequences of the conflict in Northern Ireland. To the extent that the broader societal consequences of the conflict are acknowledged, however, this is within a short list of 'Society Issues', namely sectarianism and young people, exiles and improved services to victims. The Report is particularly concerned with the potential for intergenerational transfer of sectarianism (Consultative Group on the Past 2009: 28). The only form of discrimination identified by the Report is sectarianism. Northern Ireland continues to be marked by high levels of discrimination against women and ethnic and sexual minorities.[58] A consideration of the impact of the conflict on these particular groups might have provided a more comprehensive picture of the societal consequences of the conflict. Such a picture might also provide a sounder basis for ensuring that efforts to deal with the past bring attention to these broader issues of discrimination.

The absence of a meaningful consideration of gender in the Consultative Group Report is also betrayed in the limited vision for the future articulated within the Report. Defining the overarching objective of the Legacy Commission as the promotion of peace and stability, without a principled commitment to justice and equality, risks reinscribing a conservative gender order in Northern Ireland through the work of the Commission. The potential for such a harmful outcome is reinforced when one considers the failure of the Report to acknowledge the critical role of women in sustaining families and communities during the conflict. In the Northern Ireland case, there is some limited understanding of structural inequalities, in terms of the planned thematic investigations; however, there appears to be no place for gender within that.

The caution sounded in the introduction, about the potential for truth processes to move forward on the basis of values that are antithetical to women's equality, takes on particular resonance in the Northern Irish case. The Consultative Group's mandate to develop proposals to 'help society towards a shared future' (Consultative Group on the Past 2009: 37) already revealed a great deal about the understanding of the conflict that underpinned the Group's work. The singular focus on sectarianism as the axis of discrimination to be 'reconciled' was inadvertently complemented by an emphasis by women's organisations in their truth campaigns on shared and common experiences of women, transcendent of sectarian divisions. The net result was to preclude women – as either a collective or as members of their respective ethnic groups – as stakeholders in the official truth process. Already 'reconciled', official truth-seeking to advance reconciliation

58 See generally Equality Commission for Northern Ireland, available at http://www.equalityni.org/sections/default.asp?secid=7 (last accessed 27 February 2013).

need not attend to the gender-specific needs of women. Instead of affirming women's political equality, gender does not constitute a relevant political identity or constituency within the official truth process.

GLOBAL STANDARDS, LOCAL TRUTHS: INTERNATIONAL LAW AND DOMESTIC TRUTH POLITICS

Recognising harms to women

Analysis in this chapter suggests that it is in the identification of women's gender-specific experiences of harm that developments in international law have had their most profound impact. In Chile, developments in international law between the first and second phases of official truth initiatives were critical in revealing women's gender-specific experiences of public harms in terms of sexual violence perpetrated against political dissidents. In Colombia, in terms of the truth emerging from the *versiones libres*, international legal developments have been incorporated doctrinally in the mandate of truth and justice mechanisms. However, doctrinal advancements are being eroded through familiar failures in the operationalisation of doctrinal developments. In Northern Ireland, the strikingly narrow understanding of international law as essentially confined to directions of the European Court of Human Rights and the Council of Europe Committee of Ministers regarding procedural requirements around the right to life, means that international law has had limited discernible impact on the recognition of gender-specific harms against women in the truth process.

Although illustrating the positive dividends of feminist-informed international legal developments in the recognition of gender as a determinative factor in women's experiences of harm, it is striking that these dividends seem confined to the recognition of public harms of sexual violence against women. This limited recognition of harm evidences the concerns of feminist theorists such as Ross and Rosser, that women's diverse experiences of harm are collapsed into a uniform experience of sexualised victimhood (Ross 2003; Rosser 2007). In this way, diverse and varied harms are refracted through a legal lens to leave a single category of harm, a category that can be 'investigated' and about which 'findings' can be made. This chapter has explored an aspirational feminist interpretation of existing legal categories, in terms of reproductive harms in Chile for example, that uses the category of sexual harm as the means by which to establish gender as a determinative factor in women's experiences of harm. From that premise, a broader articulation of harm that recognises the exacerbating effect of political violence on women's private experiences of harm might be reached. In practice, the only evidence of this journey being made is the work of the Colombian Group on Historical Memory. However, it is in this least formally 'legal' aspect, with no express connection to international legal categories, that we see this journey being travelled. On the whole, the impact of international legal categories on domestic truth processes suggests that it operates as a useful floor to ensure that the complete absence of women as primary victims of political violence in the first phase of truth in Chile, and the more recent truth initiative in Northern Ireland, is not replicated. However, international law should not be allowed to act as a ceiling, preventing more creative approaches to truth initiatives, such as in the Colombian GMH.

Revealing structural gender inequalities

It is in the revelation of structural gender inequalities that international law is arguably least effective. International law has proven useful in recognising public harms against women in a more forensic approach to truth in transition and the documentation of particular harms. However, it is this type of forensic approach to truth that appears least well equipped to identify and describe larger questions of structural inequality (Orford 2006). This gap is best evidenced by the Chilean case, in which the grounding of the Torture Commission in international legal categories lent itself to forensic revelations of sexualised public harms against women, but provided no platform for interrogating the structural inequalities that produced those harms. This conclusion is also borne out by the Colombian experience of the *versiones libres*. Both are compelling examples of the limits of international law, and the limits of a focus on sexualised harms.

In Northern Ireland, by contrast, there was some attempt to deal with 'structural inequalities' in the conflict. However, these structural inequalities were confined to a discussion of sectarianism. The absence of patterns of sexual violence in the conflict limited the potential of international law to affirm women's experiences of public harms. Without that prerequisite, there seems to have been little prospect of the truth process investigating the structural gender inequalities that gives rise to such harms.

Affirming women's agency

In assisting the recognition of women's primary victimhood, developments in international law have expanded recognition of women's political subjectivities in truth initiatives beyond an exclusive focus on secondary victimhood. Feminist commentators are legitimately concerned at the continuing focus on women as passive victims of political violence, and not as perpetrators of, and active resistors to, that violence. Nevertheless, international legal developments have substantially expanded the range of political subjectivities of women that are recognised in truth in transition. This impact lies less in the domestic legal implications of international law, rather in the political implications of international law as a mobilising framework for feminist engagement with official truth processes. The Chilean and Colombian cases evidence the language, framework and vocabulary yielded to women's organisations by international law. The dramatic change in the political context can be seen, from the early Chilean case where the past agenda was resolutely eschewed by the women's movement, to the contemporary context in Colombia, Northern Ireland and Chile, where political and legal disagreements over the past have been resolutely claimed as legitimate and important sites of feminist activity.

Even in Northern Ireland, where a remarkably narrow understanding of international law was adopted, United Nations Security Council Resolution 1325 has provided a valuable mobilising framework for women's organisations seeking to influence that process. The markedly less successful experience of women's organisations in Northern Ireland in having feminist-informed developments in international law penetrate the legal framework of the official truth process may reflect the limitations of the international law developments around sexual violence in opening up the door to official processes in which sexual violence is not acknowledged to have been a feature of the political violence. Where the local context is resistant to truth, international law may provide a useful tool to insist on the recognition of, at least, women's gender-specific experiences of public harms. In this regard, international law can be regarded as a useful 'floor' for feminist truth campaigns, below which official truth processes cannot fall. The major caveat to that conclusion, however, is evident from the Northern Irish case, in which sexual violence is not regarded as having been a feature of the conflict. Where sexual violence is not a significant feature of political violence, international legal categories appear to provide very limited traction indeed to feminist truth campaigns.

In Colombia, the work to date by the GMH – through the recognition of women's gender-specific victimhood *and* political subjectivity, the recognition of the impact of the violence not just on narrowly defined victims, but on broader society, in attending to the construction of femininity *and* masculinity in society as a result of the violence, and in proposing reparations as a means to address the material and political consequences of the violence – is exemplary in its attention to women and gender and the affirmation of women's multiple political subjectivities.[59] The work of the GMH can clearly be contrasted with the manifold gendered shortcomings of the Chilean TRC two decades earlier, to demonstrate the enormous expertise gathered in the interim. The major caveat to this positive assessment, however, is that the Report does not directly link to the distribution of justice or reparations in the justice and peace process. And so the recognition of women's multiple and diverse forms of political subjectivity has emerged in the case in which official truth processes are most clearly de-linked from formal criminal accountability and reparations, and without any clear link to international law. Where truth could be regarded as unthreatening in terms of legal or material

59 This has been acknowledged in local feminist response to the Report. See, for example, Corporación Humanas (2008a).

implications, the process and output were most clearly feminist. There is an ominous familiarity about this formula: to quote Elizabeth Vallance 'where power is [in terms of binding legal obligations, and legal and material implications], women are not' (Vallance 1982: 218–19). This conclusion draws a serious question mark under the ostensible feminist gains delivered by the GMH truth process.

Part IV

Reparations

Chapter 7

Women's movements claiming repair

INTRODUCTION

Reparations have arguably been the area of most creative feminist scholarly analysis in transitional justice (see especially Rubio-Marin 2009), but, as this chapter demonstrates, have been slower in engaging women's movements in the case studies. Reparations constitute material and symbolic redress to victims of human rights violations.[1] In the aftermath of widespread political violence, reparations are typically delivered through judicial or administrative programmes. This chapter examines feminist political engagement with the issue of reparations and focuses in particular on women's movement demands for reparations in Chile, Northern Ireland and Colombia. The chapter advances three claims: first, that scholarly optimism about the transformative potential of reparations for women might usefully be contextualised within the political and economic cost to states that accompany such reparations; second, women's movements seeking to build collaborative relationships with the new or reformed state may not wish to prioritise oppositional issues such as reparations for past harms (in particular in light of the documented gap between women's and human rights organisations and the failure of the latter to document harms against women during periods of political violence); third, for all of these reasons, women's movements may instead opt to focus on private harms in their engagement with the transitional state.

WHY REPARATIONS MATTER FOR WOMEN, AND FOR WOMEN'S MOVEMENTS

The prominence of reparations within feminist analysis can be attributed to several factors: first, the uniqueness of reparations in transitional justice, as 'a

1 See generally United Nations Basic Principles and Guidelines on the Right to a Remedy and Reparation for Victims of Gross Violations of International Human Rights Law and Serious Violations of International Humanitarian Law, GA Res. 60/147 UN Doc. A/RES/60/147 (21 March 2006) [hereinafter Basic Principles and Guidelines on Reparations].

measure on behalf of victims, rather than in response to perpetrators' (de Greiff 2006: 2). The preponderance of women as secondary victims, in particular as living survivors of those killed and disappeared by political violence, casts women disproportionately as potential and actual beneficiaries of reparations to victims of political violence (Rubio-Marin 2009). Moreover, the intended comprehensiveness of reparations, as both individual and collective, moral and material, monetary and non-monetary, as judicial and administrative, offers particular promise to a feminist agenda in transitional justice that advances a more nuanced and comprehensive understanding of the public and private harms that result from political violence. The discussion in Chapter 4 of non-legal dividends to women's movements of retributive justice indicated the importance of looking beyond the relatively narrow gains of retributive legal processes to a broader understanding of feminist gains. Reparations embrace just such a broader understanding of benefits and gains, as material and symbolic, collective and individual. In addition, and importantly, the right to reparations is affirmed in multiple intersecting and overlapping instruments of international law that relate to women and victims of political violence (Evans 2012). The right to reparations is said to be 'attaining customary status in international law' (Evans 2012: 13). Moreover, it is clear that the right to reparations consists of obligations that must be discharged, first and foremost, by the state.[2] In this regard, reparations provide not just a comprehensive framework of entitlements through which women's movements in transitional states can frame their demands and advance their political claims; reparations also provide a clear institutional target for advocacy and influence, namely the state. Importantly, reparations affirm women as rights-holders, and not as merely the beneficiaries of voluntary welfarist measures of the state. Finally, reparations bear an important relationship to the truth aspect of transitional justice already explored. Truth commissions often make recommendations regarding reparations.[3] Reparations programmes often rely on the list of victims in official truth initiatives in order to identify beneficiaries for reparations. The harms identified and investigated in truth processes will typically underpin the categorisation of harms entitled to reparations. The feminist learning curve in the gendered significance of official truth processes has provided some ready insights into how to engage reparations and why this should be done.

Highly developed feminist theoretical scholarship of reparations gives great emphasis to the importance of reparations as acts in the creation of the new or renewed democratic unit. Because reparations are delivered by the newly (re) formed state, the delivery of reparations establishes and validates a bond between the political community and the individual victims (de Greiff 2007: 154). Moreover, the fair and transparent design and delivery of such reparations can (re)establish civic trust and victims' confidence in the state (de Greiff 2007: 156). Importantly,

2 See Basic Principles and Guidelines on Reparations, Article 16.

3 See Hayner (2002: 170–82) on the relationship of truth commissions to reparations.

reparations are also an expression of solidarity amongst citizens, as non-victims will contribute through taxation to the delivery of reparations to victims (de Greiff 2007: 158). In this regard, reparations have both a vertical state–citizen and horizontal citizen–citizen element (de Greiff 2007: 160). By valuing women equally within reparations design and delivery – more specifically, by avoiding overtly discriminatory measures (Rubio-Marin 2006a), by ensuring that patriarchal values do not 'leak into' reparations delivery (Rubio-Marin 2009: 66; O'Rourke 2011), by optimising the 'modest' potential of reparations to subvert prevailing discriminatory norms (Rubio-Marin 2009: 66) and by forging a progressive relationship to other aspects of transitional justice (Rubio-Marin 2009: 66) – the delivery of reparations can provide an effective opportunity to establish women as equal citizens within the (re)new(ed) democratic unit.

This chapter argues that the reasons for sustained feminist engagement with reparations are sound, but need to be considered in light of the overwhelming reluctance of the transitional state to accept liability for past harms, which is inherent to the state awarding reparations to victims of political violence. As Naomi Roht-Arriaza asks:

> Why the discrepancy between word and deed? If reparations are so universally accepted as part of a state's human rights obligations, why have so few states emerging from periods of conflict or mass atrocity put viable programs into place?'
>
> (Roht-Arriaza 2004: 158)

While the state may be the principal bearer of legal obligations in respect of reparations, the transitional state is also, at the same time, seeking to re-establish its legitimacy and to distance itself from past state wrongs. Hence, such overt admissions of liability as are evident in the delivery of reparations are highly costly, economically as well as politically. Reparations to indigenous groups in Australia are a popular example of this tension, in which political claims for reparations encounter conceptual difficulty in disagreements about who (if anyone) now counts as a perpetrator, including the problem of explaining why existing citizens of a political society owe reparation for injustices that they had no role in perpetrating (Thompson 2007: 71).

As the case studies reveal, the transitional state is typically highly motivated by the need to obscure its liability for past harms. This presents particular tensions for women's movements seeking to advance their claims through official reparations processes, while also seeking to establish constructive relationships with newly (re) formed state institutions. To quote Sonia Alvarez in her pathbreaking study of women's movements and the democratisation transition in Brazil: 'The State, heretofore widely perceived to be women's worst enemy, is suddenly portraying itself as "women's best friend" ' (Alvarez 1990: 12). In terms of the web of gender-based harms against women, women's movements may be seeking repair to both public and private harms against women, but find greater traction with the state on the issue of private harms that are not overtly connected to fraught political questions of state liability for past wrongs.

CHILE

This section observes that reparations have never been a key mobilising issue in feminist organising in Chile. It is difficult to locate evidence of the issue of reparations ever having been central to feminist concerns throughout the period of dealing with the past in Chile. The belated accountability efforts for the victims of torture and political imprisonment motivated more co-ordinated interventions than in the past; for example, the issue of reparations was amongst feminist concerns raised in the Chilean state's 2004 Report to the UN Committee Against Torture.[4] Even the contemporary feminist pursuit of prosecutions for sexual violence has not, however, focused concerted feminist attention on the question of reparations. This is significant for our theoretical understanding of reparations, because it suggests that feminist scholarly optimism and energy in this area may underestimate the political obstacles, in terms of a hostile political opportunity structure and difficulties in the mobilisation of resources to delivering on feminist ambitions in reparations. Instead, feminist framing may focus on forward-looking concerns that resonate more comfortably with the transitional state.

Political opportunity structure: the new democratic state looks forward

Reparations are typically identified as the one thing Chile has done well in terms of accountability for dictatorship harms. The Chilean reparations programme is widely regarded as one of the most comprehensive programmes ever to have been implemented by a successor government (Kritz 2009: 14). The broad acceptance of the Report of the Truth and Reconciliation Commission (TRC) marked an auspicious start to the process of reconciliation in post-authoritarian Chile. However, the expectation was that the Commission's report would lead to prosecutions of the responsible state agents. Instead, the 1978 amnesty law cast a long shadow over the courts, as an unreformed judiciary continued to construe the amnesty law as prohibiting even the investigation of the military's human rights violations. The continued broad jurisdiction of the military courts bolstered this impunity.[5] In this context, state efforts to deal with the past shifted to a focus on reparations. As recommended by the TRC Report, the Reparations Corporation

4 As noted in Fundación Instituto de la Mujer *et al.* (2004).

5 See further Amnesty International (2001b).

(Corporación Nacional de Reparación y Reconciliación, CNRR) was established in 1992.[6]

With the shift to reparations, however, high-profile demands for accountability transformed into individualised delivery of psychosocial services, pensions and educational benefits. Moreover, the 'problem' of the past increasingly came to be popularly viewed as resolved, as victims and survivors were provided with material redress – though not accountability – for the harms suffered. As a result, the motherist and human rights groups seeking accountability for the wrongs of the dictatorship grew increasingly marginalised from the political mainstream in post-authoritarian Chile (Wilde 1999). The groups were viewed as intransigent, and as disruptive to the Chilean transition (e.g. Jaquette 1994). They were expected to 'move on', and as the question of the past receded further from the public sphere, accountability for the past moved to the private concerns of a relatively small number of victims and survivors.

Resource mobilisation

Studies of the fragmentation of the Chilean women's movement during the transition reveal the strain that changing state formations put on formerly unified social movements (Waylen 1996). Feminists had to decide whether to take power within the state, for example as 'double militants' within political parties and in new state institutions, or to pursue an autonomous feminist path (Baldez 2002: 180–83). In contrast to the diminishing prominence of past-focused accountability and human rights groups, the Chilean 'double militants' found themselves in a new and closer relationship with the democratic state. The onset of the new democratic state coincided with substantial targeted – and effective – feminist energy around the issue of domestic violence. The concentration of feminist energies on private harms was illustrated in the prominence of domestic violence within demands made by feminists of the first democratic government, in particular in terms of demands for legal reform.[7] Moreover, these feminist demands secured a great deal of traction with the new democratic state. A National Service for Women (Servicio Nacional de la Mujer, SERNAM) contained and worked with prominent women from the Chilean women's movement (Waylen 1996), and quickly adopted intra-family violence as its priority area of concern (Larrain Heiremans 1994; Servicio

6 Ley No.19.123, Diario Oficial, 8 February 1992.

7 See further Fundación Instituto de la Mujer and Colectivo 'Mujeres de Chile y Canada' (1991). At the time of the transition, the laws that applied to domestic violence were contained in the Criminal Code that had been in effect since 1873. Under the Code, domestic violence was identified as a crime of 'injury' (*lesiones*), and no bespoke remedies existed in civil law. Therefore, the only possible judicial 'satisfaction' for reported incidents of domestic violence was the incarceration of the offender. Consequently, there was a very high incidence of women withdrawing complaints (Gonzales 1992).

Nacional de la Mujer 1995: 18; Waylen 1996). Evidencing this new collaborative relationship of the Chilean women's movement and the state, in 1994 a legislative initiative led by SERNAM and the civil society Chilean Network against Domestic and Sexual Violence (Red Chilena Contra la Violencia Domestica y Sexual) resulted in the first dedicated Chilean Domestic Violence Law.[8]

In contrast with this collaborative relationship between the women's movement and the democratic state, the distance between the Chilean women's movement and human rights groups persisted. For example, the continued difficulty of articulating domestic violence as a human rights issue was noted in a 1996 publication by the Chilean Network against Domestic and Sexual Violence. In an explicit challenge to the prevailing definition of peace in the country, the Network entitled the publication *Challenges for Peace: a Country without Injured Women* (Red Chilena Contra la Violencia Domestica y Sexual 1996). When discussing challenges for the coming years, the need to challenge the locally prevailing understanding of human rights in Chile featured prominently. The important developments in the recognition of women as rights-holders at the international level was contrasted with the common understanding of human rights in Chile, as only concerning the human rights violations of the past.

These divergent fates of the motherist human rights groups and the women's movement within the new democratic regime reflected and perpetuated the earlier divide between these movements during the period of the dictatorship, in which the women's movement agitated on issues of direct concern to women, while motherist groups dominated the past-focused human rights agenda.

Changes made to the Programme of Reparations and Comprehensive Health Care for Victims of Human Rights Violations (Programa de Reparación y Atención Integral de Salud para las Víctimas de Violaciones de Derechos Humanos, PRAIS) in 1994 usefully illustrate both the new state's receptiveness to the domestic violence demands of the women's movement and its continuing attempt to 'move on' from past-focused questions of accountability. This programme was established in 1991 to provide comprehensive physical and psychological health care for those most severely affected by human rights violations. With the passage of the domestic violence law in 1994, a subprogramme on intrafamily violence was added to PRAIS by ministerial decision. For many, the introduction of attention to domestic violence affected the symbolic character of the programme within the health service as a programme of reparation to victims

8 Ley No.19.325 (Ley de Violencia Intrafamiliar), Diario Oficial, 27 August 1994. Domestic violence was made punishable by law, specifically applying to 'misdemeanour' offences, between relatives or persons cohabiting. Offences under the law were within the purview of civil, not criminal, courts. Consequently, the police could not detain suspected aggressors without a judicial order. Cases of grave physical or sexual violence, because they were considered crimes, were for the attention of the Penal Court.

of the military regime.[9] In the perception of PRAIS employees and beneficiaries, the programme lost the definition or distinction of its function as a reparations programme for the victims of human rights violations and was thus deemed limited and diluted, as evidenced in their public statement that:

> in 1994, the inclusion of the intrafamily violence programme diminished the capacity of the [PRAIS] teams. These events reflect the variation in political will regarding the programme, which has resulted in the programme losing its identity.
>
> (Quoted in Lira and Loveman 2005: 390)

The broad perception of staff and beneficiaries of PRAIS was that the inclusion of domestic violence victims was an overt attempt by the state to de-politicise the programme, through the inclusion of 'private' violence within the family, which was perceived to be 'apolitical'. These dynamics left little prospect of an alliance around reparations between human rights groups and the women's movement.

Framing

While 'framing' refers to the resonance of women's movement demands with the dominant understanding of the transition, in the case of reparations in Chile we can identify a dialectical relationship between the state's framing of gender within reparations programming and the framing of feminist demands upon reparations: in the first instance, the issue of reparations was not prioritised by the Chilean women's movement. Rather, the focus on domestic violence – private harms for which the state cannot be held directly culpable – resonated with the state's framing of the new democratic state. In time, with the shift from truth to reparations in the state's approach to the past, where benefits were awarded to family members on the basis of their secondary victimhood, increasing awareness of women's secondary victimhood is apparent amongst the motherist human rights groups. Finally, the minimal reparations made to women recognised as primary victims under the Torture Commission after 2005 prompted a more concertedly feminist response to reparations by the women's movement. An examination of the framing adopted by motherist and feminist organisations in reparations activity in Chile reveals that feminist organisations have never given prominence to reparations demands.

The shift in focus from truth to reparations reflected a discernible shift in interventions by motherist groups into official efforts to deal with the past. The shift to reparations, in which benefits were awarded to (largely female) surviving family members of victims, coincided with the emergence of greater consciousness

9 For the dynamics of this debate, see Lira and Loveman (2005: 380).

amongst the affected women of their experiences of secondary harms. This dynamic can be traced through the mid-nineties, in which women relatives of the disappeared and tortured sought recognition for their contribution and suffering as 'indirect' victims of the dictatorship, primarily in their maternal roles in sustaining their communities and in suffering the loss of their children 'disappeared' by the regime. Significantly, interventions by women into the reparations process did not just focus on their experience as relatives of the disappeared. There has also been an attempt to seek recognition for the sustaining role that women played in the community through the period of repression. For example, in 1995 the women's programme of the Chilean Commission on Human Rights published a report entitled *Women, Memory, and Human Rights.*[10] This report brought together women from a range of relatives' organisations to reflect on women and the dictatorship. The issues raised in this report split evenly between women's experience in justice demands and the burden borne by women during the dictatorship in meeting the subsistence demands of the community. Notably, the women writing regarded both aspects of this work as acting in the defence of human rights: 'The loss of democracy in our country did not just give rise to pain and death, but also to an increase in unemployment, hunger and misery.'[11]

The next and final stage in this reparations activity was the coming together of feminist consciousness and motherist group priorities in reparations, with the statement of ex-political prisoners upon the announcement of the reparations plans for the Torture Commission. In particular, the state's decision to award only half-reparations to those primary victims under the Torture Commission who had already benefitted under the earlier reparations programme to secondary victims prompted acute feminist criticism. In the Statement of Women Ex-Prisoners, the women asserted: 'We are not simply "mothers of" or "sisters of", we experienced the harms in our own right.'[12] Over time, therefore, reparations provided a site for the tentative bridging of feminist and human rights concerns in transitional justice.

NORTHERN IRELAND

Political opportunity structure

In Northern Ireland, the state's determined resistance to acknowledge the political violence that prevailed in the jurisdiction for three decades as a 'conflict' under

10 The non-governmental organisation was established in 1980. See further Comisión Chilena de Derechos Humanos (Programa de Mujeres) (1995: 64).

11 'La perdida de la democracia en nuestra patria, no solo repercutio en dolor y muerte, sino aumento la cesantia, el hambre y la miseria' (Comisión Chilena de Derechos Humanos (Programa de Mujeres) 1995: 36), contribution of Sola Sierra, Presidente de la Agrupación.

12 See Agrupación de Mujeres ex Prisoneras Políticas Sobrevivientes de la Red de Centros de Tortura Clandestinos del Régimen Militar de Pinochet (2004: 3).

international law meant that reparations to victims during the conflict were delivered through criminal injuries compensation. The state has made no official commitment in respect of 'reparations' per se. Instead, amendments to the Criminal Injuries Compensation Scheme, and the establishment of dedicated statutory bodies to provide services and monetary assistance to victims and survivors of the Troubles, have formed the substance of an ad hoc approach to reparations in Northern Ireland.

The subsidence in the conflict in the mid 1990s resulted in greater attention and resources of statutory bodies being directed to the network of victims' organisations that now exist in Northern Ireland. Further, material and symbolic reparations to victims emerged as a more prominent issue in the latter stages of the peace negotiations. In 1997 the Northern Ireland Secretary of State appointed the civil servant Kenneth Bloomfield:

> to lead the Commission and to examine the feasibility of providing greater recognition for those who have become victims in the last thirty years as a consequence of events in Northern Ireland.
>
> (Bloomfield 1998: 8)

Further to the Bloomfield Report, the Review of Criminal Injuries Compensation, also led by Kenneth Bloomfield, was established in October 1998 to examine the fitness for purpose of the existing arrangements. On foot of the review, a criminal injury compensation scheme similar to that of England and Wales was introduced in Northern Ireland.[13]

So, while there has been substantial state activity to redress private material concerns of victims, there has been little overt state activity on reparations. Just as the Chilean case revealed a dialectical relationship between state activity on reparations and the framing of women's movement reparations demands, the absence of a clear programme of state activity on reparations in Northern Ireland has worked to limit the terrain for engagement on the issue by women's organisations and to diminish the importance afforded to it by those organisations.

Resource mobilisation

During the conflict, exclusionary problems for women arising from the criminal injury compensation scheme featured (though surprisingly rarely)[14] in feminist mobilisation against violence. Overall, this suggests a relative lack of interest or expertise in this area, or a decision to not identify the question of reparations as an important area of feminist concern.

13 Criminal Compensation (Northern Ireland) Order 2002.

14 See, for example, Women's Law and Research Group and Rape Crisis Centre (1985), which raises the issue of 'rape and compensation'.

In the post-conflict context, the potential for reparations to act vertically (state–victim) and horizontally (citizen–victim) to affirm the citizenship and democratic equality of all women was mooted in the theoretical elaboration at the outset of the chapter. The gendered division of labour in dealing with the past in Northern Ireland takes on particular resonance in the discussion of feminist strategies in reparations. Through their involvement in the women's and victims sector, women deal with the (private) material consequences of the conflict (such as trauma, poverty, lack of education and training) deemed to be 'apolitical'; men deal with the 'political' consequences of the conflict (prosecutions, public enquiries, police investigations) (Potter 2004: 57). Women-led victims' organisations do not self-identify as women's organisations, and are structurally largely separate from women's sector networks in the jurisdiction (Potter 2004: 48). The consequence of the gendered division of labour in dealing with the past, and the absence of alliances between women's sector and victims' organisations, has been to undercut the necessary mobilisation of resources to articulate a distinctively *feminist* intervention into reparations demands.

Framing

Ultimately, the passage of time between the Belfast Agreement and the establishment of the Consultative Group on the Past was to prove crucial in initiating a conversation on reparations among women in Northern Ireland. The outcome of this conversation was, however, to continue a deliberately non-political and instrumentalist approach to dealing with the past.

More recent framing efforts in women's sector interventions into the past have linked the question of reparations to the contemporary funding needs of the women's sector.[15] So, for example, a comprehensive civil society study of the impact of the conflict on women identifies 'priority issues' for concern by the state as mental and general health provision, safer streets and communities, with an emphasis on improved education funding and access to education, community regeneration and job creation.[16] Adequate mental health services (Coiste na n-Iarchimí and Relatives for Justice 2010) are prominent in reparations demands. 'The need for specialist legal advice and services should be added to the need for services, funding, healthcare and compensation' (Women's Support Network 2009: 11). This framing, with its emphasis on the private material consequences of the conflict, resonates with the dominant state approach, but does little to advance more transformative feminist objectives in reparations, in terms of affirming and advancing women's political equality.

15 See Women's Resource and Development Agency and Women's Centres Regional Partnership (2008); Women's Support Network (2009).

16 See Women's Resource and Development Agency and Women's Centres Regional Partnership (2008: 58–60).

COLOMBIA

Political opportunity structure

Colombia constitutes a highly dynamic political context for the pursuit of reparations. Whereas the justice and peace process, and the demobilisation of paramilitaries, is embedded within a systematic process of the state distancing itself from paramilitaries, this has become particularly pronounced in political and legal debates about the responsibility for reparations. Throughout the justice and peace process – and before – the Colombian state has resisted liability for conflict violence. Indeed, the Colombian approach to reparations has been, in the words of Gustavo Gallon, to cast the 'state as victim' by shifting the responsibility to make reparation to paramilitary and guerrilla groups (Gallon 2007: 353). The election in 2010 of a new president, Manuel Santos, has led to new political dynamics in reparations, with the state agreeing to reparations for a much larger victim group and much larger distribution of benefits, through the 2011 Victims Law.[17] The peculiarly Colombian approach to the question of reparations and state liability has been to cast the Victims Law, and this novel state commitment to reparations to conflict victims, in the language of state 'solidarity' with victims,[18] and not state responsibility for or to victims.

Resource mobilisation

The internal tensions within the Colombian women's movement noted throughout the study also exist in relation to reparations. Notable also are the continued alliances, unique in terms of the cases under study in this book, between human rights and women's movements. The Women and Armed Conflict (Mujer y Conflicto Armado) Working Group, which continues to report annually on conflict patterns and their impact on women, has made specific demands around reparations (Mesa de Trabajo Mujer y Conflicto Armado 2012), most notably in recent times through its participation in the broad-based monitoring group for the decisions of the Constitutional Court and rights of women displaced by the conflict, Auto 092.[19] Within this tapestry of civil society organisations, established

17 Ley 1448 de 2011.

18 Ley 1448 de 2011, Article 14.

19 Constitutional Court, Auto 092 of 2008. See Working Group to Monitor Compliance with Auto 092 of 2008 of the Colombian Constitutional Court (2011). The Working Group consists of The Center for the Study of Law, Justice and Society, the Colombian Commission of Jurists, the Consultancy for Human Rights and Displacement, the Foundation 'Casa de la Mujer', the Foundation 'Sisma Mujer', the José Alvear Restrepo Lawyers' Collective, the League of Displaced Women, the Movement 'Ruta Pacífica de las Mujeres', the Observatory for Gender, Democracy, and Human Rights, the Partnership 'Colombian Women's Initiative for Peace' and the Working Group on Women and Armed Conflict. Members of the Working Group monitor compliance with

human rights NGOs, such as the Colombian Commission of Jurists, participate in all of these alliances of women's organisations. Corporación Humanas and Sisma Mujer belong to the Women and Armed Conflict Working Group, along with the more oppositional groups, such as La Ruta Pacifica. In this reporting work, they can find common ground in their articulation of demands on the reparations process (Working Group to Monitor Compliance with Auto 092 of 2008 of the Colombian Constitutional Court 2011).

In addition to concerns raised by legally engaged feminist NGOs, La Ruta Pacifica, with other like-minded women's organisations, has attempted to articulate transformative components of a national administrative programme for reparations, premised on the principle that 'reparation should include restitution of the rights historically denied [to women] and which recognise us as citizens with full rights' (La Ruta Pacifica *et al.* 2009). For example, the League of Displaced Women (Liga de Mujeres Desplazadas) has proposed abortion services as a form of reparation where pregnancy has resulted from sexual violence committed in the course of the armed conflict (Mesa de Trabajo Mujer y Conflicto Armado 2005: 107).

Framing

In their interventions into the contemporary truth and reparations process in Colombia, both feminist technical and transformative articulations of harm have been far removed from those set out in the Justice and Peace Law. Indeed, the technical and transformative feminist visions for the reparations process have been much closer to each other than to the legal operation of the justice and peace process. For example, the truth-telling and historical memory work being pursued by Vamos Mujer in the 'Scrutinize the Skin' campaign also has the interim purpose of preserving women's accounts of the conflict until a future process that they find legitimate emerges to deliver reparations in Colombia.[20] The practical interim function of their work suggests that the distance between technical and transformative feminist engagement with the contemporary process may not, in practice, be so great. Importantly, the existence of both types of feminist interventions into the contemporary truth and reparations process ensures that, in a clearly flawed process, feminist input is present within *and* against the process, in technical *and* transformative accounts of how the process can be improved.

Of particular interest in this section is the way in which Colombian feminist organisations articulate the relationship between public and private harms in their

the order remitted to the Office of the Prosecutor General of the Nation and the invitation to the Office of the Inspector General of the Nation as regards the confidential annex to Auto (Order) 092 of 2008 of the Colombian Constitutional Court. It is supported by the Office in Colombia of the United Nations High Commissioner for Human Rights and UN Women.

20 Olga Lucía Ramírez, Vamos Mujer, Medellín, 23 July 2009, personal communication.

advocacy. The introductory chapters to the book revealed the established preoccupation of international human rights law and transitional justice with public political harms and how this preoccupation worked to exclude the 'private' harms routinely experienced by women. Feminist interventions therefore focused on expanding state liability for private harms. How we understand private harms has, of necessity, implications for how we understand public harms and state liability for those harms. Thus, this section argues, the state's receptiveness to campaigns for an improved state response to private harms may problematically be linked to state efforts to eschew accountability for public harms.

The framing of feminist interventions into the reparations debate in Colombia has to be understood within the broader tapestry of the ongoing justice and peace process. The emphasis on linking public *and* private harms in Colombian feminist interventions into reparations should be contextualised within the following dynamics: first, the transitional justice process has made available international funding to women's organisations to work on conflict-related issues;[21] second, the urgency of the conflict situation, in particular the massive number of internally displaced persons, has made this the priority issue for feminist organisations.[22]

The prominence of sexual violence against women across feminist advocacy is striking.[23] For example, reports of the Women and Armed Conflict Working Group have been, on occasion, entirely dedicated to reporting on incidences of sexual violence (Mujer y Conflicto Armado 2008). However, this Report documented violence against women both within the armed conflict, and not ostensibly related to the armed conflict. The decision was justified on the basis of a feminist articulation of gender-based violence as operating along a 'continuum' from public to private incidences of violence (Mujer y Conflicto Armado 2008: 6). The language of a 'continuum of violence' is recurrent in Colombian feminist

21 This was a recurring issue in interviews. It is amply demonstrated by the remarkable publication of a network of women's organisations making very specific recommendations on the different aspects of the justice and peace process, funded by the United States Agency for International Development (USAID) (Grupo de Trabajo Mujer y Género, 2008). USAID has taken an active role in funding several implementation-focused initiatives of the Justice and Peace Law, such as an Inter-Institutional Justice and Peace Information System, which will serve as the clearing house of information for the eight government agencies working on the justice and peace process in Colombia. See http://www.iom.int/cms/en/sites/iom/home/news-and-views/press-briefing-notes/pbn-2012/pbn-listing/iom-usaid-and-colombian-government-laun.html (last accessed 29 March 2013).

22 'The conflict situation is so urgent.' Alexandra Quintero, SISMA Mujer, Bogotá, personal communication, 10 December 2008.

23 See, for example, the prominence of sexual violence in other reports of Colombian feminist organisations: Corporación SISMA Mujer (2008); Corporación Humanas (2008b); Mesa de Trabajo Mujer y Conflicto Armado (2005); Mujer y Conflicto Armado (2005, 2008).

advocacy.[24] Within this continuum, the focus on sexual violence is regarded as a way to bridge public and private incidences of gender-based violence. As Corporación Humanas staff member Cecilia Barraza acknowledges: 'One theme which for me is a complete link [between conflict and non-conflict-related gender issues] is sexual violence.'[25]

There is evidence, therefore, that many feminist issues in Colombia are being refracted through the conflict lens. However, this trend in Colombian feminist advocacy, of using gender issues in conflict and transition as the vehicle through which to articulate a broader feminist agenda, is not without costs. For example, the focus on the conflict and its harms to women risks the neglect of other feminist issues:

> Of course. This is the eternal concern of feminists in this country. We are very worried about this. We are very worried because the conflict makes invisible other important issues.[26]

It is a complex example, but the 2006 strategic litigation brought by local and international feminist organisations to liberalise access to abortion in Colombia is illustrative of some of these tensions, and of the potential risks of refracting every feminist issue through a conflict lens. The abortion litigation was brought to the Colombian Constitutional Court because of perceived liberal appointments to the bench and because of the deference to the state's international human rights commitments enshrined within the Colombian Constitution.[27] It was hoped that the court would deliver a liberal judgment, articulating access to abortion as an implicit right of the prohibition on non-discrimination under Colombia's international human rights commitments. Progressive Colombian interpretation of its equality commitments under international human rights obligations could then underpin more progressive interpretation of access to abortion under international human rights law more generally (Jaramillo Sierra and Sierra 2008: 44–62). The application was designed to be grounded in an equality argument – that the adverse impact of the ban on women's lives was in violation of the prohibition on discrimination – in order to advance claims for women's equality more broadly beyond the specific question of abortion. As a secondary aim, the applicants hoped that, by establishing that the prohibition on abortion was leading to clandestine abortions and these were key causes in Colombia's high level of maternal mortality,

24 For example Cecilia Barraza, Corporación Humanas, Bogotá, personal communication, 9 December 2008. Also Claudia Gomez, SISMA Mujer, Bogotá, personal communication, 10 December 2008.

25 Cecilia Barraza, Corporación Humanas, Bogotá, personal communication, 9 December 2008.

26 Cecilia Barraza, Corporación Humanas, Bogotá, personal communication, 9 December 2008.

27 The decision was the result of the challenge brought by Women's Link Worldwide. See Jaramillo Sierra and Sierra (2008: 47).

this could form the basis of legal challenge to the ban per se, and not just to the quite restrictive circumstances of threat to life or health of the pregnant women, or rape or fatal foetal abnormality, in which an abortion could be sought. The applicants argued that the right to life imposed a positive obligation on the state to protect the lives of women, and that the high levels of maternal mortality as a consequence of the abortion ban meant that the Colombian state was in breach of this duty.[28]

The Court itself gave no real consideration to the general question of high levels of maternal mortality resulting from the general prohibition. Instead, the Court noted that state agencies supporting the Women's Link claim did so because of the particular toll that the health consequences of botched abortions were taking on displaced women.[29] Ultimately, the specific circumstances of the Colombian conflict were to feature prominently in the Court's decision.[30] The application and the Court's decision included prominent and detailed discussion of the prevalence of sexual violence in the Colombian armed conflict. The consequent impact on high numbers of unwanted pregnancies resulting from rape was central to the Court's reasoning.[31] By grounding the application, the amicus briefs and the contributions of state agencies to the judgment in the specific circumstances of the conflict, the judgment was particularised to the Colombian situation. This was contrary to Women's Link's broader international objectives with the litigation (Jaramillo Sierra and Sierra 2008: 44–62). Further, critically, there was a strong sense in the judgment that the conflict narrative – the specifics of how women experienced the conflict, sexual violence and unwanted pregnancy – moved the reasoning further and further from an assertive endorsement of women's right to equality, and made it more an exceptional issue of women's reproductive rights in conflict situations. Therefore, rather than consolidating a progressive trajectory in the interpretation of regional Latin American human rights obligations in respect of abortion, the exceptionality of the Colombian case due to the internal conflict is emphasised. Isabel Cristina Jaramillo, one of the architects of the litigation strategy, although not a member of the litigation team, explains that when the litigation team sought evidence of the negative and discriminatory impact of the abortion ban on women's lives in Colombia, 'the data was all the recent work – it was all about the war'.[32] The resonance here with the relationship

28 Compare La Demanda del 14 de abril de 2005 with La Demanda del 12 de diciembre de 2005, available at http://www.womenslinkworldwide.org/ (last accessed 8 March 2013).

29 Corte Constitucional de Colombia, *Sentencia No. C–355/06* (2006), 4.1.5.

30 Corte Constitucional de Colombia, *Sentencia No. C–355/06* (2006). The challenge to Article 123 of the Criminal Code (Ley No. 599 (Código Penal), Diario Oficial, 24 June 2000), which reduced the penalty for abortion in the case of pregnancy resulting from rape, relied entirely on an argument of human dignity – not equality – and drew almost entirely on the conflict situation.

31 See especially Corte Constitucional de Colombia, *Sentencia No. C–355/06* (2006), 4.1.3 Intervención de la Corporación Sisma Mujer.

32 Isabel Cristina Jaramillo Sierra, Universidad de los Andes, personal communication, 2 December 2008.

tracked between issues prioritised in human rights advocacy and the harms prioritised for prosecution in transitional justice is clear. In this Colombian case, however, the gender dynamics are even more complex. The framing of gender inequality in Colombia as a consequence of the violent conflict, rather than the conflict as a consequence of deep structural inequality within Colombia, is ultimately a framing that serves the state, its belligerent response to non-state violence and its prioritisation of ending violence over ending inequality. While delivering critical gains to women, the framing of the abortion litigation reinforces a discourse deeply embedded in the rejection of state liability for conflict harms.

CONCLUSION

Political opportunity structure

The findings from the case studies suggest that feminist theoretical optimism in the area of reparations might usefully be contextualised within a political opportunity structure that is typically hostile to acknowledging state liability for past harms.

Resource mobilisation

This state posture further impacts the effectiveness with which groups seeking reparations for past harms can mobilise resources and secure allies in other areas of civil society. The reticence that typifies feminist political approaches to reparations across the case studies suggests that women's movements are not likely to be at the vanguard of oppositional demands on the state for reparations or in step with past-focused human rights groups in their preoccupation with reparations. Feminist theoretical optimism in the capacity of reparations to recognise and affirm women's political equality might well be revisited in light of this reticence amongst feminist groups and women's movements to prioritise the issue of reparations.

Framing

Ultimately, the difficulty of framing reparations demands within the dominant state narrative of transition and state transformation means that feminist political energies may be better directed to questions of redress for *ongoing* private harms against women than reparations for *past* harms.

Chapter 8

Reparations in transitional justice and harms against women

INTRODUCTION

This chapter examines the strengthening norm in international law of the right to reparation, focusing in particular on the role of international law in defining harms, benefits and beneficiaries. The chapter observes a regulatory gap in terms of reparations for women victims of gender-specific conflict harms. States, such as Northern Ireland, that are positioned to exploit this regulatory gap, frame reparations not as rights of victims, but as voluntary welfarist measures of the state. When the delivery of these voluntary welfarist measures to victims relies principally on the unpaid labour of women, reparations negatively impact women's political equality. As with truth, even progressive norms in international law are vulnerable to regressive domestic gender norms in the local interpretation of international law, which points to an enforcement gap in international law. Moreover, despite evidence in some cases of domestic political commitment to meaningful reparations, the difficulty of the local context, in particular ongoing violence and a weak state, may result in an implementation gap in the transformative elements of reparations.

THE INTERNATIONAL FRAME: INTERNATIONAL LAW, THE RIGHT TO REPARATIONS AND HARMS AGAINST WOMEN

There is increasing consensus about the right to reparations within international law for serious violations of human rights. The origins of reparations in human rights law stem from the adoption of the Universal Declaration of Human Rights in 1948, as Article 8 states that:

> Everyone has the right to an effective remedy by the competent national tribunals for acts violating the fundamental rights granted him by the constitution or the law.

The International Covenant on Civil and Political Rights gives this provision legally binding force in Article 2(3a): 'any person whose rights of freedoms as herein recognised are violated shall have an effective remedy'.[1] Further, the Covenant guarantees reparations for unlawful arrest, detention and conviction.[2] The right to reparation is similarly guaranteed in the Convention Against Torture[3] and the Convention on the Elimination of All Forms of Racial Discrimination.[4] The definitive articulation of the right to reparations under international human rights law is codified in the 2005 Basic Principles and Guidelines on the Right to Remedy for Serious Violations of International Human Rights and Humanitarian Law.[5] The right to reparations is said to include five constituent elements: restitution (restoring the victim to their original situation before the violation, if possible), compensation (monetary compensation for economically assessable harm), rehabilitation (medical and psychological care as well as legal and social services), satisfaction (disclosure of the truth) and guarantees of non-repetition (such as civilian control of the military, judicial independence and necessary legal reform).[6]

It is acknowledged that gender-specific rights and requirements in reparations are under-articulated. Signalling the early gender exclusions of the right to reparations, the CEDAW is unique among the international human rights treaties in not specifically enumerating a right to reparation for victims of rights violations.[7] Claims for reparations for women are instead based within the existing guarantees of reparations, coupled with the prohibition on discrimination, in the Covenant on Civil and Political Rights and the regional instruments.[8] Even with this limited frame of civil and political rights, Yakin Ertürk has noted during her office as UN Special Rapporteur on Violence Against Women, when it comes to the implementation of the due diligence obligation to reparation, 'very little information is available regarding State obligations to provide adequate reparations for acts of violence against women . . . this aspect of due diligence remains grossly

1 International Covenant on Civil and Political Rights, 16 December 1966, 999 UNTS 171, Article 2(3)a [hereinafter ICCPR].
2 ICCPR, Articles 9(5) and 14(6).
3 Convention Against Torture and Other Cruel, Inhuman or Degrading Treatment or Punishment, 10 December 1984, 1465 UNTS 85, Article 14.
4 International Convention on the Elimination of All Forms of Racial Discrimination, 21 December 1965, 660 UNTS 195, Article 6.
5 United Nations Basic Principles and Guidelines on the Right to a Remedy and Reparation for Victims of Gross Violations of International Human Rights Law and Serious Violations of International Humanitarian Law, G.A. Res. 60/147 U.N. Doc. A/RES/60/147 (21 March 2006), [hereinafter Basic Principles and Guidelines], Principle 15.
6 Basic Principles and Guidelines, Principle 21.
7 See United Nations Special Rapporteur on Violence Against Women: Rashida Manjoo (2010: para 22).
8 See United Nations Special Rapporteur on Violence Against Women: Rashida Manjoo (2010: para 23).

underdeveloped.'[9] Consequently, there have been substantial scholarly and policy efforts to elaborate the application of the principles of compensation, restitution, rehabilitation, satisfaction and the guarantee of non-recurrence to the specific reparations needs and experiences of women in the aftermath of political violence.[10] These interventions have operated at three levels: conservative and formalist efforts seek to ensure the absence of overtly discriminatory language and provisions in reparations programming; more optimistic determination to ensure that patriarchal values do not 'leak into' reparations delivery; and more transformative ambitions to optimise the ('modest' (Rubio-Marin 2009: 66)) potential of reparations to subvert prevailing discriminatory norms (Rubio-Marin 2009: 66).

While the Basic Principles are themselves acknowledged to be deficient in their elaboration of reparations that meaningfully redress gender-specific harms experienced by women, there has been some significant elaboration of how the constituent elements of reparations could be adapted to the experience of, for example, violence against women. Importantly, the obligation to provide reparations to women subjected to violence is much more clearly spelled out in the UN General Assembly Declaration on the Elimination of Violence against Women.[11] Most notably, United Nations Special Rapporteur on Violence Against Women, Rashida Manjoo, has elaborated the application of the constituent elements to the experience of violence against women.[12] For example, she has noted that women who are victims of gender violence are often revictimised by their families and communities, so restitution may require measures that target the women's wider communities.[13] Moreover, rehabilitation measures often need to overcome gender biases that are entrenched within national modes of benefit delivery.[14] In parallel, the Nairobi Declaration on Women's and Girls' Right to a Remedy and Reparation is a civil society initiative providing concrete guidance on the reparative needs of women and girls.[15] Moreover, the work of the CEDAW Committee,[16] as well as the Inter-American and European human rights courts, to recognise

9 See United Nations Special Rapporteur on Violence Against Women: Yakin Ertürk (2006: para. 55).

10 See United Nations Special Rapporteur on Violence Against Women: Yakin Ertürk (2006); United Nations Committee on the Elimination of Discrimination against Women (2011).

11 United Nations General Assembly Declaration on the Elimination of Violence against Women, 20 December 1993, A/RES/48/104, Article 4(d).

12 See United Nations Special Rapporteur on Violence Against Women: Rashida Manjoo (2010). This report is dedicated to examining reparations for violence against women.

13 See United Nations Special Rapporteur on Violence Against Women: Rashida Manjoo (2010: para 50).

14 See United Nations Special Rapporteur on Violence Against Women: Rashida Manjoo (2010: para 56).

15 Nairobi Declaration on Women's and Girls' Right to a Remedy and Reparation (2007).

16 United Nations Committee on the Elimination of Discrimination Against Women, General Recommendation No. 19, 1992, A/47/38.

violence against women as a violation of their underpinning treaties, has led incrementally to a gender-specific body of law underpinning the right of women to reparations for gender-specific human rights violations.[17] Particularly significant in this elaboration of gender-inclusive reparations has been the recognition and redress of reproductive harms 'that take place through practices such as forced pregnancy, abortion, or sterilisation and includes physical or psychological violence that interferes with men's or women's biological ability to reproduce or effectively parent' (Duggan and Jacobson 2009: 125).

All normative and legal instruments in this area recognise that '[t]he quantitative and qualitative differences between individual and gross and systematic violations might affect the scope and nature of remedies that can and should be afforded'.[18] In such contexts, remedies may have to be 'adjusted to achieve goals other than that of compensating each individual victim in proportion to harm, including prioritising the recognition of victims and promoting interpersonal trust and trust in the institutions of the new State order'.[19] Administrative reparations programmes are a popular mechanism to this end. Typically, they focus on the most serious violations and they do not align to all five of the constituent elements of reparations. Rather, they are structured around the delivery of material and symbolic benefits to individual and collective beneficiaries.[20]

More specifically, reparations is an area of identified under-regulation in international law in terms of gender and gross and systematic human rights violations. This is acknowledged in, for example, the 2011 Concept Note of the CEDAW Committee on a General Recommendation for the Rights of Women in Conflict and Post-Conflict Situations (UN Committee on the Elimination of Discrimination against Women 2011: 18–19). This lacuna has been ameliorated by normative standards such as United Nations Security Council Resolution 1325 (2000) and its successor resolutions, in particular United Nations Security Council Resolution 1820 (2008), which makes specific provision around reparations for conflict-related sexual violence.[21] Nevertheless, gaps and oversights persist. There are grounds for feminist unease at some of the abiding core tenets of the right to reparations, in terms of the material scope of the right. Questions remain concerning what harms activate the right to reparations and to what extent harms against women fall within this scope; the treatment of collection harms: to what extent does the right to reparation recognise collective harms against women and

17 For the most comprehensive and up-to-date account of this right, see United Nations Special Rapporteur on Violence Against Women: Rashida Manjoo (2010).

18 See United Nations Special Rapporteur on Violence Against Women: Rashida Manjoo (2010: para 18).

19 See United Nations Special Rapporteur on Violence Against Women: Rashida Manjoo (2010: para 18).

20 De Greiff (2007) provides a neat summary of these dynamics. De Greiff (2006) provides a comprehensive analysis of state practice in this area.

21 United Nations Security Council resolution 1820 (2008), 19 June 2008, S/RES/1820.

redress the structural gender inequalities that made women vulnerable to these harms; and the political impact of reparations: to what extent do reparations recognise women as rights-holders and affirm women's political equality.

CHILE: EXPLOITING AN ENFORCEMENT GAP IN INTERNATIONAL LAW

Introducing a recent study of gender and administrative reparations programmes, Ruth Rubio-Marin explains the decision not to include analysis of Chile, Brazil or Argentina on the grounds that 'all of these had the great disadvantage that, at the time of their initial conception, gender was not even part of the conversation' (Rubio-Marin 2006a: 27). Similarly, international law in the general area of reparations was substantially under-developed. The Declaration on the Elimination of Violence against Women, which affirmed the right to reparations for victims of violence against women,[22] had not yet been adopted by the UN General Assembly. Moreover, state practice in reparations programming at this time was limited and organised around 'the traditional catalogue of civil and political rights' (de Greiff 2006: 7).

While there may have been little overt discussion of women in the design and execution of the Chilean reparations programme, it nevertheless carried important gender implications. As recommended by the Truth and Reconciliation Commission Report, the Reparations Corporation (Corporación Nacional de Reparación y Reconciliación) was established in 1992. The Reparations Corporation made a Final Report in 1996 (Corporación Nacional de Reparación y Reconciliación 1996) and was subsequently disbanded. Its task was taken up by the Programme for Continuity of Law 19.123 (Programa de Continuidad de la Ley 19.123), now the Human Rights Program of the Ministry of the Interior (Lira 2006a: 6). Finally, the later Torture Commission led to a further administrative reparations programme in Chile (Lira 2006a: 18). Each phase of reparations in Chile therefore occurred within a different international frame, in terms of the level of recognition and redress for gender-specific harms to women. As this chapter demonstrates, the local gender values that structured the truth process cut against progressive doctrinal developments in international law.

Doctrinal: defining harms, determining beneficiaries and benefits

The Chilean reparations programme is widely regarded as one of the most comprehensive programmes ever to have been implemented by a successor

22 United Nations General Assembly Declaration on the Elimination of Violence against Women, 20 December 1993, A/RES/48/104.

government (see, for example, Kritz 2009: 14). The decision to include only those disappeared or executed by the dictatorship within the mandate of the Truth and Reconciliation Commission resulted in a heavy gender imbalance towards males being recognised as direct victims of the regime. However, the decision to award reparations to the families of victims meant that beneficiaries were largely surviving female relatives.[23] As a means of acknowledging and compensating for harm caused by the state, the Reparations Corporation established a reparation allowance to be given to family members of the detained–disappeared and of those who had been executed for political reasons. The Reparations Law also provided for medical benefits, including psychological counselling for the families. The health benefits extended beyond the families of those killed and those who disappeared, to cover families in which a member was detained and tortured, as well as returning exiles. Finally, the law provided a subsidy for high school and college education and waived tuition fees at public institutions of higher education for the children of the victims (Lira 2006a).

Nevertheless, consistent with the enduring valorisation of the family, surviving female relatives were obliged to conform to 'conventional' family forms in order to receive these reparations. Mothers of victims who were born outside of marriage were not entitled to pensions awarded under the reparations programme (Casas 2003: 149). The mothers of victims who were born within marriages that were subsequently annulled were similarly excluded (Casas 2003: 149).

The 'leakage of patriarchal values' (Duggan and Abusharaf 2006: 625) into reparations programming was further evidenced in the unexpected prominence in the final report of the Reparations Corporation in dealing with the 'interruption of intrauterine life' (Corporación Nacional de Reparación y Reconciliación 1996: 40–41). It is worthwhile to quote the section at some length:

> The section includes four cases in which pregnancies were aborted as a result of blows and maltreatment, inflicted by agents of the state on pregnant women.
>
> In learning of this situation, the Superior Council formed the conviction that illegitimate violence exercised by state agents against a pregnant woman, producing as a consequence the interruption of the intrauterine life of the foetus carried in the belly, constituted a violation of the right to life of the foetus.
>
> In conformity with the stipulations of Article 19 of the Constitution and Article 4.1 of the Inter-American Convention on Human Rights, which according to Article 5 of the Constitution is part of the Chilean legal order, *the basic right to life of every person begins at the point of conception.* Therefore, the foetus found in the maternal belly already qualifies for this right, and to be

23 Ley No.19.123, Diario Oficial, 8 February 1992.

> deprived of this acquired right, from that moment, is to be a victim of a human rights violation, forming the basis of an obligation to repair the harm to the mother.
>
> (Corporación Nacional de Reparación y Reconciliación 1996: 40–41, emphasis added)

The loss of the pregnancies was no doubt devastating for the women involved. The Corporation's decision to include lost pregnancies involved the recognition of new 'victims' of the regime and new female beneficiaries of the reparations programme. Further, the Corporation's decision could be said to acknowledge and reflect the articulation of harm promoted by feminist and human rights organisations in their consistent invocation of the disappeared pregnant woman as the iconic female victim of the repression (CODEPU 1990, 2002). Nevertheless, there are worrying aspects of the Corporation's reasoning and decision in this aspect of the reparations programme. As already noted, due to the restrictive mandate of the Truth and Reconciliation Commission and the reparations programme, the abuse and violence suffered by these four women on their own bodies, independent of their pregnant condition, is given no recognition in this formulation of the 'interruption of intrauterine life'. These women exist in the reparations programme only as vessels for the 'unborn child',[24] and the harm that these women experienced is only recognised as vicarious through the ending of the pregnancy.

Redressing structural gender inequalities

The Corporation's decision that the ending of the pregnancy constituted a violation of the right to life – of an equivalent standing in the reparations programme as those who were disappeared or executed by the regime – reflected and reinforced a grander Chilean legal narrative of foetal rights that has been experienced punitively by women seeking to exercise reproductive choice in Chile. In a clear distortion of international human rights law,[25] the Corporation based its decision to recognise the equal right to life of the foetus in Article 4.1 of the American Convention on Human Rights, which protects the right to life 'in general, from the moment of conception'.[26] The Corporation ignored the jurisprudence of the Inter-American Commission, which from as early as 1981

24 '*Hijo neonata*' is the language used in the Report when detailing each individual pregnancy in the list of victims appended to the report. See Corporación Nacional de Reparación y Reconciliación (1996: 852–4).

25 For a comprehensive statement of the status of the foetus in international human rights law, see Copelon *et al* (2005).

26 American Convention on Human Rights, 22 November 1969, OASTS No. 36, 1144 UNTS 123, Article 4.1.

had consistently interpreted the Article not to confer an equivalent right to life on the foetus.[27]

This narrative of foetal rights continued into the reparations provision made by the Torture Commission in 2005. The Report of the Torture Commission deals at some length with the definitions of victimhood, and states that a decision was made not to design a reparations programme based on a ranking of types of torture suffered, or length of time spent in detention. Rather, all those determined to be 'victims' would share the same entitlements. The Commission classified children who were detained along with their parents as victims, entitling the children to a half-share of reparations; similarly for those children born in prison (Comisión Nacional sobre Prisión Política y Tortura 2005: 74). As with the Reparations Corporation Report, the issue of 'intrauterine life' features prominently in the Torture Commission Report:

> The Commission also received testimonies from individuals who were in gestation when their mothers were being tortured, as well as individuals who were the product of rape committed while their mothers were in detention, which also constitutes a form of torture. In all of these cases, the mothers gave birth after their release from detention. The Commission is of the conviction that these individuals must also be considered victims. Whoever was in gestation when their mothers suffered torture are included in the same category as children born in prison and of children detained together with their parents [i.e. entitled to half-reparations]. Those who were born as a result of rape are considered direct victims [and therefore entitled to full reparations].
>
> (Comisión Nacional sobre Prisión Política y Tortura 2005: 74–5)

Affirming women's agency

Chapter 7 identified a role for reparations programmes in advancing moral values and establishing the basis of citizenship in post-conflict and post-authoritarian societies. The highly partial recognition of reproductive harm to women throughout reparations programming suggests considerable limitations on the basis of women's citizenship in post-authoritarian Chile. The award of reparations to individuals who were in gestation when their mothers were subjected to torture constitutes the only occasion on which legal creativity was used to actually *expand* the number of women to benefit from the programme, and must be contrasted with the exclusion of surviving female relatives who did

27 *Baby Boy v United States*, Inter-Am. C.H.R., Case 2141, Report No. 23/81, OEA/Ser.L/V/II.54, DOC.9 REV.1 (1981). See further Corporación Nacional de Reparación y Reconciliación (1996: 124–5).

not conform to 'conventional' family forms, or the failure to even contemplate the inclusion of women who died under the military regime as a result of unsafe abortions.[28]

The approach to the 'unborn' in the reparations programme is also usefully viewed in contrast to the treatment of women who were recognised by the reparations programme of the Torture Commission as primary victims of sexual violence in detention. There was an angry response to the decision to make reduced reparations payments to torture victims who had already been beneficiaries of the reparations programme. The women were determined to assert their direct political involvement in the opposition to the dictatorship, and that they were tortured for this reason:

> The militant women and opposition do not accept being treated in our new political dispensation, as 'the mothers or wives of . . .'. We suffered the torture independently of being single or married to militants, therefore, there cannot be confused or subtracted from the reparation [already received] for the assassination or disappearance of a spouse, the reparation to be awarded for having been an individual victim of torture.
>
> (Agrupación de Mujeres ex Prisoneras Políticas Sobrevivientes de la Red de Centros de Tortura Clandestinos del Régimen Militar de Pinochet 2004: 3)

NORTHERN IRELAND: EXPLOITING A REGULATORY GAP IN INTERNATIONAL LAW

In Northern Ireland, the state's determined resistance to acknowledging the political violence that prevailed in the jurisdiction for three decades as a 'conflict' under international law had implications also for the delivery of reparations in the jurisdiction. Due to the particular nature of the Northern Ireland conflict, and its legal characterisation as an 'internal criminal matter', reparations to victims during the conflict were delivered through criminal injuries compensation. The state made no official commitment to reparations per se, but has instead relied on a criminal injuries compensation model to deliver the financial component of reparations. The state therefore resisted external regulation of its conduct of conflict, while also opting out of some key external regulatory mechanisms of civil and political rights violations subscribed to by states not experiencing political violence. The UK refrained from ratifying the Optional Protocol to the International Covenant on Civil and Political Rights (ICCPR) (which provided

28 For a discussion of a state's due diligence requirements and potential liability for reparations in the case of restrictive abortion regimes, see Getgen (2008).

for individuals to petition the Human Rights Committee for violations of the Covenant) until the peace process was well in hand.[29] The state thereby positioned itself to exploit a regulatory gap.

Doctrinal: defining harms, determining beneficiaries

Reparations for conflict-related harms in Northern Ireland have remained curiously immune from international legal developments in the area. The European Convention on Human Rights refers in its Article 41 to the right to 'just satisfaction' and only 'if necessary'. The European Convention approach to reparations has meant, in practice, that the European human rights regime has lagged well behind its Inter-American counterpart in the development of reparations broadly under international human rights law, and more specifically in terms of reparations for conflict-related harms against women.[30] The reparations framework traditionally embraced by the European Court is narrow and has not allowed full recognition of the moral and material harm that women subjected to violence experience.[31] No measures of satisfaction, symbolic recognition, rehabilitation or guarantees of non-repetition have been ordered. Additionally, the treatment of pecuniary damages has been very narrow, as it requires high standards of proof and fails to include future expenses, even in cases where they are foreseeable.[32] According to the UN Special Rapporteur on Violence Against Women, 'This approach does not reflect an understanding of either the true material harm following a violation, or its sex-specific dimension.'[33] To illustrate, reparations awarded by the European Court in the landmark *Jordan* decision, finding the UK in violation of its procedural obligations under Article 2 of the Convention, was limited to financial compensation: the applicants were awarded £10,000 for the 'frustration, distress and anxiety' caused by the state's failure to carry out a prompt and effective investigation into their son's death.[34] This most egregious of violations was considered by the Court to merit only compensation, without

29 The UK government ratified the Optional Protocol in 1998. Optional Protocol to the International Covenant on Civil and Political Rights, 19 December 1966, 999 UNTS 171.

30 See, for example, the reparations awarded by the European Court in the landmark *Aydin* case, the Court's first decision to recognise rape as torture. *Aydin v Turkey*, ECHR, Application No. 57/1996/676/866 (1997).

31 See United Nations Special Rapporteur on Violence Against Women: Rashida Manjoo (2010: para 79).

32 See United Nations Special Rapporteur on Violence Against Women: Rashida Manjoo (2010: para 79).

33 See United Nations Special Rapporteur on Violence Against Women: Rashida Manjoo (2010: para 79).

34 *Jordan v United Kingdom*, 2001-III ECHR, paras 170–71.

comparable entitlements to, for example, rehabilitation. Thus, the regulatory regime of the European Convention has provided few practical or legal boundaries to the UK adoption of a criminal injuries compensation model in lieu of reparations for conflict harms.

Compensation for criminal injuries in Northern Ireland has traditionally been determined by a statutory scheme administered by the Northern Ireland Office, and the awards could be challenged in the courts (Bloomfield *et al* 1999). Evidence consistently showed that the Northern Irish approach delivered larger amounts of money to qualifying victims than the English and Welsh approach to criminal injuries. However, the Northern Irish approach operated highly inequitably in its definition of 'qualifying victims'. These iniquities impacted both criminal injuries resulting from conflict violence, and criminal injuries resulting from sexual and domestic violence not directly related to the conflict (Bloomfield *et al* 1999). Many of the modernisation initiatives implemented to the tariff scheme in England and Wales had consequently not been implemented in Northern Ireland. For example, eligibility for a bereavement award was limited to spouses and parents of unmarried minors, and excluded the fathers of minors born outside of marriage and cohabiting couples. In respect of sexual violence, the statutory time limit of three years (extendable to age 21 for injuries suffered in childhood but with no other discretion), was widely viewed as grossly unjust because of its effect on victims of child sex abuse who did not come forward about their experiences until over the age of 21. In terms of domestic violence, criminal injury compensation operated highly inequitably during the conflict. Under the 1977 legislation no claim could be made if the assailant was a member of the same household,[35] with obvious consequences for domestic violence victims. In 1988 the Order was repealed, and the relevant provision amended to provide for compensation to victims of criminal injury inflicted by a member of the same household, but only in incidences in which the victim had ceased to live in the same household and was 'unlikely to live in the same household again'.[36] Victims who were members of 'unlawful associations' were entirely excluded from criminal injury compensation.[37]

This highly partial domestic framework for the delivery of reparations, with manifold gendered iniquities, finally began to receive greater attention with the subsidence of the conflict in the mid 1990s. Greater attention and resources of statutory bodies began to be directed to the network of victims' organisations that now exist in Northern Ireland. Further, material and symbolic reparations to victims emerged as a political issue in the latter stages of the peace negotiations. In 1997 the Northern Ireland Secretary of State appointed the civil servant Kenneth Bloomfield:

35 Criminal Injuries (Compensation) (Northern Ireland) Order 1977, 3(2)(b).
36 Criminal Injuries (Compensation) (Northern Ireland) Order 1988, 5(2)(a)(ii).
37 Criminal Injuries (Compensation) (Northern Ireland) Order 1988, 5(9)(a).

> to lead the Commission and to examine the feasibility of providing greater recognition for those who have become victims in the last thirty years as a consequence of events in Northern Ireland.
>
> (Bloomfield 1998: 8)

Further to the Bloomfield Report, the Review of Criminal Injuries Compensation, also led by Kenneth Bloomfield, was established in October 1998 to examine the fitness for purpose of the existing arrangements. On foot of the review, a criminal injury compensation scheme similar to that of England and Wales was introduced in Northern Ireland.[38] In the new compensation scheme, provisions dealing with domestic and sexual violence have been brought into line with England and Wales. Hence, the eligibility criterion – that in domestic violence cases the offender must cease living in the same household as the victim before compensation can be paid – was amended to apply only to cases of violence between adults (The Compensation Agency 2002: Part 9). In terms of childhood sexual abuse, the normal time limit for applications was actually reduced from three to two years; however, it was now possible for discretion concerning the time limit (The Compensation Agency 2002: Part 9). Also, on the grounds that the England and Wales scheme operated a more flexible approach to considering refusal or reduction of compensation based on previous convictions, the complete automatic disqualification on the grounds of terrorist involvement was removed (Bloomfield *et al* 1999: Recommendation 18). Thus, by extending the English and Welsh model to Northern Ireland, the 2002 reforms addressed many of the most egregious gendered iniquities in the system.

Nevertheless, the Bloomfield approach left little space for addressing the specific conflict-related circumstances of criminal injuries in Northern Ireland, and might readily be viewed as part of a larger state discourse that denied the existence of a conflict. The recommendations of the Review of Criminal Injuries Compensation relating to the specific circumstances of the Northern Ireland conflict were not adopted in the new scheme. For example, the Review recommended 'top-up' payments to certain categories of victim who claimed compensation prior to the introduction of the 1988 Order. These recommendations were rejected in favour of financial support for a wider category of victims (Bloomfield *et al* 1999: 2). Further, the recommendation that payments be made to the families of the 'disappeared' was accepted, but such exceptional payments would be made outside the new schemes (Bloomfield *et al* 1999: Recommendation 3).

By consistently framing conflict-related reparations as a matter of 'criminal injury', the state effectively evaded all international scrutiny of its reparations activity.

38 Criminal Compensation (Northern Ireland) Order 2002.

Normative: redressing structural gender inequalities

Another important dynamic underpinning reparations initiatives in Northern Ireland is the approach to the question of victims adopted in the Belfast Agreement. Under the Agreement, the participants committed 'to acknowledge and address the suffering of the victims of violence as a necessary element of reconciliation'.[39] Recognising the extensive services that already existed independently or semi-independently of the state, the Agreement stated:

> The provision of services that are supportive and sensitive to the needs of victims will also be a critical element and that support will need to be channelled through both statutory and community-based voluntary organizations facilitating locally-based self-help and support networks. This will require the allocation of sufficient resources, including statutory funding as necessary, to meet the needs of victims and to provide for community-based support programmes.
>
> (Agreement Reached in the Multi-Party Negotiations, Ir–UK, 10 April 1998, Chapter 6, para 12)

From the outset, therefore, there was no official commitment to a comprehensive programme of reparations. Instead, compensation would continue to be delivered through the criminal injury model. Rehabilitation would be largely channelled through existing civil society organisations. The issue of satisfaction or disclosure of truth was not mentioned at all.

In 2000 the newly established Northern Ireland Executive published its draft Programme for Government, which included a commitment to agree the first cross-departmental strategy 'for ensuring that the needs of victims are met'.[40] Two years later, the strategy *Reshape, Rebuild, Achieve* was published, setting out how the Northern Ireland administration would 'deliver practical help and services to those who have suffered most over more than 30 years of violence' (Office of the First and Deputy First Minister 2002: Ministerial Foreword). The strategy dealt exclusively with issues of material and psycho-social needs of victims, within a welfare model (as opposed to a rights-based) approach.[41] (Indeed, as Brice Dickson (2003: 49) notes, 'I do not think the word "rights" appears even once in the document.') Any question of truth-seeking was deferred to the community-based *Healing through Remembering* project, which was due to report that same year.

39 Agreement Reached in the Multi-Party Negotiations, Ir–UK, 10 April 1998, Chapter 6, para 11.

40 Northern Ireland Executive, Programme for Government, 2000, quoted in Hamber and Wilson (2003: 5).

41 On these dynamics, see further Dickson (2003: 49).

Issues such as access to justice for victims were entirely absent from the report. Thus, concludes O'Rawe, *Reshape, Rebuild, Achieve* was 'an attempt to compartmentalize' service provision for victims separately from accountability (O'Rawe 2003: 52). This compartmentalisation has continued through the operation of statutory funding initiatives such as the Northern Ireland Memorial Fund[42] and the Commission for Victims and Survivors, who address material though not legal needs of victims.[43] It is a 'compartmentalisation' that, not coincidentally, reinforces the identified gendered division of labour between (women-led) work to ameliorate the material consequences of the conflict and (male-led) work in the pursuit of accountability.

Political: affirming women's agency

Feminist theoretical contributions to the study of transitional justice rightly identify reparations as a potentially critical tool for the affirmation of women's full citizenship and political equality in post-conflict and post-authoritarian states (de Greiff and Rubio Marin 2007). De Greiff and Rubio-Marin eloquently capture this four-fold potential: first, to use the involvement of women in the design of reparations programmes to promote women 'as valuable agents of political and social transformation' (2007: 154) in post-conflict societies; second, to disrupt practices and norms that are frequently part of pre-existing gender hierarchies, for example by departing from iniquitous laws of inheritance to ensure women a fair apportionment of benefits (2007: 154); third, to accompany reparations for sexual violence 'by a serious effort to encompass other forms of victimisation that also have a disparate impact on women', such as forced domestic labour (2007: 155); and finally, to systematically address the needs of certain groups who are particularly vulnerable before, during, and after conflict (2007: 156).

Measured against these four-fold feminist ambitions for reparations, the Northern Irish case appears particularly disappointing in its failure to affirm women's political equality and equal citizenship. Rather than recognise women as important stakeholders in the design of reparations, there has been no official acknowledgement of the disproportionate role that women play in the delivery of rehabilitation to victims. Rather than disrupt entrenched state reliance on women's voluntary organisations to deliver state services, reparations delivery continues to rely on the under- and unremunerated work of women-led victims organisations. This further naturalises the position of women in 'apolitical' care-taking roles. Rather than systematically address the needs of women as a group through reparations, there has been persistent official denial to women of any gender-specific stake in reparations. Ultimately, reparations in Northern Ireland

42 See further http://www.nimemorialfund.co (last accessed 29 March 2013).

43 See further www.cvsni.org/ (last accessed 8 March 2013).

have involved the state devolving to the women-dominated victims sector its own duties to provide services to victims.

COLOMBIA: THE IMPLEMENTATION GAP

Colombia has been the site of very substantial reparations activity. The negotiated settlement of a partial peace process to demobilise pro-state paramilitaries was given legislative effect through the Justice and Peace Law of 2005. This law included provision for demobilised paramilitaries to compensate victims from their illegally earned gains. While providing a critical opportunity to insert reparations into efforts to resolve the Colombian conflict, reparations provision within the Justice and Peace Law was highly partial, in particular as it addressed only the victims of demobilised paramilitaries, rather than conflict victims more broadly. In response to this partial domestic reparations activity, international actors have proved important catalysts for broadening reparations activity in Colombia. The International Criminal Court began to scrutinise the legal framework for individual and collective demobilisation of illegal armed groups that was initiated in the country in 2002. At the same time, the Permanent Council of the Organization of American States invited the Inter-American Commission on Human Rights to provide technical advice to the Colombian government in order to adopt a comprehensive legal framework for demobilisation that respected victims' rights to truth, justice and reparation.[44] Annual reports on the situation of human rights in Colombia by the UN Office of the High Commissioner for Human Rights reiterated the need for victims' rights to truth, justice and reparation to be respected within the demobilisation process. Moreover, the Inter-American Court has ordered landmark reparations awards to victims of conflict violence in Colombia in certain high profile cases.[45]

In response to the identified failures of that provision, an administrative reparations programme was established in 2008.[46] Both the justice and peace process and the administration programme included only victims of paramilitary violence and excluded a much broader universe of victims. In 2011, with the election of a new Colombian president, the Victims Law was adopted by the Colombian parliament.[47] This important innovation in reparations activity in Colombia uniquely recognises victims of state violence as also entitled to reparations. The law establishes a universe of victims limited only to anyone

44 Permanent Council of the OAS, Resolution CP/RES. 859 (1397/04).

45 Most notably, *Case of the 'Mapiripán Massacre' v Colombia* (Merits, Reparations and Costs), IACtHR, Series C No. 134 (2005). See also *Case of 19 Merchants v Colombia* (Merits, Reparations and Costs), IACtHR, Series C No. 109 (2004).

46 Decree 1290 of 22 April 2008.

47 Ley No. 1448, Diario Oficial, 10 June 2011.

suffering rights violations related to the internal armed conflict, occurring after 1 January 1985.[48]

In all phases of reparations activity in Colombia, international law has been an important catalyst (or stick) and the institutions of international law have provided substantial technical input and oversight in the design and delivery of reparations. While initial reparations efforts by the government were regarded with suspicion by victims, more recent efforts have evidenced some commitment and goodwill from the government (Comisión de Seguimiento a la Política Pública sobre Desplazamiento Forzado 2011: 5). Indeed, in some respects the Colombian process has been exemplary in its progressive interpretation of its international obligations (for example, the Constitutional Court's ruling that same-sex partners are entitled to reparations on the same basis as heterosexual couples[49]). Nevertheless, even in the context of improving state commitment to reparations, challenges to implementation persist. There is an important distinction to be made between the Northern Ireland case, where state recalcitrance limits the delivery of reparations, and the Chilean case, where regressive gender norms infuse an otherwise comprehensive reparations programme, from the Colombian case, where the severity of the ongoing violence and the scale of need overwhelms state capacity to deliver reparations.

Doctrinal: defining harms, determining beneficiaries

The Justice and Peace Law (Ley 975) established a judicial procedure for the pursuit of reparations claims by individual victims against an individual perpetrator.[50] To claim reparations, the harms must be the consequence of illegal activity of armed groups affected by Ley 975.[51] Awarding reparations is the final stage in the justice and peace process before sentencing. The award of reparations is considered only in the case of an express petition by the victim.[52] The law therefore imposes a considerable burden on victims. As well as having to bring the petition, the victim must indicate the reparation that he/she wants, providing

48 Ley No. 1448, Article 3.

49 Corte Constitucional de Colombia, *Sentencia No. C-029/09* (2009).

50 For the purpose of claiming reparations, the law establishes a relatively broad definition of victim, as 'a person who individually or collectively suffered direct harm such as temporary or permanent injury giving rise to any type of physical, mental and/or sensorial (vision and/or hearing) disability, emotional suffering, financial loss, or violation of one's fundamental rights' Ley No. 975, Diario Oficial, 25 July 2005, Article 23.

51 Also understood as a victim is the spouse, partner or immediate family member of a direct victim who has been murdered or disappeared: Ley No. 975, Diario Oficial, 25 July 2005, Article 5.

52 The prosecutor also has discretion to make a petition for reparations on behalf of an individual victim, although the law provides little clarity as to the circumstances in which this discretion should be exercised (Barraza Morelle and Guzmán, 2008).

evidence that supports this quantification of the harm. The victim is then expected to agree the amount of the reparations with the perpetrator through a process of conciliation. If an agreement cannot be reached, the court can make this determination.

Colombian feminist NGOs have been vocal in their criticism of the operation of the reparations procedure established by the Justice and Peace Law. A number of procedural concerns have been raised by feminist organisations that have attempted to engage Ley 975 in the interest of victims. Criticisms have centred on the requirement that the victim request that the offence be considered for reparations; the difficulties for victims to satisfy the evidential requirements in order to be awarded reparations; and in particular, the fear of victims of participating in the process of conciliation with the perpetrators of the violence they experienced (Barraza Morelle and Guzmán 2008: 130). In practice, paramilitaries are presenting themselves at the justice and peace hearings as individuals without resources. After almost six years of operation of the Justice and Peace Law providing for judicial reparations, only three partial sentences have been dictated, the first of which was declared null and the most recent of which waits resolution of an application being considered by the Criminal Court. Thus no reparations have been paid through this process (Barraza Morelle and Guzmán 2008: 119).

Nevertheless, the Colombian administrative reparations programme has demonstrated good practice in registering high numbers of claimants. It has functioned effectively to register a large number of claims (approximately 300,000), the vast majority of which have come from women (87 per cent).[53] Of the 200,000 million Colombian pesos paid to date through the administrative reparations programme, 242 million (0.1 per cent) has been paid to victims of sexual offences. Further, although the law establishing the administrative reparations programme provides for comprehensive reparations, to date only indemnity (monetary compensation) has been awarded. In that sense, the programme has become one of administrative compensation, not reparation.

Normative: redressing structural gender inequalities

One of the potentially radical elements of reparations activity in Colombia has been the attention to land restitution. Land restitution has been a prominent issue for feminist advocates in Colombia, because of the close relationship between conflict-related sexual violence and the forced displacement of women (Meertens

53 It is not yet clear how successful the registration process has been in registration of claims for sexual violence, as the available data shows that only 11,000 claims have been processed and adjudicated upon to date, and data on the claims that have not yet been processed is very limited (Procuraduría General de la Nación 2010). However, anecdotal evidence is that one-third of reparations claims for conflict-related sexual violence have come from men. See interview testimony from officials of the administrative process in Roth *et al* (2011).

2006: 28–32). Sexual violence against rural dwellers and their families is frequently part of the tactics used by armed groups to forcibly displace the rural population in conflict-affected regions. Moreover, the threat of further sexual violence discourages the return of the displaced either to their own lands or to alternative rural locations. Finally, amongst women's civil society leaders targeted for violence, those demanding land restitution have been targeted with particular frequency (Meertens 2006: 28–32).

Proving women's ownership of land, and thus their loss of land rights through the conflict-related violence and displacement, is a persistent challenge in implementing land restitution to women, due to embedded gender norms of land ownership. In most rural areas directly affected by the conflict, land title in practice passes between men. Formal records of land ownership – to the extent that they exist – are often destroyed or lost through displacement (Meertens and Zambrano 2010: 190). Moreover, when asked, women tend to be much more concerned with the ability to work the land than to own it per se. When calculating their losses due to the conflict and displacement, women seldom speak of 'their' property, and so do not account for lands, nor the harvest (that they worked), nor the animals (that they tended), nor the houses (that they maintained) (Meertens 2006: 68). Between 1996 and 2005 the numbers receiving benefits under the land restitution policy were tiny, because victims did not want to return to land that continues to be subjected to conflict violence. In addition, many of the families who took up the land abandoned it again due to continuing insecurity, and women landowners in particular faced additional barriers to making productive use of land (Meertens 2006: 53–4). Female-headed households, especially widows, are more vulnerable to uncertainty of tenancy, for example threats to losing their parcel of land due to debt, because they are less able to mobilise family labour to increase productivity on the land and because of their lack of experience/access to credit (Meertens 2006: 55).

These embedded gender iniquities determine women's access and control of land in contemporary Colombia. In terms of effective rights to land, favourable adjudication of claims and assignment of land to women, without capacity-building and support, will not meet equitable objectives of reparations activity. Such patterns suggest a need for conscientisation of victims and their rights. Against this backdrop, fair and effective land restitution to women through contemporary reparations activity stands to potentially transform the status and citizenship of women in Colombia.[54] The normative 'confusion' (Comisión de Seguimiento a la Política Pública sobre Desplazamiento Forzado 2011: 16) that has defined reparations activity in the country to date, in particular in terms of the consistent rejection of state liability for conflict harms[55] and the apparent muddling

54 See further Meertens and Zambrano (2010).

55 Victims Law, Article 9 explicitly precludes state culpability for any harms compensated.

of humanitarian assistance and comprehensive reparations,[56] suggests limited grounds for optimism about the potential of current land restitution efforts to redress structural gender inequalities in the country.

Political: affirming women's agency

The demobilisation of guerrilla groups in the 1980s and early 1990s was conducted without any judicial process. Today, the Colombian state has acknowledged the international legal requirement that some minimum standards of justice must be observed in the demobilisation of armed actors. The transformation of the international legal context is noteworthy and heartening in several respects. Nevertheless, the significance of these gender gains is tempered when considered against the backdrop of the highly problematic process of transitional justice currently taking place in Colombia. The extent to which the justice and peace process has survived international legal scrutiny, of both the ICC and the Inter-American human rights regime, contrasts tellingly with local accounts of the consequences of the justice and peace process. The normalisation of violence within demilitarisation zones, combined with overwhelming evidence that the current process is ineffective in dismantling paramilitary structures of violence and criminality, is alarming. Thus the adjudication of international bodies, taking issue with details of the current process while largely affirming the legality of the overall process, has operated to obscure broader challenges to the effectiveness and legitimacy of that same process from domestic and civil society constituencies. Contemporary events in Colombia pose serious questions to assumptions that the convergence of international law and the state practice concerning reparations is per se a good thing. These questions have a clear gender component, as Colombian feminists have traditionally drawn on the international human rights framework to underpin a comprehensive articulation of gender-based harms in Colombia. This can be found, for example, in the work of the Mujer y Conflicto Armado group to secure a visit from the UN Special Rapporteur on Violence Against Women. This same framework, however, now perversely operates to legitimate a process with which many Colombian feminist organisations have deep reservations.

Challenges confronting local feminist and women's organisations in seeking either to improve the technical operation of gender components of the process, or to transform the entire understanding of peace and justice that underpins the

56 Similar inconsistencies are replete throughout the law, for example Article 123 provides that housing restitution will come out of the fund for housing subsidies for the displaced, while the Constitutional Court has established that housing subsidies to the forcibly displaced will be in addition to the fund for housing subsidies for the displaced. The Victims Law further provides that humanitarian assistance given in the form of money for deaths and personal injuries in the application of the 1997 Law on Internal Displacement will now be understood to be monetary compensation as part of reparations (Comisión de Seguimiento a la Política Pública sobre Desplazamiento Forzado 2011: 16–19).

process, are enormous. Nevertheless, the review of the difficult legal and political context to transitional justice in Colombia also reveals the sophistication of feminist engagement with that process. The divergent approaches of feminist NGOs and social movements, while premised on deep political and ideological divisions between those groups, has engendered a richness to feminist engagement with reparations in Colombia that surpasses the other cases in the book. Diverging feminist approaches to the contemporary process ensures that feminist input is present within *and* against the process, in both technical *and* transformative accounts of how the process can be improved. Clearly, the final chapter on reparations in Colombia has yet to be written; nevertheless, the likelihood of the process eventually delivering transformative reparations for women lies not in the unity of feminist interventions, but in their diversity, democracy and difference.

CONCLUSION

The introduction to the book noted Antonio Cassese's salutary assertion that 'the *normative* role of [international] law is more powerful and effective than its *repressive* function' (Cassese 2008: 8). This admonition is arguably more true of reparations than any other area of transitional justice. Together, the case studies have evidenced a regulatory gap, an enforcement gap and an implementation gap, despite the substantial progressive doctrinal developments in the right to reparations and harms against women under international law.

The chapter began by observing a regulatory gap in international law in terms of reparations to women victims of gender-specific conflict harms. While the relevant regulatory framework has been substantially augmented, and stands to be further enhanced by the CEDAW General Recommendation on the Situation of Women in Situations of Conflict and Post-conflict, the Northern Irish case illustrates the pernicious problem of states that are positioned to exploit this regulatory gap. In Northern Ireland, reparations have been framed, not as a right of victims, but as voluntary welfarist measures to victims of (non-state) criminal violence. Even more problematically in terms of women's political equality, the delivery of these voluntary welfarist measures to victims relies principally on the unpaid labour of women.

Legal analysis of reparations in the aftermath of political violence rightly identifies a progressive trajectory in terms of international law and state practice (Evans 2012). Nevertheless, the Chilean case evidences the vulnerability of progressive norms in international law to regressive domestic gender norms in the local interpretation of international law. It is powerful evidence of an enforcement gap in international law and institutions in their vindication of women's right to remedy.

Finally, as the Colombian case illustrates, even where there is evidence of some domestic political commitment to reparations, the difficulty of the local context, in particular ongoing violence and a weak state, makes the implementation of the transformative elements of reparations difficult. This implementation gap may be the most critical obstacle to achieving transformative reparations in societies exiting political violence.

Part V

Institutional reform

Chapter 9

Women's movements seeking institutional reform

INTRODUCTION

Women's organisations tend to be at the forefront of campaigns for forward-looking institutional reforms in transitional societies, to address a range of private harms such as domestic violence and reproductive rights violations. Because it depends on a defined vision for the future, institutional reform is an area of transitional justice in which divisions and differences within women's movements become more apparent. More than elsewhere in the book, this chapter confronts the major fault-lines within the women's movements in the three case studies.

International human rights law is prominent in the framing adopted by the women's movements across the case studies. This chapter advances a number of claims in this regard. First, this prominence signals the positive feminist-informed progress made in the international human rights canon during the interventions under study. Moreover, the prominence of an international feminist political agenda within local feminist advocacy evidences the power of an internationally forged feminist framework for institutional reform to transcend local political divisions amongst women. Finally, the identified improvements in the international human rights canon, in terms of the recognition and redress to both public and private harms, resonated importantly with local feminist efforts across the case studies to address a broad range of harms against women through institutional reform.

WHY INSTITUTIONAL REFORM MATTERS FOR WOMEN AND FOR WOMEN'S MOVEMENTS

Feminist approaches to institutional reform in transitional justice need to be understood within the context of two larger dynamics: first, feminist approaches to the state, and second, feminist critique of the 'from' and 'to' of transition.

A review of early feminist approaches to the state largely reveals either suspicion or rejection of the state. Catharine MacKinnon's work is paradigmatic in this regard:

> The rule of law and the rule of men are one thing, indivisible, at once official and unofficial – officially circumscribed, unofficially not. State power, embodied in law, exists throughout society as male power at the same time as the power of men over women throughout society is organised as the power of the state.
>
> (MacKinnon 1989: 170)

More recent approaches, adopting poststructuralist insights, challenge the idea of the state as a unitary body that acts with specific intent. In an influential essay, Judith Allen argued that:

> 'The state' is a category of abstraction that is too aggregative, too unitary and too unspecific to be of much use in addressing the disaggregated, diverse and specific (or local) sites that must be of most pressing concern to feminists. 'The state' is too blunt an instrument to be of much assistance (beyond generalizations) in explanations, analyses or the design of workable strategies.
>
> (Allen 1990: 22)

This recognition of the diverse and disaggregated nature of the state did not, however, lead to an abandonment of the state as an object of feminist theoretical and political energies. Instead, it led to a recognition of the state as a site of contestation, with both regressive and progressive elements, and thus as an important site of feminist engagement (Banaszak *et al* 2003). At one (important) end of this feminist engagement, feminists have entered the state either as individual actors (femocrats),[1] or seeking the institutionalisation of feminist agendas and women's policy concerns within the state through state women's machineries (Rai 2003).

This trajectory of feminist approaches to the state adopts, interestingly, a particular resonance when applied to the transitional state. There are unique dynamics of the transitional state that offer greater potential opportunity and threats to feminists seeking to advance their political agenda through the state. In positive terms, the transitional state is attempting to (re)build popular legitimacy. Because civil society formed the locus of past dissent from the state, one means to achieving popular legitimacy is by securing the buy-in of influential social movements, such as women's movements. States may actively court social movements. Women's organisations may, therefore, find themselves with unprecedented access and influence to policy-making. This gender dynamic has been identified across transitional states:

1 This phenomenon is particularly associated with Australia. See further Squires (2007: 11).

> Competitive electoral politics and the control of the state by an elected government offer women's movements the possibility to forge new relationships with governments, political parties, and some parts of the state.
>
> (Waylen 2007: 79)

But all feminist approaches to the state must confront the embodiment of the public/private divide that defines the state. As Sonia Alvarez observes, drawing on the Brazilian case:

> [T]he fundamental contradiction that women's movements have encountered, in past and present times, is that the very institutional arenas in which many such changes must be sought are fundamentally premised upon the continued confinement of women to the private sphere, the sphere that is the structural foundation of both politics and production.
>
> (Alvarez 1990: 28)

These dynamics around public/private take on particular significance when considered in the context of transitional justice. Transitions are defined by the ending of political violence and the reassertion of a (liberal) democratic state. Feminist critique of this defined 'from' and 'to' of transition focuses on narrow conceptions of the problem that results from a focus on public political violence, and limited ambitions for the future that aspire to replicate the embedded gendered failings of established liberal democratic states (Bell and O'Rourke 2007). This links to a point already established in this book, concerning the contingent understanding of justice in transition ('what is deemed just is contingent and informed by prior injustices' (Teitel 2000: 6)). Institutional reform in transitional justice rests on a particular – and limited – understanding of past harms. The gendered shortcomings identified in the discussion of justice, truth and reparations in transitional justice can easily be replicated in shaping reform to state institutions. Into this tapestry, as this chapter documents, women's movements attempt to articulate a vision of institutional reform that redresses a broader range of public and private harms against women.

This chapter examines mobilisation by women's organisations seeking reform to state institutions across the three case studies. Some themes are prominent: first is the importance of *being there* and attempting to build ideas of women's equality and human rights 'in with the bricks' of new institutions (Mackay 2011). The importance of actors – women's movements establishing 'conjuntural alliances' (Waylen 2011) with key insiders and influential outsiders – is also noted, as is the resounding dynamic across the case studies, namely the importance of acknowledging difference, both between women and within women's movements. Given the broad scope of areas potentially addressed in institutional reform, this area evidences little by way of common agendas among women, but international human rights law and standards are particularly prominent in this area of women's mobilisation.

CHILE: DEMOCRATISATION OVER JUSTICE

Political opportunity structure

Implementing institutional reform has proven a long and arduous road in Chile. Institutional resistance to change, combined with the in-built veto of the conservative political parties over all proposed change, made the reform agenda articulated by the Truth and Reconciliation Commission around the development of a human rights culture and establishment of institutions for the protection of human rights difficult to implement (Chilean TRC 1993: Part Four, Chapter Two, A). Human rights in Chile continue to be perceived as an issue of the past. This acts as a double obstacle to reform: first, the general populace prefers to avoid discussions of the past, so there is little widespread support for a campaign to make contemporary institutions human rights-compliant (Saba 2002); second, having made some improvements in their response to justice demands of the past, state organs (most notably the judiciary) regard these developments as the extent of their human rights obligations.[2] Human rights, therefore, are not relevant in contemporary legal issues such as the detention conditions of prisoners, Mapuche land rights, or access to contraception.

Another legacy of Chile's pacted transition, since the return to democracy, is the country's binominal ('two seat') electoral system.[3] In practice, the system exaggerates the strength of the minority opposition party, as it only needs one-third of the vote in each district to win one-half of the parliamentary seats. The system has guaranteed the right-wing parties sufficient parliamentary membership to block substantive changes to the Constitution, which require the support of three-fifths of the members present and voting of each Chamber.[4] The binominal system has been the main obstacle to institutional reform in Chile. It has fostered the practice of political parties forming coalitions – the centre-left Concertación de los Partidos por la Democracia and the conservative coalition of National Renewal and Democratic Independent Union – to contest elections, in order to avoid splitting the vote. As each coalition list can contain no more than two parliamentary

2 These dynamics are best discussed by Alexandra Huneeus in her outstanding dissertation of 2006.

3 Each of the country's 60 lower-chamber electoral constituencies returns 2 members. The Upper Chamber consists of 36 elected members and 8 appointees. Each of the country's 18 Upper Chamber constituencies returns 2 members. Only if the leading party outpolls the second-place party by a margin of more than two-to-one does the winning party gain both seats. For a detailed discussion of the Chilean Electoral System, see http://www.psr.keele.ac.uk/docs/chile.htm (last accessed 11 March 2013).

4 Chilean Constitution, Chapter XIV – Reform to the Constitution, Article 116. Changes to Articles I (Bases of Institutionality), III (Constitutional Rights and Duties), VII (Constitutional Court), X (Armed Forces, Public Order and Security), XI (Council of National Security) and XIV (Reform to the Constitution) require the support of two-thirds of members present and voting. Otherwise, a three-fifths majority is sufficient.

candidates in each constituency, a high degree of negotiation and consensus is required to reach agreement on the nomination of candidates. Its operation has fostered party coalitions, and by guaranteeing the substantial presence in Congress of right-wing parties, it has been instrumental in perpetuating the 'politics of agreement' that characterised the transition.

Resource mobilisation

The women's movement in Chile has, historically and currently, been at the forefront of efforts to broaden the understanding of harms underpinning the transition from military rule, and to heighten ambitions for the post-authoritarian state. To illustrate, in February 1988, 13 oppositional political parties came together to form the campaign for a no vote (Concertación por el No) in the upcoming referendum on the military's continued control of government. The campaign eventually grew to 18 parties. It was dominated by the Christian Democrats (as the largest party) but also included a range of socialist and centre-left political parties (Oxhorn 1995: 248). These same parties would later form the Concertación de los Partidos por la Democracia to contest the subsequent congressional elections. Political party control of the no campaign marked the reassertion of political power over social movements by the dormant though enduring Chilean political parties.[5]

Studies of the fragmentation of the Chilean women's movement during and after the transition to democracy are replete (Waylen 1993; Jaquette 1994; Baldez 2002). The fragmentation is typically attributed to three dynamics: first is the reassertion by political parties over political power. Social movements that had learned to rely on political parties as allies in opposition to the government now had to channel their demands on power through these political parties that controlled government (Alvarez 1998: 182). Second, feminists had to decide whether to take power within the state, for example as 'double militants' within political parties and in new state institutions, or to pursue an autonomous feminist path (Baldez 2002: 180–83). Finally, as the new democratic government endured the limitations of the political structures designed by the military dictatorship in the 1980 Constitution, democratic parties of the centre and left were forced to moderate their policies to secure the necessary support of parties on the right. Human rights groups and popular sector women's organisations felt increasingly alienated from the new government that they pointedly labelled 'a disgrace' ('esta democracia es una desgracia' (Baldez 2002: 190)). As feminists and women's organisations pursued different paths, either within or against the state, opposition to the dictatorship no longer formed a unifying frame for organisations with different visions and priorities for the new democratic regime. These differences translated into very different priorities for institutional reform.

5 See further Waylen (1994).

Framing

To ensure the presence of a feminist influence in the transition, on 1 July 1988, 22 feminist groups and 11 well-known individuals took out a full-page advertisement in a major Santiago newspaper, *La Epoca*, calling on Chilean women to make their voices heard in demands for democracy:

> As feminist women, we are aware of the times we are living in. To all Chilean women, young and old, organized and independent, we would like to propose that we unite to express our own demands of democracy. We further propose that these demands become part of the democratic project to which the majority of us aspire. We think that the series of basic demands we propose below represent justice for all women. We invite you to support them and propose that together we take them to democratic political parties, to social organizations and unions, to religious institutions and the Chilean Human Rights Commission. Our objective is that these organizations develop a commitment to include our demands as a non-negotiable part of the democracy that all of us, women and men alike, are constructing.[6]

Chilean feminist demands for the ratification of the CEDAW, and – drawing on the Nairobi Declaration[7] – the creation of a national women's machinery with ministerial rank, in addition to the requirement that 30 per cent of decision-making positions in government be held by women, clearly drew on developments in human rights of women at the international level. Further demands addressed more specifically the Chilean context, namely the elimination of the reproduction of sexism in the educational system (in which the military had been dominant). These demands were maintained with the creation of the autonomous Coalition of Women for Democracy (Concertación de Mujeres por la Democracia) in 1988.

Feminist campaigns in the closing stages of the military regime demanded 'Democracy in the Country and in the Home', attempting to link public and private incidences of repression. However, the prevailing human rights narrative in Chile quickly collapsed into 'the fight for truth and justice' ('*la lucha por justicia y verdad*'), with an exclusive focus on serious civil and political rights violations under the dictatorship. Similarly, official responses to the human rights violations of the past have offered limited gains to women because of their focus on civil and political rights violations. Further, and more pragmatically, past-related human

6 Quoted in Chuchryk (1994: 84).

7 United Nations World Conference to Review and Appraise the Achievements of the UN Decade for Women, Nairobi 1985, Nairobi Forward-looking Strategies for the Advancement of Women, available at http://www.un.org/womenwatch/confer/nfls/ (last accessed 11 March 2013).

rights advocacy has for many years encountered substantial societal and institutional opposition in Chile (Saba 2002). Thus dealing with the past has offered little traction for a feminist articulation of violence and injustice. In this context, feminist mobilisation has endeavoured to 'recuperate' (Red Chilena Contra la Violencia Domestica y Sexual 1996) the local human rights agenda in order to bring local traction to feminist gains made in international human rights, while generally finding greater campaigning traction in the democratisation agenda. The political agenda of the Concertación de los Partidos por la Democracia when competing in the 1990 presidential election demonstrated the success of women within the coalition in advancing gender issues. The programme included a commitment to establishing a national women's machinery to advance a women's agenda within the new democratic government. Further, there was an overt commitment to advancing women's legal equality. Tackling intrafamily violence[8] featured explicitly, while even at this stage any likely advancement in reproductive rights issues proved fraught. The success of the Concertación por Democracia de las Mujeres was given early institutional recognition by the new democratic government through the establishment of the National Service for Women (Servicio Nacional de la Mujer, SERNAM).[9]

The prominence of international human rights law in feminist advocacy for institutional reform is also demonstrated in the women's movement's engagement with reform to the criminal justice system, campaigns to establish an Ombudsman Office and pursuit of the adoption of international human rights treaties by the Chilean government. With its forward-looking focus, the democratisation agenda has offered more rhetorical space at least for feminist campaigning. Women have worked to establish, variously, equal political participation, an end to partner violence and greater reproductive freedom as the true 'test' of democratisation in Chile. Campaigns for justice, however, belong to a small number of men, and their mothers.

NORTHERN IRELAND

The avowed forward-looking focus of the Belfast Agreement has proven auspicious to the institutional reform aspirations of women's organisations in Northern Ireland. De-linking demands for institutional reform from fraught and highly divisive questions of state liability for past harms has created a space for more

8 '*Violencia intrafamiliar*' is the term most commonly used by both women's organisations and the state to reference domestic violence. Similarly, the corresponding legislation in Chile consists of three distinct Leys de Violencia Intrafamiliar.

9 The Chilean state explicitly acknowledged the link between the Concertación por Democracia de las Mujeres and the establishment of SERNAM in its report to the Beijing Conference in 1995 (SERNAM, 1995: 18).

comprehensive and holistic feminist articulation of the need to address both public and private harms in any process of institutional transformation.

Political opportunity structure

The early 1990s in Northern Ireland witnessed the nascent détente between constitutional nationalism and physical force republicanism. The détente manifested in secret talks between Sinn Féin President Gerry Adams and leader of the nationalist Social Democratic and Labour Party (SDLP), John Hume. The talks proved critical to securing the 1993 Downing Street Joint Declaration of the British and Irish Governments,[10] stating that the two governments were willing to enter peace talks with any group not engaged in the violent pursuit of their political objectives. The Joint Declaration was followed in 1994 by the announcement of ceasefires by, first, the IRA, and shortly thereafter the main loyalist paramilitary groups. After a stumbling and slow starting process, the peace talks proper began in 1996. When the British government announced its intention to hold elections to a multi-party forum and peace talks in 1996, an unexpected opportunity presented itself. Chiefly in order to ensure the election of at least some representatives of the newly formed Loyalist political parties, a novel 'top-up' electoral mechanism was adopted for the elections, which favoured the election of representatives of smaller parties. The Belfast Agreement emerged on 10 April 1998.[11] Ten political parties in the jurisdiction, representing a spectrum of political opinion, and the British and Irish governments were parties to the Agreement. It was subsequently endorsed by popular referendum in the jurisdiction.

The Belfast Agreement provided for major reforms to policing and criminal justice institutions in the jurisdiction,[12] the creation and strengthening of human rights protections[13] and the consolidation of paramilitary ceasefires through provision for early prisoner release[14] and the inclusion of the full range of political representatives in a power-sharing Assembly.[15] Notably, however, the Agreement did not provide for an accountability mechanism to deal with the legacy of Northern Ireland's conflict. No provision for truth-telling, amnesty or special inquiries into unresolved deaths by either state or non-state actors was made. The Agreement was therefore avowedly forward-looking. It mandated an agenda of

10 Mr Albert Reynolds An Taoiseach, T.D., and The Rt Hon. John Major, The British Prime Minister, MP, 'Downing Street Declaration' (1993).

11 Agreement Reached in the Multi-Party Negotiations, Ir–UK, 10 April 1998 [hereinafter Belfast Agreement].

12 Belfast Agreement, Annex A and Annex B.

13 Belfast Agreement, Rights, Safeguards, Equality of Opportunity. See also Bell (2000).

14 Belfast Agreement, Prisoners.

15 Belfast Agreement, Strand One.

aggressive institutional reform, with the objective of securing the confidence of all communities in state institutions. By securing the inclusion in state institutions of formerly excluded actors, the Agreement was to establish mechanisms for the peaceful expression of conflict (Bell 2000: 173).

Resource mobilisation

When the closed and secretive manner of peace negotiations in the early 1990s became apparent, a range of initiatives to intervene into the incipient peace process and to influence institutional reform through the peace talks were undertaken by women, from both within and across their political communities.

Republican feminist interventions

The first such initiative in response to the Downing Street Declaration emerged from Republican women, who were concerned that the exclusion of women would continue into future negotiations. Clár na mBan began with a series of small meetings among nationalist and Republican women as the basis of securing a more active role in the peace negotiations. The highest point of the group's activity was a major conference held in Derry in 1994, four months before the IRA declared its ceasefire. Trenchant criticism was made of the unfolding process, its exclusionary nature and the absence or silencing of dissenting voices, noting that:

> women's voices have largely been absent from the formal political discussion and debate that will determine our future and the future of our children.
>
> (Clár na mBan 1994: Introduction)

The organisation and conference encountered criticism from both feminists and, in particular, from mainstream Republicans. The fact that the conference took place with the explicit objective of Irish unity was considered divisive by some women.[16] In reality, however, the criticism and opposition of mainstream Republicanism to the initiative was stronger and more pronounced. The public expression of dissent from the peace process entered into by Sinn Féin was deemed damaging and 'disloyal' (Hackett 1995: 113).

Ultimately, Clár na mBan proved to be a short-lived initiative. Shortly after the 1994 Conference, in order to reduce the influence and prominence of dissenting Republican feminist voices in Belfast, Sinn Féin's Women's Department was relocated from Belfast to Dublin (Hackett 1995).

16 For an account of this criticism, see Hackett (1995).

Women's cross-community interventions

The unfolding peace process did not provoke a response just from Republican women. The broader women's sector also recognised this period as an opportunity to impact the peaceful settlement and future political dispensation in Northern Ireland. Notable in these interventions, in common with Chile, was the prominence of the international women's human rights agenda in framing local demands. In 1995 a conference was organised by the University of Ulster Centre for Research on Women concerning women in decision-making, and funded (controversially) by the Northern Ireland Office. Debate centred on how best women could influence developments around the peace process. It was at that point that the prospect of a women's political party was first mooted.[17] No consensus for action emerged from the conference. However, when elections to the 1996 peace talks were announced, with a novel electoral mechanism designed to ensure the inclusion of smaller political parties, the result would be the election of Northern Ireland Women's Coalition (NIWC) members to the Multi-Party Forum and the peace talks.[18] The party did not take a position on the national question; rather it adopted the principles of equality, inclusion and human rights, and each policy of the party was proofed against those values. The party was avowedly cross-community, with two leadership figures, one Catholic (Monica McWilliams) and one Protestant (Pearl Sagar). However, the party's decision to permit a diversity of opinion on the national question provoked vocal dissent from Republican women. In a letter published in *Women's News* June/July 1996 edition:

> The Women's Coalition is not agreed on a policy on future constitutional arrangements for this island . . . Inevitably, they will not be able to represent the views of all the people who have voted for them . . . [the] Women's Coalition inability to agree on fundamental issues of policy reflects the inherent weakness of a women's political party.
>
> (Quoted in Fearon 1999: 13)

'Unworthy women'?[19]

The effectiveness of the NIWC in securing access to the peace talks must be contrasted with the exclusion of partisan or combatant women from the peace talks. This is a tremendous tribute to the talent and organisational skills within the NIWC. Further, the party's success demonstrates that a political constituency existed at the time for the articulation by women of a non-partisan perspective on the conflict. However, the contrasting fates of the non-partisan Women's Coalition, with the disruptive voices of Republican or Loyalist women, reinforce

17 Avila Kilmurray, personal communication, 2 July 2007.
18 For a detailed account of these events, see Fearon (1999).
19 Roulston (2003).

feminist concerns about the selective inclusion of women in peace negotiations. Perceptions continue that it was 'non-partisan, peace-brokering women who were included, rather than partisans and combatants' (McEvoy 2009: 282). Women's inclusion is permitted or fostered to the extent that it is consistent with a perceived link between femininity and peacefulness:

> Women included in peace processes are often those women who play roles traditionally associated with femininity, advocating for and brokering peace agreements rather than being invested in the conflict.
>
> (McEvoy 2009: 282)

This selective inclusion of women is consistent with the British government's historical approach to funding and validating the work of women's organisations in the jurisdiction. Further, this selective inclusion of women deemed inherently peaceful and non-partisan signals the later obstacles to recognising women as stakeholders in the political debate over how to deal with Northern Ireland's violent past.

Framing

Across these different interventions by women into the peace process, and efforts to shape the state institutions that would result, clear efforts to expand the notion of harms underpinning the process were evident. Moreover, in the case of the Women's Coalition at least, these interventions drew strongly on international standards.

Clár na mBan, or the Women's Agenda for Peace, sought to explore '[i]f there's an agenda for change about to happen, what kind of changes do women want to see?'[20] The agenda that emerged was founded on the principle of self-determination. Conceding that the term was 'better known for its nationalist than its feminist connotations', Clár na mBan nevertheless emphasised the importance of the concept to a feminist discourse about:

> the right and ability to make real choices about our lives: our fertility, our sexuality, childcare, the means to be independent and all the areas in which we are currently denied autonomy and dignity in our various identities as women.
>
> (Hackett 1995: 111)

In its preparatory position papers for the peace talks, the NIWC called for comprehensive review of emergency policing and the judiciary, and for a 'gender

20 Marie Mulholland, Belfast, personal communication, 7 August 2007.

dimension' to this review (Northern Ireland Women's Coalition 1996/7). An end to all forms of violence was called for:

> It is a basic human right to live free from violence and the Women's Coalition calls for an end to the use of violence for whatever purposes.
>
> (Northern Ireland Women's Coalition 1996/7)

Building on the important consensus-building work undertaken within the party, the NIWC explicitly and comprehensively addressed the issue of detention and the treatment of prisoners:

> A series of initiatives should be taken in relation to prisoners with a review of sentencing, release and licensing arrangements for all prisoners in the context of a reduced risk of re-offending. Transfers of prisoners should be granted as a humane action for both prisoners and their families. An effective and resourced programme for resettlement of ex-prisoners should be developed.
>
> (Northern Ireland Women's Coalition 1996/7)

In terms of broader activism on violence against women during this period, decommissioning and arms were a major stumbling block throughout the period of the peace talks: whether, when and how paramilitary (particularly IRA) weapons would be permanently put beyond use. The Women's Coalition did try, however, to inject a specifically gendered understanding of this issue during this period. On the basis of their principle of inclusion, the NIWC called for the inclusion of Sinn Féin and Loyalist parties in the Talks without the precondition of decommissioning, thereby demonstrating that the party could maintain a united position on difficult political issues. More significantly, however, the party leader Monica McWilliams had a long-standing record of research and advocacy on domestic violence, and constantly made the point during these negotiations that: 'you can't decommission the poker in front of the fire' – a reference to a common weapon used against women by abusive partners (McWilliams 2005). While such an understanding of weapons and violence did not appear to penetrate the peace talks or the resulting agreement, it was nevertheless a noteworthy feminist attempt to expand the conversation beyond the prevailing meta-narrative of 'political' violence.

The party's willingness to confront the range of divisive political issues such as the exclusion of political parties from the peace talks was to contrast somewhat with the party's position on reproductive rights. The origins of the NIWC lay very much in the fledgling peace process, and the imminent prospect of peace talks. Consequently, party co-founder Avila Kilmurray defends the party's decision not to broach the issue of reproductive rights within the party during the peace process on pragmatic grounds:

> What we were going into at that stage was the peace talks, where, to be honest, *abortion wasn't going to be a paragraph in the agreement* . . . There's a time and place for that issue as well, but the peace talks wasn't really that.
>
> (Avila Kilmurray, Director of the Community Foundation for Northern Ireland and Founder Member of Northern Ireland Women's Coalition, personal communication, 2 July 2007)

The narrow gendered terms within which peace processes tend to unfold are apparent in this quote. However, the political interplay of the peace negotiations and the legal regulation of abortion in Northern Ireland was in fact very direct in this period. Northern Ireland continued to be governed by direct rule from Westminster during this period. The election of a British Labour government in a major landslide in 1997, to replace 18 years of Conservative Party rule, prompted great optimism among pro-choice advocates in Northern Ireland. The Labour Party had a long-standing policy supporting the extension of the Abortion Act to Northern Ireland. Both the new Prime Minister, Tony Blair, and Secretary of State for Northern Ireland, Mo Mowlam, while in opposition had voted to extend the Act to Northern Ireland. There is strong consensus among pro-choice advocates in Northern Ireland that the concurrence of the ostensibly improved prospects of liberalisation of abortion with the crunch period in the peace process worked to effectively stall any progress on abortion. ('I definitely think the peace process was used as a way of keeping people quiet.'[21]) A statement was later made by the Secretary of State, Mo Mowlam, that she could not have raised abortion at that time, because it would 'stir up the tribal elders', referring to senior political figures in Northern Ireland (McCann 2007). Conservative consensus on abortion among the political parties in the jurisdiction was used in this instance to shore up an otherwise fragile political consensus around the shape of institutional reform.

COLOMBIA: FEMINISTS WEAVING A WEB

The story of institutional reform in Colombia begins long before the most recent phase of transitional justice initiated by the Justice and Peace Law of 2005. The most dramatic and lasting efforts at institutional reform in the country concerned the 1991 process of negotiating and ratifying a new constitution.

Political opportunity structure: 'We can still save Colombia'

As in Northern Ireland, the Colombian transition offered a clear conjunctural moment of institutional reform with an open process for feminist intervention.

21 Goretti Horgan, Alliance for Choice, personal communication, 24 July 2007.

'We can still save Colombia' was the slogan used by Colombia's student movement to call for the inclusive drafting of a new constitution in the country. The movement was prompted by developments surrounding the 1990 election campaign. In this period the urban-based left-wing guerrilla movement M-19 re-emerged, however this time as a formal political organisation called Alianza Democratica M-19 seeking election to Congress. At the same time, a slate of Conservative social groups known as the Movement of National Salvation emerged. It was felt that, by incorporating these social movements into the political system, the basis for a more inclusive and peaceful democratic state could be forged (Morgan 1992). Led by law students at Bogotá's El Rosario University, Colombian voters were called upon to express their views by voluntarily casting a so-called 'seventh ballot' in the legislative elections of 11 March 1990. Two million voters marked and deposited this non-binding 'seventh ballot', voicing their support for a constitutional assembly (Morgan 1992). On 27 May a massive majority (88.89 per cent) of the voters of Colombia approved the convocation of a constitutional assembly. In August of that year, César Gaviria Trujillo assumed the Colombian presidency, and quickly issued a decree calling for elections to the Constituent Assembly (see especially Alvarez and Banks 1991). Significantly, while conceding that the decree did not accord with the provisions for amendment to the Constitution, the Supreme Court held that the utility of legal norms should be judged by their capacity 'to accomplish certain ends that are deemed valuable to the community . . . One of those values is peace.'[22]

This assertion by the Supreme Court signalled the clear purpose of the new constitution: to secure peace. Colombian feminists quickly recognised the importance of shaping this peace.

Resource mobilisation: old divisions re-emerge

The accelerated pace of events – with only three weeks to the elections – found Colombian feminists not fully prepared to contest the elections. Further, old tensions between feminist double militancy and autonomy re-emerged in response to the Constituent Assembly (Morgan 1992). Some sought to pursue an autonomous strategy, organising women as women and proposing a women-only slate to elections to the Constituent Assembly. Under the election rules, any organisation that obtained 10,000 signatures could field a slate of candidates for the 70 elected assembly seats (four seats were reserved for representatives of guerrilla groups). Sufficient signatures were obtained for a women's list and a separate NGO list led by a woman. The double-militants thought it best to concentrate their efforts in ensuring the election of women and feminists, particularly within the newly

22 Decision of 9 October 1990, Corte Suprema, 19 J. & D. 985 (Colombia). For an account, see Alvarez and Banks (1991: 59).

formed left organisation, Alianza Democratica M-19. With a generally progressive agenda, AD M-19 included 8 women among its list of 58 candidates, although the party's commitment to gender issues was always questioned (Morgan 1992: 374).

Ultimately, four women were elected to the Constituent Assembly, two from the AD M-19 list and one each from the party lists of the Liberals and leftist Unión Patriótica. The women's list and NGO list received only about a thousand votes each. The poor showing of women candidates was largely attributed to poor organisation and lack of consensus among women on electoral strategies (Morgan 1992: 374). Nevertheless, women's organisations regrouped in the aftermath of the elections to influence the Constituent Assembly from outside. The autonomous strategy was led through Mujeres a la Asamblea Nacional Constituyente, the organisation established to co-ordinate feminist interventions into the National Constituent Assembly.[23] It began as 10 organisations from 6 cities. Within two weeks, 90 women's groups had affiliated to the Network, adopting the slogan 'Without the rights of women, democracy doesn't work' (La Mesa por la Vida y la Salud de las Mujeres 2009: 19).

Framing

The fundamental demand was that principles of the CEDAW, which had been ratified by Colombia in 1981, be elevated to constitutional rank. Women's reproductive freedoms were prioritised.[24] Efforts to enshrine comprehensive reproductive rights was an important mobilising cause for women outside of the Assembly seeking to influence its deliberations. The Women and the Constituent Assembly National Network was determined not to reduce their reproductive rights demands to abortion and so formulated the concept of 'free motherhood':

> Article G: Maternity and paternity serve a social function. The State will protect in a special manner the free choice of women to maternity and all biological, psychological, and socio-cultural processes that are derived from this.

While not specifically seeking to enshrine the state's duty to end violence in the family, the proposals of Mujeres a la Asamblea Nacional Constituyente included:

> Article E: The State will guarantee the physical and psychological integrity of all persons. All forms of degrading treatment that damage human dignity are prohibited.

23 Reproduced in Morgan (1992: 376).

24 For discussion, see La Mesa por la Vida y la Salud de las Mujeres (2009: 18–19).

> Article J: All family structures and forms of union of women and men rest in voluntary agreement in respect, solidarity, and equality of rights and responsibilities, and produce civil effects that the State will guarantee.

Thus the comprehensive articulation of violence consistently promoted by Colombian feminists, addressing public and private incidences, was continued in their engagement with the drafting of the new Constitution. Indeed, in her assessment of the role of women and gender in the process of agreeing the new Constitution, feminist constitutional lawyer Martha Morgan concluded in 1992 that:

> The most important contribution of Colombian feminists to the country's contemporary political affairs may be their emphasis on understanding the relationship between the many forms of violence and their persistent call for an end to this violence.
>
> (Morgan 1992: 412–13)

CONCLUSION

In contrast to reparations, this chapter reveals that institutional reform is an issue that motivates substantial mobilisation by women and is prioritised across women's movements. This finding is unsurprising, given the consistent emphasis on forward-looking concerns made by women's movements across the processes of transitional justice under study.

Political opportunity structure: the openness of the process

The political opportunity structure for women's movements to influence institutional reform varied across the case studies, in terms of their openness to civil society and their openness to women's movement demands. Chile's pacted transition meant that the demands of the pro-democracy movement became marshalled through the resurgent political parties. As the transition proceeded, the women's movement became more and more distant from the fulcrum of power. In Northern Ireland, by contrast, elements of the women's organisations were able to institutionalise themselves within the talks by becoming a political party. While the process emerged from a closed and exclusionary process, the need to broaden the peace process to a wider political constituency also presented an opportunity for women to become recognised stakeholders in the peace talks. In Colombia democratic elections to peace talks again provided spaces for the women's movement to develop a feminist agenda and the negotiation process provided a forum and site to press these demands.

Resource mobilisation: defined political cleavages and the invisibility of gender

Waylen identifies the need for women's movements to establish a 'conjunctural alliance' with political parties, institutional insiders and other social movements in order to influence institutional reform (Waylen 2011). But the case studies reveal challenges from all sides to the development of an autonomous feminist agenda in institutional reform. The case studies evidence the difficulties of articulating a feminist agenda in a political context defined by political cleavages that has ostensibly little to do with gender. In Chile, efforts to forge a united agenda amongst women could not withstand the fragmentation of the broader pro-democracy movement with the return to democratic government. In Northern Ireland, efforts within and across the main political constituencies to articulate a feminist agenda encountered severe opposition (much of it from women). In Colombia, the double militants and the *autonomas* differed on whether a feminist agenda should be pursued within or without the established political parties.

Moreover, across the case studies it is clear that different women were in different relationships to established power-holders. In Chile and Colombia, women's movements gained some influence on the official process of institutional reform through left-wing political parties. In Northern Ireland, influence was principally exercised through a dedicated women's political party, as women's organising within the main political groupings gained little prominence or autonomy.

Framing: an international frame

The prominence of international human rights law in the framing adopted by the women's movements across the case studies is particularly notable. This prominence signalled the positive feminist-informed progress made in the international human rights canon during the interventions under study. Moreover, the prominence of an international feminist political agenda within local feminist advocacy suggests the power of the internationally forged framework for institutional reform to transcend local political divisions amongst women. Finally, the identified improvements in the international human rights canon, in terms of the recognition and redress to both public and private harms, resonated importantly with local feminist efforts across the case studies to address a broad range of harms against women through institutional reform.

Chapter 10

Institutional reform and harms against women

INTRODUCTION

The last chapter documented the substantial feminist mobilisation precipitated by the prospect of institutional reform in states undergoing processes of transitional justice. Institutional reform is identified, arguably more than any other area of transitional justice, as holding genuine transformative potential for women and the human rights of women, as well as for institutionalising recognition and redress for a web of public and private harms against women. In this way, this chapter reveals isolated gender gains in institutional reform. Though the case studies evidence overt commitment to international human rights law as a guiding frame for domestic institutional reform, this overt commitment is often undermined by informal gender constraints that manifest during the implementation phase.

THE INTERNATIONAL FRAME: THE GUARANTEE OF NON-RECURRENCE

All of the areas of transitional justice examined so far in this book (justice, truth and reparations) have revealed substantial malleability. Institutional reform is the most opaque of all of the mooted 'pillars' of transitional justice. Closely related to reparations, institutional reform forms part of obligations on transitional states to guarantee the non-recurrence of past violations. This is most comprehensively articulated in Principle 23 'guarantees of non-repetition' of the Basic Guidelines and Principles on Reparations. The state obligations elaborated in Principle 23 somewhat narrowly pertain to civilian control of military and security forces, human rights education for law enforcement officials and judicial independence.[1]

1 United Nations Basic Principles and Guidelines on the Right to a Remedy and Reparation for Victims of Gross Violations of International Human Rights Law and Serious Violations of International Humanitarian Law, GA Res. 60/147 UN Doc. A/RES/60/147 (21 March 2006), Principle 23(a), (c) and (e).

Policy initiatives go beyond this to address a broader range of institutions and reforms (International Center for Transitional Justice 2009: 12; UN Secretary General 2004).

The feminist critique

The established feminist critique regarding the guarantee of non-recurrence is the limited catalogue of civil and political rights to which these obligations are interpreted to apply, in particular in the context of widespread and endemic human rights violations (Hamilton and Ní Aoláin 2009; Ní Aoláin *et al* 2011: 197–222). Nevertheless, in its 'Concept Note' on the application of the CEDAW to the rights of women in conflict and post-conflict contexts, the CEDAW Committee has elaborated the material scope of the rights guaranteed under the Convention to include institutional reform for states in the aftermath of grave or systematic violations of the Convention.[2] In addition, the question of post-conflict institutional reform and gender has motivated a flurry of policy-driven 'toolkits' on security sector reform, justice reform and penal reform,[3] which provide valuable insight into state practice in this area.

As well as this feminist technical critique and proposals for incremental reform, there are grounds for more profound feminist concern with the process of institutional reform in transitional justice. Feminist legal theory is particularly valuable in analysis in this regard, because feminist legal theory is constructed around the premise that law and legal institutions are not autonomous from politics (Lacey 1998: 7). Contrary to traditional assumptions of judicial independence and the rule of law, feminist legal inquiry is acutely mindful of judicial actors and the engrained gender biases of legal institutions. In particular, the gap between ostensibly progressive legislative reform that is clawed back, or operates unevenly through state enforcement and judicial interpretation, has caused feminist legal theorists to be highly attentive to the individuals and institutions who operate the law. As Lacey cautions:

2 Grounded in Article 2 of the Convention, which contains the core obligations undertaken by States Parties, the Concept Note establishes an important framework for establishing institutional protection of women's human rights in transitional justice. In addition to the identified importance of functioning national judicial systems, the Concept Note also cites national legislative arena and gender policy machinery as important institutional sites for the advancement of women in post-conflict situations (United Nations Committee on the Elimination of Discrimination against Women 2011: 8, 14).

3 See, for example, Organization for Security and Co-operation in Europe/Office for Democratic Institutions and Human Rights (2008).

> [T]he risks attendant on legal strategies are acute where we try to use new legal regulation instrumentally, to realise values which command little acceptance among those who will administer the laws in question.
>
> (Lacey 1998: 96)

All discussion of institutions and institutional reform recognise that there is no single 'institutional designer'[4] and no single moment of institutional reform determining the substance and outcomes of institutional reform. In North's paradigmatic analysis of institutions, he identifies the 'formal rules' (constitutions, laws, rights) and the 'informal constraints' (sanctions, taboos, customs, traditions and codes of conduct) that structure institutions (North 1991: 97). Informal rules structure all institutions and these rules have their gendered content and implications. As this chapter reveals, it is in the longer-term operation of institutions and the implementation of institutional reforms that these informal gendered rules of operation become apparent. North's typology of formal and informal institutional rules has proven fruitful terrain for feminist scholars of institutions to explore the way gender, operating as an informal constraint, structures and frames institutions, in particular in terms of 'the role of institutional processes and practices in reinforcing and reproducing gender inequality' (Krook and Mackay 2011: 2 and generally). The thesis here, which will be familiar to gender scholars, is that while formal institutional rules may guarantee equality and rights for all, informal gender constraints operate to undercut formal rules of equality and importantly to 'fill in' the institutional spaces where strict formal rules of equality are absent or un(der)enforced.[5] Moreover, empirical analysis of informal gender constraints reveals their tenacity, even in the face of ostensibly dramatic changes to formal rules of institutions (see especially Mackay 2009; Chappell 2011).

In an insightful contribution to the study of institutional reform in transitional justice, feminist political scientists question the very 'newness' of the supposedly new post-conflict or post-authoritarian state. Ostensibly new institutions are identified as carrying gendered legacies or 'hangovers' from their prior incarnations (Mackay 2006). Informal gender rules of operation leak into later institutions. Waylen asks: 'How new are these new institutions? How bounded are they by the institutional legacies of the past regime?' (Waylen 2011).

These questions are usefully applied to studies of institutional change and legal reform in transitional justice. Because legal norms are embedded within the dominant ideology, Martha Fineman argues that seeking legal reform:

> is more likely to operate as a conservative force, serving to tame or domesticate discourses by exerting a confining pressure on their initial development,

4 Bob Goodin (1996), cited in Mackay (2011).

5 On gender and under-enforcement, see Ní Aoláin and Rooney (2007).

> ultimately channeling even the most radical ideas into categories approved by the existing conceptual system.
>
> (Fineman 1995: 21)

Women and the meta-conflict: interrogating the 'to' of transition

McGarry and O'Leary identify the 'meta-conflict' that characterises periods of political violence, that is 'multiple disagreements over what kind of conflict it is, and about whether it is "one" or "many" ' (McGarry and O'Leary 1995: 1). In Northern Ireland, the meta-conflict was embodied by fundamentally opposing understandings of the political violence that prevailed. In one reading the violence was an expression of the legitimate grievances of the minority nationalist population. In another reading the violence was attributable to the criminal activities of the IRA and the state's proportionate response to that criminality. In a further reading the conflict was a violent manifestation of ethnic hostility between Catholic and Protestant communities, while the British state attempted to secure peace. Similar meta-conflicts can be identified in Chile and Colombia. In Chile, the military dictatorship could be interpreted either as a necessary response to the upheaval of the Allende administration or as the brutal suppression of dissent by the military regime. In Colombia, political violence could be attributed to the guerrilla violence and the development of self-defence paramilitary groups in response, or to the grossly unequal distribution of wealth and resources and the state's violent exercise of power to maintain that unequal distribution.

The contours of institutional reform in transitional justice will reflect particular positions on the meta-conflict. So too will women adopt different positions within the meta-conflict, depending on their prior political allegiances to community and political identity. What is clear from these alternative readings of the violence in each of the case studies, however, is that women do not constitute a collective in the meta-conflict. To reiterate Phillips' point: 'no one really expects women to secede' (Phillips 1995: 15). Women qua women, and gender as a political identity, are not recognised stakeholders in this meta-conflict. As this chapter reveals, it is highly challenging to insert an agenda of gender equality and women's human rights into a body of 'transitional jurisprudence' (Teitel 2000: 191–211) that is dedicated to ending political violence.

Plan of the chapter

One of the key challenges in examining the implications of institutional reform for women's human rights is the identification of relevant institutions. Because of the lack of definitional clarity in this area, regarding both the specifics of institutions to be reformed and the reforms to be made, this chapter combines inductive and deductive methods to examine state practice in the case studies. It examines judicial reform, security sector reform, legal entrenchment of rights and development of new institutions (including constitutional courts) for the protection of those rights. This is by no means, however, a comprehensive list of institutions cited for reform in these scenarios. Rather, they are sites of institutional reform that have proved important, both in terms of their gender dynamics and human rights outcomes for women, in the case studies.

CHILE: INTERNATIONAL FORM, LOCAL SUBSTANCE

Institutional reform in Chile was implemented by very limited change to formal rules of state institutions. The political dynamics identified in Chapter 9, in which the binominal electoral system guaranteed disproportionate presence in the Chilean Congress of right-wing political party representatives sympathetic to the military dictatorship, determined a consensus politics that undermined any potential for dramatic institutional reform. Indeed, the transition occurred within the framework of the 1980 Constitution put in place by the military regime. Despite the trenchant critique made of the judiciary in the Report of the Truth and Reconciliation Commission (TRC), the judiciary was the only branch of government left intact by the military regime in 1973, and then again by the new democratic government in 1990. In terms of international law, the only substantive legal change guaranteed in the domestic realm was the addition of Article 5 to the Constitution, which required state institutions to act in compliance with the international human rights treaties ratified by the state (Montes and Vial 2005).

Doctrinally: defining harms

In Chile, the definition of harms underpinning institutional reform can be traced through the concluding chapter of the TRC Report. The Report identified manifold institutional failings in the protection of human rights in Chile: the incompatibility of the domestic legal order with international human rights law, the absence of a bespoke institution to protect and defend human rights, lack of judicial will and capacity to defend human rights, and the security sector's rampant disregard for human rights.[6] These were all areas of priority concern in the Commission's recommendations for institutional and legal change to guarantee the non-recurrence of the human rights violations identified in the Report. Further, the Report found that 'the true cause of human rights violations is an insufficient respect for those rights in a national culture fostering a genuine culture of respect for human rights' (Chilean TRC 1993: Part 4, Chapter 2, A).

Given the shortcomings around the documentation of harm in the Chilean TRC, it is clear that women's experiences of human rights violations during the

6 See generally Chilean TRC 1993: Part 4, Chapter 2.

dictatorship did not underpin the need for reform of institutions identified in the TRC Report (see generally Mackay 2006; Chappell 2011). For example, the Report notes that 'victims' family members, human rights agencies, the main universities and centers of learning, the political parties, the churches, and other moral authorities', as well as international human rights organisations, were all asked by the Commission to propose 'measures that might strengthen the legal order and institutional framework' and promote human rights in order to ensure the non-recurrence of events recorded in the Report (Chilean TRC 1993: Part 4, Chapter 2, B). Women's organisations were not consulted. The series of recommendations made by the Commission displayed a heavy focus on civil and political rights. The thrust of these recommendations involved measures to strengthen habeas corpus in the jurisdiction.[7]

Institutional reform in Chile became yet another site revealing the consequences of the prioritisation of civil and political rights in the international human rights regime and gaps in the documentation of harm that occurred throughout human rights reporting under the dictatorship.

Normatively: redressing structural gender inequalities

Examining the definition of harms in the TRC and its recommendations for reform is convenient shorthand for revealing the extent to which women's experiences of harm informed the institutional reform agenda. Revealing the normative underpinnings of institutional reform, however, requires closer attention to the values that underpinned the interpretation of the doctrinal changes adopted.

Change to the state's formal rules was intended to engender a broader cultural change that would ensure the respect and protection of human rights across state institutions (Chilean TRC 1993: Chapter 4, A). In the Chilean case, the judiciary was cited for particular priority attention in the area of judicial reform. In identifying institutional shortcomings under the dictatorship, the Report makes a lengthy and trenchantly critical account of the behaviour of the judicial branch:

> During the period in question the judicial branch did not respond vigorously enough to human rights violations ... The judiciary, which in view of the Constitution, the law, and the nature of its functions, was the government institution called to protect those rights, failed by not acting more forcefully ... [T]he judicial branch as a whole proved ineffective in both protecting human rights and punishing their violation during the period in question.
>
> (Chilean TRC 1993: Chapter 4, A)

7 For an overview of the recommendations, see Chilean TRC 1993: Part 4, Chapter 2, B.

Finally, in 1997 a series of judicial reforms took place. Significantly, a mandatory retirement age of 75 was introduced for Supreme Court judges, and the Court membership was expanded from 17 to 21. In that year 11 new faces joined the Supreme Court. Thus, the notable shift in the judiciary's response to Pinochet-era cases discussed in Chapter 4 is attributed in part to these modest judicial reforms. However, extensive doctrinal and empirical research into the Chilean judiciary has established that its adoption of a more robust defensive role for human rights has been limited to past-focused cases (see especially Huneeus 2006; Hilbink 2007). There is little evidence of a comprehensive or meaningful penetration of human rights into Chilean judicial reasoning. Alexandra Huneeus observes:

> [T]he 'human rights issue' is not viewed [by the judiciary] . . . as part of an abstract category that includes other fundamental civil and political liberties, but more narrowly as the plight of victims who directly suffered the violence of the military dictatorship.
>
> (Huneeus, 2006: 44)

Having made some improvements in their response to justice demands of the past, as documented in the discussion of prosecutions in Chile, the judiciary regard these developments as the extent of their human rights obligations.[8] Human rights, therefore, are not relevant to contemporary gender issues such as the legal regulation of the family or access to contraception.[9]

The continuing conservatism of the Chilean judiciary, its ongoing resistance to the meaningful judicial protection of human rights and the informal gender rules that structured its operation, is perhaps nowhere more obvious than in the 'saga' of emergency contraception referred to in the last chapter. Since 2001 the Chilean Court of Appeal, Supreme Court and Constitutional Court have consistently invoked international human rights protections of the right to life to justify restrictions on the distribution of emergency contraception. Relevant jurisprudence from the major international human rights bodies has consistently rejected this interpretation of the right to life as applying to the foetus (Casas 2008).[10] Thus, in their reasoning, the Chilean judiciary has invoked the rhetoric of international human rights without any reference to the substantive legal doctrine of human

8 These dynamics are best discussed by Alexandra Huneeus in her outstanding dissertation of 2006.

9 See, for example, *Atala Riffo and daughters v Chile*, Merits, Reparations and Costs, Judgment, IACtHR, Series C No. 239 (2012), para 271–2.

10 See, for example, decision of the Inter-American Commission on Human Rights: *Baby Boy v United States*, Case 2141, Inter-Am. C.H.R. 25/OEA/Ser.L/V/II.54, DOC.9 REV.1 (1981). See also decisions of the European Court of Human Rights precluding the right to life of the foetus: *Vo v. France*, App. No. 53924/00, ECHR, 8 July 2004, (2004) (holding that Article 2 right to life does not apply to a foetus); and *Paton v UK*, App. No. 8317/78, ECHR, (1980) (rejecting the applicant's claim to bring an action on behalf of the foetus against a pregnant woman seeking an abortion).

rights. The 1991 finding of the TRC Report on judicial attitudes to human rights rings true today:

> Experience in the area of human rights in recent years has shown that under the pretext of a supposed obligation to apply the law in a strictly literal manner, institutions for protecting human rights have been emptied of their true meaning.
>
> (Chilean TRC 1993: Part Four, Chapter Two, 2.a.1)

Further, the case of Karen Atala, the Chilean criminal judge who lost custody of her three daughters to their father due to her sexual orientation, and lost subsequent appeals to the decision up to and including the Chilean Supreme Court, reveals the extraordinary degree of embedded gender bias within the Chilean judiciary. Due to the use of discriminatory prejudices in the exercise of public power, in particular, in the judicial resolution of family relationships, as recently as 2010 the state was found to be in breach of equal protection guarantee by the Inter-American Court and obliged to undertake human rights education of the judiciary.[11]

These dynamics reflect well the phenomenon identified by Fiona Mackay of 'nested newness', in which ostensibly new or reformed institutions continue to operate to the same informal gender rules that structured precursor institutions (Mackay 2006). While the form of international human rights obligations might be transposed to the domestic legal regime, the substance of international human rights commitments are hollowed out and filled instead with the established gender rules.

Politically: affirming women's agency

The discussion of women's mobilisation to influence institutional reform identified the consistent priority given by women's movements to women's presence in both the design and implementation of institutional reform. The pacted and negotiated nature of the Chilean transition, compounded by the reassertion of political authority by the political parties, worked to diminish the influence of social movements on designing institutional reform. In addition to being the main obstacle to institutional reform in Chile, the binominal system was shown to militate heavily against the election of women candidates. It has fostered the practice of political parties forming coalitions – the centre-left Concertación de los Partidos por la Democracia and the conservative coalition of National Renewal and Democratic Independent Union – to contest elections, in order to avoid splitting the vote. As each coalition list can contain no more than two parliamentary candidates in each constituency, a high degree of negotiation and consensus is required to reach

11 *Atala Riffo and daughters v Chile*, para 271–2.

agreement on the nomination of candidates. Typically, women have lost out in this formula. This concern was raised by the CEDAW Committee in its Concluding Observations to the Chilean state report:

> The Committee urges the State party to intensify its efforts to reform the binominal electoral system, which is unfavourable for women's political representation.
>
> (Committee on the Elimination of All Forms of Discrimination Against Women, 2006: para 14)

Chilean institutions remain resistant to women's movements or progressive understandings of women's agency. The entrenched conservatism of the judiciary, and its resistance to the meaningful integration of Chile's international human rights commitments into the domestic legal order, sets the context in which the Chilean women's movement has not identified the courts as a useful site to advance a progressive feminist agenda. Engagement with the courts has been confined to rearguard actions to further encroachment on the rights of women, such as mobilisation around the emergency contraception litigation. Rather, the Chilean women's movement has found greater promise in the creation of 'popular' pseudo-legal fora, in particular the series of women's human rights tribunals from 1997 to 2003, for their symbolic, educative and mobilising capacity. Legal arguments in the tribunals are consistently grounded in Chile's international human rights obligations. The substantially more hospitable, though legally less robust, realm of international human rights has proven more accommodating to Chilean feminist demands. This explains the prominence of Chilean feminists in campaigns for the ratification of further international human rights treaties by Chile.

First recommended by the TRC Report in 1991, legislation to establish a national human rights institution (Instituto Nacional de Derechos Humanos) was finally adopted by the Chilean Congress in 2009.[12] Importantly, the Instituto has been given both a backward- and forward-looking function, as it was charged to be the guardian and archive for the records of the TRC, Torture Commission and Reparations Corporation, monitor reparations and reports on Chile's ongoing human rights obligations. The formation of the Instituto has revealed some important gender dynamics, in particular in the affirmation of women's agency and the affirmation of women's political activism as human rights activism. Carolina Carrera, Corporación Humanas Director, is a member of the Instituto's executive, while long-standing feminist human rights advocate Lorena Fries was elected by the executive to be the first Director of the Instituto. These latter dynamics in institutional reform in Chile reveal the tentative bridging of long-standing divisions between the human rights and women's movements, as the backward- and forward-looking functions of the Instituto offers potential for a shared human rights agenda.

12 Ley No. 20.405 del Instituto Nacional de Derechos Humanos (2009).

NORTHERN IRELAND: INTERNATIONAL LAW AND LOCAL POLITICAL EXPEDIENCY

The Belfast Agreement provided for major reforms to policing and criminal justice institutions in the jurisdiction,[13] the creation and strengthening of human rights protections,[14] the consolidation of paramilitary ceasefires through provision for early prisoner release[15] and the inclusion of the full range of political representatives in a new power-sharing Assembly.[16] The Agreement mandated an agenda of aggressive institutional reform, with the objective of securing the confidence of all communities in state institutions. By securing the inclusion in state institutions of formerly excluded actors, the Agreement was to establish mechanisms for the peaceful expression of conflict.

Doctrinally: defining harms

The Belfast Agreement is regarded as unique in the centrality given to human rights throughout the document. The Agreement commits the British and Irish governments and institutions within Northern Ireland to the integration of human rights throughout all institutional reforms. To illustrate: human rights were mainstreamed throughout the Belfast Agreement, featuring in the Declaration of Support made by the parties, safeguards on the new democratic institutions and provisions on policing and human rights. The Belfast Agreement provision on 'Rights, Safeguards and Equality of Opportunity' contained a list of rights affirmed 'in particular' by the parties to the Agreement. This included rights to free political thought, freedom of religious expression, to pursue democratically national and political aspirations, to seek constitutional change by peaceful and legitimate means, to choose one's place of residence, equal opportunity in all social and economic activity, freedom from sectarian harassment and, significantly, the right of women to full and equal political participation.[17]

Reforms to the security and justice sector were prominent in the Belfast Agreement, which provided for an independent commission to 'make recommendations for future policing arrangements in Northern Ireland including means of encouraging widespread community support for these arrangements'.[18] To that end, the proposals were to ensure that the police service would be accountable to the law and 'to the community it serves; representative of the society it polices, and operates with a coherent and cooperative criminal justice system, which conforms

13 Agreement Reached in the Multi-Party Negotiations [hereinafter 'Belfast Agreement'], Ir–UK, 10 April 1998.
14 Belfast Agreement 1998: Rights, Safeguards and Equality of Opportunity.
15 Belfast Agreement 1998: Prisoners.
16 Belfast Agreement 1998: Strand One: Democratic Institutions in Northern Ireland.
17 Belfast Agreement 1998: Rights, Safeguards and Equality of Opportunity: Human Rights.
18 Belfast Agreement 1998: Policing and Justice.

with human rights norms'.[19] In parallel with the independent review of policing, the Agreement also provided for a 'wide-ranging review of criminal justice'.[20] In terms of judicial reform, the review was mandated to bring forward proposals for future criminal justice arrangements including judicial appointments and independence.[21]

In terms of constitutional reform for the enhanced protection of rights, the Agreement provided for the establishment of a human rights commission, tasked with consulting and advising on a Bill of Rights to supplement the European Convention and tailored to 'the specific circumstances of Northern Ireland'.[22] Among the issues for consideration by the Commission would be:

> The formulation of a general obligation on government and public bodies fully to respect, on the basis of equality of treatment, the identity and ethos *of both communities* to Northern Ireland; and
>
> A clear formulation of the rights not to be discriminated against and to equality of opportunity in both the public and private sectors.
>
> (Belfast Agreement 1998: Rights, Safeguards and Equality of Opportunity: United Kingdom Legislation, emphasis added)

Moreover, embracing a more plural understanding of equality, the Agreement provided for the British government to create a statutory obligation on all public bodies in Northern Ireland to promote equality of opportunity in relation to religion and political opinion, gender, race, disability, age, marital status, dependants and sexual orientation.[23]

While the Agreement is embedded in a language of human rights, the rights of women were not prominent. For example, while the European Convention and the ICCPR were mentioned, the CEDAW was not. The commissions established for the reform of policing and criminal justice did not include any reference to enhancing the protection of women's rights in their mandates. 'The right of women to full and equal political participation' was the only gender-specific provision in the entire agreement, but without any enforcement mechanism attached.

Normatively: addressing structural gender inequalities

Regarding the Agreement, Bell observes that:

19 Belfast Agreement 1998: Policing and Justice.
20 Belfast Agreement 1998: Policing and Justice.
21 Belfast Agreement 1998: Policing and Justice.
22 Belfast Agreement 1998: Strand One: Democratic Institutions in Northern Ireland.
23 Belfast Agreement 1998: Rights, Safeguards and Equality of Opportunity: Human Rights.

> many of the rights issues are not dealt with substantively. Instead general principles for the institutions are agreed and a series of commissions established to work to agreed remits and recommend ways forward. Thus the agreement provides only a broad framework which establishes processes for how detail is to be filled out.
>
> (Bell 2000: 214)

In this regard, then, the general provisions for equality and human rights might, in the implementation stage, turn out to enhance the protection of women's rights. To quote Bell: 'what was lost can still be won' (Bell 2005). Examining implementation of the reforms outlined in the Agreement reveals much about the informal gender rules that 'filled out' the many details left unspecified.

For example, measures to secure greater religious pluralism in the police force[24] have also, importantly, resulted in a greater number of women police recruits. Moreover, in contrast to the Royal Ulster Constabulary's alleged 'suspicion of outsiders',[25] its successor, the Police Service of Northern Ireland, has now recognised the expertise of Women's Aid. This organisation plays a role in police training (Beare 2004). Women are well represented in the District Policing Partnerships established to enhance community ownership of the police service.[26] On the other side, due to the relative absence of paramilitary violence and greater police legitimacy, it is no longer fraught for organisations such as Women's Aid to engage with the police. The decision of Foyle Women's Aid to deliver domestic violence training to the police with the IRA ceasefire in 1994 was controversial with local Republicans, and when the IRA ceasefire broke the next year, Women's Aid workers were informed that they were now under a security threat.[27] These conflict-specific obstacles no longer factor in Women's Aid engagement with the police. Moreover, the substantial increase in reported incidences of domestic violence that accompanied both the ceasefires and the policing reform demonstrate increased confidence in the police from the community broadly and from women victims of domestic violence in particular.

These benefits have been incidental rather than the key function of the police reform. Nevertheless, taken together they demonstrate distinct, if modest, feminist gains on private harms and domestic violence that have been secured through policing reform. These incidental benefits to women are usefully contrasted with the fate of women's rights in an area of institutional reform that was forced to avowedly consider questions of women's rights, namely prison reform.

Prisons have been a key site of conflict in Northern Ireland (McEvoy 1999). The Belfast Agreement did not provide for a comprehensive review of the Prison

24 Belfast Agreement 1998: Declaration of Support, 2.

25 Eileen Calder, Belfast Rape Crisis Centre, personal communication, 29 June 2007.

26 Beare 2004.

27 Marie Brown, Foyle Women's Aid, personal communication, 15 March 2007.

Service. However, in discharging its mandate, the Criminal Justice Review 'read into' its terms of reference some aspects of the organisation of the Northern Ireland Prison Service (Criminal Justice Review Group 2000: 12.1). The Review dedicates a short discussion to the specific situation of female prisoners and noted one specific problem: all classes of female prisoners (high and low security, short and long sentence, convicted and unconvicted, and adult and young offenders) were being contained in a single unit. This pattern of detention was attributed to the small number of female prisoners and the wish of the authorities to avoid effectively imposing solitary confinement on female prisoners by separating them according to prisoner class. Rather remarkably, and in a tone distinctly out of step with the rest of the 457-page report and its 294 recommendations, the Review concluded that on this issue: 'It is difficult to know what remedial action could be taken' (Criminal Justice Review Group 2000: 12.77). In drawing this conclusion, the Review sought support from one aspect of the Council of Europe Prison Rules, which suggests that in certain isolated circumstances 'there may be some value' to allowing younger and adult prisoners, and adult men and women prisoners, to mix (Criminal Justice Review Group 2000: 12.77). The Review did not, however, dwell on the manifold ways in which the detention conditions did not meet Council of Europe standards or international best practice. Though the full scale of the violation would take some time to emerge, with a series of deaths in custody of women (Northern Ireland Human Rights Commission 2004a, 2005), the Review's handling of this very serious violation of women's human rights resonates with what Deborah Rhode identified over two decades ago as 'the "no-problem" problem', that is the denial of existence of gender inequality and the consequent denial of any responsibility to end such inequality (Rhode 1991). The 'no-problem' problem accurately locates women within the meta-conflict of institutional reform in Northern Ireland. Women as a political force were not likely to be able to interrupt the process of institutional reform or the de-prioritisation of women's rights therein.

The selective invocation of international human rights, at the expense of women's human rights, is not unique to this feature of the Criminal Justice Review. It has been evident also in the judiciary's entrenched resistance to recognising women's reproductive autonomy as a human rights issue, even in the very limited terms of the right of women to access information to abortion. In a 2009 judicial review, the Northern Ireland High Court took the mistaken view that providing non-directive counselling to women seeking information about the availability of abortion in another jurisdiction was 'arguably unlawful'.[28] In the judgment, the Court disregarded the high-profile 1992 case of *Open Door and Dublin Well Woman v Ireland*,[29] in which the European Court affirmed that providing such information

28 *Society for the Protection of Unborn Children, Re Judicial Review* [2009] NIQB 92 (30 November 2009), para 37.

29 *Open Door and Dublin Well Woman v Ireland*, ECHR, Application No. 64/1991/316/387-388 (1992).

is lawful and is protected under Article 10 of the European Convention on Human Rights. The Department of Health's implementation of this High Court judgment is a chilling limitation on the civil and political rights of women. The subsequent Guidance advises counsellors that:

> [while] the provision in Northern Ireland of factual information relating to such services would not be unlawful . . . [c]ounsellors should nevertheless appreciate that this issue has not been tested before the courts of Northern Ireland, and that if they provide such information they do so at their own risk. If in doubt they should seek their own legal advice.[30]

Moreover, the process of consultation and drafting on a Bill of Rights for Northern Ireland has evidenced a steady diminution of the proposed protection to women's reproductive rights. Throughout the process of consultation, the Northern Ireland Human Rights Commission (NIHRC) has maintained that abortion is one of the 'most controversial' issues in the Commission's consultation process (e.g. Northern Ireland Human Rights Commission 2001: 34) and that it should not be resolved through the Bill of Rights (Northern Ireland Human Rights Commission 2001: 35). The Commission's 2001 proposals did, nevertheless, guarantee 'equal and free access to sexual and reproductive health care and to information and education relating to sexual and reproductive matters at all levels, free of coercion, discrimination and violence' (Northern Ireland Human Rights Commission 2001: 35). The Commission retained this same provision in its 2004 proposals (Northern Ireland Human Rights Commission 2004b: 34). However, the advice made to the Secretary of State in 2008 moved even further away from an assertive guarantee of women's reproductive rights. The proposed provision on the right to health no longer made specific reference to sexual and reproductive health and instead asserted that: 'Women and girls have the right to access gender-sensitive and appropriate healthcare services and information' (Northern Ireland Human Rights Commission 2008: 45).

The close imbrication of reproductive harms to women with political violence in the jurisdiction and the negotiated exit from that violence was evident in the constant invocation of the issue of abortion by the British government to consolidate consensus amongst otherwise opposing parties in Northern Ireland. In this area, perhaps more than any other, the ways in which the political exigencies of exiting violence cut across progressive assertion of women's human rights are compellingly clear.

The limitations around the proposed protection of women's reproductive rights within the Bill of Rights should be considered within the context of the fraught

30 In July 2010 the Department of Health, Social Services and Public Safety (DHSSPS) distributed, for consultation, another version of the Guidance including revisions to the two disputed sections (DHSSPS 2010: para 5.13).

drafting process. After considering the 2008 advice of the NIHRC for a year, the Northern Ireland Office (NIO) published its consultation document on a bill of rights for Northern Ireland on 30 November 2009. It its report, the NIO rejected the majority of the NIHRC's recommendations on the basis that the rights suggested by the NIHRC were not specific to the circumstances of Northern Ireland (as required by the terms of reference) but rather would be more appropriately addressed as part of the debate over a UK bill of rights (Northern Ireland Office 2009).

The NIO consultation document focuses on rights that in the government's view 'can be argued to reflect the particular circumstances of Northern Ireland and the principles of mutual respect for the identity and ethos of both communities' (Northern Ireland Office 2009). This is essentially limited to rights related to sectarian and community issues. The long shadow of the meta-conflict now poses an ominous challenge to robust local civil society mobilisation to ensure that the social and economic causes and consequences of the conflict were understood to constitute part of 'the particular circumstances of Northern Ireland'.[31]

Politically: affirming women's agency

The language of 'community' is recurrent throughout the text of the Belfast Agreement. The new political and legal institutions established by the Agreement were designed with the avowed objective of securing the participation and confidence of all sections of all communities. The understanding of community penetrating the Agreement is clearly concerned with issues of ethnic identity (as tellingly captured by repeated reference to 'both communities' and 'the two communities').[32] Thus the discourse and politics of 'community' have been prominent in the implementation stage of the Belfast Agreement. As members of the community, and as prominent actors in community-based activism, it is women who arguably stand to gain most from this emphasis on 'community'. Feminists, however, have seldom endorsed the community as the central organising unit of the political system. Recognising the potentially exclusionary and conservative politics of defining the membership and values of the 'community', a highly developed critique of communitarianism is evident in feminist theory (Lacey and Frazer 1993; Young 2000). First, there is a disturbing privileging of homogeneity in 'community' that works to exclude or oppress those who are different (Lacey and Frazer 1993: 145). Further, the idealisation of community tends to lead to the suppression of internal dissent (Lacey and Frazer 1993: 137) and an inattention to the dynamics of power involved in defining both the terms of membership and the communal values to be privileged in 'community' (Lacey and Frazer 1993: 142–5). There is little awareness of the domination and inequality within 'community'

31 Civil society initiatives in this direction proliferate but see, for example, Marshall *et al* (2010).
32 Belfast Agreement 1998: Strand One: Democratic Institutions in Northern Ireland.

that systematically gives the voices of certain groups – such as women – lower status in the articulation of communal values. These theoretical concerns foreshadow some of the most exclusionary dynamics of institutional reform in Northern Ireland that has, with remarkable consistency, denied any status to gender as the basis of political identity.

Reform to institutions in Northern Ireland, such as that seen in policing, was clearly predicated on the need to enhance cross-community support for the institution and to make the police force more representative (in sectarian terms) of the population. Indeed, some of the proposals to this end were quite radical. The 50/50 recruitment of officers from Catholic and Protestant backgrounds is probably the most famous of these reforms. The legality of the 50/50 recruitment of Catholics and non-Catholics to the police service was tested, unsurprisingly, in the Northern Irish High Court. The complexity of the measure required an explicit exception to the European Union Equality Directive.[33] The measure was challenged instead as a violation of freedom of religion and the prohibition on discrimination guaranteed in Articles 9 and 14 respectively of the European Convention on Human Rights.[34] In finding that the differential treatment of Catholic and non-Catholic recruits constituted a justifiable limitation on the prohibition of discrimination, the Court held that the measure pursued a legitimate aim and was proportionate to that aim:

> It cannot seriously be disputed that a police force should be representative of the community that it serves. That had been recognised and endorsed by all the parties who supported the Belfast Agreement. That agreement had in turn been endorsed by 71% of the voting population of Northern Ireland. These circumstances provide formidable support for a method of recruitment that would strike at the heart of the problem.
>
> (*In the Matter of an Application by Mark Parsons for Judicial Review* (2002), NIQB 46, para 34)

This purposive jurisprudence, which departed from the strict interpretation of formal equality in pursuit of a more substantive and meaningful vision of equality within the police force, is tellingly contrasted with the decision of the High Court in 2000, in which the issue of gender equality within the regulation of parading was considered. The applicant was a resident of the mainly nationalist Garvaghy Road in Portadown (the site of a very contentious Loyalist Orange March). She argued that the Secretary of State had acted unlawfully by failing to appoint any women to the Northern Ireland Parades Commission. The legislation establishing the Parades Commission stipulated that 'as far as practicable the membership of

33 European Union Directive 2000/78/EC, Article 15 (1).

34 *In the Matter of an Application by Mark Parsons for Judicial Review* (2002), NIQB 46, para 2.

the Commission is representative of the community in Northern Ireland'.[35] The applicant argued that, because of the absence of female members, the membership of the Commission could not be said to be representative of the community in Northern Ireland. Further, it was argued that the provision of the Public Processions (Northern Ireland) Act 1998 had to be interpreted in light of the statutory equality duty on public bodies, imposed by section 75 of the Northern Ireland Act 1998. Dismissing the application, then Northern Ireland Lord Chief Justice Carswell held:

> The phrase in question does not refer to gender or to the make-up of the population of the Province. It refers specifically to 'the community', which in the context of parades is constantly used to denote the different sectarian blocks . . . In the context of the 1998 Act, therefore, it is in my view a tenable proposition . . . that paragraph 2(3) imposes a requirement only to ensure sectarian balance in the composition of the Commission.
>
> (*In Re An Application by Evelyn White for Judicial Review*, The High Court of Justice in Northern Ireland, CARE3208 (Transcript), 18 May 2000)

This restrictive and clearly value-laden interpretation of whose participation matters in reformed institutions, and whose does not, was reached by the Court with the express disregard of instruments for the protection of women's rights in international human rights law. The Northern Ireland Human Rights Commission sought leave to intervene in the case. This was denied by the High Court, although the Commission was granted leave to make a written submission. In dismissing the application, Justice Carswell not only held that failure to appoint any women to the Parades Commission was consistent with the equality duty imposed on public bodies by section 75, he also observed that:

> [None] of the provisions of the several conventions cited by the Human Rights Commission [ICCPR, CEDAW, Convention on Political Rights of Women] adds anything of consequence to those of domestic law . . . To dilate further on these conventions would be an unnecessary elaboration.
>
> (*In Re An Application by Evelyn White for Judicial Review*, The High Court of Justice in Northern Ireland, CARE3208 (Transcript), 18 May 2000)

While human rights have become increasingly effective as a unifying mobilising discourse amongst Northern Irish women, success in securing domestic legal traction to the internationally guaranteed human rights of women has been much more limited. International protection of women's human rights have not proven

35 Public Processions (Northern Ireland) Act 1998, Schedule 1, para 2(3).

sufficient to shift or broaden the established understanding of political identity in the jurisdiction.

COLOMBIA: CONSTITUTIONAL REFORM TO REDRESS A WEB OF HARMS

The 1991 Constitution was designed to establish mechanisms for the peaceful management of political conflict and to bolster the legitimacy of the state, both by guaranteeing respect for human rights of all citizens and securing broad political participation in state institutions.[36] The 1991 Constitution was both a peace agreement and the most significant legal mechanism for facilitating the transition away from conflict in Colombia. The Constitution elevates 'peace' to the status of a constitutional right in the Colombian legal order. Indeed, the Constitutional Court has held that the right to peace 'occupies a transcendent place in the Colombian constitutional order'.[37]

Doctrinally: defining rights, defining harms

The status of the 1991 Constitution as a peace agreement was demonstrated by the guaranteed inclusion of representatives of demobilising guerrilla organisations in the Constituent Assembly.[38] The prominence of peace as the motivating value for the new Constitution was nowhere more evident than in the text of the Constitution itself. For example, Article 22 asserts that: 'Peace is a right and duty of complementary obligation.' Chapter 5 sets out 'obligations on the person and the citizen', which include: 'To propose the achievement and maintenance of peace'.[39] Further, the Constitution contained a number of transitory articles to facilitate the amnesty or peace, as well as incorporation into the political life of former combatants.[40]

In terms of the state's international human rights obligations, Article 93 of the new Constitution provided for the international treaty commitments to prevail in the domestic legal order and for rights and duties under the Constitution to be interpreted in accordance with the state's international human rights obligations. The 1991 Constitution defined Colombia as a social state of law ('*estado social de derecho*'), and included a broad 'three generational' panoply of both negative and

36 This characterisation of the 1991 Constitution is frequently made in the Court's own jurisprudence. See for example Corte Constitucional de Colombia, *Sentencia No.* C-225/95 (1995), magistrado ponente Alejandro Martínez Cabellero.

37 Corte Constitucional de Colombia, *Sentencia No.* C-055/95 (1995), magistrado ponente Alejandro Martinez Caballero.

38 On constitutions as peace agreements, see Bell (2008).

39 Colombian Constitution, Article 95 (6).

40 Colombian Constitution, Transitory Article 12.

positive rights, including civil, political, social, economic, cultural and collective rights.[41] 'Fundamental rights' include the right to life, the right to live free from forced disappearance, torture and cruel, inhuman or degrading treatment. Article 86 established the *tutela* for protecting fundamental rights. The *tutela* is designed to provide:

> immediate protection of . . . fundamental constitutional rights, when any of these [rights] are violated or threatened by the action or omission of any public authority.
>
> (Colombian Constitution, Article 86)

Guarantees of peace also reached into the private realm of violence within the home:[42]

> Whatever form of violence within the family is considered destructive of its harmony and unity, and will be punished according to the law.
>
> (Colombian Constitution, Article 42)

The Constitution's guarantees of justice include reference to reproductive justice. Article 42 of the Constitution enshrines the right of couples 'to freely and responsibly decide the number of their children'. Article 43 provides that:

> During pregnancy and after birth [women] shall enjoy special assistance and protection from the State, and will receive support benefits from it if they then become unemployed or abandoned.

Article 43 further states that: 'The State shall provide help in a special manner to women heads of family.' In its attention to the family, the Constitution makes substantial public guarantee of the rights of individuals within the private realm of the family.

Normatively: addressing structural gender inequalities

As well as the important juridical value of the Court's jurisprudence, analysis in this section asserts the important symbolic value of the jurisprudence. Adopting a

41 This characterisation of the constitution is taken from Morgan, 1998: 258.

42 At the time of the Constituent Assembly meeting, domestic violence was not expressly dealt with in Colombian legislation. Under the then penal code, domestic violence was criminally punishable only when falling within the general category of *lesiones personales* (personal injuries) requiring that the injury leave visible scars or marks. The then penal code also provided that those charged with crimes of sexual violence could escape criminal liability if they offered to marry their victims (Morgan 1998: 388).

feminist legal deconstructive strategy, analysis here approaches the judgments as narratives (Conaghan 2001: 721). As has been cogently argued by Colombian feminist lawyers in their analysis of constitutional jurisprudence:

> The judgments of the Constitutional Court, as with all judgments, are discourses. That is, networks of words connected by certain rules and certain values. As discourse, they reflect and mould ways of seeing the world which determine the limits, as much as the possibilities, of human activity. [The judgments] demonstrate different perspectives inevitably located within human relationships that develop in cultural contexts. But they also give form to cultural contexts, in the way that they constitute new representations, with possibilities of modifying that which exists and is accepted.
>
> (Centro de Investigaciones Sociojurídicas 1998: 33)

This section therefore interrogates not only the legal substance of the right to 'peace' in the Court's jurisprudence, but also the vision of peace advanced discursively in the Court's jurisprudence.

The political pact that underpinned the 1991 Constitution, which initially held the political and military elites to principles of non-violence, quickly disintegrated. In this context, the strong trend in the Court's jurisprudence was to interpret the right to peace as attaching to the collective and to serve the larger interest of allowing the state to reassert its authority and to monopolise violence within the national territory. The Court did so, for example, by holding that the right to peace imposed a duty on all citizens to accept the violent consequences of having a police station in close proximity to their homes.[43]

This interpretation of the right to peace as collective has also worked to undermine the individual right to peace and to reprivatise violence against women. This is evident, for example, in the endorsement of conciliation as an appropriate mechanism for resolving domestic violence offences. The Constitutional Court has interpreted the right to peace not as the absence of conflict, but rather as the guarantee of a social and institutional space for the peaceful resolution of conflict.[44] Interpreting 'conciliation in equality'[45] as a mechanism for alternative dispute resolution for all matters susceptible to extrajudicial conciliation, including cases of domestic violence,[46] the Court held:

43 Corte Constitucional de Colombia, *Sentencia No. T-139/93*, magistrado ponente Jorge Arango Mejía. See also Corte Constitucional de Colombia, *Sentencia No. T-255/93*, magistrado ponente Fabio Morón Diaz.

44 Corte Constitucional de Colombia, *Sentencia No. T-139/93*, magistrado ponente Jorge Arango Mejia. See also Corte Constitucional de Colombia, *Sentencia No. T-255/93*, magistrado ponente Fabio Morón Diaz.

45 Colombian Constitution, Article 116.

46 Ley 640, Article 105.

> Conciliation is not only congruent with the 1991 Constitution, but can be understood as a projection, at the juridical level, of the pacifist spirit that informs the Constitution in its entirety. This mechanism carries the conviction that – from the confrontation of opposing points of view – a compromise position can be reached, without needing a third party to decide what the parties themselves can agree.
>
> (Court's decision, Corte Constitucional de Colombia, *Sentencia No.* C-165/93 (1993), magistrado ponente Carlos Gaviria Diaz)

Feminists reject that conciliation or mediation provides sufficient recourse in cases of domestic violence, as it lacks sufficient safeguards for the victim (Howe and McIsaac 2008), ignores the inequality that characterises family and societal relationships marked by violence (Howe and McIsaac 2008: 1569) and substitutes justice for 'harmony' (Nader 1992). These arguments made little impression on the Court, despite the documented circumstances of the weak Colombian state, in which non-compliance with conciliation agreements is estimated at rates of 80–85 per cent (Lemaitre Ripoll 2002: 82). In interpreting the right to peace to attach to the collective, the Court's reasoning worked to reprivatise domestic violence, taking it out of the criminal justice realm into which feminists have long campaigned to have it inserted.

When interpreted as an individual right, by contrast, the right to peace has been powerful in its vindication of women's rights. In 1997 the Court was to make its first major decision concerning sexual violence. In the application, the more lenient penalty for sexual violence committed within marriage was challenged as a violation of the rights of family members[47] and children[48] within the Constitution.[49] In allowing the claim, the Court dwelled on the social function of the domestic violence law, as grounded in Article 42 of the Constitution:

> The said protection has the objective, as well as to guarantee the rights of the weakest members of the population (minors, elderly people, women), to eradicate violence in the family, an objective which is committed to the general interest, given that the family is the basic institution and fundamental nucleus of society, and *an essential space for the consolidation of peace.*
>
> (Corte Constitucional de Colombia, *Sentencia No.* C-285/97 (1997), magistrado ponente Carlos Gaviria Diaz, emphasis added)

47 Colombian Constitution, Article 42.

48 Colombian Constitution, Article 44.

49 Corte Constitucional de Colombia, *Sentencia No.* C-285/97 (1997), magistrado ponente Carlos Gaviria Diaz.

The family is identified as a critical realm for 'the consolidation of peace'. The right to sexual liberty is also guaranteed within this family realm. In this decision, the Court offers a very progressive delineation of the public/private divide: the Court breaches the family's private veil in order to guarantee the right of sexual liberty to individual family members within the family.

The right to peace has assumed unprecedented prominence in the Constitutional Court's jurisprudence concerning the legality of the transitional justice process put in place by President Uribe. The Constitutional Court's decision in Sentencia No. C-370 of 2006, the lead decision on the constitutionality of the Justice and Peace Law, Ley 975, marked the most extensive consideration to date of the right to peace. The substance of Ley 975 was modified by the Court, in order to strengthen the rights of victims. For example, the Court required that the *version libre* must be true and complete. Otherwise the demobilised combatant would lose all benefits under the Justice and Peace Law. The judgment also strengthened the reparations provision in the law. The Court's ruling brought the process closer to the required international standards of human rights concerning truth, justice and reparations. In reaching this decision, the Court made its longest exposition ever of the right to peace, its guarantee within international human rights law and international humanitarian law, the status of the right in domestic constitutional order as a right of the collective and of the individual, that satisfaction of the right to peace depends on the effective guarantee of all of the other civil and political rights of individuals and the right to peace as a right against the state and a duty on all Colombians.[50] Ultimately, the Court concluded that rights to justice, truth, reparations and non-recurrence had to be balanced with the collective right to peace, which permitted certain restrictions on the rights of victims.[51] Notable in terms of the gender significance of this decision is the prominence given by women's organisations to the negative impact of the justice and peace process on women, in particular in terms of harms occurring to women within the demilitarisation zones. By affirming the constitutionality of the justice and peace process and its consequent restrictions on the individual rights of victims, the judgment is powerful in its affirmation of new zones of private harm to women.

Politically: affirming women's agency

Further affirming women's individual rights, the Colombian Constitutional Court has proven an important backstop to state inactivity to protect women political

50 Corte de Colombia, *Sentencia No. C-370/06*, magistrados ponentes Manuel Jose Thorny Cepeda Espinosa, Jaime Cordova Triviño, Rodrigo Escobar Gil, Marco Gerardo Monroy Cabra, Alvaro Tafur Galvis, Clara Inés Vargas Hernandez, 4.1 El derecho a la Paz.

51 Corte de Colombia, *Sentencia No. C-370/06*, magistrados ponentes Manuel Jose Thorny Cepeda Espinosa, Jaime Cordova Triviño, Rodrigo Escobar Gil, Marco Gerardo Monroy Cabra, Alvaro Tafur Galvis, Clara Inés Vargas Hernandez, 5.5.

activists. In response to the high-profile assassinations of four women leaders in 2007, the Court held that the existing programme for protection of victims and witnesses was inadequate to protect the applicants' constitutional rights to life and security.[52] Additionally it held that the Minister for Justice and National Office of the Prosecutor were under a legal obligation to establish a programme of protection within six months that specifically addressed the added vulnerability of women victims seeking to avail themselves of the justice and peace process.[53]

When the Court has affirmed women's individual rights, it has been a powerful proponent for women's equality in Colombia. As such, the Colombian Constitution and the Constitutional Court have proven to be a potent 'enabling framework' (Waylen 2011) for rights demands of individual women. An examination of Colombian feminist mobilisation since the adoption of the 1991 Constitution reveals increasing engagement with the law and, more specifically, with the Constitutional Court. The emergence of organisations such as SISMA Mujer in 1998 'to do work with a greater interest in targeting the law, the legal, the juridical'[54] is exemplary of this trend. The establishment of feminist NGOs such as SISMA demonstrated an ideological shift in Colombian feminism to considering law 'as a realm of emancipation, as a realm where certain advances could be made'.[55] The reorientation towards specifically legal mechanisms in feminist mobilisation was replicated and fostered within the Colombian legal academy. Colombian feminist legal academics, based in particular at the Universidad de los Andes School of Law, set about monitoring Constitutional Court jurisprudence for its treatment of women and issues of gender (see especially Motta 1998).

The reasons for the effectiveness of the Colombian Constitution and Court as an enabling framework for women's rights demands are both internal-institutional and external-political. The internal-institutional factors can be identified as threefold: first, the availability of the *tutela* as a preventative and reactive measure providing immediate access to the Court in the case of actual or potential rights violation, combined with the relatively liberal membership of the Court,[56] means that Colombians have come to view the Court as a protective institution against violations perpetrated by other state institutions (Sánchez Gómez 2008: 26). Second, the broad standing granted by the Constitution and the Court has made the Court highly amenable to advocacy groups. Finally, the domestic legal status given to the state's international human rights commitments, reinforced by the frequency and willingness of the Inter-American Commission and Court to find Colombia in violation of its international human rights obligations, means that the

52 Corte Constitucional de Colombia, *Sentencia No.* T-025-04 (2004).

53 Corte Constitucional de Colombia, *Auto 092 de 2008* (2008).

54 Claudia Gomez, SISMA Mujer, Bogotá, personal communication, 10 December 2008.

55 Alexandra Quintero, SISMA Mujer, Bogotá, personal communication, 10 December 2008.

56 This has also resulted in several attempts by the Executive to limit the Court's powers. See, for example, International Crisis Group (2003: 6).

Constitutional Court is highly cognisant of the need to consider the international human rights jurisprudence in its reasoning. Chief amongst the external factors for the effectiveness of the Colombian Constitution and Court as an enabling framework for women's rights is the dynamic identified throughout this book, namely the long-standing collaborative relationship between women and human rights groups in Colombia. This relationship has contributed to a high level of legal literacy in Colombian feminist advocacy.

CONCLUSION: INSTITUTIONAL REFORM, THE INTERNATIONAL FRAME AND THE LOCAL FIT

Defining harms

The case studies evidence an overt commitment to international human rights law as a guiding international frame for domestic institutional reform. The Chilean transition was underpinned by a constitutional amendment requiring state institutions to act in compliance with Chile's international human rights commitments. In Northern Ireland, human rights commitments were fundamental to the peace agreement and an underpinning value to all of the institutional reforms mandated in the agreement. The Colombian Constitution of 1991 gave prominence and legal precedence to the state's international human rights obligations. However, closer scrutiny of institutional reform in each of the case studies reveals the highly selective invocation of international human rights law. The case studies evidence the judicial invocation of the language of human rights, with little fealty to the substance of those international human rights obligations. In Northern Ireland, the European system was dominant, with little status given to the CEDAW either by the courts or in the development of a Bill of Rights for the jurisdiction. In Chile, the courts invoke the guarantee of the right to life in the Inter-American Convention without any reference to the regional system's interpretation of that right. The persistence of discriminatory prejudices in the exercise of public power, in particular in the judicial resolution of family relationships, operates in complete defiance of the values and doctrine of the Inter-American system. In Colombia, the domestic 'right to peace' has been interpreted to make international human rights of individual Colombian citizens subservient to the exigencies of the state's conflict strategy.

Redressing structural gender inequalities

This selective invocation of international human rights commitments consistently buttressed the grander political trajectory of transition at the expense of the progressive assertion of women's human rights. The findings across the case studies evidenced teleological jurisprudence that works in complex, though mutually reinforcing, ways against the human rights of women. The space between the formal adoption of international human rights commitments and the daily practical implementation of these commitments is the space in which the vulnerability of formal human rights commitments becomes apparent. The informal gender constraints of higher courts demonstrate a need for stability. Traditional gender norms are highly effective stabilising forces in states otherwise experiencing dramatic changes.

Affirming women's agency

The introduction to this chapter posited the ambition that institutional reforms in transitional justice create an enabling framework for women's movements to advance their political claims. In Chile, institutional reform has shown some belated recognition of women's agency and of the political value of women's social mobilisation. The establishment and personnel of the hard-fought-for and long-awaited Instituto de Derechos Humanos suggests that the defining dichotomy in Chile between women's rights and human rights may be beginning to diminish. The senior courts continue, however, to offer little promise to feminist advocates or to the women's movement. In Northern Ireland, the overwhelming dominance of the sectarian narrative, that posits religion and nationality as the only meaningful political identity, continues to cast women's rights as oppositional to community rights. This leaves little space for the affirmation of a gender or feminist identity *within* one's political community. In Colombia, uniquely of the case studies, constitutional reform and the Constitutional Court have provided an important site and target of feminist mobilisation for the affirmation of women's rights. The Colombian Constitutional Court has led the American continent in its progressive interpretation of the rights of women. Yet the gap between the promise of the Court's judgments and the peril of the unwillingness and inability of state institutions to discharge these judgments is chillingly illustrated in the ongoing assassinations of women political activists.

Part VI

Conclusion

Conclusion

PART ONE: A FEMINIST LAW OF TRANSITIONAL JUSTICE?

Restoring connections: revealing a web of gender-based harms

The book has explored the connections between the harms recognised within transitional justice and those harms deemed 'private', less serious or 'apolitical' within transitional justice. By eschewing established legal categories, and by valuing feminist articulations of harm, a web of harms linking women's public and private experiences of violence and injustice has emerged. This web was demonstrated in the more prosaic details of domestic violence in Northern Ireland: the greater number of legally and illegally held guns in Northern Ireland meant that gun use was more common in incidences of domestic violence. The web of public and private harms is also apparent in so-called 'demilitarisation' initiatives in Colombia: contemporary initiatives to end the 'public' violence of paramilitaries are contingent on the transfer of violence to private spheres of women's homes and bodies. The web of harms is apparent in the punitive politics of personal morality that emerged in transitions in Northern Ireland and Chile, whereby fragile political consensus in these transitional societies was shored up by increasing legal regulation of women's reproductive lives. The web of gender-based harms reveals continuities and relationships between different harms and the manifold ways in which public political violence impacts and exacerbates a range of private harms. Centrally, through extensive empirical research of three separate transitions, the book has demonstrated the continuities between harms that are recognised within transitional justice and harms that are overlooked by the prevailing legal paradigm. We see that legal categorisations of harms in transitional justice, by seeing only the public and the political, retrospectively impose a public/private distinction that is not consistent with the lived reality of conflict and repression.

Revealing continuities of public and private harms reflects work ongoing outside of law for several years. Considerable work has been done by anthropologists (e.g. Parson 2005), sociologists (e.g. Lira n.d.) and psychologists (see especially Herman 2001) to explore and expose the similarities and continuities between the violence and trauma of sexual and domestic violence and the violence of an authoritarian state. Most notably, the work of psychiatrist Judith Herman has been pathbreaking in this regard. She examines the characteristics of traumatic disorders suffered by combat veterans (largely male) and by victims of sexual and domestic violence (largely female). In *Trauma and Recovery*, Herman formulates clinical and social concepts that unify these apparently divergent experiences of trauma. She focuses on the disconnection from human relationships, 'the damage to relational life' caused by a traumatic experience, and how this undermines one's sense of safety in the world (Herman 2001: 51). Captivity – the real or perceived inability to escape from traumatic circumstances – gives rise to intense anger accompanied by a constant fear of retribution (Herman 2001: 94–5). In an intricate account of the nature and impact of combat violence, rape and domestic violence, Herman documents the commonality of disconnection and captivity to each of these forms of violence.

Herman's work has been adopted by Elizabeth Lira to explore the similarities in the nature of fear induced by violence within a family and violence within a society, and how this fear operates to paralyse opposition or resistance in both contexts (Lira n.d.). The anthropologist Nia Parson examines women's experiences of domestic violence within the broader economic inequalities and structural violence that women face, establishing how these different forms of violence operate synergistically to determine the impact on the victim and her chances of healing (Parson 2005).

Moreover, Herman documents how clinical recognition of different traumatic disorders has consistently been accompanied by a political movement. This is evidenced, for example, by the anti-war movement and recognition of post-traumatic stress disorder among Vietnam combat veterans, or the feminist movement and recognition of the psychological trauma of sexual and domestic violence: 'The study of trauma in domestic and sexual life becomes legitimate only in a context that challenges the subordination of women' (Herman 2005: 9). Significantly, therefore, Herman demonstrates that securing recognition of these diverse harms as related and qualitatively similar is intrinsically political and that feminist mobilisation has been critical to securing that recognition.

Each of these feminist scholarly interventions seeking the recognition and definition of gender-based harms is dedicated to revealing the relationships between diverse forms of harm experienced by women. Thus, the continuities of individual and collective harms, of physical and mental harms, and of political, cultural and economic harms are revealed. The avowed objective of this work is:

> restoring connections: between the public and private worlds, between the individual and community, between men and women. [Describing] commonalities: between rape survivors and combat veterans, between battered women and political prisoners, between the survivors of vast concentration

camps created by tyrants who rule nations and the survivors of small, hidden concentration camps created by tyrants who rule their homes.

(Herman 2005: 2–3)

Acknowledging the gender of the 'justice gap'[1]

Recognition of a web of gender-based harms presents a set of normative and legal challenges for transitional justice. Transitional justice is understood as 'partial justice', or as a 'justice gap' (Gray 2006: 2621), that requires deviation from conventional understandings of accountability. Thus, the pursuit of individual criminal liability for each offence committed is not feasible. Rather, the pursuit of individual criminal liability is restricted to leadership figures and to the harms designated 'most serious'. Analysis here has revealed how, in order to secure an end to the incidences of violence and injustice in the public sphere, harms deemed private can be overlooked and ultimately even exacerbated. Otherwise, the reconstruction of the public sphere can be premised on the denial of a private sphere to women in respect of their reproductive lives. For example, 'demilitarisation' zones in Colombia are sites of extraordinary levels of violence and coercion within the private sphere of homes and communities. In Northern Ireland and Chile, the larger political meta-goals of transition are bolstered by increasing legal regulation of women's reproductive lives. The early constitutional jurisprudence emerging from Colombia demonstrated the same tendency, namely to bolster 'public order' by making women's reproductive lives subject to the public morality of the collective. In each of these cases, domestic processes of transition deferred to international law in categorising harms that were either 'most serious', on the one hand, or less serious and therefore amenable to amnesty, on the other. The same international legal categories provide the normative and legal framework of transitional justice more generally and, consequently, the gender dynamics of the cases under study are unlikely to be confined to those cases only.

'Pragmatic' approaches to transitional justice contend that the objectives of transitional justice should not be 'overloaded'.[2] In this reading, the objective of transitional justice is, first and foremost, to facilitate the transition away from mass human rights violations of violent conflict or political repression. To require transitional justice to deliver improvements in accountability or redress for domestic violence and women's reproductive rights is – at best – naïve. At worst, such requirements risk derailing transitions from situations of mass human rights violations by insisting on 'the perfect peace' (Anonymous 1996: 249). Analysis in this book has demonstrated, however, that irrespective of one's normative expectations of transitional justice, transitional justice does in fact heavily impact the legal

1 See Gray (2006: 2621).

2 Compare Hannum (2006: 36–8), advocating clearer distinction between the pursuit of accountability for past harms and reform to institutions of the rule of law.

treatment of violence against women experienced in the home and the legal regulation of women's reproductive lives. Nominally past-focused legal mechanisms, and the political compromise at the heart of transitional justice have a resounding impact on women's post-conflict and post-authoritarian gender-based experiences of violence in their homes and in their reproductive lives. Acknowledgement of this fact transforms the very nature of the so-called peace versus justice dilemma. The question is no longer: why should transitional justice, directed at securing some measure of accountability for mass violence, address a broader range of human rights violations concerning violence against women in the home or women's reproductive lives? With recognition of a web of gender-based harms, and the potential for political compromise on public harms to exacerbate women's experiences of private harms, the question becomes: why should the partiality of transitional justice so consistently take its toll on the bodies of women? Is this gendered pattern of compromise not contrary to even the most modest goals of transitional justice?

IMAGINING A FEMINIST LAW OF TRANSITIONAL JUSTICE

Recognition of the gendered nature of the justice gap prompts a feminist reconsideration of transitional justice: is there a way for changes to legal norms and institutions in transitional justice to move away from a gendered and exclusionary focus on 'most serious harms' and to account for the web of public and private harms that occurs in violent and repressive societies? Can the prevailing legal paradigm be made more accommodating to a transformative feminist goal of ending the web of harms experienced by women in violent and repressive societies? In particular, it is notable that the substantial feminist gains secured in international human rights law over the past two decades, in expanding the range of harms recognised as human rights violations to reflect the diverse experiences of women, have had a limited impact on transitional justice. Is there potential to more effectively integrate progressive developments in the international human rights framework into the legal framework of transitional justice?

Although advanced in a different discipline, the work of Herman and others does posit some novel terrain for a feminist reformulation of transitional justice. By focusing on the harms experienced by the victims – as opposed to the actions of the perpetrator(s) – a feminist law of transitional justice need not be exclusively preoccupied with securing individual criminal liability for each of the public and private harms experienced by women. (It is acknowledged that establishing individual criminal liability can play an important role in ending cycles of impunity for gender-based violence) (Askin 2003: 346). Establishing the 'political motivation' of the perpetrator would not be the prerequisite to recognising the harm experienced. Rather, the priority of a feminist law of transitional justice would be to secure an end to the web of public and private harms experienced by the victims.

The next section sketches the outline of a feminist-informed law of transitional justice. The outline is drawn directly from the findings of the three case studies. The differing outcomes of the case studies, in terms of the impact of transitional justice devices on the legal treatment of violence against women and the legal regulation of women's reproductive lives, reflect to a large extent whether transitional justice was pursued with an emphasis on truth-telling, justice, reparations or institutional reform. Further, the emphasis of transitional justice was linked to the underlying causes of mass violence and the nature of the transition. Hence, both the particular points of good practice and the failings of transitional justice initiatives in each of the case studies undoubtedly reflect the particular political context from which they emerged. Nevertheless, transitional justice in the case studies was pursued through a familiar repertoire of justice, truth, reparations and institutional reform. The feminist law of transitional justice proposes how, by adopting the good practice identified and avoiding negative aspects, transitional justice initiatives can be made to work more effectively for women in diverse political contexts.

Justice

Achievements in the criminalisation and prosecution of sexual violence have set an important precedent in securing broad recognition that gender is a determining factor in one's experience of violent conflict and political repression. The pursuit of retributive justice for individual acts of gender-based violence can set an important marker for the post-conflict and post-authoritarian society of the moral repugnance and legal prohibition of these offences. Retributive justice can therefore be considered for its symbolic effects in demonstrating the illegality of gender-based violence, as well as its educative value as an opportunity to build capacity within the criminal justice system for dealing with crimes of sexual violence more generally. Moreover, the pursuit of retributive justice can be an important basis for mobilising women to intervene in the operation of transitional justice. The reawakening of justice demands in Chile with the arrest of General Pinochet prompted the first domestic feminist interventions into past-focused justice demands. While not delivering justice for gender-based violence in the sense of criminal prosecutions, renewed official efforts to deliver justice finally provided an enabling environment for the formulation of feminist demands on the past and official recognition of the sexual torture of female political dissidents.

The selective pursuit of a small number of prosecutions is premised on the existence of a much larger-scale amnesty or highly qualified accountability. The reintegration of former combatants into civilian life is an integral part of the demilitarisation objectives of transitional justice and is facilitated by amnesty. Perversely, however, the compromises made on justice and accountability in contemporary Colombia have been shown to engender further forms of violence against women, particularly against women living within demilitarisation zones. The pursuit of alternative forms of justice, for example through conciliation in

Colombia, is with the avowed objective of advancing peace in this transitional context. Nevertheless, such initiatives risk reprivatising gender-based violence experienced by women within their homes and communities. Together, these incidents demonstrate the clear potential for the ending of violence in transition to be a chimera, dependent on the movement of violence from public to private spheres.

A feminist reformulation of the justice component in transition would emphasise the symbolic and educational, as well as retributive, components of such justice initiatives. Further, a minimum commitment to at least *do no harm*, informed by an understanding of the web of gender-based harms and an awareness of the potential for violence to move between public and private spheres, might usefully guide the design of such initiatives. Hence, compromises on justice and accountability should not be conceded at the cost of increased gender-based violence in the homes and communities to which demobilised combatants return. Further, the formulation of alternative forms of penalties should resist the tendency to reprivilege formerly violent actors within the community, particularly where this is done at the expense of long-established women's organisations.

Truth

The recognition of women's political subjectivity in official accounts of the past has been shown in this book to have significance for the longer-term equal citizenship of women in societies emerging from conflict or repression. The legacy of the failures of the Chilean Truth and Reconciliation Commission to acknowledge and affirm women's political subjectivity still resonates in Chile today. Recognition of women as 'mothers of' or 'sisters of' direct victims, while important, can only ever be a partial account of the diverse forms of women's political participation. Further, the denial of a truth or a past to former combatant women, as in Colombia, forms the basis of gendered, unequal and exclusionary forms of citizenship. Official truth-seeking initiatives in Northern Ireland seem destined for the same fate. The Colombian example, by contrast, demonstrates the potential for official truth-seeking initiatives to subvert dominant understandings of the past and the conflict, and to offer alternative formulations of 'before' and 'after' that recognise the continuities of gender-based violence and the web of gender-based harms. The work of the Colombian Group on Historical Memory has demonstrated that it is possible for official truth-seeking initiatives to acknowledge and affirm women's political subjectivity in its diverse forms.

Official definitions of the violence and injustice to be ended by transition should seek to account for the web of public and private harms articulated in this book. Truth-seeking mechanisms should provide a forum and mandate to explore and articulate the relationships of public or political violence to private incidences of harm. Central here is providing an account of the past that captures the complexity of gender-based harms, rather than sacrificing that complexity to legal absolutes such as 'most serious violations' and 'political motivation'.

Reparations

The potential for reparations programmes to perpetuate gender inequalities has been clearly demonstrated in each of the case studies under analysis. In Chile, the initial design of the reparations programme privileged traditional family forms and reaffirmed a legal narrative of foetal rights that is experienced punitively by women. In Colombia, making reparations payments contingent on the outcome of a conciliation process between the perpetrator and the victim perpetuates the violence and inequality of power relations between these two actors, rather than restoring the victim to a position of civic trust and dignity.[3] In Northern Ireland, the state devolving of its duties to provide services to victims in the women-dominated victims sector further naturalises the position of women in 'apolitical' caretaking roles. Reparations programmes have done little to establish women's equal citizenship in these transitional societies.

By contrast, a feminist-informed approach to reparations might begin with the question: how can the design of an administrative or judicial programme of reparations contribute to the recognition of women as equal citizens in transitional societies? Recent feminist analysis has considered the potential of reparations programmes: to use the involvement of women in the design of reparations programmes to promote women 'as valuable agents of political and social transformation' in post-conflict societies (de Greiff and Rubio-Marin 2007: 321); to disrupt practices and norms that are frequently part of pre-existing gender hierarchies, for example by departing from iniquitous laws of inheritance to ensure women a fair apportionment of benefits (de Greiff and Rubio-Marin 2007: 325); to accompany reparations for sexual violence 'by a serious effort to encompass other forms of victimisation that also have a disparate impact on women', such as forced domestic labour (de Greiff and Rubio-Marin 2007: 325); or to systematically address the needs of certain groups who are particularly vulnerable before, during and after conflict (de Greiff and Rubio-Marin 2007: 325). Importantly, this analysis has started from the premise that 'in situations of large-scale violence and repression, reparations are best conceptualised as rights-based political projects aimed at enhancing civic trust both among citizens and between citizens and state institutions' (de Greiff and Rubio-Marin 2007: 321). This work signals the capacity of appropriately designed reparations programmes to advance women's equal citizenship in transitional justice.

Institutional reform

Reform to state institutions in transition is premised on the need to prevent the recurrence of past harms. Feminist-informed institutional reform considers exactly

3 The key scholar in the area, Pablo de Greiff (2006), characterises the purpose of reparations as to enhance civic trust among citizens and between citizens and actors.

which harms are to be ended by transition. As the Northern Ireland case demonstrates, institutional reform can deliver an improved state response to, for example, domestic violence. The post-authoritarian Chilean government established a bespoke institution for the advancement of women, with a priority focus on addressing domestic violence. Further, the 1991 Colombian Constitution established a range of new rights protections, affirmed women's right to equality in the family, work and political life, and established the Constitutional Court, which has acted as an assertive and progressive guardian of those rights. These very promising institutional reforms were avowedly undertaken to address the armed conflict in the country. Hence, there is nothing inevitable about institutional reform being structured along a public/private divide that ignores women's experiences of violence within the home.

Further, institutional reform is premised on securing the inclusion of groups formerly excluded from the political process, in order to ensure that mechanisms exist for the peaceful expression of conflict between opposing groups. Again, feminist-informed institutional reform would consider exactly which groups are recognised as 'formerly excluded'. Who counts in 'inclusion'? The Northern Irish case of *In re White*,[4] in which the High Court held that the obligation on public bodies to be 'representative of the community' referred to Catholic and Protestant communities in the context of parading, and not to women and men, provides a stark example of just who tends to count when defining 'formerly excluded groups'. Feminist-informed institutional reform would, however, value and facilitate the inclusion of a diversity of groups, including women, in the political process.

Further, it is important to consider political participation not only in terms of new democratic institutions. Transitional justice mechanisms and new legal institutions should themselves be understood as targets and sites of political participation. The resounding impression from each of the case studies is the deeply political work of defining harm in transitional justice, whether these definitions address past or future harms, public or private harms. The contours of institutional reform constitute important sites of political contestation over the definition of harm in transitional justice. This contestation plays out long into the implementation phase of any political pact underpinning transitional justice. Institutional reform in transitional justice should therefore facilitate this contestation in an inclusive and meaningful way. Institutional reform that reprivileges already privileged actors should be challenged on those grounds.[5]

4 *In Re An Application by Evelyn White for Judicial Review*, The High Court of Justice in Northern Ireland, CARE3208 (Transcript), 18 May 2000.

5 These arguments are developed more fully in O'Rourke (2009).

PART TWO: . . . OR A FEMINIST POLITICS OF SEEKING GENDER JUSTICE IN TRANSITION?

The introduction to the book established two factors as the book's motivation. First, the proliferation of transitional justice mechanisms and the recognition of their significance for women's status and gender relations in post-conflict and post-authoritarian contexts. Second, growing feminist unease about the gap between ostensible feminist gains in international law and the actual impact of international law on women's daily lives. This final section reflects on the findings and their implications for both feminist confidence in the transformative potential of transitional justice and feminist engagement with international law. While these reflections refer principally to the internally driven transitions under study in the book, they hold some tentative applicability to the ever-increasing number of internationally driven processes of transitional justice.

Transitional justice as transformative for women?

Analysis in the three cases under study suggests that the participation of women, and explicit recognition of gender, is alone no panacea in transitional justice. In many respects, the findings from the case studies are surprising: the prominence of domestic violence in institutional reform in Northern Ireland; the prominence of the conflict's toll on women in the liberalisation of abortion law in Colombia; and the political expediency for the women's movement in Chile of dissociating itself from past-focused justice claims. Nevertheless, the book's findings suggest that isolated improvements in the state response to private harms against women seemed to be consistently linked to the elision of state accountability for public harms. Transitional states in Chile and Northern Ireland can bolster their human rights credentials by beginning to target domestic violence, while resisting any meaningful measure of accountability for state-perpetrated harms of the past. In Colombia, the state's determination to portray every human rights and equality issue as a consequence of the conflict – a position supported by the Constitutional Court's reasoning in liberalising abortion law in the country – perversely works to deny the state's own role in human rights violations, inequality and ultimately the conflict itself. The consistency with which states resist meaningful accountability for the wrongs in which they are complicit suggests that the dynamics in the case studies are far from unique. The findings here posit the worrying conclusion that positive human rights outcomes for women in transitional justice might be secured at the expense of legitimating a process that is in fact contrary to a broader feminist objective of gender justice in transition, where gender justice is understood as addressing a web of public *and* private harms.

These findings prompt a number of questions for feminist engagement with transitional justice. For example, to what extent do positive developments in the gender aspect of transitional justice legitimate other less benign goals of transition? How does an officially sanctioned desire for transitional justice to 'include women' and be 'gender-sensitive' relate to the need to bolster the legitimacy of transitional states, *without* those states substantially addressing inequality or injustice? To quote Anne Orford: 'Does gender work as a category in such situations, and if so, *whose work does it do*?' (Orford 2002: 293, emphasis added).

These dynamics around state legitimacy adopt additional complexity within the political opportunity structure of most contemporary internationally driven transitions. In the case of failed states, international intervention is the prerequisite to any official process of transitional justice. These internationalised processes are typically either resisted or heavily manipulated by local power elites (Sajjad 2013). Against this backdrop, the involvement of women and of local women's organisations can be an effective short-cut for international actors to secure ostensible popular legitimacy for internationally driven processes (Tickner 2002), but can also posit women as either outsiders or enemies to local political constituencies. The resources to be mobilised by women's organisations in their engagement with official transitional justice processes may be entirely external. This will have serious consequences in terms of their ability to mobilise domestic resources as the transition beds down and becomes increasingly controlled by local political elites. International actors may well frame their operation of domestic transitional justice processes in terms of women's equality and advancing women's human rights; however, the gains to local women's movements from the resonance with the framing of international actors may be very short-term. These tentative observations point to the value of further in-depth qualitative and legal research into the interaction of the local fit and international frame in internationally driven processes of transitional justice so as to understand the human rights outcomes for women of such processes.

Read together, these findings and observations make a strong case against legal templates for ensuring feminist outcomes in transitional justice. Legal templates, applied uniformly across very different transitional contexts, will inevitably fail to consider the political dynamics driving transitional justice in a particular context. Ultimately, the case studies demonstrate that gender justice for women looks very different in each transitional justice process. In Northern Ireland, more sophisticated state response to the intersectional identities of women might form the basis of gender justice for women, manifesting in an end to the privileging of women's 'apolitical' activity and, amongst a range of outcomes, the improved detention conditions of women. In Chile, an end to the punitive valorisation of maternity might underpin gender justice for women, in the form of vindicating women's reproductive autonomy and recognising equal though diverse forms of women's citizenship. In Colombia, official acknowledgement of the conflict's roots in inequality and human rights violations, that explores and addresses the structural underpinnings of violence in the country, might form the basis of gender justice for women. Transitional justice and its human rights outcomes for women can only really be understood and evaluated with reference to the surrounding political context.

Consequently, although the book sets out the potential design of a feminist law of transitional justice, these proposals should be considered only to the extent that they support and advance a feminist politics of seeking gender justice in transition. A feminist politics of seeking gender justice in transition cannot, by definition, be captured by legal templates.

Analysis in this book has demonstrated the complexity of public/private distinctions in a state undergoing transition. Formerly private concerns of violence within the family can assume unexpected prominence in the public sphere of a transitional state. Classically public concerns of state-perpetrated violence can be forced into the private sphere and become the exclusive concern of a small number of surviving relatives of victims. The most intimate parts of a woman's life, maternity and reproduction, can become subject to public ownership and control. The consistency with which these gendered shifts in the division of public and private occurred across three very different case studies indicates the heavy manipulation to which the public and private are subjected by states seeking to create a rehabilitated public sphere through transitional justice. Nevertheless, for women's movements seeking to make gains through the state, the overall project of rehabilitating the public sphere is helpful. The state can thereby become a legitimate site of feminist activity and feminist gains.

The web of gender-based harms, which includes a full range of harms whether deemed public or private and understands the relationship between them, is a useful tool when considering public/private distinctions in the transitional state. Sharp distinctions (borne of political expediency) between harms of the past and harms of the future operated in Chile and Northern Ireland to deny recognition or redress to the public harms experienced by women detained in periods of conflict and repression. The improved response of the 'new' state to traditionally private harms within homes was secured at the expense of accountability for harms against political dissidents perpetrated by the state in the past. The damaging disaggregation of harms into public and private and past and future should be resisted by feminists, even when such disaggregation provides the basis of select gender gains in relation to particular harms. A principled feminist commitment to gender justice in transition would continue to articulate and seek redress for the web of gender-based harms.

Feminism and international law

Contrasting the early Chilean transition with the contemporary process of transitional justice in Colombia demonstrates just how much the international legal landscape has shifted in the intervening two decades. Women and gender are now on the agenda, in no matter how partial or unsatisfactory a way. Inclusion in the transitional justice agenda did not come about spontaneously or through the unprompted enlightenment of the international community. Recognition of women and gender as important to the transitional justice agenda has principally come about through decades of transnational feminist campaigning to demand change in international law and human rights. These achievements have been remarkable.

Yet it is critical to understand the limits of law's reach. Certain harms are more amenable to definition and recognition by legal categories. As shown, physical harms to the individual body, perpetrated within a narrow understanding of political violence, fall most easily within the existing purview of transitional justice. This is particularly the case where the focus is individual criminal liability. Feminist critiques of the narrow range of recognised legal harms in transitional justice, however, should not inexorably lead to the pursuit of the *criminalisation* of another range of harms, such as socio-economic, non-bodily or perceived non-political harms. Decades of feminist engagement with rape law teach us the duplicitous nature of criminal law reform (Smart 1989: 26–49).The criminalisation of certain harms often does little to effectively discontinue the harm, or secure a remedy for the victim. The criminalisation of a wider range of gender harms reprivileges law in the identification and definition of harms. Where minor gains are made in broadening legal categories, this reinforces the diminished status of a wider range of harms. Legal categories are not well suited to the subtleties and complexities of harms experienced due to familial separation and disruption to family life, or the denigration of community esteem. The failure of law to characterise certain harms does not, however, mean that such harms need be entirely invisible or unaddressed. For example, Judith Herman's work demonstrates the importance of clinical recognition of a range of harms and their consequences as intrinsic to valuing women's lives, and remedying harms experienced by women. Moreover, her work emphasises the importance of a social movement to securing clinical recognition of these complex harms experienced by women.

Hard-won gains in feminist campaigning secured leverage and access to processes of international law formerly marked by their exclusion of women. And with this leverage and access comes responsibility. Findings here reveal women as agents in transitional justice processes, with influence, clout and leverage. This suggests that examining where women are in fact included, and which actors and dynamics are being legitimated in the process, might provide a better basis for principled engagement with transitional justice than default assumptions of women's marginality or exclusion. This is not an easy conceptual shift to make. It challenges the self-perceptions of many women's and feminist organisations of being '*utterly without power*' (Halley 2006: 9, original emphasis). It requires feminists to take ownership of the consequences of our advocacy and participation in transitional justice processes. However, the conceptual shift proposed here is also liberating: in recognising that, through participation and inclusion, feminists wield influence on the shape and contours of transitional justice, we recognise that feminists can also wield influence in our absence and self-exclusion from such processes. Moreover, in attending to non-legal categories and categorisation of harms, more accommodating space for feminist articulations of harm may be uncovered. Ultimately, strengthening that recognition may inspire feminist articulations of justice in transitional justice that are even more creative and transformative than those seen to date.

Bibliography

Books and Articles

Acuña Moenne, M. E. (2005) 'Embodying memory: women and the legacy of the military government in Chile', *Feminist Review* 79: 150–61.

Albertyn, C. (1994) 'Women and the transition to democracy in South Africa' in Murray, C. (ed), *Gender and the New South African Legal Order*, Cape Town: Juta & Co, Ltd.

Allen, J. (1990) 'Does Feminism Need a Theory of "The State"?' in Watson, S. (ed), *Playing the State*, London: Verso.

Alvarez, E. and Banks, W. C. (1991) 'The new Colombian constitution: democratic victory or popular surrender?', *University of Miami Inter-American Law Review* 23: 39–92.

Alvarez, S. (1990) *Engendering Democracy in Brazil: Women's Movements in Transition Politics*, Princeton, NJ: Princeton University Press.

Alvarez, S. (1999) 'Advocating feminism: the Latin American feminist NGO "boom"', *International Feminist Journal of Politics* 1(2): 181–209.

Anonymous (1996) 'Human rights in peace negotiations', *Human Rights Quarterly* 18: 249–58.

Arthur, P. (2009) 'How "transitions" reshaped human rights: a conceptual history of transitional justice', *Human Rights Quarterly* 31: 321–67.

Askin, K. (1997) *War Crimes Against Women: Prosecution in International War Crimes Tribunals*, The Hague: Martinus Nijhoff.

Askin, K. (2003) 'Prosecuting wartime rape and other gender-related crimes under international law: extraordinary advances, enduring obstacles', *Berkeley Journal of International Law* 21: 288–349.

Backer, D. (2003) 'Civil society and transitional justice: possibilities, patterns and prospects', *Journal of Human Rights* 2(3): 297–313.

Baldez, L. (2001) 'Coalition politics and the limits of state feminism', *Women and Politics* 22(4): 1–28.

Baldez, L. (2002) *Why Women Protest: Women's Movements in Chile*, Cambridge: Cambridge University Press.

Banaszak, L. A., Beckwith, K. and Rucht, D. (2003) 'When Power Relocates: Interactive Changes in Women's Movements and States', in Banaszak, L. A., Beckwith, K. and Rucht, D. (eds), *Women's Movements Facing the Reconfigured State*, New York: Cambridge University Press.

Barraza Morelle, C. and Guzmán, D. E. (2008) 'Proceso de Reparación para las Mujeres Víctimas de Violencia en el Marco del Conflicto Armado Colombiano', in Corporación

Humanas (ed), *Sin Tregua: Políticas de reparación para mujeres víctimas de violencia sexual durante dictaduras y conflictos armados*, Santiago: Corporación Humanas, Centro Regional de Derechos Humanos y Justicia de Género.
Bedont, B. and Hall Martinez, K. (1999) 'Ending impunity for gender crimes under the International Criminal Court', *The Brown Journal of World Affairs* 6(1): 65–85.
Bell, C. (2000) *Peace Agreements and Human Rights*, Oxford: Oxford University Press.
Bell, C. (2003) 'Dealing with the past in Northern Ireland', *Fordham International Law Journal* 26: 1095–147.
Bell, C. (2005) 'Women and the Problems of Peace Agreements: Strategies for Change', in Coomaraswamy, R. and Fonseka, D. (eds), *Peace Work: Women, Armed Conflict and Negotiation*, New Delhi: Women Unlimited.
Bell, C. (2008) *On the Law of Peace: Peace Agreements and the* Lex Pacificatoria, Oxford: Oxford University Press.
Bell, C. (2009) 'Transitional justice, interdisciplinarity and the state of the "field" or "non-field"', *International Journal of Transitional Justice* 3(1): 5–27.
Bell, C. and Keenan, J. (2004) 'Human rights nongovernmental organizations and the problems of transition', *Human Rights Quarterly* 26: 330–74.
Bell, C. and Keenan, J. (2005) 'Lost on the way home? The right to life in Northern Ireland', *Journal of Law and Society* 32: 68–89.
Bell, C. and O'Rourke C. (2007) 'Does feminism need a theory of transitional justice? An introductory essay', *International Journal of Transitional Justice* 1(1): 23–44.
Blofield, M. (2006) *The Politics of Moral Sin: Abortion and Divorce in Spain*, New York: Routledge.
Boon, K. (2001) 'Rape and forced pregnancy under the ICC Statute: human dignity, autonomy and consent', *Columbia Human Rights Law Review* 32: 625–76.
Borzutzky, S. and Oppenheim, L. H. (eds), *After Pinochet: The Chilean Road to Democracy and the Market*, Gainesville, FA: University of Florida Press.
Brownmiller, S. (1993) *Against Our Will: Men, Women and Rape*, New York: Fawcett Columbine.
Brysk, A. (1993) 'From above and below: social movements, the international system, and human rights in Argentina', *Comparative Political Studies* 26(3): 259–85.
Buckley-Zistel, S. and Stanley, R. (eds) (2011) *Gender in Transitional Justice*, Basingstoke: Palgrave Macmillan.
Bunch, C. (1990) 'Women's rights as human rights: toward a re-vision of human rights', *Human Rights Quarterly* 12: 486–98.
Bunch, C. and Reilly, N. (1994) *Demanding Accountability: The Global Campaign and Vienna Tribunal for Women's Human Rights*, New York: UNIFEM.
Bunster, X. (1985) 'Surviving beyond Fear: Women and Torture in Latin America', in Nash, J. and Safia, H. (eds), *Women and Change in Latin America*, South Hadley, MA: Bergin & Garvey.
Bunster, X. (1991) 'Sobreviviendo más allá del miedo', in ISIS *et al* (eds), *La mujer ausente: Derechos humanos en el mundo*, Santiago: ISIS Internacional.
Burgerman, S. D. (1998) 'Mobilizing principles: the role of transnational activists in promoting human rights principles', *Human Rights Quarterly* 20: 905–23.
Campbell, C. and Ní Aoláin, F. (2005) 'The paradox of transition in conflicted democracies', *Human Rights Quarterly* 27: 172–213.
Campbell, C. and Turner, C. (2008) 'Utopia and the doubters: truth, transition and the law', *Legal Studies* 28(3): 374–95.

Casas, L. (2003) 'Derechos Humanos de las Mujeres', in Universidad Diego Portales Facultad de Derecho (ed), *Informe Anual sobre Derechos Humanos en Chile 2003*, Santiago: Universidad Diego Portales Facultad de Derecho.

Casas, L. (2004) 'Women and reproduction: from control to autonomy? The case of Chile', *American University Journal of Gender, Social Policy and the Law* 12: 427–51.

Casas, L. (2008) 'La Saga de la anticoncepción de emergencia en Chile: avances y desafíos', *Serie Documentos Electrónicos N°2, Noviembre, Programa Género y Equidad*, Santiago: FLACSO Chile and UNFPA.

Cassese, A. (2008) *International Criminal Law*, New York and Oxford: Oxford University Press.

Chappell, L. (2011) 'Nested Newness and Institutional Innovation: Expanding Gender Justice in the International Criminal Court', in Krook, M. L. and Mackay, F. (eds), *Gender, Politics and Institutions: Towards a Feminist Institutionalism*, Basingstoke: Palgrave Macmillan.

Charlesworth, H. (1993) 'Alienating Oscar? Feminist Analysis of International Law', in Dallmeyer, D. (ed), *Reconceiving Reality: Women and International Law*, Washington DC: American Society of International Law.

Charlesworth, H. (1998) 'The unbearable lightness of customary international law', *American Society of International Law Proceedings* 92: 44–7.

Charlesworth, H. and Chinkin, C. (2000) *The Boundaries of International Law: A Feminist Analysis*, Manchester: Manchester University Press.

Charlesworth, H., Chinkin, C and Wright, S. (1991) 'Feminist approaches to international law', *American Journal of International Law* 85: 613–45.

Chinkin, C. (1994) 'Rape and sexual abuse of women in international law', *European Journal of International Law* 5: 326–41.

Chuchryk, P. (1989) 'Subversive Mothers: the Women's Opposition to the Military Regime in Chile', in Charlton, S. E., Everett, J. and Staudt, K. (eds), *Women, the State, and Development*, Albany: State University of New York Press.

Chuchryk, P. (1994) 'From Dictatorship to Democracy: The Women's Movement in Chile', in Jaquette J. (ed), *The Women's Movement In Latin America: Participation And Democracy*, Boulder, San Francisco and Oxford: Westview Press.

Cockburn, C. (1998) *The Space Between Us: Negotiating Gender And National Identities in Conflict*, London: Zed Books.

Cockburn, C. (2007) *From Where We Stand*, London: Zed Books.

Cohen, S. (1996) 'Government responses to human rights reports: claims, denials, and counterclaims', *Human Rights Quarterly* 18: 517–43.

Collins, C. (2006). 'Grounding global justice: international networks and domestic human rights accountability in Chile and El Salvador', *Journal of Latin American Studies* 38: 711–38.

Collins, C. (2010) *Post-Transitional Justice: Human Rights Trials in Chile and El Salvador*, University Park, PA: University of Pennsylvania Press.

Collins, C., Herbst, J. *et al* (2011) 'Verdad, Justicia y Memoria: Las Violaciones a los Derechos Humanos del Pasado', in *Informe Annual*, UDPF d. Derecho, Santiago.

Conaghan, J. (1996) 'Gendered harms and the law of torts: remedying (sexual) harassment', *Oxford Journal of Legal Studies* 16: 407–31.

Conaghan, J. (2001) 'Wishful thinking or bad faith: a feminist encounter with Duncan Kennedy's *Critique of Adjudication*', *Cardozo Law Review* 22: 721–46.

Constable, P. and Valenzuela, A. (1991) *A Nation of Enemies: Chile Under Pinochet*, New York: W. W. Norton & Company.

Cook, R. (ed) (1994) *Human Rights of Women: National and International Perspectives*, Philadelphia: Pennsylvania University Press, Pennsylvania Studies of Human Rights.

Copelon, R. (1994) 'Surfacing gender: re-engraving crimes against women in humanitarian law', *Hastings Women's Law Journal* 5(2): 243–66.

Copelon, R. (2003) 'Tortura bajo el Régimen de Pinochet: Violencia Sexual Contra las Mujeres', in Fundación Instituto de la Mujer (ed), *4° Tribunal de Derechos de las Mujeres Chilenas*, Santiago: Fundación Instituto de la Mujer.

Copelon, R., Zampaz, C., Brusie, E. and Devore, J. (2005) 'Human rights begin at birth: international law and the claim of fetal rights', *Reproductive Health Matters* 13(26): 120–29.

Corcoran, M. (2006) *Out of Order: The Political Imprisonment of Women in Northern Ireland, 1972–1998*, Cullompton and Portland: Willan Publishing.

Cover, R. (1983) 'Nomos and Narrative I', *Harvard Law Review* 97: 4–67.

Craske, N. (1998) 'Remasculinisation and the Neoliberal State in Latin America', in Randall, V. and Waylen, G. (eds), *Gender, Politics and the State*, London and New York: Routledge.

Craske, N. (2003) 'Gender, Poverty and Social Movements', in Chant, S. and Craske, N. (eds), *Gender in Latin America*, London: Latin America Bureau.

De Greiff, P. (2006) 'Introduction, Repairing the Past: Compensation for Victims of Human Rights Violations', in de Greiff, P. (ed), *The Handbook of Reparations*, Oxford and NY: Oxford University Press:.

De Greiff, P. (2007) 'Justice and Reparations', in Miller, J. and Kumar, R. (eds), *Reparations: Interdisciplinary Inquiries*, New York and Oxford: Oxford University Press.

De Greiff, P. and Rubio-Marin, R. (2007) 'Women and reparations', *International Journal of Transitional Justice* 1: 318–37.

De Londras, F. (2009) 'Prosecuting Sexual Violence in the Ad Hoc International Criminal Tribunals for Rwanda and the former Yugoslavia', UCD Working Papers in Law, Criminology and Socio-Legal Studies, Dublin.

Diaz, C. (2007) 'Colombia's Bid for Justice and Peace', *Building a Future on Peace and Justice*, International Conference, Nuremberg, 25–27 June 2007.

Dickson, B. (2003) 'Victims' Rights', in Hamber, B. and Wilson, R. (eds), *Recognition and Reckoning: The Way Ahead on Victims Issues*, Belfast: Democratic Dialogue.

Dobrowolsky, A. (2000) *The Politics of Pragmatism: Women, Representation, and Constitutionalism in Canada*, Toronto: Oxford University Press.

Dobrowolsky, A. and Hart, V. (2003) 'Women Making Constitutions: New Politics and Comparative Perspectives', in Dobrowolsky, A. and Hart, V. (eds), *Women Making Constitutions: New Politics and Comparative Perspectives*, Basingstoke and New York: Palgrave Macmillan.

Dugard, J. (2005) *International Law: A South African Perspective*, 3rd edn, Cape Town: Jutta & Co.

Duggan, C. and Abusharaf, A. (2006) 'Reparation of Sexual Violence in Democratic Transitions: the Search for Gender Justice', in de Greiff, P. (ed), *The Handbook of Reparations*, New York and Oxford: Oxford University Press.

Duggan, C. and Jacobson, R. (2009) 'Reparation of Sexual and Reproductive Violence: Moving from Codification to Implementation', in Rubio-Marin, R. (ed), *The Gender of Reparations: Unsettling Sexual Hierarchies While Redressing Human Rights Violations*, Cambridge and New York: Cambridge University Press.

Elshtain, J. B. (1981) *Public Man, Private Woman: Women in Social and Political Thought*, Princeton and Chichester: Princeton University Press.

Engle, K. (2005) 'Feminism and its (dis)contents: criminalizing wartime rape in Bosnia and Herzegovina', *American Journal of International Law* 99: 778–816.

Evans, C. (2012) *The Right to Reparation in International Law for Victims of Armed Conflict*, Cambridge: Cambridge University Press.

Ewing, K. and Gearty, C. (1990) *Freedom Under Thatcher: Civil Liberties in Modern Britain*, Oxford: Clarendon Press.

Father Dennis Faul (1983) *The Stripping Naked of the Women Prisoners in Armagh Prison 1982/83*, Belfast.

Fearon, K. (1999) *Women's Work: The Story of the Women's Coalition*, Belfast: Blackstaff.

Fineman, M. (1992) 'Feminist theory in law: the difference it makes', *Columbia Journal of Gender and Law* 2: 1–23.

Fineman, M. (1995) *The Neutered Mother, the Sexual Family, and other Twentieth Century Tragedies*, New York and London: Routledge.

Fitzsimmons, T. (2000) *Beyond the Barricades: Women, Civil Society, and Participation after Democratization in Latin America*, New York and London: Garland Publishing.

Fletcher, L., Weinstein, H. and Rowen, J. (2009) 'Context, timing and the dynamics of transitional justice: a historical perspective', *Human Rights Quarterly* 31(1): 163–220.

Foster, R. F. (1988) *Modern Ireland 1600–1972*, London: Penguin.

Foucault, M. (1980) *Power/Knowledge: Selected Interviews and Other Writings*, New York: Pantheon Books.

Fraser, N. (1998) 'Sex, Lies, and the Public Sphere: Reflections on the Confirmation of Clarence Thomas', in Landes, J. (ed), *Feminism, the Public and the Private*, New York and Oxford: Oxford University Press.

Friedman, E. (2003) 'Gendering the Agenda: The Impact of the Transnational Women's Rights Movement at the UN Conferences of the 1990s', *Women's Studies International Forum* 26(4): 313–31.

Frühling, H. (1983) 'Stages of repression and legal strategy for the defense of human rights in Chile: 1973–1980', *Human Rights Quarterly* 5: 510–33.

Fullard, M. (2004) *Dis-placing Race: The South African Truth and Reconciliation Commission and Interpretations of Violence*, Cape Town: Centre for the Study of Violence and Reconciliation.

Furedi, A. (ed) (1995) *The Abortion Law in Northern Ireland*, Belfast: Family Planning Association Northern Ireland, with support from Europe Region, International Planned Parenthood Federation.

Fuszara, M. (1991) 'Legal regulation of abortion in Poland', *Signs: Journal of Women in Culture and Society* 17(1): 117–29.

Gallon, G. (2007) 'Human Rights: A Path to Democracy and Peace in Colombia', in Welna, C. and Gallon, G. (eds), *Peace, Democracy, and Human Rights in Colombia*, Notre Dame, IN: University of Notre Dame, 353–409.

Gardam, J. (1997) 'Women and the law of armed conflict: why the silence?', *International and Comparative Law Quarterly* 46: 55–80.

Garretón, R. (2005) 'La Defensa de los Derechos Humanos y la Agresion Sexual a Mujeres Presas durante la Dictadura', in Fundación Instituto de la Mujer and Centro Regional de Derechos Humanos y Justicia de Género (eds), *Memorias de Ocupación: Violencia Sexual contra Mujeres Detenidas durante la Dictadura*, Santiago.

Gaviola, E., Largo, E. *et al* (1994) *Una Historia Necesaria: Mujeres en Chile: 1973–1990*, Santiago: Aki & Aora Ltda.

Geiger, R. (1998) 'The German border guard cases and international human rights', *European Journal of International Law* 9(3): 540–49.

Getgen, J. E. (2008) 'Reproductive injustice: an analysis of Nicaragua's complete abortion ban', *Cornell International Law Journal* 41: 143–77.

Gonzales, N. (1989) *Violencia Domestica: Analisis Critico de Sentencias y Expedientes*, Santiago: Oficina Legal de la Mujer.

Gonzales, N. (1992) 'A New Concept of Mediation: An Interdisciplinary Approach to Domestic Violence in Chile', in Schuler, M. (ed), *Freedom from Violence: Women's Strategies from Around the World*, New York: UNIFEM.

Gray, D. (2006) 'An excuse-centered approach to transitional justice', *Fordham Law Review* 74: 2621–93.

Green, J., Copelon, R. *et al* (1994) 'Affecting the rules for the prosecution of rape', *Hastings Law Journal* 5: 171–241.

Greer, S. (1995) *Supergrasses: A Study in Anti-terrorist Law Enforcement in Northern Ireland*, Oxford: Clarendon Press.

Goodin, R. (1996) 'Institutions and Their Design', in Goodin, R. (ed), *The Theory of Institutional Design*, Cambridge: Cambridge University Press.

Hackett, C. (1995) 'Self-determination: the Republican Feminist Agenda', *Feminist Review* 50: 111–16.

Hadfield, B. (1989) *The Constitution of Northern Ireland*, Belfast: Servicing the Legal System.

Halley, J. (2006) *Split Decisions: How and Why to Take a Break from Feminism*, Princeton and London: Princeton University Press.

Halley, J. (2008) 'Rape at Rome: feminist interventions in the criminalization of sex-related violence in positive international criminal law', *Michigan Journal of International Law* 30: 1–123.

Hamber, B. (2009) *Transforming Societies After Political Violence: Truth, Reconciliation, and Mental Health*, New York: Springer.

Hamber, B. and Wilson, R. (eds) (2003) *Recognition and Reckoning: A Way Ahead on Victims' Issues*, Belfast: Democratic Dialogue.

Hamilton, M. and Ní Aoláin, F. (2009) 'Gender and the rule of law in transitional societies', *Minnesota Journal of International Law* 18: 380–402.

Hannum, H. (2006) 'Human rights in conflict resolution: the role of the Office of the High Commissioner for Human Rights in UN peacemaking and peacebuilding', *Human Rights Quarterly* 28: 1–85.

Harris-Rimmer, S. (2010) *Gender and Transitional Justice: The Women of East Timor*, Sydney: Routledge.

Hayner, P. (2002) *Unspeakable Truths: Facing the Challenge of Truth Commissions*, London and New York: Routledge.

Hegarty, A. (2011) 'Briefing on the Status of UNSCR 1325,' available at http://www.wrda.net/Documents/Briefing%20on%20the%20legal%20Status%20of%20UN%20SCR%201325.pdf (last accessed 27 February 2013).

Heise, L. (1995) 'Freedom Close to Home: The Impact of Violence Against Women on Reproductive Rights', in Peters, J. and Wolper, A. (eds), *Women's Rights: International Feminist Perspectives*, London and New York: Routledge.

Herman, J. (2001) *Trauma and Recovery: From Domestic Abuse to Political Terror*, New York: Basic Books (Reprint, originally published 1992).

Hilbink, L. (2007) *Judges beyond Politics in Democracy and Dictatorship: Lessons from Chile*, New York: Cambridge University Press.

Howe, W. J. and McIsaac, H. (2008) 'Response', *Family Court Review* 46: 592–594.

Htun, M. (2003) *Sex and the State: Abortion, Divorce, and the Family Under Latin American Dictatorships and Democracies*, New York: Cambridge University Press.

Huneeus, A. (2006) *The Dynamics of Judicial Stasis: Judges, Pinochet-Era Claims, and Judicial Legitimacy in Chile (1998–2005)*. Jurisprudence and Social Policy. Berkeley, University of California. Doctor of Philosophy.

Huneeus, A. (2010) 'Judging from a guilty conscience: the Chilean judiciary's human rights turn', *Law and Social Inquiry* 35(1): 99–135.

Huntington, S. (1991) *The Third Wave: Democratization in the Late Twentieth Century*, Norman, OK and London: University of Oklahoma Press.

Jackson, J. and Doran, S. (1995) *Judge without Jury: Diplock Trials in the Adversary System*, Oxford: Oxford University Press.

Jaquette, J. S. (ed) (1989) *The Women's Movement in Latin America: Feminism and the Transition to Democracy*, Boston, MA and London: Unwin Hyman.

Jaquette, J. (ed) (1994) *The Women's Movement in Latin America: Participation and Democracy*, 2nd edn, Boulder, San Francisco and Oxford: Westview Press.

Jaramillo Sierra, I. C. and Sierra, T. A. (2008) *Mujeres, Cortes y Medios: La Reforma Judicial del Aborto*, Bogotá: Siglo del Hombre Editores, Universidad de los Andes.

Joachim, J. M. (2007) *Agenda Setting, the UN, and NGOs: Gender Violence and Reproductive Rights*, Washington DC: Georgetown University Press.

Keck, M. E. and Sikkink, K. (1998) *Activists beyond Borders: Advocacy Networks in International Politics*, London and Ithaca, NY: Cornell University Press.

Kirkwood, J. (1983) 'El Feminismo Como Negación del Autoritarismo', in *Material de Discusion, Programa FLACSO – Santiago de Chile, Número 52*.

Kouvo S. and Pearson, Z. (eds) (2011) *Feminist Perspectives on International Law: Between Compliance and Subversion*, Oxford: Hart Publishing.

Kritz, N. (2009) 'Policy Implications of Empirical Research on Transitional Justice', in van der Merwe, H., Baxter, V. and Chapman, A. R. (eds), *Assessing the Impact of Transitional Justice: Challenges for Empirical Research*, Washington DC: United States Institute of Peace.

Krook, M. L. and Mackay, F. (2011) 'Introduction: Gender, Politics, and Institutions', in Mackay, F. and Krook, M. L. (eds), *Gender, Politics and Institutions: Towards a Feminist Institutionalism*, Basingstoke: Palgrave Macmillan.

Lacey, N. (1998) *Unspeakable Subjects: Feminist Essays in Legal and Social Theory*, Oxford: Hart.

Lacey, N. and Frazer, E. (1993) *The Politics of Community: A Feminist Critique of the Liberal–Communitarian Debate*, Hemel Hempstead: Harvester Wheatsheaf.

Lagos, R. (2003) *No Hay Mañana sin Ayer*, Santiago: Government of Chile.

Landes, J. (ed) (1998) *Feminism, the Public and the Private*, New York and Oxford: Oxford University Press.

Laplante, L. and Theidon, K. (2007) 'Transitional justice in times of conflict: Colombia's Ley de Justicia y Paz', *Michigan Journal of International Law* 28: 49–108.

Lawther, C. (2013) 'Denial, silence and the politics of the past: unpicking the opposition to truth recovery in Northern Ireland', *International Journal of Transitional Justice* 7(1): 157–77.

Lees, S. (1997) *Ruling Passions: Sexual Violence, Reputation and the Law*, Buckingham: Open University Press.

Lemaitre Ripoll, J. (2002) 'Justicia injusta: una crítica feminista a la conciliación en violencia conyugal' *Derecho Privado* 16(27): 73–98.

Lira, E. (2006a) 'Human Rights in Chile: The Long Road to Truth, Justice, and Reparations', in Borzutzky, S. and Oppenheim, L. H. (eds), *After Pinochet: The Chilean Road to Democracy and the Market*, Gainesville, FA: University of Florida Press.

Lira, E. (2006b) 'The Reparations Policy for Human Rights Violations in Chile', in de Greiff, P. (ed), *The Handbook of Reparations*, Oxford and New York: Oxford University Press.

Lira, E. (n.d.) 'Violencia en la Familia, Violencia en la Sociedad: Impacto sobre los Terapeutas', 147–82.

Lira, E. and Loveman, B. (2005) *Políticas de Reparación, Chile 1990–2004*, Santiago: LOM Ediciones.

Londregan, J. (2000) *Legislative Institutions and Ideology in Chile*, Cambridge and New York: Cambridge University Press.

Loughran, Christine (1988) 'Armagh and feminist strategy: campaigns around republican women prisoners in Armagh Jail', *Feminist Review*: 59–79.

Lundy, P. (2009) 'Can the past be policed? Lessons for the Historical Enquiries Team, Northern Ireland', *Law and Social Challenges* 11: 109–71.

Lundy, P. and McGovern, M. (2008) 'Whose justice? Rethinking transitional justice from the bottom up', *Journal of Law and Society* 35(2): 265–92.

Luz María Londoño, F. and Yoana Fernanda Nieto, V. (2007) *Mujeres No Contadas: Procesos De Desmovilización y Retorno a La Vida Civil De Mujeres Excombatientes En Colombia 1990–2003*, Medellin: La Carreta Editores.

Mackay, F. (2009) 'Institutionalising "New Politics" in Post Devolution Scotland: "Nested Newness" and the Gendered Limits of Change'. *European Conference on Politics and Gender*, 27–29 January, Queen's University Belfast.

Mackay, F. (2011) 'Response and Reflection', 25 May 2011, *Women, Transition and Institutional Reform: Northern Ireland and Beyond*, Transitional Justice Institute, University of Ulster.

MacKinnon, C. (1983) 'Feminism, Marxism, method, and the state: toward feminist jurisprudence', *Signs: Journal of Women in Culture and Society* 8(4): 635–58.

MacKinnon, C. (1989) *Toward a Feminist Theory of the State*, Cambridge, MA: Harvard University Press.

MacKinnon, C. (1993) 'On Torture: A Feminist Perspective on Human Rights', in Mahoney, K. and Mahoney, P. (eds), *Human Rights in the Twenty-first Century: A Global Perspective*, Dordrecht and London: Martinus Nijhoff.

MacKinnon, C. (1994) 'Rape, genocide and women's human rights', *Harvard Women's Law Journal* 17: 5–16.

Mallinder, L. (2007) 'Can amnesties and international justice be reconciled', *International Journal of Transitional Justice* 1(2): 208–30.

Mallinder, L. (2008) *Amnesties, Human Rights and Political Transitions: Bridging the Peace and Justice Divide*, Oxford: Hart Publishing.

Mani, R. (2002) *Beyond Retribution: Seeking Justice in the Shadows of War*, Cambridge: Polity.

McAdam, D., Tarrow, S. and Tilley, C. (2001) *Dynamics of Contention*, Cambridge and New York: Cambridge University Press.

McCafferty, N. (1980) 'It Is My Belief that Armagh Is a Feminist Issue', *Irish Times*, 17 June.

McCann, E. (2007) 'Voodoo voices on the rise', *Belfast Telegraph*, 15 March.

McCann, M. (ed) (2006) *Law and Social Movements*, Aldershot: Ashgate.

McCoy, G. (2000) 'Women, Community and Politics in Northern Ireland', in Davies, C. and Roulston, C. (eds), *Gender, Democracy, and Inclusion in Northern Ireland*, Basingstoke and New York: Palgrave.

McEvoy, K. (1999) 'Prisoners, the agreement and the political character of the Northern Ireland conflict', *Fordham International Law Journal* 22: 153–76.
McEvoy, K. (2000) 'Law, struggle, and political transformation in Northern Ireland', *Journal of Law and Society* 27(4): 542–71.
McEvoy, K. (2001) *Paramilitary Imprisonment in Northern Ireland: Resistance, Management, and Release*, Oxford: Oxford University Press.
McEvoy, K. (2007) 'Beyond legalism: towards a "thicker" understanding of transitional justice', *Journal of Law and Society* 34(4): 411–40.
McEvoy, S. (2009) 'Loyalist women paramilitaries in Northern Ireland: beginning a feminist conversation about conflict resolution', *Security Studies* 18(2): 262–86.
McGarry, J. and O'Leary, B. (1995) *Explaining Northern Ireland: Broken Images*, Oxford: Blackwell.
McWilliams, M. (2005) Comments. *Women, Transition, and Transformation Conference*, 10 March, Transitional Justice Institute, University of Ulster, Belfast.
McWilliams, M. and Kilmurray, A. (1997) 'Athene on the loose: the origins of the Northern Ireland Women's Coalition', *Irish Journal of Feminist Studies* 2(1): 1.
McWilliams, M. and McKiernan, J. (1993) *Bringing It Out in the Open: Domestic Violence in Northern Ireland*, Belfast: HMSO.
Meertens, D. and Zambrano, M. (2010) 'Citizenship deferred?', *International Journal of Transitional Justice* 4: 189–206.
Meehan, E. (2003) 'From Government to Governance, Civic Participation and "New Politics"', presented at *Women in Parliament: Reflections on Representation*, Queen's University of Belfast, 28 February.
Meintjes, S. (2009) '"Gendered truth"? Legacies of the South African Truth and Reconciliation Commission', *African Journal on Conflict Resolution* 9(2): 101–11.
Meron, T. (1993) 'Rape as a crime under international humanitarian law', *American Journal of International Law* 87: 424–8.
Merry, S. E. (1997) 'Global human rights and local social movements in a legally plural world', *Canadian Journal of Law and Society* 12: 247–71.
Merry, S. E. (2003) 'Rights talk and the experience of law: implementing women's human rights to protection from violence', *Human Rights Quarterly* 25: 343–81.
Mertus, J. (2000) 'Considering nonstate actors in the new millennium: toward expanded participation in norm generation and norm application', *New York University Journal of International Law and Politics* 32: 537–66.
Mill, J. S. (1859) *On Liberty*, London: J. W. Parker.
Miller, Z. (2008) 'Effects of invisibility: in search of the "economic" in transitional justice', *International Journal of Transitional Justice* 2(3): 266–91.
Molyneux, M. (1985) 'Mobilization without emancipation? Women's interests, state, and revolution', *Feminist Studies* 11(2): 227–54.
Molyneux, M. (1998) 'Analyzing women's movements', *Development and Change* 29: 219–45.
Montes, J. E. and Vial, T. (2005) *The Role of Constitution-Building Processes in Democratization: Case Study Chile*, Stockholm: International IDEA Democracy-Building & Conflict Management (DCM).
Montgomery, P. and Bell, V. (1985) *Police Response to Wife Assault: A Northern Ireland Study*, Belfast: Northern Ireland Women's Aid Federation.
Morgan, M. (1992) 'Constitution-making in a time of cholera: women and the 1991 Colombian Constitution', *Yale Journal of Law and Feminism* 4: 353–413.

Morgan, M. (1998) 'Taking machismo to court: the gender jurisprudence of the Colombian Constitutional Court', *University of Miami Inter-American Law Review* 30: 253–342.

Morison, J. and Livingstone, S. (1995) *Reshaping Public Power: Northern Ireland and the British Constitutional Crisis*, London: Sweet and Maxwell.

Motta, C. (1998) 'Observatorio Legal de la Mujer: el Legado de la Constitución', in *Estudios Ocasionales Centro de Investigaciones Sociojurídicas*, Bogotá, Colombia, Universidad de los Andes Facultad de Derecho, Dirección Nacional de Equidad para las Mujeres.

Munro, V. E. (2007) *Law and Politics at the Perimeter: Re-evaluating Key Debates in Feminist Theory*, Oxford: Hart Publishing.

Murphy, R. (2003) 'Constitutional Rights Discourse: Canadian and South African Feminist Engagements', in Dobrowolsky, A. and Hart, V. (eds), *Women Making Constitutions: New Politics and Comparative Perspectives*, Basingstoke and New York: Palgrave Macmillan.

Nader, L. (1992) 'From legal process to mind processing', *Family and Conciliation Courts Review* 30: 468–73.

Nelken, D. (2005) 'Doing Research into Comparative Criminal Justice', in Banaker, R. and Travers, M. (eds), *Theory and Method in Socio-legal Research*, Oxford and Portland, OR: Hart Publishing.

Nesiah, V. (2006) 'Discussion lines on gender and transitional justice: an introductory essay reflecting on the ICTJ Bellagio Workshop on Gender and Transitional Justice', *Columbia Journal of Gender and Law* 15: 799–812.

Ní Aoláin, F. (1997) 'Radical rules: the effects of evidential and procedural rules on the regulation of sexual violence in war', *Albany Law Review* 60: 883–905.

Ní Aoláin, F. (2000a) 'Sex-based violence and the Holocaust – a reevaluation of harms and rights in international law', *Yale Journal of Law and Feminism* 12: 43–84.

Ní Aoláin, F. (2000b) *The Politics of Force: Conflict Management and State Violence in Northern Ireland*, Belfast: Blackstaff Press.

Ní Aoláin, F. (2002) 'Truth telling, accountability and the right to life', *European Human Rights Law Review* 5: 571–90.

Ní Aoláin, F. (2006) 'Political violence and gender during times of transition', *Columbia Journal of Gender and Law* 15(3): 829–49.

Ní Aoláin, F. (2008) 'A Feminist Theory of Harm', paper given at *Conflict and Transitional Justice: Feminist Perspectives*, Emory University School of Law, Atlanta, GA, 19 September 2011.

Ní Aoláin, F. (2009) 'Women, security, and the patriarchy of internationalized transitional justice', *Human Rights Quarterly* 31(4): 1055–85.

Ní Aoláin, F. and C. O'Rourke (2010) 'Gendered Transitional Justice and the Non-State Actor', in Lyons, A. and Reed, M. (eds), *Contested Transitions: Dilemmas of Transitional Justice in Colombia and Comparative Experience*, Bogotá: International Center for Transitional Justice.

Ní Aoláin, F. and Rooney, E. (2007) 'Underenforcement and intersectionality: gendered aspects of transition for women', *International Journal of Transitional Justice* 1: 338–54.

Ní Aoláin, F. and Turner, C. (2007) 'Gender, truth and transition', *UCLA Women's Law Journal* 16: 229–79.

Ní Aoláin, F., Haynes, D. and Cahn, N. (2011) *On the Frontlines: Gender, War and the Postconflict Process*. New York and Oxford: Oxford University Press.

North, D. (1991) 'Institutions', *The Journal of Economic Perspectives* 5(1): 97–112.

Northern Ireland Civil Rights Association, *'We Shall Overcome'. The History of the Struggle for Civil Rights in Northern Ireland 1968–1978*, Belfast: NICRA, 1978.

Northern Ireland Women's Coalition (1996/7) *Information and Policy Papers*, Belfast.
O'Donnell, G., Schmitter, P. C. and Whitehead, L. (1986) *Transitions from Authoritarian Rule*, Baltimore, MA: Johns Hopkins University Press.
O'Rawe, M. (2003) 'Truth and Justice', in Hamber, B. and Wilson, R. (eds), *Recognition and Reckoning: The Way Ahead on Victims Issues*, Belfast: Democratic Dialogue.
O'Rourke, C. (2009) 'The shifting signifier of "community" in transitional justice: a feminist analysis', *Wisconsin Journal of Gender, Law and Society* 23: 269–91.
O'Rourke, C. (2011) 'Transitioning to What? Transitional Justice and Gendered Citizenship in Chile and Colombia', in Buckley-Zistel, S. and Stanley, R. (eds), *Gender in Transitional Justice*, Basingstoke: Palgrave Macmillan.
O'Rourke, C. (2012) 'Dealing with the past in a post-conflict society: does the participation of women matter? Insights from Northern Ireland', *William & Mary Journal of Women and the Law* 19(1): 35–68.
Olsen, F. E. (1985) 'The myth of state intervention in the family', *University of Michigan Journal of Law Reform* 18(4): 835–64.
Orentlicher, D. F. (1991) 'Settling accounts: the duty to prosecute human rights violations of a prior regime', *Yale Law Journal* 100: 2537–615.
Orentlicher, D. (2005). 'Report of the Independent Expert to Update the Set of Principles to Combat Impunity, Addendum: Updated Set of Principles for the Protection and Promotion of Human Rights through Action to Combat Impunity United Nations Commission on Human Rights'.
Orford, A. (2002) 'Feminism, imperialism and the mission of international law', *Nordic Journal of International Law* 71: 275–96.
Orford, A. (2006). 'Commissioning the truth', *Columbia Journal of Gender and Law* 15: 851–82.
Osiel, M. (1997) *Mass Atrocity, Collective Memory and the Law*, New Brunswick, NJ and London: Transaction Publishers.
Otto, D. (2009) 'The exile of inclusion: reflections on gender issues in international law over the last decade', *Melbourne Journal of International Law* 10: 11–26.
Oxhorn, P. (1995) *Organizing Civil Society: The Popular Sectors and the Struggle for Democracy in Chile*, Philadelphia: Pennsylvania State University Press.
Parson, N. (2005) *Gendered Suffering and Social Transformations: Domestic Violence, Dictatorship and Democracy in Chile*, New Brunswick: State University of New Jersey, unpublished PhD Dissertation.
Pateman, C. (1988) *The Sexual Contract*, Cambridge: Polity.
Petchesky, R. P. (1986) *Abortion and Woman's Choice: the State, Sexuality, and Reproductive Freedom*, London: Verso.
Phillips, A. (1995) *The Politics of Presence*, Oxford: Oxford University Press.
Plata, M. I. (1994) 'Reproductive Rights as Human Rights: the Colombian Case', in Cook, R. (ed), *Human Rights of Women: National and International Perspectives*, Philadelphia: University of Pennsylvania Press.
Potter, M. (2004) *In Their Own Words: A Research Report into the Victims Sector in Northern Ireland*, Belfast: Training for Women Network.
Rai, S. M. (ed) (2003) *Mainstreaming Gender, Democratizing the State? National Machineries for the Advancement of Women*, Manchester: Manchester University Press.
Reilly, N. (2009) *Women's Human Rights: Seeking Gender Justice in a Globalizing Age*, Cambridge and Malden, MA: Polity.
Requa, M. (2007) 'Truth, transition, and the Inquiries Act 2005', *European Human Rights Law Review* 12(4): 404–26.

Rhode, D. (1991) 'The "no-problem" problem: feminist challenges and cultural change', *Yale Law Journal* 100(6): 1731–93.

Roht-Arriaza, N. (1990) 'State responsibility to investigate and prosecute grave human rights violations in international law', *California Law Review* 78: 451–513.

Roht-Arriaza, N. (2004) 'Reparations decisions and dilemmas', *Hastings International and Comparative Law Review* 27: 157–219.

Roht-Arriaza, N. (2005) *The Pinochet Effect*, New York and Oxford: Oxford University Press.

Rolston, B. (2006) 'Dealing with the past: pro-state paramilitaries, truth and transition in Northern Ireland', *Human Rights Quarterly* 28(3), 652–75.

Rolston, B., and Scraton, P. (2005) 'In the full glare of English politics: Ireland, inquiries and the British state', *British Journal of Criminology* 45(4): 547–64.

Rooney, E. (1995) 'Political division, practical alliance: problems for women in conflict', *Journal of Women's History* 6/7(4/1): 40–49.

Rooney, E. (2006) 'Women's equality in Northern Ireland's transition: intersectionality in theory and place', *Feminist Legal Studies* 14: 353–75.

Ross, F. (2003) *Bearing Witness: Women and the Truth and Reconciliation Commission in South Africa*, London and Sterling, VA: Pluto Press.

Rosser, E. (2007) 'Depoliticized speech and sexed visibility: women, gender and sexual violence in the 1999 Guatemalan *Comisión para el Esclarecimiento Histórico* Report', *International Journal of Transitional Justice* 1(3): 391–410.

Rossiter, A. (2001) *The Other Irish Journey*, London: Marie Stopes International.

Roth, F., Guberek, T. and Hoover Green, A. (2011) *Using Quantitative Data to Assess Conflict-Related Sexual Violence in Colombia: Challenges and Opportunities*. Report of the Benetech Human Rights Program (Palo Alto, CA) and Corporación Punto de Vista (Bogotá: Colombia).

Roulston, C. (1997) 'Gender, nation, class: the politics of difference in Northern Ireland', *Scottish Affairs* 18(Winter): 54–67.

Roulston, C. (2003) 'Unworthy Women?' *Conference of the Centre for the Advancement of Women in Politics*, 24 February, Queen's University Belfast.

Rubin, G. (1984) *Power and Danger*, London: Routledge.

Rubio-Marin, R. (2006a) 'Introduction: The Gender of Reparations: Setting the Agenda', in Rubio-Marin, R. (ed), *What Happened to the Women: Gender and Reparations for Human Rights Violations*, New York: Social Science Research Council.

Rubio-Marin, R. (ed) (2006b) *What Happened to the Women: Gender and Reparations for Human Rights Violations*, New York: Social Science Research Council.

Rubio-Marin, R. (2009) 'The Gender of Reparations in Transitional Societies', in Rubio-Marin, R. (ed), *The Gender of Reparations: Unsettling Sexual Hierarchies While Redressing Human Rights Violations*, Cambridge and New York: Cambridge University Press.

Saba, R. (2002) *El Movimiento de Derechos Humanos y el Trabajo Actual en Derechos Humanos en Chile*, Santiago: Ford Foundation.

Sajjad, T. (2013) *Transitional Justice in South Asia: A Study of Afghanistan and Nepal*, New York: Routledge.

Sánchez Gómez, O. A. (2008) *Las Violencias contra la Mujeres en una Sociedad en Guerra*, Bogotá: La Ruta Pacifica.

Schild, V. (1997) 'New subjects of rights? Gendered citizenship and the contradictory legacies of social movements in Latin America', *Organization* 4(4): 604–19.

Schirmer, J. G. (1988) '"Those who die for life cannot be called dead": women and human rights protest in Latin America', *Harvard Human Rights Yearbook* 1: 41–76.

Schneider, E. M. (1986) 'The dialectic of rights and politics: perspectives from the women's movement', *New York University Law Review* 61: 589–652.

Shirlow, P. and McEvoy, K. (2008) *Beyond the Wire: Former Prisoners and Conflict Transformation in Northern Ireland*, London: Pluto Press.

Sikkink, K. (1993) 'Human rights, principled issue-networks, and sovereignty in Latin America', *International Organization* 47(3): 411–41.

Sikkink, K. and M. Finnemore (1998) 'International norms dynamics and political change', *International Organization* 52(4): 887–917.

Simmons, B. (2009) *Mobilizing for Human Rights: International Law in Domestic Politics*, Cambridge and New York: Cambridge University Press.

Smart, C. (1989) *Feminism and the Power of Law*, London and New York: Routledge.

Sokhi-Bulley, B. (2006) 'The Optional Protocol to CEDAW: First Steps', *Human Rights Law Review* 6(1): 143–59.

Spelman, E. (1990) *Inessential Woman: Problems of Exclusion in Feminist Thought*, London: Women's Press.

Squires, J. (2007) *The New Politics of Gender Equality*, Basingstoke: Palgrave Macmillan.

Sternbach, N. S., Navarro-Aranguren, M., Chuchryk, P. and Alvarez, S. E. (1992) 'Feminisms in Latin America: from Bogota to San Bernardo', *Signs* 17(2): 393–434.

Teitel, R. (2000) *Transitional Justice*, New York: Oxford University Press.

Thomas, D. Q. and Beasley, M. E. (1993) 'Domestic violence as a human rights issue', *Human Rights Quarterly* 15(1): 36–62.

Thompson, J. (2007) 'Coming to Terms with the Past in Australia', in Miller, J. and Kumar, R. (eds), *Reparations: Interdisciplinary Inquiries*, Oxford and New York: Oxford University Press.

Tickner, J. A. (2002) 'Feminist perspectives on 9/11', *International Studies Perspectives* 3: 333–50.

Uprimny Yepes, R., Botero Marino, C. *et al* (2006) *¿Justicia Transicional sin transición? Verdad, justicia y reparación para Colombia*, Bogotá: Centro de Estudios de Derecho, Justicia y Sociedad-DeJuSticia.

Uprimny, R. and Saffon, M. P. (2008) 'Usos y Abusos de la Justicia Transicional en Colombia', *Universidad de Chile Centro de Derechos Humanos Anuario del Centro de Derechos Humanos* 4: 165–95.

Urban Walker, M. (2009) 'Gender and Violence in Focus: A Background for Gender Justice in Reparations', in Rubio-Marin, R. (ed), *The Gender of Reparations: Unsettling Sexual Hierarchies While Redressing Human Rights Violations*, Cambridge and New York: Cambridge University Press.

Valenzuela, J. S. (1992) 'Democratic Consolidation in Post-Transitional Settings: Notion, Process, and Facilitating Conditions', in Mainwaring, S., O'Donnell, G. and Valenzuela, J. S. (eds), *Issues in Democratic Consolidation: The New South American Democracies in Comparative Perspective*, South Bend, IN: University of Notre Dame Press.

Vallance, E. (1982) 'Where power is, women are not', *Parliamentary Affairs* 35(2): 218–19.

Van Boven, T. (1993) *Study Concerning the Right to Restitution, Compensation and Rehabilitation for Victims of Gross Violations of Human Rights and Fundamental Freedoms: Final Report*, UN Doc. E/CN. 4/Sub.2/1993/8.

Walker, N. (2000) *Policing in a Changing Constitutional Order*, London: Sweet & Maxwell.

Ward, M. (1991) 'The Women's Movement in Northern Ireland: Twenty Years On', in Hutton, S. and Stewart, P. (eds), *Ireland's Histories: Aspects of State, Society and Ideology*, London and New York: Routledge.

Waylen, G. (1994) 'Women and democratization: conceptualizing gender relations in transition politics', *World Politics* 46: 327–54.

Waylen, G. (1996) 'Democratization, Feminism and the State in Chile: The Establishment of SERNAM', in Rai, S. and Lievesley, G. (eds), *Women and the State: International Perspectives*, London and Bristol: Taylor and Francis.

Waylen, G. (2003) 'Gender and transitions: what do we know?', *Democratization* 10(1): 157–78.

Waylen, G. (2004) *What Can the South African Transition Tell us about Gender and Democratization?*, Belfast: Centre for the Advancement of Women in Politics, Queen's University of Belfast.

Waylen, G. (2006) 'Constitutional Engineering: What Opportunities for the Enhancement of Gender Rights?', in *UK Political Studies Association Women and Politics Annual Conference* 'Feminist Ethics, Feminist Politics and the State We're In: Critical Reflections in Uncertain Times', University of Edinburgh, 11 February.

Waylen, G. (2007) *Engendering Transitions: Women's Mobilization, Institutions, and Gender Outcomes*, New York and Oxford: Oxford University Press.

Waylen, G. (2011) 'New Democratic Institutions and State Women's Machineries'. Paper given at *Women, Transition and Institutional Reform: Northern Ireland and Beyond*. Transitional Justice Institute, University of Ulster, 26 May.

Welna, C. and Gallon, G. (eds), *Peace, Democracy, and Human Rights in Colombia*, Notre Dame, IN: University of Notre Dame.

West, R. (1991) 'The Difference in Women's Hedonic Lives: A Phenomenonological Critique of Feminist Legal Theory', in Fineman, M. and Thomsaden, N. (eds), *At the Boundaries of Law: Feminist and Legal Theory*, New York: Routledge.

Whelan, L. J. (1992) 'The challenge of lobbying for civil rights in Northern Ireland: the Committee on the Administration of Justice', *Human Rights Quarterly* 14: 149–70.

Wilde, A. (1999) 'Irruptions of memory: expressive politics in Chile's transition to democracy', *Journal of Latin American Studies* 31(2): 473–500.

Wilford, R. A. (1996) 'Women and Politics in Northern Ireland', in Lovenduski, J. and Norris, P. (eds), *Women in Politics*, Oxford: Oxford University Press.

Wills, M. E. (2007) *Inclusión sin Representación: Irrupción Política de las Mujeres en Colombia 1970–2000*, Bogotá: Grupo Editorial Norma.

Wilson, R. (2001) *The Politics of Truth and Reconciliation in South Africa: Legitimizing the Post-Apartheid State*. Cambridge and New York: Cambridge University Press.

Young, I. M. (2000) *Inclusion and Democracy*, New York and Oxford: Oxford University Press.

Yuval-Davis, N. (1997) *Gender and Nation*, Thousand Oaks and New Delhi: Sage Publications.

Reports

Agrupación de Mujeres ex Prisoneras Políticas Sobrevivientes de la Red de Centros de Tortura Clandestinos del Régimen Militar de Pinochet (2004), *Declaración de las Mujeres ex Presas Políticas bajo la Dictadura*.

Americas Watch (1982) *Human Rights in the Two Colombias: Functioning Democracy, Militarized Society*, New York: Americas Watch.

Americas Watch (1983a) *Chile Since the Coup: Ten Years of Repression*, New York: Americas Watch.

Americas Watch (1983b) *The 'MAS Case' in Colombia: Taking on the Death Squads*, New York: Americas Watch.

Americas Watch (1986) *Human Rights in Colombia: As President Barco Begins*, New York: Americas Watch.
Americas Watch (1987) *The Vicaria de Solidaridad en Chile*, New York: Americas Watch.
Americas Watch (1988) *Chile: Human Rights & the Plebiscite*, New York, Americas Watch.
Americas Watch (1989) *Informe sobre Derechos Humanos en Colombia: The Killings in Colombia*, Bogotá: Centro de Estudios Internacionales de la Universidad de los Andes: Instituto de Estudios Políticos y Relaciones Internacionales, Universidad Nacional de Colombia.
Americas Watch (1991) *Chile: Human Rights and the 'Politics of Agreement'*, New York: Americas Watch.
Americas Watch (1992) *La Violencia Continúa: Asesinatos Políticos y Reforma Institucional en Colombia*, Bogotá: Tercer Mundo, Universidad Nacional, Instituto de Estudios Políticos y Relaciones Internacionales, Universidad de los Andes, Centro de Estudios Internacionales.
Amnesty International (1983) *Chile: Evidence of Torture*, London: Amnesty International.
Amnesty International (1985) *USSR: Conditions for Women Prisoners of Conscience in the 'Small Zone' (of Mordovian Corrective Labour Colony No. 3)*, London: International Secretariat.
Amnesty International (1986) *Women: Victims and Fighters*, London: Amnesty International.
Amnesty International (1988a) *Colombia Briefing*, London: Amnesty International.
Amnesty International (1988b) *Killings by Security Forces and 'Supergrass Trials'*, London: Amnesty International.
Amnesty International (1991a) *Colombia: Further Evidence of Army Responsibility for 'Disappearances'*, London: Amnesty International.
Amnesty International (1991b) *United Kingdom: Allegations of Ill-Treatment in Northern Ireland*, London: Amnesty International.
Amnesty International (1991c) *Women in the Front Line*, New York: Amnesty International.
Amnesty International (1992a) *Human Rights Defenders under Attack*, London: Amnesty International.
Amnesty International (1992b) *Women in the Frontline: Appeal Cases 1992*, London: Amnesty International.
Amnesty International (1994a) *Political Killings in Northern Ireland*, London: Amnesty International.
Amnesty International (1994b) *Political Violence in Colombia: Myth and Reality*, London: Amnesty International.
Amnesty International (2001a) *Broken Bodies, Shattered Minds: Torture and Ill-treatment of Women*, London: Amnesty International.
Amnesty International (2001b) *Chile, Testament to Suffering and Courage: the Long Quest for Justice and Truth*, London: Amnesty International.
Barraza Morelle, C. and Guzmán, D. E. (2008). 'Proceso de Reparación para las Mujeres Víctimas de Violencia en el Marco del Conflicto Armado Colombiano', in Corporación Humanas (ed), *Sin Tregua: Políticas de Reparación para Mujeres Víctimas de Violencia Sexual durante Dictaduras y Conflictos Armados*. Santiago: Corporación Humanas: Centro Regional de Derechos Humanos y Justicia de Género.
Beare, N. (2004). Press Release: 'Beare Slams Self-Serving Women's Coalition Proposals for Council Reform'. Belfast: Democratic Unionist Party.
Bill of Rights Women's Working Group (2008) *Final Report of Women's Working Group*, Belfast.
Bloomfield, K. (1998) 'We Will Remember Them', Report of the Northern Ireland Victims Commissioner, Sir Kenneth Bloomfield, Belfast, Northern Ireland Office.
Bloomfield, K., Gibson, M. and Greer, D. (1999) *Criminal Injuries Compensation in Northern Ireland: A Report to the Secretary of State for Northern Ireland*, Belfast, available at http://www.

ofmdfmni.gov.uk/report_of_the_review_of_criminal_injuries_compensation_in_ni.pdf (last accessed 27 February 2013).

Casa de la Mujer (1988) *Violencia en la Intimidad*, Bogotá, Colombia.

Center for Reproductive Law and Policy and Open Forum on Reproductive Health and Rights (1998) *Women Behind Bars: Chile's Abortion Law, a Human Rights Analysis*, New York and Santiago.

Centro de Investigaciones Sociojurídicas, Universidad de los Andes (1998), available at http://cijus.uniandes.edu.co (last accessed 3 April 2013).

Chilean National Commission on Truth and Reconciliation (TRC) (1993) *Report of the Chilean National Truth and Reconciliation Commission: Final Report*, Notre Dame: University of Notre Dame.

Coiste na n-Iarchimí and Relatives for Justice, *Report of the Workshop*, 4 December 2010.

Comisión Chilena de Derechos Humanos (Programa de Mujeres) (1995) *Mujeres, Memoria y Derechos Humanos*, Santiago, Chile.

Comisión de Estudios sobre la Violencia (1987) *Colombia: Violencia y Democracia, Informe Presentado al Ministerio de Gobierno*, C. Members: Jaime Arocha R., Alvaro Camacho M. *et al*, Bogotá: Universidad Nacional de Colombia – Centro Editorial.

Comisión de Seguimiento a la Política Pública sobre Desplazamiento Forzado (2011), *Balance Aproximativo de la Ley de Victimas Aprobada por el Congreso de la República* (Ley 1448 de 2011), Bogotá.

Comisión Nacional de Reparación y Reconciliación y Grupo de Memoría Historica (2007) *Plan de Acción del Área de Memoria Histórica de la Comisión Nacional de Reparación y Reconciliación*, Bogotá: Comisión Nacional de Reparación y Reconciliación.

Comisión Nacional de Reparación y Reconciliación y Grupo de Memoría Historica (2008a) *Trujilla: Una Tragedia que no Cesa. Primer Informe del Grupo de Memoria Histórica de la CNRR*, Bogotá, Colombia.

Comisión Nacional de Reparación y Reconciliación and Grupo de Memoría Historica (2008b) *Narrativas y Voces del Conflicto: Programa de Investigación*, Bogotá: Comisión Nacional de Reparación y Reconciliación.

Comisión Nacional sobre Prisión Política y Tortura (2005) *Informe de la Comisión Nacional sobre Prisión Política y Tortura*, Santiago: Ministerio del Interior, El Gobierno de Chile.

Committee on the Administration of Justice (CAJ) (1983) *Emergency Laws: Suggestions for Reform in Northern Ireland*, Belfast.

Committee on the Administration of Justice (CAJ) (2009) 'Defending Human Rights Defenders, Defending Human Rights', available at http://www.caj.org.uk/files/2009/01/01/2009February.pdf (last accessed 27 February 2013).

Committee on the Administration of Justice (CAJ) (2012) 'CAJ's Response to the Department of Justice Consultation on Governance and Accountability of the Public Prosecution Service', Belfast.

Committee on the Elimination of All Forms of Discrimination Against Women (2005) *Report on Mexico produced by the Committee on the Elimination of Discrimination against Women under Article 8 of the Optional Protocol to the Convention, and Reply from the Government of Mexico*, UN Doc. CEDAW/C/2005/OP.8/MEXICO.

Consultative Group on the Past (2009) *Final Report*, Belfast.

Corporación de Promoción y Defensa de los Derechos del Pueblo (CODEPU) (1990) 'Todas Íbamos a ser Reinas: Estudio sobre nueve mujeres embarazadas que fueron detenidas y desaparecidas en Chile', Santiago, available at http://www.derechos.org/nizkor/chile/libros/reinas/ (last accessed 27 February 2013).

Corporación de Promoción y Defensa de los Derechos del Pueblo (CODEPU) (2002) *Todas Íbamos a ser Reinas: Estudio sobre Diez Embararazadas que fueron Detenidas y Disaparecidas en Chile*, Santiago: LOM Publicaciones.

Corporación Humanas (2007) *Mujeres entre Mafiosos y Señores de la Guerra: Impacto del Proceso de Desarme, Desmovilización y Reintegración en la Vida y Seguridad de las Mujeres en Comunidades en Pugna*, Autoras: Caso Villavicencio. Cecilia Barraza Morelle and Luz Piedad Caicedo, Bogotá, Colombia.

Corporación Humanas (2008a) 'Trujillo' in *Boletín Informativo.*

Corporación Humanas (2008b) *Sin Tregua: Políticas de Reparación para Mujeres Víctimas de Violencia Sexual Durante Dictaduras y Conflictos Armados*, Santiago: Centro Regional de Derechos Humanos y Justicia de Género.

Corporación Humanas (2009) *Guia para Llevar Casos de Violencia Sexual: Propuestas de Argumentación para Enjuiciar Crímenes de Violencia Sexual Cometidos en el Marco del Conflicto Armado Colombiano*, Bogotá, Colombia.

Corporación Humanas and UNIFEM (2005) *Riesgos para la Seguridad de las Mujeres en Procesos de Reinserción de Excombatiente – Estudio sobre el Impacto de la Reinserción Paramilitar en la Vida y Seguridad de las Mujeres en los Municipios de Montería y Tierralta Departamento de Córdoba*, Bogotá: Corporación Humanas Centro Regional de Derechos Humanos y Justicia de Género.

Corporación Nacional de Reparación y Reconciliación (1996) *Informe Final de la Corporación Nacional de Reparación y Reconciliación*, Santiago, Chile.

Corporación SISMA Mujer (2008) *Más Allá de la Cifras: Cuarto Informe de la Red Nacional de Mujeres*, Bogotá, Colombia.

Corporación Vamos Mujer (2006–2007) 'Deletrear la Piel', available at http://www.vamosmujer.org.co/campanas/deletrearlapiel.htm (last accessed 27 February 2013).

Cory, P. (2004) *Cory Collusion Inquiry Report*, London: The Stationery Office.

Criminal Justice Review Group (2000) *Review of the Criminal Justice System in Northern Ireland: A Guide*, Belfast: Stationery Office.

Department of Health, Social Services and Public Safety (DHSSPS) (2010) 'Guidance on the Termination of Pregnancy: The Law and Clinical Practice in Northern Ireland (Draft)'. Belfast: DHSSPS, available at http://www.dhsspsni.gov.uk/guidance_on_the_termination_of_pregnancy__the_law_and_clinical_practice_in_northern_ireland.pdf (last accessed 27 February 2013).

DOMOS and Corporación de Desarrollo de la Mujer (1999) *Violencia Domestica En Chile: Avances, Dificultades y Propuestas*, Santiago, Chile.

Equality Commission for Northern Ireland, 'Equality Survey: Awareness, Attitudes, Perceptions,' available at http://www.equalityni.org/sections/default.asp?secid=7 (last accessed 27 February 2013).

Fundación Instituto de la Mujer (1997) *Actas del Primer Tribunal de Derechos de las Mujeres*, Santiago, Chile.

Fundación Instituto de la Mujer (1999) *Actas del Segundo Tribunal de Derechos de las Mujeres Chilenas*, Santiago, Chile.

Fundación Instituto de la Mujer (2001) *Tercer Tribunal de Derechos de las Mujeres Chilenas*, Santiago, Chile.

Fundación Instituto de la Mujer (2003) *4° Tribunal de Derechos de las Mujeres Chilenas*, Santiago, Chile.

Fundación Instituto de la Mujer and Centro Regional de Derechos Humanos y Justicia de Genero (2005) *Memorias de Ocupacion: Violencia Sexual contra Mujeres Detenidas durante la Dictadura*, Santiago (Anexos pp. 123–134: Declaración Pública de Mujeres Detenidas

durante la Dictadura con Motivo de la Denuncia de Violencia Sexual Ejercida por un Alto Funcionario de Investigaciones (2003) – Conclusiones y Recomendaciones del Comité contra la Tortura de Naciones Unidas. Caso de Chile.
Fundación Instituto de la Mujer and Colectivo 'Mujeres de Chile y Canada' (1991) 'Legalidad y violencia doméstica. Las experiencias de "El Instituto de la Mujer" y de la "Oficina Legal de la Mujer" en Chile', in *Mujer y Violencia Domestica*, Santiago, Chile.
Fundación Instituto de la Mujer, La Morada *et al* (2004) 'Shadow Report respecting the Third Periodic Report of the Government of Chile, submitted to the Committee Against Torture, Geneva, Switzerland, 32nd Session, 10–11 May 2004', Santiago, Chile.
Grupo de Memoría Historica (2010) *La tierra en Disputa: Memorias de Despojo y Resistencia Campesina en la Costa Caribe (1960–2010)*, Bogotá, Colombia.
Grupo de Trabajo 'Mujer y Género, p. l. v., la justicia, la reparación y la reconcilación' (2008) *Recomendaciones para Garantizar los Derechos a la Verdad, la Justicia y la Reparación de las Mujeres Víctimas del Conflicto Armado en Colombia*, Bogotá: Alianza Iniciativa de Mujeres Colombianas por la Paz-IMP, Corporación Humanas, Corporación Humanizar, Confluencia Nacional Mujeres, Democracia y Paz, Corporación de Investigación y Acción Social y Económica, Red Nacional de Iniciativas Ciudades por la Paz y contra la Guerra, Beatriz Quintero (de la Red Nacional de Mujeres), Yoana Nieto.
Healing Through Remembering (2002) *The Report of the Healing Through Remembering Project*. Belfast.
Helsinki Watch (1991) *Human Rights in Northern Ireland*, New York: Human Rights Watch.
Human Rights Watch (2003) *You'll Learn Not to Cry*, New York: Human Rights Watch.
Human Rights Watch (2004) *Chile: Former Political Prisoner Convicted of Defamation*, New York: Human Rights Watch, available at: http://www.hrw.org/en/news/2004/04/28/chile-former-political-prisoner-convicted-defamation (last accessed 27 February 2013).
Independent Commission on Policing for Northern Ireland (1999) *A New Beginning: Policing in Northern Ireland (Sep)*, Belfast: HMSO.
Iniciativa de Mujeres Colombianas por la Paz (2009) *Observaciones a la Repuesta Oficial a la Sentencia T-496 de 2008: Mesa de Trabjajo por un Plan de Protección Integral a Víctimas y Testigos de Graves Violaciones de los Derechos Humanos e Infracciones al Derecho Internacional Humanitario, con Enfoque Diferencial de Género*, Bogotá: Iniciativa de Mujeres Colombianas por la Paz.
Inter-American Commission on Human Rights (1974) *Report on the Status of Human Rights in Chile: Findings of 'on-the-spot' observations in the Republic of Chile, July 22–August 2, 1974*, San Jose, Costa Rica: Organization of American States.
Inter-American Commission on Human Rights (1981) *Report on the Human Rights Situation in Colombia*, Washington DC: Organization of American States.
Inter-American Commission on Human Rights (2004) *Report on the Demobilization Process in Colombia*, Washington DC.
Inter-American Commission on Human Rights (2005) *Press Release No 26/05 – IACHR Issues Statement Regarding the Adopting of the 'Law of Justice and Peace' in Colombia*, Washington DC: IACHR.
Inter-American Commission on Human Rights (2006) *Statement by the Inter-American Commission on Human Rights on the Application and Scope of the Justice and Peace Law in Colombia*, Washington DC: IACHR.
Inter-American Commission on Human Rights (2007) *Report on the Implementation of the Justice and Peace Law: Initial Stages in the Demobilization of the AUC and First Judicial Proceedings*, Washington DC: IACHR.

International Center for Transitional Justice (2006) *Truth Commissions and Gender: Principles, Policies, and Procedures*, New York: ICTJ.

International Center for Transitional Justice (2009) *Overview of the Conflict 2009 Factsheet*, available at http://www.ictj.org/our-work/regions-and-countries/colombia (last accessed 3 April 2013).

International Commission of Jurists (1974) *Report on Mission to Chile*, Geneva: ICJ.

International Commission of Jurists (1976) *Arrests and Detention and Freedom of Information in Chile*, Geneva: ICJ.

International Criminal Law Review (2011) 'Special Edition – Women and International Criminal Law', *International Criminal Law Review* 11(3): 365–662.

International Crisis Group (2003) *Colombia: President Uribe's Democratic Security*, ICG Latin America Report No 6, Brussels/Bogotá.

International Federation for Human Rights (2007) *Colombia: La Desmovilización Paramilitar, en los Caminos de la Corte Penal Internacional*, Bogotá: Colombia.

Irish National Caucus (1993) *Congressional Briefing Paper*, Washington DC.

La Mesa por la Vida y la Salud de las Mujeres (2009) *Un derecho para las mujeres: La Despenalización parcial del Aborto en Colombia*, eds C. Barraza Morelle and C. Gómez López, Bogotá, Colombia.

La Ruta Pacifica, Corporación Vamos Mujer, *et al* (2009) *Declaración Final, Foro Internacional Verdad, Justice y Reparación Integral: una Deuda Pendiente con las Mujeres Víctimas de las Violencias*, Bogotá, 25 June 2009.

Larrain Heiremans, S. (1994) *Violencia Puertas Adentro: La Mujer Golpeada*, Santiago: SERNAM.

Lawyers Committee for Human Rights (1993) *Human Rights and Legal Defense in Northern Ireland*, New York: Lawyers Committee for Human Rights.

Lawyers Committee for Human Rights (1996) *At the Crossroads: Human Rights and the Northern Ireland Peace Process*, New York: Lawyers Committee for Human Rights.

London Armagh Group (1984) *Strip Searches in Armagh Jail*, London.

Lord Saville (2010) *Report of the Bloody Sunday Inquiry*, London: The Stationery Office.

Marshall, C., Scraton, P. *et al* (2010), *Consultation Response*, Childhood, Transition and Social Justice Initiative, School of Law, Queen's University Belfast.

Maturana, P. (2011) 'Violencia sexual como tortura', 11 April 2011, Corporación Humanas – Centro Regional de Derechos Humanos y Justicia de Género, available at http://www.humanas.cl/?p=5136 (last accessed 3 April 2013).

Meertens, D. (2006). *Informe Final de la Consultoría sobre Derechos de las Mujeres a la Tierra*. Bogotá: Programa de Paz y Seguridad UNIFEM Región Andina, Oficina de Colombia.

Mesa de Trabajo Mujer y Conflicto Armado (2005) *La Tradición, La Semilla y La Construcción: Sistematización de Tres Experiencias de Resistencia de Organizaciones de Mujeres Frente al Conflicto Armado en Colombia*, Bogotá: Corporación de Apoyo a Comunidades Populares (Codacop); Programa Mujer de la Asociación de Cabildos Indígenas del Norte del Cauca; Instituto Latinoamericano de Servicios Legales Alternativos; Liga de Mujeres Desplazadas; Liga Internacional de Mujeres por la Paz y la Libertad (Limpal Colombia); Asociación Mis Esfuerzos; Grupo de Mujeres por un Mejor Futuro; Asociación de Artesanas de San Jacinto; Mujeres Ejemplares; Mujeres Unidas de San José del Peñón; Mujeres de Villa Alegría en Acción.

Mesa de Trabajo Mujer y Conflicto Armado (2008) 'Según la Defensoría del Pueblo', en una publicación de Julio de 2008, eran 11 los casos de violencia sexual enunciados.

Mesa de Trabajo Mujer y Conflicto Armado (2012) *XI Informe sobre Violencia Sociopolítica contra Mujeres, Jóvenes y Niñas en Colombia*, Bogotá: La Mesa de Trabajo.

Mujer y Conflicto Armado (2001a) *Preview of the Report on Violence Against Women and Girls in the Colombian Armed Conflict*, Bogotá, Colombia.

Mujer y Conflicto Armado (2001b) *Second Report on Sociopolitical Violence Against Women and Girls in Colombia*, Bogotá: Working Group on Women and Armed Conflict.

Mujer y Conflicto Armado (2004) *Report on Social and Political Violence Against Women in Colombia*, Bogotá: La Mesa de Trabajo.

Mujer y Conflicto Armado (2005) *Women and Armed Conflict: Report on Social and Political Violence Against Women in Colombia, Fourth Report, January 2003–June 2004*, Bogotá, Colombia.

Mujer y Conflicto Armado (2008) *VIII Informe sobre Violencia Sociopolítica contra Mujeres, Jóvenes y Niñas en Colombia, 2007–2008 Violencia Sexual*, Bogotá: Mesa de Trabajo Mujer y Conflicto Armado.

National Council for Civil Liberties (1986) *Strip Searching: an Inquiry into the Strip Searching of Women Remand Prisoners at Armagh Prison between 1982 and 1985*. Belfast.

Northern Ireland Human Rights Commission (2001) *Making a Bill of Rights for Northern Ireland: A Consultation by the Northern Ireland Human Rights Commission*, Belfast: NIHRC.

Northern Ireland Human Rights Commission (2004a) *The Hurt Inside: The Imprisonment of Women and Girls in Northern Ireland*. Belfast: NIHRC.

Northern Ireland Human Rights Commission (2004b) *Progressing a Bill of Rights for Northern Ireland: An Update*, Belfast: NIHRC.

Northern Ireland Human Rights Commission (2005) *The Hurt Inside: The Imprisonment of Women and Girls in Northern Ireland*, Revised Edition. L. Moore and P. Scraton. Belfast: NIHRC.

Northern Ireland Human Rights Commission (2008) *A Bill of Rights for Northern Ireland: Advice to the Secretary of State for Northern Ireland*, Belfast: NIHRC.

Northern Ireland Office (2007) Press Statement: 'Hain Announces Group to Look at the Past,' 22 June 2007.

Northern Ireland Office (2009) *A Bill of Rights for Northern Ireland: Next Steps, Consultation Paper*, November 2009.

Northern Ireland Women's European Platform (2004) 'UNSCR1325 on Trial,' available at http://www.niwep.org.uk/id42.html (last accessed 3 April 2013).

Observatorio Derechos Humanos, Universidad Diego Portales, available at http://www.icso.cl/observatorio-derechos-humanos/ (last accessed 27 February 2013).

Office of the First and Deputy First Minister (2002) *Reshape, Rebuild, Achieve*, Belfast.

Orentlicher, D. (2005) *Report of the Independent Expert to Update the Set of Principles to Combat Impunity, Addendum: Updated Set of Principles for the Protection and Promotion of Human Rights through Action to Combat Impunity United Nations Commission on Human Rights*, UN Doc. E/Cn.4/2005/102/Add.1.

Organization for Security and Cooperation in Europe/Office for Democratic Institutions and Human Rights (2008) *Gender and Security Sector Reform Toolkit*, available at http://www.osce.org/odihr/30652 (last accessed 27 February 2013).

Police Ombudsman for Northern Ireland (2008) *Annual Report and Accounts for Year Ended March 2008*, Belfast: HMSO, HC 648.

Presidencia de la República Ministerio de Defensa Nacional República de Colombia (2003) *Política de Defensa y Seguridad Democrática*, Bogotá, Colombia.

Procuraduría General de la Nación (2010). *Informe de Seguimiento al Programa de Reparación individual por Vía Administrativa*, Bogotá.

Red Chilena Contra la Violencia Doméstica y Sexual (1996) *Desafíos para la Paz: Un País Sin Mujeres Agredidas*, Santiago, Chile.

Red Chilena Contra la Violencia Doméstica y Sexual (2008) *Violencia Sexual y Aborto: Conexiones Necesarias*, Authors: Gloria Maira Vargas, Paula Santana Nazarit and Siomara Molina Sáez, Santiago, Chile.

Rosemary Nelson Inquiry (2011) *The Rosemary Nelson Inquiry Report*, No. 0947 2010–12, London: The Stationery Office.

Rosemary Nelson Inquiry, 'Chairman's Initial Statement,' available at http://www.rosemarynelsoninquiry.org/current-key-documents/4/ (last accessed 27 February 2013).

Servicio Nacional de la Mujer (1995) *Chile: Informe Nacional. IV Conferencia Mundial*, Santiago: SERNAM.

Sierra Leone Truth and Reconciliation Commission (2004) *Witness to Truth: Report of the Sierra Leone Truth and Reconciliation Commission*, Freetown, Sierra Leone.

Standing Advisory Commission on Human Rights (1986) *Strip Searching Women Prisoners*, Belfast: SACHR.

Standing Advisory Commission on Human Rights (1993) *Abortion Law in Northern Ireland: the Twilight Zone*, Belfast: SACHR.

The Compensation Agency (2002) *A Guide to the Northern Ireland Criminal Injuries Compensation Scheme 2002*, available at http://www.nidirect.gov.uk/tariff_guide_02.pdf (last accessed 3 April 2013).

United Kingdom Government National Action Plan (2012) 'UNSCR 1325 Women, Peace and Security – November 2010 to November 2013,' available at http://www.peacewomen.org/assets/file/NationalActionPlans/unitedkingdom_nationalactionplan_feb2012revised.pdf (last accessed 27 February 2013).

United Nations Committee against Torture (2004) *Conclusions and Recommendations of the Committee Against Torture to Chile*, UN Doc CAT/C/CR/32/5.

United Nations Committee on the Elimination of Discrimination against Women (2011) *Concept Note: General Discussion on the Protection of Women's Human Rights in Conflict and Post-conflict Contexts*, available at http://www2.ohchr.org/english/bodies/cedaw/docs/GRConceptNote.pdf (last accessed 27 February 2013).

United Nations High Commissioner for Human Rights (2005) *Report on the Human Rights Situation in Colombia*, UN Doc E/CN.4/2005/10, 28 February 2005.

United Nations Human Rights Committee (1996) *Concluding Observations of the Human Rights Committee: Guatemala*, UN Doc. CCPR/C/79/Add.63.

United Nations Secretary-General (2004) *The Rule of Law and Transitional Justice in Conflict and Post-conflict Societies*, New York: United Nations.

United Nations Secretary-General (2010) *Report on Women's Participation in Peacebuilding. Report of the Secretary General*, New York: United Nations.

United Nations Special Rapporteur on Violence Against Women, Radhika Coomaraswamy (2001) *Report of the Special Rapporteur on Violence Against Women, its Causes and Consequences*, submitted in accordance with Commission on Human Rights Resolution 2001/49, Addendum: mission to Colombia (1–7 November 2001), United Nations Economic and Social Council Commission on Human Rights.

United Nations Special Rapporteur on Violence Against Women, Yakin Ertürk (2006) *The Due Diligence Standard as a Tool for the Elimination of Violence Against Women: Report of the Special Rapporteur on Violence against Women, its Causes and Consequences*, submitted to the Commission on Human Rights, Sixty-second session, Item 12(a) of the provisional agenda of the Human Rights Council, E/CN.4/2006/61, 20 January 2006.

United Nations Special Rapporteur on Violence Against Women, Rashida Manjoo (2010) *Promotion and Protection of All Human Rights, Civil, Political, Economic, Social and Cultural Rights, Including the Right to Development: Report of the Special Rapporteur on Violence Against Women, its Causes and Consequences* (Advance Edited Version), submitted to the Human Rights Council, Fourteenth session, Agenda item 3, A/HRC/14/22, 19 April 2010.

Women's Law and Research Group and Rape Crisis Centre (1985) *Victims on Trial: The Law on Rape in Northern Ireland and the Case for Change*, Belfast.

Women's Resource and Development Agency and Women's Centres Regional Partnership (2008) *Women and the Conflict: Talking about the 'Troubles' and Planning for the Future*, Belfast.

Women's Support Network (2009) *A Response to Dealing with the Past in Northern Ireland: The Recommendations of the Consultative Group on the Past*, Belfast.

Working Group to Monitor Compliance with Auto 092 of 2008 of the Colombian Constitutional Court (2011) *Access to Justice for Women Victims of Sexual Violence: Fourth Follow-Up Report to Auto 092 of the Colombian Constitutional Court*, Bogotá, Colombia.

Index

Page references referring to information in tables are in **bold**.